"We have long been gifted by the l.... foundational writings in humanistic psychology, but *Personality and Growth* is a new genre of his work that yields fresh insights into his remarkable talks in the classroom. With this work Bassett has unearthed a treasure-trove of heretofore unpublished presentations Maslow made to his Brandeis students highlighting an experiential understanding of personality development. This understanding covered self-actualization, love, transcendence, being-motivation vs. deficit motivation, and so on. I highly recommend this book to any readers, academic or otherwise, who value Maslow's key illuminations of what it means to be fully, experientially human, and who relish, as I do, the enlivening seminars he held on these matters."

~ **Kirk J. Schneider, Ph.D.,** Adjunct Faculty, Saybrook University and Teachers College, Columbia University, and author of *The Spirituality of Awe*, *The Polarized Mind*, and (with Fraser Pierson and James Bugental) *The Handbook of Humanistic Psychology*

"*Personality and Growth* offers a fascinating, detailed, and unprecedented picture of this brilliant thinker in the college classroom during the 1963-1964 period. The unabridged transcriptions of the classes particularly reveal Maslow's evolving ideas on peak-experiences, strengthening positive emotional expression, and the importance of self-awareness in forging close relationships with others. I strongly recommend this book to all interested in Maslow's work and its legacy for the 21st century."

~ **Edward Hoffman, Ph.D.,** author of *The Right to Be Human: A Biography of Abraham Maslow*

"After reading *Personality and Growth* you may recognize changes in yourself and your perspective. In fact, I have good reason to believe you will never be the same again. How can I make this prediction with such assuredness? Simple: I took the same class with 'Abe' three years after these recordings were made. It changed my life in ways I never imagined possible, profoundly and for the good. This book is more than an historic account of events occurring over half a century ago. It is a powerful retelling of those Maslowian concepts that, when actualized, can change both you and your world."

~ **Louis Ari Kopolow, M.D., DLFAPA, ACP,** Asst. Clinical Professor of Psychiatry at George Washington University, President Emeritus Suburban Maryland Psychiatric Society, and author of the forthcoming book *Reaching Your Peak: Following Maslow's Path to Self-Actualization and Happiness*

"Maurice Bassett has done a masterful job in framing and presenting Abraham Maslow's style of teaching and the methods he used to stimulate creative thought and self-exploration about how we are wired up as human beings. Unlike other books written about or by Maslow himself, *Personality and Growth: A Humanistic Psychologist In The Classroom* uses classroom transcripts to allow a reader to actually "become a student" in one of Maslow's classes and to authentically engage and experience the unfolding, self-exploratory discussions and exercises related to personality and growth. A reader, therefore, gets to experience the "authentic voice" of Maslow as he engages inquisitive learners about aspects of "the self" and our human potential for growth. Many gems can be found in this book in terms of what became known as the Human Potential Movement. A very intriguing, very insightful, and very creatively presented read!"

~ **Carroy (Cuf) Ferguson, Ph.D.,** Co-President of the Association for Humanistic Psychology, Full Professor in Psychology and Human Services Program Director at University of Massachusetts-Boston, and author of *Evolving The Human Race Game, Transitions in Consciousness from An African American Perspective, A New Perspective on Race and Color,* and *Innovative Approaches To Education and Community Service*

"Fifty years ago reading an article by Maslow changed the course of my life, but I never had a chance to meet him in person. Now I have. Through this book, I feel like I've been able to sit down with him in the same room and have a conversation. Personable, brilliant, engaging, provocative, genuine, and always on the cutting edge of understanding human beings at their very best."

~ **Robert McGarey, M.A.,** Co-President of the Association for Humanistic Psychology and Founder/Executive Director of the nonprofit Human Potential Center in Austin, Texas

"This gem of a book conveys more than just information about early approaches in humanistic psychology and is more than an historical record of a prominent leader in psychological thought. It brings readers into the classroom, immersing them in a learning experience that at the time was revolutionary. These are not lectures but facilitated dialogues and shared inquiries into the nature of our human condition. What Maslow was offering in these classes is a pedagogical experience still relevant today. In 1968 I had the good fortune to hear Maslow give a talk at SUNY at Buffalo, where I was an undergraduate. I was so inspired that I was determined to work with him for my graduate studies. Unfortunately Maslow left Brandeis on sabbatical and within the year had passed away. With this publication my dream of being in the classroom with Maslow has been realized in many ways. And like me, you too can now have an experience of being taught by Maslow."

~ **Jeff Kelton, Ph.D.,** Clinical Psychologist, GlobalWalkabouts Coaching

PERSONALITY AND GROWTH

PERSONALITY AND GROWTH

A Humanistic Psychologist in the Classroom

ABRAHAM H. MASLOW

WITH ILLUSTRATIONS BY SAUL STEINBERG

MAURICE BASSETT

Maurice Bassett
P.O. Box 839
Anna Maria, FL 34216

Contact the Publisher:
MauriceBassett@gmail.com
www.MauriceBassett.com

Edited by Hung-Min Chiang & Chris Nelson
Cover designed by David Michael Moore

ISBN: 978-1-60025-078-1

Library of Congress Control Number: 2019941972

~ Dedicated to ~

Abraham H. Maslow

ACKNOWLEDGMENTS

THE PUBLISHER ACKNOWLEDGES AND THANKS the following people:

Ann Kaplan for her years-long support of my work and for trusting me with so much of her father's work, both published and unpublished.

Colin Wilson for the book, *New Pathways in Psychology*, the reading of which was the opening of a treasure chest for me.

Hung-Min Chiang for his work with Abraham H. Maslow and his extensive efforts on the project.

Chris Nelson for his masterful editing, layout and project management.

Michael Pastore for his superb indexing.

Katrina Greeley for her flawless proofreading.

Katie Söderlind for the typing of the manuscript.

Lou Judson, our audio engineer, for digitizing and improving the audio recordings.

David Michael Moore for our cover design.

Michelle Nassau and Trinity for the essential research and administrative support necessary to make this project a success.

TABLE OF CONTENTS

FOREWORD

Maurice Bassett

If I were dropped into the ocean 1,000 miles from anyplace,
I'd start swimming the 1,000 miles!

Abraham H. Maslow
The Journals of A. H. Maslow

IT IS BOTH AN HONOR AND A JOY to be able to publish this book.

Personality and Growth was intended for publication half a century ago but for reasons I discuss below it is only now seeing the light of day. Personally, I consider it to be a kind of time machine that takes us back to the world of Abraham H. Maslow and America in the early 1960s.

I first discovered the audiocassettes upon which this book is based in November, 2010, on my long drive across the U.S. from the West Coast to Florida. A few days after leaving Seattle, I arrived at the home of Maslow's daughter, Ann Kaplan. I had met Ann at her home once before, but this time I thought to ask about any audios or videos she might have on hand of her father. She gave me permission to look around, and I soon found numerous audiocassettes packed away in a storage closet in her living room.

This was an amazing discovery in itself—previously unknown recordings by Maslow. But the real treasure surfaced the following year when I flew out to visit Ann once again in the spring of 2011 to have her review and sign various publishing agreements.

After a dinner of lasagna one night there was plenty of food left over; I asked Ann where I could store it for her, and she directed me to a giant freezer in the basement. I had been to her home twice before but for some reason had never realized it had a basement . . .

Adjacent to the freezer was an old, Army-green filing cabinet that looked like something from the 1940s. Back upstairs, I mentioned it to Ann, who told me that, yes, it had belonged to her father, and I was welcome to look through it if I liked.

Down I went at around eight o'clock. Two hours later Ann opened the door at the top of the stairs and shouted, "Maurice, are you all right down there?"

I was more than alright. I was amazed. The filing cabinet was filled with Maslow's personal papers, including things like his birth certificate, driver's license, numerous family photos and negatives, and—deep in the bottom drawer—a giant, unpublished manuscript sat in a box. I could hardly believe my eyes when I dug out the pages of what is now *Personality and Growth*.

I immediately recognized that this manuscript was based on Maslow's semester-long, 1963-'64 class on personality at Brandeis University, the very same one for which I had found the cassette recordings the previous year. A cover letter (buried in another folder in the file cabinet) indicated that it was transcribed and compiled by Maslow's graduate student, Hung-Min Chiang ("Min"), who'd prepared it for publication sometime in the late 1960s or early 1970s. He'd sent it to Maslow's wife, Bertha, in 1976, writing that he had transcribed the recordings of Maslow's class but was not sure what to do with the resulting manuscript. As it turned out, he published an introductory essay (included in the present book) and an extract from the transcript in the second edition of *The Healthy Personality* in 1977 (the first edition had been prepared with Maslow in 1969). The vast majority of the transcript—hundreds of pages of material— disappeared into Maslow's file cabinet.

Once the initial shock waves of the enormity of the discovery had passed over me, I began thinking about publication. Min and Bertha had already been contemplating this and it seemed likely that Ann would appreciate seeing it in print after so many decades. And I knew

I could help get it out into the world.

As it turned out, Ann had neither seen nor heard of the manuscript, but she was excited as well. We duly photocopied it the next day. Sometime after that, I got in touch with Min and exchanged a series of emails with him regarding the manuscript. He was happy to answer my questions and even sent me several photos of Maslow that I'd never seen before. Needless to say, this project owes so much to Min, and I am so grateful to him for all his work on it, both as Maslow's assistant in the course and for his transcriptions and editor's commentary.

To create the definitive version of the manuscript, we have painstakingly listened to the audios once again and corrected and updated the transcriptions. The cassettes were digitized, allowing for improved clarity and the ability to slow down and better understand previously unintelligible portions.

Thanks to a special licensing arrangement with the Artists Rights Society, it gives me great pleasure to be able to include the very same Saul Steinberg illustrations that Maslow himself used in the class. You will find those seven illustrations in the "Laboratory for Self-Knowledge" class session held on January 6, 1964 (pp. 351-372).

So take a seat in the front row for the class "Experiential Approaches to the Study of Personality," as taught by Dr. Abraham H. Maslow at Brandeis University in 1963-'64. You'll find a course rich in both content and engaging discussions between Maslow and his students.

No doubt the original class was a remarkable experience, a once-in-a-lifetime opportunity. We ourselves may not have been afforded the chance to participate directly, way back in 1963, but I trust you will find this book the next best thing. Enjoy!

And look for future Maslow-related projects, including the forthcoming *Early Diaries*—Maslow's unpublished journals from the 1920s and '30s.

Experiential Approaches to the Study of Personality

A survey of efforts at self-analysis, self-therapy and self-growth.
Dreams and symbol psychology; peak, mystic and psychedelic
experience; archaic and prerational cognition.
Recovery of the preconscious.

The course description as it appeared in the
1963 Brandeis University Course Catalog

INTRODUCTORY NOTE:
CONTEXTUALIZING AND EDITING THE TRANSCRIPTS

Chris Nelson

The Source Material

IN HIS ORIGINAL NOTES TO THE TRANSCRIPT of this volume, Hung-Min Chiang writes:

> This book contains a chronological report of the course "Experiential Approaches to the Study of Personality" given in the fall semester of 1963 at Brandeis University. It was a class of 24 students (11 males and 13 females), mostly juniors and seniors majoring in psychology. Because of a previous agreement on confidentiality, none of the participants (except Maslow) are identified in the transcript and pseudonyms are used throughout. There were 12 sessions altogether. As a rule, each session consisted of a two-hour lecture followed by a laboratory for self-knowledge of one hour. A sound recording was kept from October 28 through the end of the semester.[1]

The present volume utilizes both Chiang's original transcript of the recordings as well as the recordings themselves (digitized for enhanced clarity) as source material.

Editing for Style

The spoken word is of course different from the written one. Perfectly acceptable habits of speech can be challenging to read verbatim on the page. For example, in the class it is common for Maslow or the students to start speaking, stop in mid-stream to reformulate their thoughts, then begin again. This can lead to a confusing mix of ideas and, often enough, grammar. To that end both Chiang and I have edited for the sake of clarity, organization and readability while still aiming to retain the natural flow of the spoken word in the context of the class. At times, ephemera such as details of scheduling, office hours and the like are also left out. In certain instances, too, papers shift, doors creak, students talk over one another, or sit too far from the recorder. So, despite the enhanced recordings, some material is still unintelligible; this is only indicated when a passage seems to lack clarity because of missing material. Ellipses are used to note when a speaker's voice has trailed off.

Editing for Content

We have not edited away occasional comments on topics such as gender roles, race, and homosexuality that modern readers will consider products of a less-enlightened time. While it is important to recognize the historical context in which these comments were made, it can nevertheless be acknowledged that several of Maslow's opinions have not aged well and will strike 21st-century readers as insensitive and ill-conceived. But to remove them would be to deny the existence of these contemporary perspectives and undermine both the historical veracity of the document as well as the meaning and flow of some of the classroom discussions.

It is also true that the informal, conversational style in the classroom did not always lend itself to a thorough and detailed explication of ideas. As Chiang points out in one of his notes, Maslow himself had nuanced views on gender, for example, that are not fully captured in the classroom discussion.[2]

In any event, the spectrum of views expressed in this book affords us an invaluable opportunity. The class was held on the cusp of major social changes in America during the late sixties and early seventies.

Some of the "radical" views regarding, for example, women's roles in society, are clearly held by the students. As a product of an earlier generation, Maslow recognized this and occasionally commented on it. For example, in the context of discussing student journals he says:

> I feel, sometimes very strongly, the gap in the generations. It's as if I don't know what's in your heads, what you're thinking of and feeling, and some of the notebooks have been very instructive for me—which is very good. I should think educating the professors is a very desirable thing to do . . . I'm grateful for it.[3]

Students often challenged Maslow's ideas and views, be they points of psychological theory, his grading system or his stance on celebrity product endorsements. Maslow embraced and encouraged this open dialogue. As twenty-first century readers, we can now retrospectively participate in this multi-generational exchange of perspectives.

What shines throughout is a picture of Abraham H. Maslow: teacher, scientist, psychologist and human being—a creative and compassionate thinker possessing a unique and lively genius. He challenges his students to think for themselves, to pursue self-knowledge, to discover their potential and fully engage with the world.

One wonders if he could have given them—and now us—any greater encouragement with which to move forward in life.

The Present Volume

The introductory essay that follows was written by Chiang in 1976 and provides a valuable context for the course and insights into Maslow's goals for it. It is followed by Chiang's summaries of the first four classes of the course—from September 30 through October 21, 1963. The transcripts begin on October 28, 1963, the first day the tape recorder was brought to class.

Introduction

A HUMANISTIC PSYCHOLOGIST IN THE CLASSROOM[1]

Hung-Min Chiang

IN THE FALL OF 1963, the present writer was given an unusual opportunity of assisting Abraham H. Maslow in one of his educational ventures. I was asked if I would be interested in helping him with "Experiential Approaches to the Study of Personality," a course he was planning to offer at Brandeis University that year. As I understood it, he was highly dissatisfied with the goals and methods of traditional education and was actively in search of some viable alternatives. I was also told that the course was a sort of pilot study in an uncharted waterway and he was eager to have its value assessed as impartially as possible.

We both felt that the best strategy was to tape the entire proceedings in the class so that the materials could be retrieved and evaluated at a later date. After some lengthy discussions, and with the consent of the other participants in the class, we taped the weekly sessions, the recordings of which were later transcribed verbatim. An early brief report of the course has been published elsewhere.[2]

It is widely acknowledged that Maslow, being a long-time spokesman and the chief architect of humanistic psychology, has left a considerable impact on the theory and practice of humanistic education. But beyond the generalities, what did Maslow have to say on certain key issues in education, and the teaching of psychology in particular? And how would he approach the practicalities of teaching in an actual classroom situation? In spite of his image as a banner bearer of the new movement in psychology and his reputation as an inspiring psychologist, surprisingly little is known about Maslow as a teacher. His voluminous writings certainly contain a wealth of ideas any educator with a humanistic bent will find most stimulating. And again the question is: how would Maslow himself apply them in the classroom? This introduction and the subsequent transcripts of Maslow's class provide some clues in this regard.

In many ways 1963—the year the course was first offered—was a pivotal period for Maslow. He had just put together his notes on social psychology, which were to be published under the title *Eupsychian Management*.[3] He was also working on the manuscript of *Religions, Values and Peak-Experiences* (1964), from which he drew a substantial amount of material for the course. The previous year marked the publication of his widely read book, *Toward a Psychology of Being* (1962c), which, along with his earlier work, *Motivation and Personality* (1954), was rapidly becoming the rallying ground of humanistic psychologists across the country. The Association for Humanistic Psychology, a brainchild of Maslow's, was formed and held its first meeting in Philadelphia in August 1961. Its official organ, the *Journal of Humanistic Psychology* (1961-) had begun publication under the auspices of the Department of Psychology, Brandeis University. The winds of change were blowing everywhere and Maslow, the visionary, had good reason to be enthusiastic about his new educational project at this particular point in time.

One remarkable sign of this "humanistic revolution" was the mushrooming of so-called "growth centers." Outside of the academic circle a number of the growth centers were springing up across the country. The most famous of these was the Esalen Institute that had opened its door on the rocky coast of California in 1962. It had as its goal the integration of humanistic psychology and various forms of Eastern thought, including Zen Buddhism and yoga. It had already launched its bold experiment (an alchemy, one might say) with radically new ideas along the lines suggested by Maslow. At Esalen, where the spirit of revolution ran high, Maslow was regarded as the father of the humanistic revolution. Maslow—still a maverick on his home ground of Brandeis—went out of his way to praise Esalen as potentially the most important educational institute in the world.

In a way, the Esalen Institute came quite close to Maslow's ideal of intrinsic education. "In the ideal college," he wrote of humanistic education, "there would be no credits, no degrees, and no required courses . . . The college would be ubiquitous—that is, not restricted to particular buildings at particular times—and the teachers would be any human beings who had something that they wanted to share with others."[4] The college would be a kind of educational retreat where people could go and find their own identity.

> What do we mean by the discovery of identity? We mean finding out what your real desires and characteristics are, and being able to live in a way that expresses them. You learn to be authentic, to be honest in the sense of allowing your behavior and your speech to be the true and spontaneous expression of your inner feelings.[5]

That is the ideal; however, the goal Maslow set for his experimentation that year was quite modest compared to Esalen. Unlike Esalen, which enjoyed the freedom of an independent institution, at Brandeis Maslow had to contend with the structural constraints imposed by a typical university. He also voiced his reservations, even misgivings, about some outlandish "growth techniques" being tried elsewhere. Being realistic as well as idealistic, he simply wanted to explore possible avenues and effective means of teaching experimental skills in the setting of a college such as Brandeis. As a description of the course reads:

> A survey of efforts at self-analysis, self-therapy, and self-growth. Dreams and symbol psychology; peak, mystic and psychedelic experience; archaic and prerational cognition. Recovery of the preconscious.

Officially, the enrollment was limited to 20 students, but it was a rule that was not strictly observed. In 1963 there were 24 registered for the course, and it soon became clear that the class was too large. At one point Maslow became keenly aware of this and remarked, "We're too big a group, it seems quite clear to me now, for the effort that we are making."[6] But no real effort was made toward a reduction in the size of the class, neither then nor after. In 1966, for instance, there were 38 participants sitting in the class, which was far too large a number for any meaningful group interactions.

Maslow's apparent reluctance to hold the class size down reflected to a large degree his uncertainty about an optimal size. Neither was he quite sure of the direction or the structure of the course at this stage. It should be noted, too, that he had the course listed not as a workshop or a group therapy, but as a survey course. It was simply announced, with no promises or fanfare, as a study of methods and means of personal growth, *period.* From the very beginning, the class was told the nature of the course: "This is not an experimental research designed in advance on purpose. This is sort of a groping exploration into the unknown, and we don't know where we're going."[7] Then he continued, "But I would like you to think of yourselves as not so much students who are beholden to a professor but rather as collaborators in an enterprise in which we all want to learn as much as we can so that we can pass this on to other people."[8]

In choosing a model for the course, Maslow had several options open to him. He could have chosen a group model and patterned the course after the sensitivity training group (T-group), or he could have chosen a psychoanalytic model and stressed the depth dimension of personality. He weighed the pros and cons of each; in the end he rejected both for practical reasons.

In the summer of 1962 Maslow visited Lake Arrowhead, California, where he observed the T-group in action for the first time. He wrote in his journal of the impressions:

> My first impression in the first group that I sat in on was one of real shock and amazement. These people behaved and talked in a spontaneous and free way that I have ordinarily associated with psychoanalyzed people, that is, with people who have been under psychoanalysis for a year or two at least.[9]

Then and there he clearly saw the far-reaching implications of the T-group for the psychology of personal growth, and yet when he returned to Brandeis, he seemed to have some doubts about the applicability of the T-group techniques in the classroom. The long and intensive group interaction necessary for a successful T-group, so he reasoned, is hardly feasible at the college with a regimented schedule. Anonymity is practically impossible to maintain in a small college community, and there is also an ethical question as to whether a student should attend a group session if he is less than willing. Maslow clearly feared that a poorly conducted group session might drive the individual against the wall where there is no possibility of graceful retreat.

There were certainly many ways of overcoming some of these difficulties, and the experience has shown that a non-structured approach can successfully be used in teaching.[10] But there were two obstacles in Maslow's way and one of them was the incompatibility of the roles of teacher and T-group leader. An ideal leader is accepting and non-judgmental, whereas a teacher is necessarily evaluative and judgmental. Maslow saw no easy way to resolve the contradiction. Another stumbling block for Maslow in leading a T-group in the class was his very ability to toy with words and concepts. This is what made him a good lecturer, but in leading a T-group it was more of a liability than an asset. Maslow was fully aware of his shortcoming and warned the students: "I'm an intellectual and you have to tone me down sometimes or the words will run away with me."[11] Upon the insistence of some students, a non-structured approach was tried out in some sessions—without desired results, however. It soon became clear to everyone that Maslow simply could not remain silent in the company of the students. The following exchange that occurred in one of the non-structured sessions is self-explanatory. One exasperated male student told Maslow:

> **Student:** You start a question which is always directed in your own terms and . . . as far as I can tell, with no consideration of the feeling of the day, place, time, what's happening, and then when there is silence you begin talking and you keep talking.

> **Maslow:** Yeah, I've been told that by practically everybody.
>
> **Student:** I'm very annoyed at this, I can't stand it and I wish you wouldn't do it.
>
> **Maslow:** You speak for many.[12]

There is no question that Maslow firmly believed in the potential benefits of the T-group. As he wrote:

> The T-group is an effort to make you aware of who you really are, of how you really react to other people, by giving you a chance to be honest, to tell what is really going on inside of you instead of presenting facades or giving polite evasions.[13]

He even made a valid comparison with psychoanalysis, saying,

> There are some kinds of things that can happen in these T-groups that can *never* [emphasis original] happen in the individual psychoanalysis, no matter how long it takes. There are certain kinds of feedback we can get from other people that we simply cannot get from just one person.[14]

In spite of such insights, Maslow's own attitude toward the T-group can at best be described as non-committal. He would point out the benefits of a T-group, but at the same time he would tell the students the course was not a group therapy, and that the group spontaneity of the T-group was not the goal. He would rather recommend a voluntary T-group run by someone other than himself outside of the scheduled class hour. It is very likely that Maslow's knowledge of the T-group at that time was basically that of an observer rather than a participant. There was no indication in his writings that he was personally affected by the experience, nor was there any hint that he appreciated the intense joy known only to the participants themselves.

Maslow's assessment of psychoanalysis, in contrast, was solidly based on his own personal experience. Earlier he had received training as a psychoanalyst and had gone through analysis with Karen Horney.[15] His appreciation of the experience was genuine and totally affirmative. His basic position was that psychoanalysis is the best proven tool for exploration of the self yet discovered by man. As late as 1968 he still could reflect back on his personal psychoanalysis as the most valuable experience that led him to the discovery of his self. Said he: "Another profound learning experience that I value more highly than any particular course or any degree that I have ever had was my personal psychoanalysis: discovering my own identity, my own self."[16] The fact that there was a wealth of information available on psychoanalysis and that Maslow was very familiar with the subject could also be a contributing factor here.

This is not to say that Maslow was taken up with psychoanalysis and tried it in the classroom without necessary modifications. Maslow regarded himself as an "epi-Freudian"[17] and was fully aware of the limitations of the psychoanalytic model in education as well as in therapy. As he saw it, psychoanalysis is essentially an individual therapy and cannot be done on a large scale. Furthermore, the recovery of the id, which is perhaps justifiable in the consulting room, may not be so desirable in the classroom. Explaining that the course was not meant to be psychotherapy, Maslow cautioned the students:

> What we must avoid doing in our class are the characteristics of a depth therapy. Ours is not a regression therapy, not built on transference analysis, placing no stress on dream interpretation, and there will be no speaking about our personal sex life.[18]

He was very cautious about any potential dangers and advised the participants not to push themselves to the edge of embarrassment in front of the group.

What, then, was the goal of the course? If it was not a course in individual or group therapy, what was it? In this scheme, the main emphasis was on the recovery of experiences—in particular, the recovery of feelings, emotions, subtle impulses and inner voices. They are believed to be the essential part of human nature and yet are so easily forgotten, denied or suppressed in the course of socialization. To be experientially alive means to renew a contact with our essential nature, and the first step in that direction is "to pay a greater attention to the concrete, pre-abstract, preverbal and the unconscious." Here Maslow could have said "preconscious" instead of "unconscious," for he did distinguish between two aspects of the unconscious, and the one he was primarily interested in is generally known as the preconscious.[19] The unconscious is said to be the seat of drives and needs—especially irrational needs—whereas the preconscious has more to do with a way of sensing and cognizing—for example, with primary process cognition.

Psychoanalysis was Maslow's starting point and though he continued using some Freudian terminology throughout that year, the main thrust of his thinking was unmistakably humanistic. He spoke of impulses, needs and sexual urges, but he postulated that the inner nature of man is neither good nor bad but is "prior to good and evil." A good psychotherapy was seen by him as an "uncovering therapy," a discovery or re-discovery of the intrinsic growth tendency in every person.

To aid recovery of the experiences, all kinds of experiential exercises were given, and the students were asked to try them out. Included in the list were exercises in sensory awareness, here-and-now, innocent perception, synesthesia, physiognomic perception, B-humor[20] and the unitive consciousness. Most of the exercises were either an extension or direct application of the ideas contained in his books (mentioned earlier). Maslow left a personal memo in which he listed over two dozen "experiential techniques and experiments" he used over the years. Here are a few typical ones:[21]

1. Exercises in Suchness and concrete experiencing, use the *Sense of Wonder*[22] by Rachel Carson.[23] A good way of recounting the ability to perceive Suchness is to do as she did, to take a little boy or a little girl to go look at the seashore or spiderwebs or surf or trees, or to look through magnifying glasses at leaves or snowflakes and the like. To help the child look means to help yourself look. Also the child's reactions to what you overlook or pay no attention to may help to pull you back to seeing the world and its Suchness as a child does.

2. Try not to label things or ask for names on a nature walk. Just look at each bird or tree or flower or leaf in itself, *per se*, as if you were seeing it for the first time, or as if no other such existed in the world. Don't try to classify it or label it or name it. It makes no difference whether it's common or not; the robin or the sparrow is just as much a miracle as the cardinal or the oriole. Try the same thing with dogs. Most people don't see "dogness" (although children do). They think in terms of pedigrees or lines or even clip their hair in particular ways which are not doglike but are dog-owner like. They fuss about "pure lines," and then of course you can tell that such a person doesn't really like dogs, but has acquired a property. The same thing is true of flowers. Make bouquets of meadow grasses or weeds and look at them as if they were quite rare. You will see them in a different way. In such looking also be sure that you push aside all questions of usefulness or uselessness, of good or bad, danger, etc.

3. Introduce Freud's concept of free-floating attention. Pair off students in the class, one to be a talker and one to be a listener, with the listener trying to acquire the ability for evenly distributed attention, or free-floating attention, non-concentrating attention, Taoistic attention, passive receptivity, non-active listening, etc.

4. It made a very good exercise to ask the students in a group to volunteer their peak-experiences. This generally touched off other people in the group. Also it tended to be progressively more intimate, i.e., starting from rather mild and not very intimate experiences, and going on to more poignant, more emotional, more shaking experiences being reported. *The same can be done for desolation experiences . . .*[24]

5. I tried deliberately to help the students recover the awareness of anxiety, of sadness or depression, of anger in whatever ways I could think of through the whole semester. Allen Wheelis's[25] book, *Illusionless Man*[26]—in

this book the peak-experience quality is missing; zest, joy in life, etc. He sees everything, he is very smart, he is fully aware, but he doesn't *feel*. What would you say to him? What can one say to a person who doesn't experience emotion, or pleasure, or joy? One can talk here about the general topic of joylessness, of the non-peaker, of emotional aridity.

6. With each such class there should be a voluntary T-group, run by someone else, I believe, rather than the teacher in charge. I lectured about feedback, about here and now, about sending out signals that could be heard, of checking back your hearing of the signals with the sender to see if you received it right, the becoming aware and conscious in the T-group situation of the actual feeling of anxiety in the face of silence, for instance, etc., etc. Of course this can be expanded a very great deal.

Within the span of some 12 weeks, a wide range of topics on personal growth were introduced. Some of these topics were Zen, mysticism, general semantics, phenomenology of love, human sexuality, masculinity-femininity, authenticity, Jungian archetypes, many Freudian concepts, dreams, peak-experiences and self-actualization. Maslow also reported his personal observations, quotations from his notes and his latest thoughts on human values, all of which he was eager to pass on. Several scores of books and dozens of articles were mentioned. Some were discussed in the class while others were recommended for future reading. Several books were specifically assigned for intensive study,[27] and two of them were *Self-Analysis*[28] by Karen Horney and *The Forgotten Language*[29] by Erich Fromm.[30] There were tests and interviews, and the students were also asked to keep a personal journal.

A weekly three-hour session was divided into two periods: the first two hours were a seminar during which the course materials were presented and discussed intellectually. The remaining third hour was put aside as an experiential workshop (or "Lab in Self-Knowledge," as it was called) where the focus was on experiential reports and exercises. It must be pointed out, however, that in the year 1963-64, which the current volume covers, the distinction between the two periods was neither clear nor scrupulously observed. As a result, a substantial portion of the class hours were taken up by discussions interspersed with experiential exercises.

The lectures by Maslow were often as stimulating as his writings—perhaps even more so. He spoke with the obvious pleasure and conviction of a man who had devoted his whole life to searching for truth. He loved to experiment with new ideas and learned as much from the ones that didn't work as from those that did. He even mused at his own verbosity by saying:

> I'm tossing out all sorts of seeds all over the place . . .
> like an old-fashioned sower with wheat grains in every
> direction. I don't know which word comes out and the
> only way I can ever find out is for you to tell me.[31]

He was definitely an intellectual—a great one—but he was also quite candid with regard to his own inner world. He talked freely about his feelings, personal experiences and, on a few occasions, offered an interpretation of his own dreams.

If there is one thing that truly distinguishes this course from many other similar ventures, it is its holistic orientation. The course was experientially oriented but was unique in its two-pronged approach to personal growth. Instead of repudiating the word and concept as the enemy of experience, as was often done elsewhere, Maslow attempted to view both experience and abstraction in a proper perspective. To be more precise, he wanted to know if the intellect could be used to facilitate or sharpen the experiential awareness. This basic position of Maslow was far from being popular among his contemporaries. Many traditionally oriented psychologists who live in the world of numbers and constructs would certainly frown at the experiential approach and its possible implications for psychology. At the other extreme, the vanguards of the human potential movement, such as Fritz Perls,[32] have gone to the point of treating the intellect with suspicion and disdain.

There is an amusing story of D.T. Suzuki,[33] a renowned Zen scholar, giving a seminar at the invitation of the Psychology Department at Brandeis when Maslow was the chairman. The story has it that no sooner had the seminar begun when a spirited discussion erupted among the participants and, amid all the intellectual excitement, the guest speaker dozed off. Suzuki was almost 90 years of age then, but this incident may well be taken as his gentle way of making a poignant point of Zen—non-verbally. Not so graceful was Perls in a well-known incident at Esalen which also involved Maslow. Maslow was giving a seminar, and right in the middle of the proceedings, Perls crawled around on his belly, and totally disrupted the seminar by his "zany" acts. This might have been Perls' way of dramatizing his boredom, but he certainly failed to see the larger issue that Maslow was deeply concerned with.

The issue at stake, which will have important ramifications for education at large, is the relationship between the two modes of knowing: experiential versus abstract. Are they mutually exclusive or are they complementary to each other? Can the words and concepts be used in such a way as to induce or enhance man's experiential awareness? Maslow firmly believed that they could, and the only question for him was how. Maslow would point out that man's cognition needs (which include both modes of knowing) are too important to be ignored, and that therefore they must be fully attended to. His view, also shared by general semanticists, was that one can use language or any other form of abstraction so long as the user is fully aware of the level of abstraction he is at. Then, by freely shifting the mental gear from one mode of knowing to the other, or alternating between the experiential and the abstract as the occasion may call for, the person might make his own life so much richer.

It has often been said that a map is not a territory and a label must not be confused with the reality. But if we can use the map in the exploration of external environment, why cannot we use the words and concepts in the discovery of inner space? Far from shying away from words, Maslow tried to make the best of them. Maslow hoped that by exposing the students to the experiential reports of others, they might hit a responsive chord within. As is seen in his memo, Maslow found doing so a very effective way to elicit a response from his audience. He often read an example or two from his large collection of peak-experiences, making comments as he went along, and then encouraged personal responses from the class.

A similar technique was applied to the "unitive consciousness" which was discussed at great length toward the end of the semester. The unitive consciousness is defined as the transcendence of the basic polarities—such as good and evil, sacred and profane—and is said to be a distinguishing characteristic of mystics and self-actualizing people. Here again Maslow wanted to discover if the basic skills involved in the higher forms of cognition, such as unitive consciousness, could be taught and developed through a combination of lectures, examples and exercises.

Maslow has called his approach to experiential education a *cognitive therapy* because of the emphasis he placed on cognition (in a broader sense) as a way to greater experiential awareness. It was called a "therapy" only for the lack of a better term, and Maslow would stress the fact that his approach is not for the sick but for the normal—in particular, in the class setting, for normal college students. It is a therapy only in the sense that it is purported to bring about a change in a person's outlook on life. A natural question is, does it work? Is it a viable alternative to a traditional method (such as meditation) which requires a long and arduous effort?

In discussing the results of the course, one can think in terms of both long- and short-term effects. The immediate feedback from the students was mixed and varied. Some students, anticipating a T-group situation, were rather disappointed. One student wrote in his journal the following impressions when the course was half over:

> The first hour everyone had to contribute, there was a great deal of comradeship felt, frankness was displayed. It was as if we were excited travelers about to explore ourselves together. The prospect of this new, exciting, perhaps terrifying business set us all aflame. Since that day, the class has been flat. The original excitement and venturousness had been lost. Now the talkers talk, the listeners listen, and the class is normal.

This nicely sums up a portion of what had happened at this time in the course. But it should also be noted that the above entry was made at the low point in the course and a number of meaningful things did happen later on. There were situations that involved the whole group in a meaningful way, and one of them was an exercise on what Maslow has called "rhapsodic communication." A rhapsodic communication is a non-structured communication which makes use of metaphors, figures of speech, analogy and poetic expression. In this type of communication, the primary process cognition, as opposed to the secondary process cognition, plays a leading role, and the words used tend to be more connotative than denotative. It is particularly suited for the expression and communication of feelings, and Maslow has attached great importance to its cultivation.

The rhapsodic communication workshop reported in this volume[34] is undoubtedly one of the most interesting sessions of the year. There are perhaps many ways to facilitate a rhapsodic communication, but in this particular instance visual materials were employed. The exercise engaged the whole class in a spirit of adventure, which is a rare achievement in a class of this size. Best of all, it is a group approach to self-knowledge, with all the participants joining in what might be called a shared journey into the twilight zone of the self. The occasion also showed Maslow in his most introspective moments, expressing his hopes and self-doubts, convictions and dilemmas. In a class where the ultimate goal is self-knowledge, such an experience is almost an education in itself.

When the course came to an end, if only too soon, there was a general feeling that many of the materials presented in the class could only be assimilated by the individual over years or even decades. And this was what Maslow apparently had in mind when he planned the course: education for life. There is also some evidence that the materials learned and the insights gained in such a course are not likely to dissipate easily, as they involve a change in attitudes, beliefs, values, and even a radical change in the fundamental outlook on life. To some students, at least, the course became a major turning point in their lives soon after it was over. The following samples of feedback solicited from the participants three months later already indicated a direction of that change, and they were by no means atypical.

One student wrote of her experience:

> I enjoyed this course very much. Every class session
> left me with a sense of exhilaration and renewed zest

for life. This course has been a major force in determining the direction I will take for a future career.

Another student also wrote of a change in personal outlook:

> It is hard to say what I learned which I value most, because so much has been assimilated in bits and pieces, all unorganized . . . It was not any specific theory; I think I learned an *attitude*, a way of treating life . . . My attitudes have changed much in many ways. I allow myself to be myself, and others to be themselves in many ways that I did not before.

Maslow had suggested to the students to keep in touch with him even after graduation, and I believe many did. They were to tell Maslow how the course may have affected their lives and how they would appraise the course in retrospect. According to our original plan, this feedback would be an important part of the follow-up study. Unfortunately, the full plan was never carried out due to the sudden death of Maslow in California in June 1970.

Although the present book is primarily concerned with Maslow's pilot course of 1963-64, it may be necessary to mention one discordant note I noticed in the closing chapter of Maslow's teaching career. There are some indications that Maslow was greatly disappointed in the student reactions to some of the courses he taught in the late 1960s. In one unusually self-critical paper,[35] he recalled how discouraged or even angry he was in one of the courses he taught in 1968. He was exasperated because he had failed, so he believed, to instill in the students the love of knowledge as well as the sense of social responsibility he himself deeply felt inside. Other teachers might shrug their shoulders and carry on teaching as if nothing had ever happened, but to Maslow it was too important to ignore. He was reaching the point when he began questioning the wisdom of remaining in the teaching profession.

In the same article he also raised many questions he had been asking himself. While he reaffirmed his basic belief in the value of humanistic education, he wondered how it would fit in with college education. He cast doubt on the efficiency of a non-structured approach in dealing with content-oriented subjects, asking if these might not be better taught by a traditional method. He understood a profound desire of the students for intimacy and community feeling, and yet he asked if college was the proper place to fulfill such basic needs as love and acceptance.

As a polemic, he even proposed to draw a distinction between what he has called "professional" and "humanistic" education. The former is more content-oriented, factual learning, while the latter deals with the problems of personal growth, identity, and values. Professional education consists of extrinsic learning, whereas humanistic education is devoted to intrinsic learning. He further proposed that early education might be devoted to humanistic education so that the college years can be spent on professional training. This suggestion of his cannot be taken as a definitive statement, however. Not only is it incongruent with the basic tenet of his theory but it also illustrates the importance he assigned to experiential and motivational aspects of learning. The idea might, furthermore, accentuate the current artificial separation between the cognitive and the affective, the extrinsic and the intrinsic, which Maslow in the main wanted to eradicate.

His definitive statement of the goals and implications of humanistic education can be found in his posthumous work, *The Farther Reaches of Human Nature* (1971). Humanistic education is here envisioned by him as encompassing the whole lifespan, a process that commences at birth and continues throughout life. Similarly, experiential learning as an integral part of humanistic education need not be limited to childhood only. He also suggested that education must refocus itself on the joy of personal discovery, the sense of awe and mystery in learning. The process of learning can then become as meaningful and exhilarating as peak-experiences.

One of Maslow's long-cherished dreams as a psychologist had always been to immerse himself in research and writing—full-time, hopefully. The wish had been latent all those years, but as he began to experience growing frustrations in teaching, his desire to follow his true inclination became irresistible. Especially after his first heart attack in 1967, he felt time was running out, and when in 1969 the Laughlin Foundation[36] offered him a four-year grant to do exactly what he wanted to do, he promptly accepted.

By all accounts, his final year in California was one of the happiest in his entire life. Relieved now of the burdens of teaching and other academic routines, he was able to devote all his time and energy to the theoretical research and writing which was now his "calling." He was full of hope and zest for his work and he seemed as optimistic as ever about the future of mankind. True, he was saddened by the ignorance, hostility and violence which plagued society, but this experience only seemed to intensify his already strong determination to work out a comprehensive theory of human nature. In the spring of 1970 he wrote and urged me to join him at the Foundation, while informing me of his plan to work on his "big systemic theory of human nature and of society." It was planned as a very large expansion of the last chapter of *Toward a Psychology of Being*, which was titled, "Some Basic Propositions of Growth and Self-Actualizing Psychology."[37]

Could a teacher like Maslow, who has taught all his life, give up a profession which is almost his mission? Definitely not. Even though he left his university post, Maslow carried on teaching in a new form, and to a new height. His pupils were no longer limited to those who were within the confines of the academic institution but to anybody who was willing to listen and share his joy of discovery. He regarded his works and writings as ongoing communications, and the whole world as his classroom. As he has said:

> Sometimes I get the feeling of my writing being a communication to my great-great grandchildren who, of course, are not yet born. It's a kind of an expression of love for them, leaving them not money but in effect affectionate notes, bits of counsel, lessons I have learned that might help them.[38]

PERSONALITY AND GROWTH

PART I

LECTURE & LAB SUMMARIES
SEPTEMBER 30 - OCTOBER 21, 1963

Hung-Min Chiang

In the following chapters, Hung-Min Chiang provides synopses of and commentaries on the first four classes that took place before the tape recorder was brought in. These consist of Maslow's lectures and the "laboratory for self-knowledge" group discussions. These classes occurred on September 30, October 7, 14, and 21, 1963.

SEPTEMBER 30, 1963

Lecture

THE AIM OF THE COURSE, as Maslow stated in the opening of the class, was to study various strategies of experiential learning. Its goal was to recover the neglected, overlooked or even—in some cases—repressed aspects of personality; to return to "raw" experience; to become aware of the unconscious and preconscious within us and gain a better understanding of ourselves. In the context of the course, being "experiential" simply meant being less abstract and bookish and becoming more concrete and preverbal.

Individual psychoanalysis was regarded by Maslow as the best means yet for the discovery of self-knowledge; nevertheless, it was also recognized as impractical in the classroom situation. If the aim was to learn and to teach personal knowledge, what would be a viable alternative to individual analysis or group therapy? Could a psychodynamic type of education be devised and taught in school? Maslow hoped that the same objectives might be attained through a proper combination of lectures, group discussions, and exercises specifically designed for the purpose. Maslow referred to the approach taken in this course as "cognitive therapy."

It needs to be pointed out that the term "cognition" used here, as elsewhere in Maslow's writings, has two mutually related meanings. Firstly, it is related to the group of needs Maslow loosely called "cognitive needs" in his need-hierarchy theory.[1] It refers to the desire to know and understand ourselves and the world around us—needs as essential as any basic need for psychological health. It consists of not only intellectual knowing, but also the learning of values, perspectives and personal identity. The thwarting of these needs, Maslow believed, may ultimately lead to "cognitive psychopathology."[2]

But in the context of the course, Maslow was particularly interested in a special form of cognition known in psychoanalysis as "primary process cognition." The functions of the primary processes are believed to be "essentially cognitive rather than conative."[3] Maslow characterized the present approach as an "intellectual approach to non-intellectual learning." Here, the intellect was seen not as an enemy but rather as a friend whose service might facilitate experiential learning. This was a very different approach from most educational endeavors attempted by others. A key to success in this approach apparently lies in knowing not only how but also when to use appropriate modes of knowing.

A number of reading assignments were given, including two papers by Maslow: "The Creative Attitude"[4] and "Lessons from the Peak-Experiences."[5] The central theme here is the need for openness to experience. The Taoist's idea of letting-be, or "Taoistic receptivity," as Maslow has called it, was cited as a defining characteristic of experiential sensitivity and as a necessary condition in the attainment of full humanness. We can learn to be receptive, to let go of our control and to permit joy and sadness to sweep over us. Trying to regain or increase experiential sensitivity by way of manipulation and control is self-defeating, as is holding back. An analogy is that tightening up is a poor way of performing natural functions such as urination, defecation, sleep or sex. One good example is found in childbirth, where relaxation has been found to reduce the birth pangs caused by the contracting tension in the muscles.

Closely related to the issue of control versus Taoistic let-be are two forms of perception based on different strategies: global vs. analytical. Ordinary perception is highly analytical and manipulative. It is an active process of categorizing—rubricizing—and it often hinders rather than facilitates a clear perception of what actually is. Total or global perception, on the other hand, is non-intrusive and non-interfering and therefore more sensitive and accurate. Some evidence supporting this contention, cited by Maslow, were the results of the "Art Test."[6] The findings of this study revealed the superiority of an open, innocent perception in detecting the finer quality of works of art.

Some issues that came up during the discussion were: Is receptivity different from mere passivity? What is child-like innocence? Is it necessarily opposed to intellectuality, sophistication or education?

Another topic presented and discussed was the resolution of dichotomies. Most of us are plagued by our own dichotomous tendencies, and the transcendence of dichotomous thinking is a necessary step in moving toward psychological health. One good example of this dichotomy is found in masculinity-femininity. It is true that to a certain degree femininity and masculinity are in inverse relationship. That is, the more femininity there is, the less masculinity there will be. But after a certain point, this no longer holds true. This is well demonstrated in self-actualizing men who are feminine and yet also the most masculine of all, and in self-actualizing women who are masculine and yet also the most feminine of all. Somehow mature people are not threatened by their own latent femininity, masculinity, or inherent bisexuality.

October 7, 1963
Lecture

THE VARIETIES OF RELIGIOUS EXPERIENCE[1] by William James was assigned for intensive reading. Maslow was obviously impressed by James' existential-phenomenological approach and called the book a good representation of a naturalistic-humanistic orientation. The parallels between Maslow and James are obvious enough. Both had broad intellectual perspectives and minds that refused to be restricted to narrow and predefined notions of science and psychology. They showed a deep and persistent interest in the frontiers of psychology. The subjective reports of mystical experience, for instance, were accepted as legitimate psychological data and were brought under the jurisdiction of science. Religious phenomena were interpreted in terms of underlying psychological processes and yet a common reductionistic error was carefully avoided.

There were also some essential differences that have been noted by Maslow himself. For instance, James studied the mystical experiences of a select few in traditional religious contexts, while Maslow studied similar phenomenon in a much wider, secular expression. For Maslow, the peak-experience is a core religious experience, but its occurrence is not limited to the religious community alone. It is universal and can be induced by a wide variety of triggers and activities.

Another point of difference between James and Maslow is found in their assessment of personality characteristics associated with the mystics and the "peakers." In Maslow's opinion, the peak-experience is more an indication of psychological health than psychopathology. It is, in his own words, "a transitory moment of self-actualization in the average person."[2] There he was in apparent company with Bucke,[3] who reported the appearance of "the cosmic consciousness" among human specimens functioning at their best. This view was in contradiction to James' observation that the religious geniuses and mystics are by nature emotionally unstable. James went so far as to suggest that it is precisely these pathological traits that were responsible for the experience. Maslow disagreed. He believed that previous depression and "the dark night of the soul" described by James were not necessary for peak-experiences. But how would Maslow explain the abundance of abnormal episodes in the religious literature? Maslow answered that the cultural expectation as well as the selection of extreme cases by James might be responsible for the observed difference.

The validation of an experience as subjective as ecstasy poses a real challenge to researchers. How could one ascertain whether any particular ecstasy is authentic? Maslow agreed with James in regarding it a very difficult problem and stated that the experience can best be judged by its fruit and by how it actually affects the person in life.

There was some discussion on the nature of triggers. Is there any relationship between the stimuli that trigger a peak-experience and the content of the experience itself? The answer was that there is no correlation. It has been found that the same trigger may lead to different experiences in different people and, conversely, a similar experience might be caused by a variety of different triggers. Maslow also observed that the actual content of peak-experiences by males and females is nearly identical, and there are no discernable sex differences in that area. There are, however, some noticeable differences in the nature of triggers for men and women. Women's peak-experiences are reported to come from love, while men's more from victory, success and conquest. How many of these sex differences could actually be attributed to the cultural expectations of the time? This is a question to ponder.

In this class, as in the previous one, there was a lengthy discussion on the importance and meaning of spontaneity. One of the questions that came up was the necessary distinction between spontaneity and impulsiveness. How can spontaneity be differentiated from impulsiveness? Maslow maintained that real spontaneity comes from the intrinsic self. A real expressiveness is ego-syntonic rather that ego-dystonic and is rooted in the biologically "real self." Impulsivity, on the other hand, is superficial and is often characterized by rigidity and tension and the lack of graceful coordination. Contrary to a common misconception, to be spontaneous does not mean to follow every impulse or desire that strikes one's fancy. Spontaneity presupposes the experiential knowing of what is real and what is not, and what is suited to us and what is contrary to our nature. It is definitely not emotionality, but it involves an active process of choosing and selecting.

What is the role of the self-observing ego in this process? Can one be spontaneous and self-observing at the same time? Spontaneity implies self-observance in the absence of the ordinary ego-function. Maslow's position on the issue (to observe oneself and be spontaneous at the same time) was that this is a difficult theoretical problem but it can be done with practice.[4]

The important thing is to become fully *aware* of whatever is going on, and awareness is not the same as ego-consciousness. Too much ego-consciousness could be crippling, but awareness is not. Maslow further stated that the best way to wear out a blind impulse or a persistent, uncontrollable impulse is not to repress it but to become fully aware of it. But the awareness and acceptance of forbidden impulses is by no means the approval of them. The point is that only if we are aware of our own unconscious processes can we do something constructive about them. And this is the best way, the only rational way, to handle the impulses.

There are many impulses which are not "bad" and yet which are repressed by culture. For instance, it is natural for men as well as women to cry, but many men cannot. Why? Maslow maintained that the over-emphasis on masculinity, competition and striving in the West has resulted in a taboo on tenderness and a subsequent loss of the ability to feel. The goal of psychotherapy, and of humanistic education, is the recovery and development of this human capacity for genuine feeling. But are the need for achievement and the need for human expression necessarily antagonistic and incompatible, and can one choose one or the other? Maslow believed that both can be integrated, as is seen in self-actualizing people in whom striving and non-striving, doing and experiencing, are well-harmonized.

OCTOBER 14, 1963

Lecture & Laboratory for Self-Knowledge

DURING THE THIRD WEEK OF THE COURSE the plan for weekly experiential labs was announced. The first two hours of this class were spent on the discussion of the aims, objectives and guidelines for the laboratory in self-knowledge. The following written statement was read out in class.

> General experiences show that the recovery of the id in the classroom, in education, does not go well. That is, psychoanalysis cannot be done on a large scale. This is, however, not clearly stated in the Freudian literature.
>
> Unconscious can be taken in two ways: one is instinctual and the other is cognitive—primary or pre-verbal. Preconscious as related to the latter has not so much to do with impulses, but it is rather a way of sensing, cognizing, and this child-like cognition of the world and of ourselves can be recovered. The latter is more subject to the influence of education than the former and results in the lowering of defenses in the long run.

The following itemized notes by Maslow were also added:

- This is not against my view on the importance of and my expectations in the expression of the instinctual process.

- You should be learning that the id or the unconscious is not a horrible thing or a source of evil things but is a source of creativeness and the ability to play—the regression in the service of the ego. Being crazy is dangerous only when you cannot come back.

- Part of this unconscious could be made more comfortable, as it is part of ourselves.

Our ability to love has been partially repressed. The recovery of feelings, to learn how to pay attention to and to perceive these inner aspects of personality, to find labels and a vocabulary for unnamable emotions, impulses, sensations and muscle tension, to practice looking inward and [to practice] concentration, to become more aware of the incipient or weak feelings before they break into the unconscious—all these help to promote a rich inner life.

The class was carefully reminded that what was being planned was *not* group therapy because the classroom situation is generally not suitable for true group therapy to take place. This is so because most school situations are not unconditional and are therefore non-therapeutic. It was hoped that in this class some characteristics of a real, deep therapy—such as regression, transference, dream interpretation or discussion of personal sex life—would be avoided. The members were encouraged to be honest with themselves, but were also advised not to push themselves to the edge of embarrassment, from which there might be no graceful retreat.

Laboratory for Self-Knowledge

This third hour began with a self-introduction by each member, followed by several individuals' experiential reports. Topics presented were: anxiety, tension, impulse for love and affection, unitive consciousness (i.e., perception of the sacred through the profane), and peak-experiences. Most of the discussion today remained at an intellectual level and truly experiential reports were few and far between. This was perhaps due to the fact that this was the first lab and the members were not quite sure of the rules and strategies. The class was then encouraged to develop skill in rhapsodic communication—communication in terms of "figures of speech, metaphors and similes." This mode of communication was said to be particularly suited for experiential reports where feelings and emotions are involved.

A major assignment in the course was the keeping of a personal journal, the purpose of which was the recording of the conscious life and the unfolding awareness of the intrinsic self. The experiential reporting consisted of, among other things, peak-experiences, desolation experiences, or anything triggered off by lectures, discussions, papers and books. The journal writing was regarded as an exercise in self-expression, in clarifying one's own thoughts and feelings, and was therefore seen as a first step in the direction of self-actualization.

OCTOBER 21, 1963

Lecture & Laboratory for Self-Knowledge

THE IMPORTANCE OF UNDERSTANDING LOVE and accepting one's own sexual feelings and impulses were the focal points of discussion. Maslow stated that there was currently a great shortage of *good* literature on sexual love. By "sexual love," he obviously meant something more than mere physical pleasure derived from the sexual act. His observation was that most of the existing literature on sex, as in sex manuals, was entirely devoid of affection and love, and there were practically no books that might teach young people what true sexual love is like. What would Maslow think of D. H. Lawrence, who had written a great many novels on the subject? Was he not a post-Freudian writer who advocated a non-repressive, sexually fulfilling way of life? Maslow replied that Lawrence was an unfortunate case of extremes, because he apparently overdid or even slightly faked the nature of sexual love. A true sexual love, Maslow contended, is as rare as any other peak-experience, and simply does not come as often as Lawrence led us to believe.

Laski's[1] recent work *Ecstasy*[2] was introduced and discussed at some length. She carried out an empirical study of secular as well as religious experiences and came up with findings that were surprisingly similar to Maslow's. A Freudian notion of ecstasy as largely a phenomenon of sexual repression was questioned and rejected. Maslow cited a case of a 44-year old sailor who had a peak-experience at the sight of the first woman he had seen in many years. Interestingly enough, it was her voice that enchanted him most. Why? Was it conditioning or repression? What constitutes female power?

Maslow believed that any life experiences, when they rise to a certain level of completion and intensity, can lead to ecstasy. This means that ecstasy could be induced not only by positive events, as Maslow previously reported, but by negative events as well. Any sad or painful experience that produces an ecstasy and a heightened sense of consciousness was referred to by Maslow and Laski as "desolation experience."

Laboratory for Self-Knowledge

The lab was more or less a continuation of the discussion started in the previous week: self-introduction, peak-experiences, anxiety and affection. The group was then asked to report their reaction to: parental affection, maternal impulses, pregnancy, childbirth and the innocence of children. Why do people like children? What is the feeling of being maternal like? These exercises were done in order to sharpen our feelings and our ability to experience fully. It was perhaps due to the nature of the topics covered that the discussion during this lab was dominated by women, while most men remained silent and contributed very little.

PART II

THE TRANSCRIPTS

October 28, 1963 – January 13, 1964

INTRODUCTION TO THE TRANSCRIPTS

Hung-Min Chiang

THE FOLLOWING IS THE RECORD of the class proceedings running from October 28 through January 13. As our intention was to reproduce and report the happenings as fully and as accurately as possible, the editing was limited. Following the wish of the late Dr. Maslow, all the events that took place in the class—be they positive or negative—are reproduced here. There were some two dozen participants in the group, but to preserve confidentiality, fictitious names have been substituted in reference to all of them but Maslow.

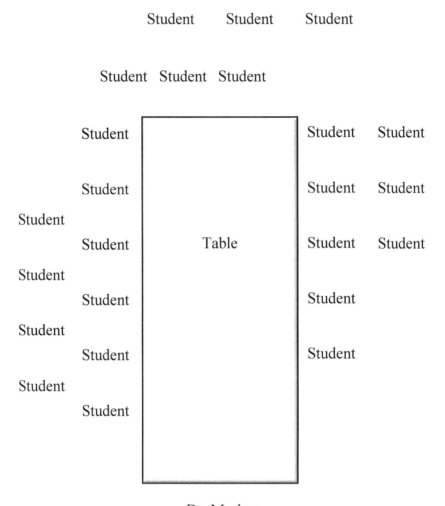

The Seating Arrangement

OCTOBER 28, 1963

Lecture

This was the fifth session of the class. A tape recorder
was brought in for the first time.

Maslow: As a matter of course they have these very fine, portable tape recorders. I've had people come into my office and simply say "how-do-you-do?" and then unpack a tape recorder and then we go on, whatever the conversation.

I feel much less uncertain about our course than I felt at the first of the semester. I thought almost constantly about what we were doing and about what we might do. In fact, I have all sorts of notes on exercises of all sorts, self-therapies of all sorts. I've been hunting through the literature on meditation and contemplation and then some of my old notes, scattered under a half-dozen different categories, and I get more impressed. I think more and more that this kind of thing can be useful and feasible.

The session that we had last Monday, for instance, seemed to me, as I went away thinking about it, to be extremely useful, as having given me the crowbar I want. That is the touchstone—the principle of differentiation between intellectualizing and experiencing. It seemed to me that as we talked, I became more conscious—and I hope you did too—of this difference, of the possibility of working out among ourselves criteria that we can all use for knowing when we are being abstract and intellectual, as most of us are most of the time. We are trying to be self-observing egos, you might say, to be aware when we are doing that and to be able to turn it on or off in favor of experiential report, which we should also be able to turn on or off as we please.

And I'd like to continue with that today, later on. I don't think it makes much difference where we start from, so we might just go ahead with that mothering and fathering experiencing of babies and children and so on, and this time I'd like to hear more from the men. I've been picking up some notes that I'll pass along to you later on about mother love, and why we don't have any parallel there for father love. That's one reason I'd like to record this more, and to be more formal—to have records so as to be able to look back to see what's happened, if anything has happened, and to make use of it and pass it on. If we've worked out techniques. We're exploring here. I don't know where I'm going and I'm sure you don't know where you're going exactly. If we do stumble across good techniques, good ways of doing things, good differentiations, then I think we ought to save them in a form that we can pass on to others.

Now this brings up another question of procedure—about that notebook, about keeping records [i.e., personal journals]. One person brought up what I hadn't thought about before, the question of privacy within the home, and it seems to me that this might be generalized. For this person it was better to do this writing—this reporting back to me about experiencing—to do it chunk by chunk rather than to save it around for a whole semester, where (it had not occurred to me) it might not be private. If you live in one of these dormitory rooms and leave a notebook around it can be a great temptation for others to read it—as it would be with personal diaries. So I would accept, as you wish, either doing what I suggested originally, either turning in that notebook—keeping everything together and then turning it in later on in a chunk—or simply turning in whatever you write, whenever you've written it. Simply put it in my box where it's safe enough, or pass it to me directly. Also you can do this with a pseudonym, if that's a help, if there are people around. If what you say is too personal, private and *sacred*—in the way that I used that word before—then you might want to do that: not have your name on it. Put some pseudonym. I suggested in the past a pretty standard pseudonym: your mother's maiden name. You'll never forget it and nobody else knows it, except your mom. Or if you prefer something else, that's alright.

And I should say again, this has nothing to do with your grades. I am trying very hard to make my peace with a situation which I consider to be contaminating of this whole enterprise, poisoning it almost. I must do grading and yet I would like to keep it as far away as possible. I should think that, for the sake of the enterprise, the third hour of ours and these reports of yours should have nothing to do with grades. And of course I repeat again, the third hour attendance is optional—very optional—and again has nothing to do with grades.

Do you have any questions about that? Or any thoughts that have occurred to you about it that I've overlooked? Now if you want to discuss these things with me, you can also write it on your journal pages when you turn them in to me, and we can set up a time to talk. Okay?

Remember that I am just as interested in negative reports as in positive reports. For instance, in retrospect I now realize what I was trying to do last Monday. I was trying to help you to differentiate between intellectualizing—abstracting, intellectual talk on the one hand—and experiencing on the other. I would like to know if you don't know what I was talking about, or if you didn't see it. I would like you to report that—the negative as well as the positive. Whatever happened, I would like it recorded. Do you have anything to respond?

Joan: I question your announcement that we are going to tape the third hour as well as the other part, knowing that this is personal and that some people just might not want what they say taped. I know in some groups there is just a general agreement that what goes on does not go out of the class.

Maslow: Remember, at the beginning of the semester I gave up the hope of keeping things private? And I explicitly . . . It never works, it hasn't, it just doesn't. And it's better to accept that as a weakness instead of trying to be perfectionistic. But this third hour, that's another story. Well, how do the rest of you feel about it? Do you have anything to say about that? [*Pause*] My own feeling is that in general, for the purposes of encouraging spontaneity and expressiveness, it would be better not to have any tape recording. On the other hand, we have something else to keep in mind; that is, the research Chiang and I are involved in. My thought here was of having kind of a compromise; I wouldn't hesitate to make my own flat promise and to ask for a flat promise from Chiang who will hear it anyhow [as he is in this class]. But if enough of you object to it, I think I would reconsider the question of the tapes. So, I would like you to talk about it.

Roslyn: I sort of register an objection.

Maslow: You don't like it.

Roslyn: I don't like it. [*Unintelligible*]

Maslow: [*Unintelligible*] Since you seemed . . . you're not saying. Does that mean you're neutral about it? That it doesn't matter?

Jayne: I see no reason why not to tape it. We won't say our names and if we say something good or something, we want to have it on tape.

Maslow: How many of your feel that way about it, that it doesn't matter? How many of you feel that it *would* matter and inhibit you some, that it would hamper you? [*Pause*] This also—if I can lecture now—I'm trying to keep my role as the passer-on of information sort of in a separate category. The experience we have with this recording and keeping notes and so on might be instructive for you, interesting for you. It has always been felt for psychotherapy that it must be entirely private. I have felt that myself; I have never taken notes. For instance, in my work on peak-experiences I never took notes. I thought it was just too sacred to have a paper and pencil, so I have no records except my memory. Well, around 1940 two people simultaneously—to everybody's horror and shock—started recording the psychoanalytic and psychotherapeutic sessions. One was Carl Rogers,[1] and this was the technique by which he opened up the whole possibility of research, and he did it for research purposes. The other was Felix Deutsch,[2] who was the old man with the beard in the psychoanalytic tribe around here. He was Freud's personal physician and was the "second messiah," let's say—highly respected. He also recorded psychoanalytic sessions. I remember when I heard about it, I was shocked and horrified and thought that they didn't understand anything about therapy and personal relationships and so on.

Now in general—and I can't get over my own objection, my own inhibition about it—I still hate to take notes when I am talking about something intimate and personal with anybody, either when I'm talking or when I'm just listening; I just feel that would be an intrusion. But the fact remains that the people who have done this report that everybody gets over the uneasiness and the distaste after a little while. It has gone so far now—people are so delicate about this—it's gone so far now that they are teaching psychoanalysis with an audience. And by gosh, they tell me it's worked out all right. It seems impossible! It's at the Menninger Clinic they have been doing this. They have a whole lineup—six or eight young psychoanalysts behind a one-way mirror and the patient knows they're there. After some difficulty for a time, the report is that if you pick the right one, the right kind of patient, that this not only makes no difference, but it raises interesting data which we have never heard of before—getting transference to a dozen analysts. [*General laughter*] Well, that's as honest as I can be about it. Everybody who has had experience with it is unanimous and they report that after the initial hesitation they get over it.

Anybody else want to say anything about this?

Ben: Just that it's acceptable to me.

Carole: I have a question: I can't understand the danger that the tape recorder poses, beyond any initial danger of somebody committing something that you say to a group.

Maslow: Which may very well happen anyway. I'm not sure that these people were thinking of danger so much as distaste. I confess I would have too. For instance, I was taped at a freshman seminar over at Harvard a couple of years ago when they started them. It was focused around autobiography, and it was a friend of mine who was running this thing. You know, I didn't *like* to do it, but I *had* to—I couldn't duck out of it. And then this whole business was present when I came there. There were these tape recorders and here I was talking about my soul, and I must confess, I felt uneasy. It wasn't for the danger so much, but for about the same reason as if I had to strip—embarrassed slightly, or hesitant. They mimeographed out the text and as I asked them, it was agreed that they wouldn't be given to anybody but the people in that class, and the tape was destroyed or erased. Now this was not any danger I was in, for there wasn't anything there that I haven't told my friends. It was just a sense of privacy.

Sharon: My objection is that whenever two people come into our house, my husband turns on the tape recorder. He tries to get reactions to his films and things of that sort. I find it is not so much danger or privacy. It is something like inhibition, in that I think people are apt to think more carefully about what they say if they know it is going to be recorded on the tape recorder. It is just really a question of spontaneity. I find it somewhat dampening, inhibiting.

Maslow: Are these the same people that come back again and again or different people?

Sharon: No, usually different people, but I know I'm always conscious of the fact.

Maslow: You are still?

Sharon: And I noticed several people that have been back before tend to talk somewhat differently.

Maslow: How about the other objectors. [*Turning to Carole*] Perhaps you could speak about that. Was yours a feeling of danger or distaste or privacy or what?

Carole: Distaste. I think you've eliminated the possibility of privacy.

Maslow: Any other . . .?

Paul: I'd just like to second the statement that the revelation itself which takes place before the group should be considered on the same level of danger as the tape recorder. I can't see why the tape recorder itself should have any extra social danger to anybody. Obviously, anything which anyone reveals in the classroom is heard by some twenty other people in here, and any one of those people is capable of using that statement slanderously. There is a liability in anything you say here but you can't live any kind of decent life without taking some kind of liability. We all seem to have agreed on some of these liabilities simply by participating in the third hour, because we have obviously been talking to one another. So I can't quite understand the feeling—I'm not even sure it's a real feeling—that spontaneity is going to be inhibited more by the presence of the tape recorder. I think that it is inhibited as it is and the recorder will be no more of a dampening factor.

Maslow: We can go into an experiential session here if you like. I think it is interesting too, that you [*Paul*] talk easily, but many people don't. They are more embarrassed, shyer; they stumble a little bit, and stammer and so on. It may be partly that this has to do with a greater sense of privacy or a lesser sense of privacy. Maybe we should take it at that level—take advantage of the situation now, and if the people who do feel slightly inhibited, even by the group or by a tape recorder, might speak up a little about it, try to express it. What's a society without trying?

Carole: I find that I speak more easily with the tape recorder on. I don't know; it makes me feel that what I am saying is more important than it would be ordinarily.

Maslow: You're surprised, eh? Anybody else feel that way? [*Pause*] Well, how about the inhibitions that you may have? Let's get them out on the table; we might just as well get used to talking about inhibitions—the feeling of inhibition. I didn't go very deep into it for myself, but if I could use my own example there about taking my clothes off—not even stripping. Supposing I sit there and take my shirt off. Wouldn't I feel a little funny? It's not quite the place for it. Well, of course, I take it off under other circumstances without any question. We are all used to stripping down almost to zero on the beach yet, especially for the girls, if I asked the girls to take their blouses off, even though they have brassieres on and whatever else, slips and so on, I'm sure you'd feel the same way—slightly inhibited, slightly embarrassed. [*Sporadic giggles from class*] Even though if we all went to the beach or in the swimming pool, they would get undressed far more drastically than that. That kind of thing now—if you can think—just try to place that feeling, reluctance perhaps. If you can put words on it. You want to try? [*Pause*]

Joan: Well, I know it influenced what I said because I didn't process it. It just came out of the discussion about tape recorders, that they would definitely inhibit me in that situation. I'm sure it would make a difference. And I think what I said is greatly a carry-over from that.

Maslow: Well, what would you compare it to as a feeling? Inhibitive in what ways? What other way in which you would feel inhibited?

Joan: [*Says something unintelligible, then chuckles*] I'm not sure. I'd have to think about it.

Maslow: Well, I would suggest to you that when you get such feelings that you make yourself aware of them and try to understand them. Your first step is simply absorbing them, simply permitting them, accepting them from the consciousness. The fact that you do feel inhibited might surprise you, or sometimes it might do the opposite, like this one, which surprised me a little bit—the opposite of inhibition there. At least be aware that the feeling *is* there and how you *do* feel about something, and be able to scrape that away, to differentiate it from the feeling that you *ought* to have in such and such a situation. The question is what feelings you actually *do*, in fact, have.

Melissa: Is it possible that because the tape recorder is a machine, the idea that a machine is receiving your soul is a kind of dehumanizing feeling? I don't think I feel that way, but because I do associate tape recorders with machines, maybe I do that somewhat.

Sophia: I was gonna say that, you know, for myself, I do get slightly inhibited when I talk with the group and say personal feelings, but my feeling towards the tape recorder isn't one of danger; it's just that I feel that there's an adjustment to make already, just being able to talk, and the tape recorder is like an additional adjustment. I think perhaps if we came in maybe two weeks later that would be enough time.

Maslow: I have a thought here that I would like to ask you. Supposing we were not using a tape recorder, but a television camera. [*Laughter*] Now that underlines it, huh? Maybe the tape recorder is like that—with that feeling we all have, we would probably get paralyzed. The tape recorder for some people, as near as I can make out, would be 1% of that feeling, but it would be the same kind in a lesser degree. Would that be for you? Does that make sense for you? Is this of the same quality, the same kind of feeling?

Sarah: Maybe nobody else in the room feels this way, but I have the feeling that television wouldn't be as bad because it would always be there. After a while you wouldn't be looking up to the camera all the time, wondering whether to smile or not to smile or just to sit there. But if the tape recorder is on when you are speaking, you are on the air, you have to be prepared. You can't really get used to it because there are certain times when you are on or when you are not.

Maslow: On—like you use that as an actress does, almost. Is that it?

Sarah: Yeah, and you have to spend so much time preparing. If you think you have to answer someone in five minutes, you listen in a very different way. And if you think that you have to prepare your speech because it is going onto the tape recorder then your mind tries to improve things. But maybe you get over that.

Maslow: The report is that you get over it. That's the report. I can't say of my own . . .Well, my own experience—as a person, yes. That television, by the way, would not bother me, or hardly at all. Well, it *hasn't.* I've been on television. It hasn't bothered me. But I think it would have. I've got detoxified after years of talking and lecturing so that I just pay no attention. But at the age of—let's say, the first year of teaching—I'm sure it would have been very difficult.

Herb: I find that as each successive statement is made about the tape recorder I become more conscious of it. [*General laughter*] I suppose the reason is that now, during any time that is going to be taped, I will be wondering whether it does or does not have these effects. It sort of involves a concentration on . . . that I just want to report on to the group, not so much endangering it.

Maslow: A little lecture footnote—take that as a parody. This is the way it hits everyone—even nice things too. As you drag them into consciousness, you get more self-conscious, more aware. This is part of the price that you pay. And then I would fit that little statement into what I said last time—you can normally expect these things to be dragged into consciousness to make you more—to be more gawky about it—but they eventually slip back into a pre-conscious state. I would expect, yes, that if I made you conscious of this tape recorder, you will be more aware at first, but eventually, I expect, that will quickly drop away.

Clara: I think there is something about a tape recorder or camera which, because it is a machine, makes it very easy to forget that it's there. It's the audience that you see that can inhibit you more and more. But with the machine itself, you don't relate in your mind how it is going to be used afterwards. It doesn't seem to me to be an inhibiting factor because you can't relate the cause and effect. You forget about it.

John: Well, I think that the people who object to the tape recorder do so definitely for a sense of danger. I think that when you say that it's not danger, but merely distaste, it is not really correct, because distaste alone is not a reason. Distaste is an expression, possibly of danger, and one danger I think is concerned with what Paul said about risk, but in a slightly different manner. What happens here is that we don't really take complete risk. It is not complete because we are in a room whose size we can see, the number of people we know, approximately, and we assume that everyone else takes a similar risk, so there is a camaraderie, a feeling that someone else will not expose you because *you* won't expose *him*, if nothing else. While with the tape recorder you are talking to an unseen audience. Even if you promised you won't let anyone hear, there is no telling who's going to hear it. [*Sounds of agreement*]

And here you are sure that people, merely because they come, they make a commitment that they won't be derisive about what you say, while this may be heard by people who *will* be derisive of what you say. Also, I think another point which causes fear is that what is said in front of the tape recorder is irrevocable. It's down there permanently, while what is said in the group is—we can sort of feel it slowly worn away by memory. Our defenses will operate with us but they won't with the tape recorder. [*General laughter*]

Sharon: This is very much what I actually feel; that on tape you make a permanent idiot of yourself. [*General laughter*] Just talking, you can hope everybody will forget what you said. This is the most honest feeling I have about it.

Maslow: Can I toss a little more into the pot here? Scopophilia. When you think about a peeping Tom—suppose you're taking a bath, both men as well as the women, and there's somebody peeping at you. You are in the bathtub, or even fully dressed in your living room or kitchen, wandering around, and suddenly you see that somebody had been looking at you all the time, in secret, private. How does that feel? Now you can make that as intense as you like, being in very private circumstances; being, let's say, in the bathtub or the shower, or even more private, like being on the toilet seat for instance, having been observed. I guess that's about the most private you can get. How about that? [*Pause*] I would think that most scopophiliacs—all scopophiliacs, all the peeping Toms—are men. Ninety-nine point something percent, maybe a hundred percent. I don't think any woman's ever been arrested for peeping, that I've ever heard, in this culture. And I say contrariwise, as all peeping Toms are men, maybe all men are peeping Toms too, to some extent. And yet if we waive that aside, the question that I have brought up for the men as well as the women is of somehow being powerless, maybe a feeling of not having full control over things, and being under someone's control. This is the way a peeping Tom feels, by the way, when he is looking—peeping through a keyhole at a naked woman, let's say. He feels as if he has a power over her, a control over her. Well, men can feel the same way if somebody's peeping at them and they don't know about it, even though it would be perfectly alright to look openly—that is, if the man, instead of peeping in through the keyhole would just walk in and sit down, and you'd know he was there. How would this feel?

John: Well, I think it would be different because then one has a choice. One can say either "Go away" or "Stay," or decide not to get dressed—and the other way one has no choice. One is seen whether one likes it or not.

Maslow: Is that a business of choice and control—power? powerlessness? Several people have mentioned the feeling of not being in charge of the situation.

John: Well, not *the* situation, but the situation of oneself in a sense. Not something that one is watching, but that one is in.

Herb: It would follow that if a peeping Tom has a feeling of power over the people that he is observing, then if he is in turn observed by other peeping Toms, he would have even a worse sense of deprivation of privacy.

Maslow: You suggested a new perversion. We're getting creative here—peeping at peeping Toms. [*General laughter*]

Charlotte: Just another analogy—different because I don't feel it is an infringement of personal privacy. I just feel like it's an inhibitory factor, like when you're a freshman. You first come to college as a freshman, you go to the first few classes, you want to say something, you want to give a good impression and you know that people are listening and watching you, especially because you are a freshman in an unusual situation. With the tape recorder you know this; besides having everyone listening, there is something there that is listening especially to you, and it can be repeated.

Sharon: My analogy that I just thought of is that we take a great many pictures, and in watching people watching pictures of themselves you see which ones they reject because it is not the impression that they want to give to people. And I think it is a question of that, perhaps. My own problem is that I don't want to accept myself in all respects, regardless of what comes out. And I withdraw my objection on two grounds: first of all, one can give up that kind of thought; second, in that first statement I made I was completely unaware that the tape recorder was on, or uninfluenced by its being there.

Maslow: We were a little sly about it. The tape recorder has been on all the time when we were talking about whether we should have it on. It is not a question! [*General laughter*]

You have been discussing the question of spontaneity, expressiveness and defense. Were you aware of that? Well, we have been talking about defenses. That's what's meant by defenses. It is a kind of screen behind which you are more safe; something which will protect you against danger. Then the question is—and this is what you would do on the psychoanalytic couch—to be aware of the fact that you are timid about being looked at, but not if you know that somebody. . . Whatever the particular answer would be for you, I think you have seen that it would be different for each of us. It has a slightly different overtone for everybody in the room, probably. I haven't even mentioned the question of exhibitionism, which we could touch off if we went into it. Many women are sort of startled when they discover that somebody is peeping at them but the peeper doesn't know that he is known, and she gets a kick out of strutting around showing herself off and being a tease and so on. This could touch off something that she might not be aware of at all in her consciousness: exhibitionism.

The question of spontaneity, I think I can now say more experientially, is spontaneity is to some extent not being aware of, that is, of making your own law so to speak, or having your behavior determined not by what's in the outside world but by what is inside of you. I think we would define certainly the greatest spontaneity as compared to the lesser, or the greater expressiveness as compared to the lesser, would be the greater ability to be naked, for instance. And this is one of the exercises I'd rather suggest later in the semester: nakedness, nudity, nudist camps, and so on, wherever it's possible to do that. Now try—you might just as well take advantage of the situation that we have sort of stumbled into here—figuring out what your own inhibitions would be in that particular situation, and this is then a greater self-awareness of what you are afraid of, what you're not afraid of, what you can do easily, what comes with difficulty. It tells you who you are.

Spontaneity in the pure sense, in the ultimate—you know, extrapolated out to the pure idea—would be simply being unaware of the whole environment altogether, just to be determined by radiation, so to speak, from within, out. You should be aware of the fact that all of us learned to do this, for cameras anyhow. Nobody gets self-conscious anymore with a camera, but when I was a child we did—when they first came in. Now we are so used to being snapshotted that it hardly bothers anyone. I'm sure everybody will get used to tape recorders eventually, as a culture.

Ben: You distinguish once in a while between spontaneity and impulsivity?

Maslow: The spontaneity would be . . . Well, it had one implication, which is full expressiveness without hindrance or inhibition—the full expressiveness of the intrinsic self, the deepest, biologically based portions of the personality. It does not apply to the expression of neurotic tendencies, for instance. Spontaneity implies that it's egosyntonic—you sort of approve of it. It is your behavior; you like it; you're just behaving, without any questions about it.

The impulsivity to some extent expresses as much the lack of necessary inhibitions as it does the impulse. It refers to the behavior coming out which should not have come out, so to speak, or which should have been delayed or controlled. Now that is just a way of speaking. That's the way the psychiatrists, psychoanalysts will use the word "impulsivity." It is a derogatory word; it implies psychopathology and the absence of control, and therefore—I don't suppose anyone has ever thought of it that way; I never have—but I suppose it implies that impulsivity would be the expression of neurotic tendencies rather than deep, core, intrinsic self-tendencies.

Okay, do you have anything else to bring up about it? Something else I want to ask you about, to throw out. I would like you to discuss my remarks, my vacillations—some of my uncertainty about the place of discussion of sex, of sexuality in the classroom. You remember that at first I had made certain terms in the class contract[3] and then rethought that situation . . . I amended that. I thought that we should have more openness about the discussion of sexuality here—the passing along of information, and so on—partly on the grounds of its lacking in communication generally, partly on other grounds too. One inhibition less. And I remember we did speak about sexuality, but I have forgotten what now. How do you feel about that? [*Long pause*] The voice of the masses!

Joan: It seems to me that where it's appropriate and when someone is willing to say something—perhaps about himself, perhaps general knowledge or common experience—he can say it in an impersonal way. But if it's something that he feels he can say about himself—"I did such and such"—well, if he is willing to say it, it seems to me that there shouldn't be any inhibiting.

Paul: On the other hand, my general experience in trying to discuss this on a group level, with a number of people with whom we haven't had an intimate friendship before coming together in a group form, is that it's generally possible to discuss sex on an impersonal level, without any references to personal experiences in a specific situation. Otherwise, it is not possible. There is too much embarrassment suffered, and I don't know any reason why this group should be different from any other group in this sense. I'm just stating a fact that I have observed in other cases and I think that it probably holds true here too. I don't think we will have any trouble discussing it on the general level. We all recognize ourselves to be sexual creatures, with all the sexually defined characteristics. We recognize sexual differences which exist between men and women without any qualms—we have been discussing them all along. It's more of an academic way of looking at it. The personal kind of introspection involves a very different phenomenon and I don't think we are capable of doing it in a group. I may be wrong but I have never seen it really occur. Of course this is a unique situation so that I mustn't . . .

Maslow: Frankly I had in mind a question also—of what you want of me, what role I play in it. It is a question that I'm not quite sure about.

In the first experiments that I did with group therapy a long time ago, around 1937—I think they were the first experiments in this country with normal people, in terms of mental health—I found that it was very, very effective as part of this group therapy to give a series of lectures about sexuality, sexual knowledge, sexology—everything that was known about the subject—because those youngsters didn't know anything—or, as a matter of fact, they knew a lot of things which weren't so.

Now, my vague impression is that that no longer holds, that you are far more sophisticated, in the sense of having more knowledge than they did in 1937. It floats in the air, it's around and there are books available. Anybody who is interested can certainly read about it, ask about it. That was partly an uncertainty on my part. If this were 1937 I know darn well that it would be useful for me simply to lecture about sexual knowledge and information. In 1937 a psych major—a young woman in New York City—got married during the semester and came into my office weeping. It was such a great tragedy: she could never have any babies. Why not? Well, she had seen her husband naked for the first time and he had no hair on his chest and she said, "Well, I will never have any children. Men without hair on their chest can't father children." [*General laughter*] 1937. I'm sure that wouldn't happen anymore. But this is one of the reasons I brought up this question. I haven't been doing this kind of work recently in sexology, but my impression is that you don't need any information about sexuality in the sense that they did.

Now how else might I serve? One of the questions that came up to mind is that we talked of trying to recover feelings of spontaneity or defense, or depression or anxiety, whatever it might be. One thing that is not investigated or not written about is, again, the recovery of the sexually erotic feelings themselves. Again, this was a long time ago when I did my studies, but it was my vague impression that while it was hard for men not to be aware of their erotic feelings, it is rather easy for women not to know what is going on inside their own bodies. I would guess again that that has changed considerably; I'm not sure.[4]

In any case I decided for myself: if it comes up naturally I think it would be better for us to permit ourselves to talk about these things. I'll see how it works out. It is not the personal stuff. Generally our professional experience is good enough. Personal talk about one's own sexuality—deliberately and specifically labelling it as such—in a group, especially in a mixed group, probably doesn't work out too well. I still think that, but we'll see how things go. [*Pause*] Any comments about that, questions, reactions to my feelings? [*Pause*]

I should tell you, by the way: it's still my impression that there is no good book on sex. It simply doesn't exist. Certainly, no good book on love exists. There isn't even a good novel on love that I'm aware of—not very good, anyway. There is practically nothing about the love-sex tie that's available. We talked about that in an earlier class but we won't start our argument about D. H. Lawrence[5] again. But this still remains to be done.

Partly, I guess, I bring this up because during the last week it happens that several books on sex came out in the mail to me. One of them I think is a good one, relatively good anyway. It's called *Sexual Behavior and Personality Characteristics*,[6] edited by M. DeMartino.[7] I have ordered it for the library. It's a collection of research papers on the subject, and it's a good selection, but it made me sad to see how few there were, how little there is, how bare-bones this treatment is. It is a most important topic for every living human being—whoever was and whoever will be—and yet it is a big blank area.

The other book was the first annual volume put out by The Society for the Scientific Study of Sexuality and it's just plain lousy, badly done studies, trivia of all sorts, little scraps of information. There is pretty definite confusion in many of the authors, in their own opinions and facts. It's very easy to do in this field.

Okay. Now we'll go back to where I started from. I want to read you, for the rest of the time that we have, some of these peak-experiences—little selections from them, done without getting too fancy about it because we don't have much time. I just want to read all sorts of things which I have picked out of this huge mass of stuff, each one for a particular reason.

Here is the question which was asked for a group study I made using a couple of hundred people, who responded anonymously:

> I would like you to think of the most wonderful experience or experiences of your life; happiest

moments, ecstatic moments, moments of rapture, perhaps from being in love, or from listening to music or suddenly "being hit" by a book or painting, or from some great creative moment. First list these. And then try to tell me how you feel in such acute moments, how you feel *differently* from the way you feel at other times, how you are at the moment a different person in some ways.[8]

First, this is a female, age 44, and her feelings about these various things. This is a very brief, anonymous response to the question. But it gives a sampling:

I feel I had quite a few of these, but I didn't know they were being institutionalized. [*General laughter*] One was making a decision to get a divorce and end an insufferable marriage situation.

Now *that* I had never seen before, possibly got her freedom or something of the sort.

Two, unconditional sexual psychic surrender during a love affair.

Usual enough.

Three, sudden bloom of insight or understanding between friends and relatives or lovers.

Now that's a general statement rather than a specific report.

Writing of a poem, sudden appreciation of an opposite point of view that is personal and happy.

Then the question: How do you feel about these things?

I feel as if a door had been opened or a rock rolled away; a sudden clearing of the atmosphere; a lifting of the spirit; heaviness, anxiety diminish; one is whole, adequate, capable, functioning, lovable; there is an awareness of self, the best side of one's self; firmness, confidence, a delight about oneself; a delicious feeling of autonomy, sufficiency, potency, identity; anything is possible.

Now a couple more I picked up partly because of the statement that I made in the very beginning of the course about the absence of the intellectual peaks, intellectual triggers. Now in personal relationships, with particular individuals, there have been intellectual peaks. The first one I picked up here—this is a student here at Brandeis, a girl:

> Two years ago while I was attempting to do some math problems in elementary calculus that I had for homework one night, I was following the long, involved procedure for finding the derivative of functions, exactly the way my teacher had told me to do. I suddenly thought I saw a quick way of finding the answer. I tried my new method, which only required inspection rather than calculation, got an answer for the next few problems, then did them again the old way. I got the same answers, showing that my perceived relationships between function and derivative was indeed correct. A day or so after this, going further in the math book, I saw an explanation of the way that I had discovered for myself. The finding out that mathematicians had known this method before I stumbled upon it, in no way marred my pleasure.

Which is something about the theory of creativeness that is very important.

> Upon finding out that my method was correct I became very excited.

Now it is also possible to become serene. This is that choice. Sometimes we get very excited and sometimes we get more calm.

> I felt very proud of myself, particularly because I had been having some trouble with math during the week or so before this experience. I ran around the house

> until I found my parents and showed them my findings, then I sat down by myself and looked over my work again. I suppose I could say that I felt creative, I certainly felt as if I "belonged." I now saw myself as having the right to be in the advanced math class that I was in. I did not feel guilty any longer, there were no longer any nagging fears of inadequacy.

One of the findings, the generalizations about this stuff, has to do with self-esteem. It is a sudden disappearance of inferiority feelings, doubts; a sudden firming up of self-esteem.

> This was not just true of my mathematical ability.

This is very interesting.

> I felt confident and sure of myself with respect to all of my studies.

She has changed; this is what you call self-esteem in general.

> I turned to working on the homework that I had in my other subjects, and the elation from the math carried over into everything I did. It helped me with my homework. But occasionally I found myself thinking about what I had done, and I would grin broadly—

To herself.

> —forgetting all about the work I was then attempting to finish. I began feeling "friendly" to the study of mathematics instead of, as before, hostile to it. I also saw it as having new importance and significance. It no longer seemed to me like a boring and unnecessary discipline.

That's a nice report, in the sense of being quite typical, very general, and that's for mankind and womankind. By the way, the reports are no different for women than men. You couldn't have told whether that was a woman or a man.

And now there are two here. One is of a very high—sort of the big moments in her life of "groupiness" with her group, her friends and so on. A feeling of communion, of closeness, of love for all of them and the feeling of belonging to the group—you know how nice a feeling that can be. She describes it very well, but it is rather long. Now this other one covers another section of the waterfront, so to speak:

> The peak-experiences that I experienced came after a night during which I'd been unable to sleep and had been thinking. I can't remember exactly what particular situation had brought me to this point, but I felt as if I were the lowest, filthiest creature on the face of the earth. At least I was trying to convince myself that I was.

This is a very nice girl. She is a very lovable girl.

> The whole world was against me for no reason other than the fact that I was so horrible a person.

It's so horrible that anybody should feel . . . She's a very wonderful person. And yet,

> All night long I wrestled, trying to make myself believe what I knew not to be true. About 4 a.m. my dog came into my room and climbed into bed with me. She usually did this but somehow this night it made me feel a sense of relief and joy that she should want to be near *me*—poor, ugly, dirty, horrible, miserable, little old me. Now I had one friend in the world, at least.

And here I have been reminded of an article which I could refer you to in the *Journal of Humanistic Psychology*, volume 1, number 1, on love.[9] It's very poignantly, poetically stated, very beautifully stated—the feeling of being loved and how curative, how therapeutic this can be. If we were interested, we could go on into the whole business of the suicidal impulse. Now I can make it very brief: mothers with babies don't commit suicide—they're too busy, they don't have any time, they can't manage, they're needed. Women without babies are much more apt to be suicidal than women with babies. Or I could say it's not just the baby. Let's say a woman with a sick husband to nurse, to take care of, it would probably be the same way. This would prevent suicide. Or it's a technique that you can use as a therapist, as a "bush league" therapist, for instance where the psychoanalyst may very well say where he's afraid of the possibility of suicide for his patient: "If you commit suicide it's going to hurt me very much. It'll make me very sad. It'll hurt me. I would feel as if I had failed you," and so on. Well another point here, there's a dissertation on this whole business if you want it: Adrian van Kaam,[10] who was here years ago. His dissertation was on "the feeling of being understood."[11] It was extremely therapeutic in this same way. This business of even a dog loving you can make the difference between living and dying.

> On an impulse I got out of bed, dressed, and putting her on a leash, went out of the house. I walked to a patch of woods high on the hill near our house, I sat down at the top of the hill where the wind was blowing fiercely, and with my dog at my side I watched the sun rise. As the sky became light and there were fewer shadows, I felt a sense of wonder, puzzlement and detachment from myself. I felt small and insignificant and yet a participant in my surroundings.

This is the kind of thought that is called "cosmic consciousness" by Bucke[12]—a cosmic consciousness in which the perception is not just of the whole world but of your place in it as well. Characteristically, there is a feeling of being very small in the world simply by comparison, and yet absolutely a member of the family—no longer estranged from the world but in it, belonging to it.

> I suddenly saw myself and my problems in their proper perspective.

That's a nice phrase: "proper perspective." That implies that it was improper before, that it wasn't true, that it wasn't correct. Now she is being correct. This raises all the questions about the veridicality of mystical knowledge ongoing for the past three thousand years. The people who report these experiences report very calmly: "Yes, now I saw the truth," and they are apt to feel very certain that this is the truth. And the business of validating that by an external kind of a validation—that's another story. That's different, but possible. I would say that this comes very close to the truth, which could be stated as the truth in such a way that nobody could possibly disagree with it. Cosmic consciousness is the truth in the sense that the universe is big, you do belong in it, you're a part of nature. By comparison with the whole, you are very small—this is certainly true—yet you belong there, you're part of it, you're not alien to it; it is not a window that you are looking through at something beyond. And it's the sense of feeling also a part of that universe in your proper perspective, meaning the amount or size that you actually do have in relationship to all the cosmos—that's the truth.

> My nightmare became just a part of living. I began to laugh inside and as I hugged my dog closer, I wanted to stand up and shout to the world, "I am."

It sounds silly, but that's very common. It's just like an affirmation of self.

> In writing these two[13] experiences down on paper, I have just let it pour out without trying to separate, in any great degree, myself from the world. I don't think I could coldly analyze these experiences without ruining the wonderful feeling I still have inside me. If I sat and thought some more I could probably think of some other experiences I have had but I feel emotionally exhausted and "if I feel any more I might bust."

Melissa: Do you ever have cases of people who have had peak-experiences and wrote about them before they ever knew about you or peak-experiences, or labeled them as "peak-experiences"?

Maslow: A few like Saint Paul [*General laughter*] It's an old story. Since anybody did any writing at all, ever, of the earliest records we have in history there were peak-experiences reported under some name or other. This girl happens to add after the whole thing was written, in ink:

I wrote my experiences and the above comment before
reading any of your books or of your papers. I am very
glad that I had not read the material because I think I
would probably have tried to make them fit into the
peak-experiences described.

Melissa: That's what I wanted to know, because I knew that from
William James, but I wondered if any of yours . . .

Maslow: I have a nice, rich mail. One of the advantages of publishing
anything is that immediately it makes you—I don't know what you'd
call it—"brothers"?—with all sorts of strangers all over the world. I
have letters from India, Poland, all places, and I may bring some of
them in sometime; it is so interesting. For instance, this one I just got
about William James, of all things. This is from a guy—I don't know
who he is—in Chicago. He mailed a copy of a letter from William
James to his wife, with a note:

> I enclose a copy of the letter from William James to his
> wife, describing an experience of his on the eve of his
> Gifford Lectures . . . It might be of interest to you.

It might! [*General laughter*]

> James repeated again and again that he had never gone
> through a mystical experience but that the descriptions
> of and his reactions to those who had done so, never
> failed to waken him responsively. And he concluded
> that innate within his consciousness was a germ or
> trace of a feeling that was responsive and compelled
> him to believe. His answer to the questionnaire, also
> enclosed, expresses this.

And, here's what James says in his letter to his wife, whom he
loved very much. It is a very nice letter. Apparently she was quite
different from him and they supplemented each other perfectly. She
was more stable and sort of more commonsensical than him. He was
out of the world half the time and she made for him a very stable life,
and his psychosomatic illnesses—which were terrible before he got

married—disappeared. Score one for marriage. [*General laughter*] She must have been a very nice woman from all the descriptions I've read. Now, this is the letter[14]:

> The temperature was perfect either inside or outside the cabin, the moon rose and hung above the scene before midnight, leaving only a few of the larger stars visible and I got into a state of spiritual alertness of the most vital description.

The language is that of 1898.

> The influences of nature, the wholesomeness of the people around me—

Which is also a trigger for peak-experiences. That's one of the nicest ways . . . You ask the question, "How can I bring these about?" Meet a nice class of people, fine people—people whom you can love, admire, are very good triggers.

> —the wholesomeness of the people around me, especially the good Pauline, the thought of you and the children, dear Harry on the wave—

Harry is his brother, Henry James; "on the wave" I suppose means traveling someplace.

> —the problem of the Edinburgh lectures, all fermented within me until it became a regular Walpurgis Nacht. I spent a good deal of it in the woods where the streaming moonlight lit up things in a magical, checkered play, and it seemed as if the Gods of all the nature mythologies were holding an indescribable meeting in my breast, with the moral gods of the inner life. The two kinds of Gods have nothing in common. The Edinburgh lectures made quite a hitch ahead.

I don't know what that means.

> The intense significance of some sort of the whole scene, if one could only *tell* the significance; the intense inhuman remoteness of its inner life, and yet the intense *appeal* of it; its everlasting freshness and its immemorial antiquity and decay; its utter Americanism and every sort of patriotic suggestiveness, and you, and my relationship to you, part and parcel of it all and beaten up with it so that memory and sensation all whirled inexplicably together; it was indeed worth coming for, and worth repeating year by year, if repetition could only procure what in its nature I suppose must be all unplanned for and unexpected. It was one of the happiest, lonesome nights of my existence and I understand now what a poet is.

That's the kind of phrase you run across every once in while in these things which gives it a nice click. That's a wonderful word. My favorite so far has been that one that I told you about, that young girl who had her first baby.[15] In that daze, she just sort of sat staring at things and her husband came in and she turned to him and said, "This has never happened to anyone before"—having a baby. And it hadn't.

> He is a person who can feel the immense complexity of influences that I felt, and make some partial tracks in them for verbal statement. In point of fact, I can't find a single word for all that significance, and don't know what it was significant of, so there it remains, a mere boulder of impression. Doubtless in more ways than one, though, things in the Edinburgh lectures will be traceable to it.

Very nice.

And then in answer to the 1904 questionnaire by Professor James Pratt[16]—this was a psychologist and philosopher who wrote several books about religious experience:[17]

The Question applied: "Is God very real to you? As real as an earthly friend, though different?"

Then James answers: "Dimly real; not as an earthly friend."

Then the next question: "Do you feel that you have experienced his presence? If so, please describe what you mean by such an experience."

Answer: "Never."

Next questions: "How vague or how distinct is it? How does it affect you mentally and physically? If you have had no such experience, do you accept the testimony of others who claim to have felt God's presence directly? Please answer this question with special care and in as great detail as possible."

Then James's answer: "Yes! The whole line of testimony on this point is so strong that I am unable to pooh-pooh it away. No doubt there is a germ in me of something similar that makes response."

And then I have some others . . . I was going to bring up some of the nutty ones. And I get some sad ones too. All sorts of schizophrenics write to me. They're seeing visions of one kind or another, and where the content of the letter sounds psychotic. So you get those, too. But on the whole, publishing a paper is almost like collecting all your friends about you, from all over the world. That is, if I am very much interested in something then all the people who are interested in that something, they will all communicate. What better bond is there between people? And you get this nice feeling: "I've met people."

Like Marghanita Laski, who wrote *Ecstasy*. When I read that book—I stumbled across it by accident—I just felt so intimate with her. I had never seen her, but I felt very, very close. I knew what she had been thinking. I could read her mind. I knew her guts. I knew what she had gone through: the fears, the ambiguities, the conflicts, the difficulties, the sleepless nights, all that. We were brothers, brother and sister, siblings. And when she showed up by accident, she felt the same way about me. She showed up here [at Brandeis]. We had never met each other, but the truth was we felt very close, very friendly, and I write to her and she writes to me. I don't know if I'll ever see her again; she lives in England. But we are companions, friends. As a matter of fact, I feel I could rely on her a lot more heavily than I could on the people who have lived next door to me, in many ways. So, that's very nice about publishing.

This is one of the lengthiest and most detailed by a fine writer, Arthur Koestler,[18] from his autobiography. It is of great interest to me because it brings up the question of the "peaker" and the "non-peaker" that we will have to introspect about. Arthur Koestler is describing here—and he's described in one other place—the mystic experience, the peak-experience. And he wrote a book, *The Lotus and the Robot*,[19] in which he went to Japan and India to investigate the gurus and the Zen Buddhists and came back rejecting the whole business as a lot of nonsense and so on. I remember my feeling as I read that book: "The poor guy; he's a non-peaker. He doesn't understand what they are getting at." Then after that I ran across these things, and this fits with one of the explanations for the non-peaker: I have found in general that the Marxians, communists and so on—the few that I have read about or known—tend to be against peak-experiences. Simone de Beauvoir,[20] for instance, has in her autobiography an excellent account of her peak-experiences and then how she rejected it, why she turned away from it. Here you have in Koestler this conflict. He was earlier a communist, then rejected and renounced communism. He was the one who had this conflict and wrote *The Yogi and the Commissar*. It's very, very good—the yogi being the peaker and the commissar the non-peaker, you might say. And here's what he says:[21]

> I met with it for the first time a day or two after I had been transferred to Seville. I was standing at the recessed window of cell No. 40—

He was in jail and was to be shot the next morning. This was during the Spanish Civil War. He had been captured by the Franco people.

> I was standing at the recessed window of cell No. 40 and, with a piece of iron-spring that I had extracted from the wire mattress, was scratching mathematical formulae on the wall.

His training was as an engineer, originally.

> Mathematics, in particular analytic geometry, had been the favorite hobby of my youth, neglected later on for many years.

This is the same guy who wrote *Sleepwalkers*—a kind of history of science. And that gives you a notion of his interests.

> I was trying to remember how to derive the formula of the hyperbola, and was stumped; then I tried the ellipse and the parabola and to my delight succeeded. Next I went on to recall Euclid's proof that the number of primes is infinite . . . Since I had become acquainted with Euclid's proof at school, it had always filled me with a deep satisfaction that was aesthetic rather than intellectual.

Koestler is very good on science for pulling in that aesthetic quality of it.

> Now as I recalled the method and scratched the symbols on the wall, I felt the same enchantment.

That's a good word for us.

> And then, for the first time, I suddenly understood the reason for this enchantment. The scribbled symbols on the wall represented one of the rare cases where a meaningful and comprehensive statement about the infinite is arrived at by precise and finite means. The infinite is a mystical mass shrouded in a haze and yet it was possible to gain some knowledge of it without losing oneself in treacly ambiguities. The significance of this swept over me like a wave. The wave had originated in the articulated verbal insight but this evaporated at once, leaving in its wake only a wordless essence—

He is doing it overdrive there.

> —a fragrance of eternity, a quiver of the arrow in the blue. I must have stood there some minutes, entranced with a wordless awareness that "this is perfect—perfect;" until I noticed some slight mental discomfort nagging at the back of my mind—some trivial

circumstance that marred the perfection of the moment. Then I remembered the nature of that irrelevant annoyance—I was, of course, in prison and might be shot. But this was immediately answered by a feeling whose verbal translation would be:

This is a very nice way of saying it's ineffable, the words won't do but you can translate it if you have to into approximately the following, which you mustn't take too literally:

"So what? Is that all? Have you got nothing more serious to worry about?"—an answer so spontaneous, fresh and unused as if the intruding annoyance had been the loss of a collar-stud. Then I was floating on my back in a river of peace under bridges of silence. It came from nowhere and flowed nowhere. Then there was no river and no I. The I had ceased to exist.

It is extremely embarrassing to write down a phrase like that—

This is the commissar coming back, after the yogi has been recharged.

—when one has read *The Meaning of Meaning* and nibbled at logical positivism and aims at verbal precision and dislikes nebulous gushing. Yet, mystical experiences, as we dubiously call them, are not nebulous, vague or maudlin; they only become so when we debase them by verbalization. However, to communicate what is incommunicable by its nature one must somehow put it into words, and so one moves in a vicious circle. When I say the "I" had ceased to exist I refer to a concrete experience that is verbally as incommunicable as the feeling aroused by a piano concerto, yet just as real only much more real. In fact its primary mark is the sensation that this state is more real than any other one has experienced before, for the first time the veil has fallen and one is in touch with "real reality" the hidden order of things, the X-ray texture of the world, normally obscured by layers of irrelevancy.

What distinguishes this type of experience from the entrancements of music, landscapes or love is that the former has a definitely intellectual, or rather noumenal, content.

"Noumenal" in Kant's[22] sense.

It is meaningful, though not in verbal terms. Verbal transcriptions that come nearest to it are: the unity and interlocking of everything that exists, and interdependence like that of gravitational fields or communicating vessels. The "I" ceases to exist because it has, by a kind of mental osmosis, established communication with, and been dissolved in the universal pool.

All figures of speech, obviously.

It is this process of dissolution and limitless expansion which is sensed as the "oceanic feeling"—

This is Freud's word for it.

—as the draining of all tension, the absolute catharsis, the peace that passeth all understanding.

The coming back to the lower order of reality.

That's just the phrase that thousands of people have used for it: "the lower order of reality."

I found it to be gradual, like waking up from anesthesia. There was the equation of the parabola scratched on the dirty wall, the iron bed and the iron table, and the strip of blue Andalusian sky, but there was no unpleasant hangover as from other modes of intoxication. On the contrary, there remained a sustained and invigorating, serene and fear-dispelling after-effect that lasted for hours and for days. It was as

> if a massive dose of vitamins had been injected into the veins or, to change the metaphor, I resumed my travels through myself like an old car with its batteries freshly recharged.

See, he is a good writer.

> Whether the experience had lasted for a few minutes or an hour, I *never knew*.

This is very characteristic.

> In the beginning it occurred two or even three times a week, then the intervals became longer.

I don't know what he means by "in the beginning."

> It could never be voluntarily induced. After my liberation—

He wasn't shot.

> —it ocurred at even longer intervals, perhaps once or twice in a year. But by that time the groundwork for a change of personality was completed.

And then he goes on from there in his autobiography. Do you want the reference? Arthur Koestler, *The Invisible Writing*, page 350 to 352. And that's about all we have time for. I think next time I'll go on—I want to discuss some drug experiences and what they have to do with this whole business. I think we'll start from there and see where we go.

OCTOBER 28, 1963
Laboratory for Self-Knowledge

Maslow: Do you want to continue from where you left off the last time—feelings for children? Or perhaps I would ask you before we start, could you respond to this question about the difference between intellectualizing and experiencing on these topics? Did you see this within yourself or with anyone else? Supposing I asked you, as an exercise in sharpening your ears, instead of my being the critic, saying now you are intellectualizing—could I ask you to do that? See if you can spot it from the first moment so that you can each learn. We *must* intellectualize, as we are intellectuals—that's our job. But to be able to do that at will, and not to do it when it seems the only way—to be able rather to report feelings, experiences, emotions, impulses, and the like, if that's necessary. And also, as you listen to someone else, watch them so as to be able to make that differentiation, so as to understand what a person is reporting, what's going on in his guts as over against what's going on in the cerebral cortex, as they call it. That's the difference.

Paul: I'm not sure I understand something, Dr. Maslow. What is the advantage, either academically or experientially—I emphasize the word "advantage"—in introspecting our own organic reactions to things? I derive a great deal of pleasure from hearing what I have in common with other people and what other people have in common with me, in terms of my psychic reactions to various phenomena and to various situations, but somehow I couldn't help at times get the feeling—that's all it was—when you went into such organic detail about reactions to various things, even though they are pleasant organic reactions, that the analogy one could so easily draw with animal pleasures themselves was so easily drawn that I often had some inkling of a slight disgust at times. Not from the way in which you said things—there was nothing in what you said that offended me—but simply the fact that I couldn't see the need to enjoy something in those terms.

Maslow: The only thing I'd add there is that I want you to be able to—well, I was talking about unpleasant things too. I'd like you to be able to know when you are being anxious, angry, or whatever, as well as pleasant. For the rest of it, I'm interested to know how you react to that.

Sarah [*to Paul*]**:** You said that you don't feel that there is any need for doing this. I think that maybe there are more people than you realize who aren't really capable of doing this except on a very superficial level. Bringing out certain feelings, you know—the more you do it, the better you get at it. It can help to experience more deeply to sort of . . . well, I don't know how to put it exactly. In a way, it's not just letting your perceptions out. It can help if you turn them over sometimes. You can always, you know, sort of *test* them. They take on a depth. I think there are too many people who go through most of their lives without really *feeling* their perceptions as much as they could.

Paul: Are you distinguishing between your organic pleasures and the psychical pleasures in saying that?

Sarah: Yes.

Paul: I mean there are two different levels of superficiality. Because if we are talking about two different levels of enjoyment which are generally intertwined, we have to differentiate them to be able to talk about them at least. There is the one case of enjoying something bodily, organically; the other case of experiencing a sense of pleasure in a—

Maslow: Anyone want to say anything about intellectualizing again?

Paul: Well, this is an intellectualizing process, obviously. This is one of the things which enables man to experience some things which animals are not capable of experiencing.

Maslow: What do you mean by "some things"?

Paul: I think the word "love," which in itself is just a verbal translation of an ineffable quality, as you put it before. I have never observed an animal to give any indication that he is capable of loving in the human sense. There are biological limitations, apparently—I should say *psychical* limitations to an animal's brain power—I don't know exactly how to put it—that seem to prevent him from going past a certain point in the act of love. It seems to be much more a biological phenomenon. An animal isn't a self-conscious creature to begin with.

Maslow: Are human beings?

Paul: We have been stating that as a premise to begin with. At least it is the potential of the human being to be self-conscious.

Maslow [*to class*]: What do you think about all this?

Melissa: Maybe one of the reasons we're doing this is so that we can get at this core-self, the inner self that we are talking about, trying to work with a better understanding. But during the week I thought of something that really kind of frightened me: what if there isn't a core-self? Why not look at it from another way: instead of there being a core-self—and I'd really like there to be—what if there are just layers and layers of self, and some layers are inner layers—more personal—and some are outer layers—less personal—but they are all self and they are all valid and legitimate self. And I think it's wrong to say that the innermost layer is the core-self because it's not, by the definition of it. This is what I'd like to get across. Can anybody work around that? I stopped working around it at that point.

Maslow: Well, the question is . . . I can work around it maybe a little. [*Pause*] It doesn't really matter, you might say. The theory of self that you have—the theory of whatever personality you have—is really irrelevant to what we're talking about. Because you can phrase what we are trying to do in a very time-honored phrasing that we started the semester with, of making believe that we don't know anything, just going back to raw facts, starting all over again. The theory of personality, which is untitled and what we're supposed to be doing today, is in a "parlous" state—that's a lot of words, of abstractions, and so on; many people feel unsatisfied with it. So then we engage in this business of saying, "Let's forget about theories and go back to the facts of human reaction, of human personality, of being whatever you are, of recognizing these feelings, or not recognizing them if you don't"—if you are anxiety-free, you'll never *feel* any anxiety. I'd say that this is independent, partly, of the theory of personality that you may or may not have and that they shouldn't get confused with each other. I'd like you to find out what's happening inside yourself.

I can be far more challenging than I have been. I doubt that any of you really knows, if I can judge by my therapeutic experience. I don't remember running across anybody who ever did know very well what was going on inside themselves. I've never met anybody who didn't have vast sets of defenses of all kinds which were in terms of a theory—an *a priori* theory that they already had. A nice girl is supposed to be such and such—therefore of course I am such and such if I am a nice girl; I am trying to be. One man I remember who pops into my head is a psychologist who was a Quaker, and hate just fell out of the world for him. He didn't want to hate. There was too much hate in the world for him. What he did was simply to deny it altogether, and claimed he never felt any hatred. I had to be skeptical about that. It turns out years later when I met him he had gone into psychoanalysis, and had to admit that he felt hatred now. But the truth was that he had been blind. I think we are all blind about certain things.

The whole psychic world, which most of the world's alive to, hasn't been explored very well. In our culture, it happens that there are specific blindnesses of all sorts which you've been brought up to, assiduously trained in. Well, simply seeing part of the world, seeing the way things are, seeing the raw facts is the way in which I can see this. There is an awful lot of talk about self, and about personality, and about human nature and so on. This is human nature; that's all it is. All the big theories, all the generalizations, all the abstractions, are built upon just raw reports of this kind. The whole Freudian structure is built like that, and it's perfectly legitimate, Freud would accept this. When you read the books about Freud, as you all have—everybody around here can spout very freely about Freud, Oedipus complexes, castration complexes—I assure you that they are meaningless unless you can give them the experiential content from which the whole business is an abstraction. Freud made all these words—he didn't make them up out of his head. Those words are supposed to be a kind of label for a whole bin-full of particular reports from particular individuals in particular circumstances, who said: "I feel funny about this. Here I just married this woman, I love her very much, I've been trying to get her to marry me for I don't know how long, and today, this morning as I was coming to the office, I suddenly found myself crossing the street"—this is one of Freud's case reports—"I ran across the street and then I looked around. Why did I run across the street? I didn't know, and then I saw my wife on the other side. Was I avoiding her, Doc? Why did I do that?" Well, Freud had a hundred thousand instances of that sort of feeling, simply the guy reporting: "Why in God's name, should I feel upset?"

I can give you one of mine which pops into my head—I guess there will have to be a lot of free association around here. It was a very powerful thing for me—it is when I first recognized anxiety in myself. When I was in psychoanalysis this very peculiar thing that had happened to me. I had been at the New York Academy of Sciences, and Mittelmann,[1] my colleague, was reporting something up there. And then I got up to make a comment; I'd been asked to make a comment when he finished speaking. Suddenly my knees got weak and I got trembly and my voice quavered and I had to hang on to the chair in front of me. My voice was very low so they couldn't hear me, and I was afraid of falling—my legs couldn't hold me up. My heart doubled in its rate—just went so rapidly pounding, I could hear it pounding. "What's the matter with me, Doc? What was this?"

What had my colleague been talking about? Well, he was

reporting—to make it brief—this man stood up and reported for the first time *my* work, which he had spiked, you might say. I had discovered this whole business of the psychosomatic questionnaire—I had been working away at it and my partner simply sold the whole goddamn business. I'd never heard of it before. I had been seeing him every day for years; we worked together, and there he was on the platform, saying something. My picture of myself was: "This didn't matter; I am a man of science, priorities don't make any difference, it doesn't matter who discovers these things, I shouldn't be selfish," and so on and so on.

And there I was and my psychoanalyst said to me: "You were having an anxiety attack." I said, "That's what it means!" I had written a book about anxiety.[2] I had read books, articles and so on; I could judge anxiety in other people. But I had just never made the connection there with these feelings, which now I could recognize in retrospect that I've had before—never so intensely, but I've had them. And now the label had come—so *that's* what you mean by "anxiety"—and suddenly there came into gear the applicability of hundreds of cases and books and everything that I had read about anxiety. For the love of Pete, if this can be for a guy who has written a book on abnormal psychology in which there is a chapter on anxiety, who had done psychotherapy for I don't know how long, I think you'll be humble enough to admit maybe there are things about yourself that you are not quite experiencing. I was blind—it was just simply a portion of my life that I didn't know about.

Of course, things come out later. All I knew was that I was having an anxiety attack. Years later an interesting question suddenly occurred to me: "Why should I be anxious about all this?" And it turned out that my impulse was to murder, you might say, at the unconscious level, and my anxiety was about my own murderous impulses. The impulses were very definite. [*Humorously*] Actually, they still are, I don't know. [*General laughter*]

And then one can get frightened of one's own impulses, and that's what happened to me; I got frightened at such a wild impulse—which I repressed altogether. I wasn't aware of being angry at him.

Are these impulses fact, part of the real world, part of the natural world? These are the raw bricks out of which you build your psychological structures, your houses, theories, and that's what I want you to be aware of, as you are not. Our culture does not have words for these things. Our culture stresses behavior. For the love of Pete, the psychologists *themselves* stress behavior. Wherever I go now they don't talk about psychology any more, they talk about "behavioral science"—what a horrible word. It's like a rejection of feelings, as if all we're interested in is behavior.

Well, let's say ours is an effort to get at the raw data. This business of concentrating on the feelings, on the experiences, on the impulses, on the emotions, good or bad, and so on. I don't really care whether they are organic or not organic or what level they are or what they mean. This is a lingering question. Real questions are: Do you have them or not? Do you know what it is to feel anxious, to feel murderous, to feel affection? Many women can't, do you know that? Anger is very sorely repressed in our society. Very much so. You're not apt to know it, especially if it's against someone whom the textbooks say you shouldn't feel angry at. Try feeling angry at someone that you feel very grateful to—it's kind of difficult. Or try feeling very angry at someone who can kill you, or someone who's really threatening—see how difficult that is. You don't *dare* to feel angry, and therefore it doesn't come up to the consciousness.

Now we know, following Freud mostly, and that whole line succeeding Freud, that it's possible to recover these feelings, these impulses. It's possible to know more about what's going on inside your belly than you now know. You might ask a question about the justification of this whole thing. To the professor this is all very intellectual: Is it a good thing, is it worthwhile, is it dangerous? I got a flavor of that. Also the word which I think you should have plucked out of what Paul said, which was the experiential part of that, when he spoke of a feeling of *disgust*—a vague, slight disgust—which many people will report as you go poking around in your intestines, you know, laying out all these introspections on the table. After a while many people get sick of it, disgusted with it. That was the *feeling* core of that which none of you picked up. That question of *justification*, I think, is an intellectual question and should be answered by the professor.

The answer is—in general, from the whole experience of fifty years of depth therapy—that for *most* people it's worthwhile. It's helpful in many different ways, including for psychological help, and in a lot of other ways too, to become more aware of what has been unconscious, what has been unaware, or what has been only dimly aware. On the whole, this is a good thing.

The few exceptions don't apply here—that'd be schizophrenic people, for instance. In such a case it's probably a good idea not to analyze but rather to build "defenses," to hang on to reality and not to tear it apart as we are doing. For people who are really afraid of losing their grip on reality, which is extremely rare in a highly-selective group like here. At your level, let's say, it all adds up. I could go on, for there's a huge amount of literature on the benefits of self-knowledge and psychotherapy, not to mention the benefits of the T-groups and sensitivity training and God knows what else. I'd say, "Yes." You may have to take it on faith for the moment. If you are interested in reading about it further, to check for yourself, I'll give you a bibliography.

I think you should be aware of this. Perhaps pick up this point about the disgust, the uneasiness and also the slight fear—Jung[3] has talked a lot about this. And we had better lay this on the table too. To go into depths can be frightening, quite legitimately frightening. Or at least it is felt as frightening by many people. Need you, in fact, be afraid of it? Most often no. I feel not very worried about even those exceptions because the defense mechanisms are so powerful anyway—they go into automatic action. And especially since I'm not pushing very hard either; it's not a one-to-one relationship. It's possible for you to keep your mouth shut if you want or to evade the questions I do ask in class. I won't push.

Okay now, let's go back to the parental feelings. I will continue my little lecture. The fact is that a huge proportion of our population don't know whether they're feeling something or it's something they've read in a book. They don't really know how to behave with their children, even the mothers. As a matter of fact, this is a problem for the whole blasted society. This is why everybody goes to child psychologists and reads books about it—Spock[4] and so on. In other cultures, this is not so. There isn't any uncertainty about what to do with children, as there is among us. Now if your feelings were very powerful, very strong, unmistakable, unequivocal, you wouldn't bother reading any books about child psychology. If you had a baby, you'd look inside your own guts; that would tell you what to do.

Sarah: What happens though if you have already read all these things first, then you are confronted with a situation where you can't tell whether it's something you've read or if it's something you are feeling?

Maslow: There is one guard for it: become doubly aware of your own impulses. Make them stronger. One phrase I have: listen to the impulse voices and let them speak out more clearly, be able to hear them more clearly. Then you can walk through situations where there are social pressures upon you, cultural expectations of all sorts. Your particular gang, your subculture, may be urging you to do this or do that, or do the other thing. But if you have recourse to the voice of your own organism, to what it says . . .

In the same way that so many . . . During the behaviorist days, when John B. Watson[5] was taken seriously by all the newspapers, and magazines, so many women were afraid to pick up their babies when they cried, or they would feed them every four hours or something like that. Well, it was very interesting to me to watch how many mothers—I'd say, on the whole, probably the good ones—simply sneaked out behind their husbands or behind John B. Watson. They wouldn't tell anyone, because of being told "It's not scientific"—but who did what their hearts told them to do, what their impulses told them to do. Well, these were people with strong feelings, strong impulses; they weren't confused. They didn't get mixed up if somebody suggested the opposite.

I was talking to Dr. Solomon Asch[6], who's in the area now. We were talking about his studies—you know those studies about the conformity business? You are like the subjects in his studies. All the studies that have been done have been done with college students. His studies were done with Swarthmore students; they were very much like you in this respect. I tell you that you can be twisted and shifted and turned. Your own opinions can be juggled until finally you deny the evidence of your own eyes, as in his experiment.

They had two lines, one was long and one was short, and because six people said the short line was longer than the long one, they agreed with them. About two-thirds of the Swarthmore college population—that's about two-thirds of you. And I can do that too if I want to. I can twist you any way I please with those suggestions.

I've done it for fun—you get a particular bottle of sherry, for instance. You get a lousy sherry, the worst sherry you can possibly find. You know its character—two gallons for 75 cents. Then you put this into a nice glass and say to your friends as they come: "I've saved this for you. I would like you to have it. I know you; I don't want to waste it on other people. You're the connoisseur." You fit your "con" to the particular person. But you know damn well that nine out of ten people who walk into your house will smack their lips and say, "Sure is wonderful sherry. Thank you for saving it for me. I'd like to get some for myself."

True?

Carole: I have a feeling that a lot of these people are doing it for your sake too. I mean, they might not want to tell you: "Look, this is real lousy stuff, but *you* don't know any better." [*General laughter*] You know—it's kind of politeness I think that goes on.

Maslow: There is a certain proportion of this. But if you read Asch's book[7] you'll see how many of these people were absolutely astonished. They finally got to see the "short" line was long. Other experiments—the Hadley Cantril[8] experiment for instance, long ago, you must know the one—is the same thing. This was done long ago in Princeton with literature majors, with the wrong labels to the poems. They were no different from you. I'd expect you to do the same thing. The people, by the way, who did not follow suggestions, the independent ones in Asch's experiment, were stronger people. One way of defining a strong person seems to be in terms of "he knows what he wants." You can say it another way, I guess: "He knows that he *is*; he knows *who* he is—the type of person he is."

You can find out for yourselves how many people dislike alcoholic drinks. Everybody drinks them, but give them permission not to have an alcoholic drink. In my own home you can drink ginger ale, for instance, if you want to. If we have a cocktail party, there is always tea and coffee, ginger ale and soda and so on, in addition to other things. And it's amazing how many people will silently leave them. [*Pause*]

In the Sherif[9] experiment[10]—another famous experiment—or the Lorge[11] experiment,[12] the same kind of thing, showing how many people are suggestible. It's about one-third to one-fourth of the population who turn out to be not suggestible. They are the ones who can tell. You can read in Asch's book, which will have the best protocols—it's a big, fat thing that'll have the exact words, and so on. What do people say? They look around; they think everybody's crazy. "This line is shorter than the other." But they may look at it carefully, they may doubt themselves for a moment and then they will go back and check, and look at everybody else, and wonder what's going on here, but they won't . . . they just won't . . . the short line looks short, and it continues to look short. For the average American intellectual citizen, the short line *changes*: it gets *long* because six people said it was.

Now your only defense against this kind of thing is to know what goes on inside you, what you like, dislike. We're talking about feelings, but the experiment I'd want to do is with tangible things—with the sherries, tea, fabrics, music and art and so on. If I can ever do it, I'd like to have people commit themselves without looking at the labels and tell me which of these two teas or coffees is nicer, and which tastes better. And then see if they can stick to the first thing they said when they see the labels. And then finally, the blessing of blessings, be able to say: "I guess I can't tell the difference between one tea and another. It makes no difference. I have got no taste." If that's the truth, it's a hard thing to say.

Do you have any comments on my lecture?

Doug: I have a friend who went through the Asch experiment and it just made it more vivid for me. He was a person I liked very much, and he was very shaken too, to realize that he would do this. I was angry that they would do this to him, but he was more concerned that he did it himself. He said it taught him something.

Maslow: I think this would be a very good form of therapy. It's just expensive in terms of time and so on, but if I can ever think of ways of doing this for you, it would simply enhance self-knowledge. If you know that you are suggestible, this is good thing to know.

Let me give you another example which may serve as a parody. David M. Levy[13] discovered, among a lot of things, the whole concept of "affect hunger." Primary affect hunger. He discovered that a main determinant for psychopaths—when he traced them back—was the absence of maternal affection. Not enough maternal affection. The response he called affect hunger is really "love hunger," and he described it very vividly in children with "kissing bugs." If you were ever in camp you know what I mean. The kid who if you smile at him he'll cling to you for the rest of the summer, desperately. It's Levy's impression that affect hunger is incurable. That is, where he finds it in an adult, it can never be changed; what is lost is lost, what is behind you is behind you. Then the question comes up: "What can we do about it?"

If a person can become aware that he has an affect hunger, he can manage it well for the rest of his life in just about the same way as if you discover that you have an allergy for strawberries or you have a slight diabetes. There are all sorts of physical examples you could use but I was going to use my own.

I had my gallbladder operation, took the darn gallbladder out, then all sorts of peculiar things happened afterwards. Apparently this darn thing had been sort of poisoning me slightly all the time and I didn't know. It would have been highly desirable if I could have been conscious of my gallbladder gnawing away at me. Unfortunately, like cancer, these are the bad things you cannot get conscious of. Now if we can take the things that we *can* get conscious of—if you get a good physical examination and find out that you have a diabetic sugar curve, for instance—in a sense it's a tragedy and in another sense it's not, because you can manage it. In the same way you can manage the affect hunger.

If a young man, let's say, knows that he has affect hunger, you know damn well the kind of wife you should have, for instance. You cannot get a cool, distant, detached wife. It would kill you; you can't stand it. You need a warm, affectionate person. Your friends have to be that way—you can just choose it. Also, you can learn from that situation to be aware of your hurts, of your sensitivities. It's like having corns on your toes: you get a particular pain then you say,

"Ah, my affect hunger—it's starting up!" Then, instead of attacking somebody for being nasty, you can say, "Well, I'm oversensitive," as you should say, because it's true.

In the same way if you have a proneness to hostility, it's better for you not to try to stamp on it. Why? Because you cannot. This is what Freud discovered: you cannot by repression make things disappear. They just go under the bed and they come up when your defenses are weak—they come up eventually. The best way to handle hostility, the best way to become a nicer person—less hating, less angry, less attacking, less murderous and so on—is to be aware of it, in the same way that you might be aware of your allergies or diabetes. If you've got it under your eyes, and consciousness, it's available for control, it's manageable. At least you don't have to fool yourself.

Sarah: What work is this in?

Maslow: You'll find some of it in his book *Maternal Overprotection*[14] but there are papers after that, very wonderful papers. One is "Primary Affect Hunger" in *Understanding Human Motivation*[15] edited by Stacey[16] and DeMartino.

Well, do you want to take another shot at the feelings? I think I have justified them enough, haven't I? And this is in spite of the fact that it's perfectly legitimate to feel whatever the truth is. There are many people who feel very private and get really quite ambivalent about introspection. They feel it to be a morbid kind of thing. My impression is that the more active, athletic, vigorous people are more apt to find it distasteful, the introspection and the kind of talk that we have in psychology courses. I think generally, they tend to stay away from psychology altogether. Well, that's legitimate; they're built in a particular way. I don't know what the chain of determinants is there, but it's the way it happens.

Well, disagreeing with me on an intellectual level, that's something we would have to fight about with experiments and data and experience, and so on. But if you say, "I hear what you say and I don't doubt the evidence but I *feel* reluctant"—those are absolutely compatible statements. Do you want to work a little on that reluctance to introspect? [*Pause*] For instance, could I ask you to start things off away from this lecture? Do any of you have any experiential reactions to report from our last meeting? Did you notice anything that happened, any sharpening of the eyes or any responses of any kind to that discussion of the feelings for children, babies, infants?

Carole: Yes, I was thinking a lot about your talking on children. I personally feel very conscious of children. I have a very strong maternal feeling. I also know my mother has it too. You were talking about where this comes from and as best as I could figure out for myself I assume that mothers teach to their children. I can recall very distinctly watching my mother with other children. One little girl I saw her with picked up three dolls and one was all upside down and cockeyed. My mother was playing with her very gently and showing her how you'd hold a baby. I was just wondering what other people felt. Is it a possibility that children are taught to be maternally conscious?

Maslow: Let me butt in for a minute and say, keep your talking about the feeling itself separate from the causes of the feelings. I mean, it's perfectly legitimate to talk about where it came from but still it doesn't make any difference where it came from so far as the diagnosis of the feeling is concerned. You know? If you feel maternal, maybe it's for one reason, maybe another. Who cares? What I'd be more interested in is if we could run across a talented introspector. If you could introspect for us, teach us: what does it *feel* like to feel maternal? *I* don't know. Is there anything you can put your finger on?

Carole: Well, I'm always very, very conscious about my own reactions towards children. How I'm going to do things, what's going to matter to me. And I find that all this stuff is somehow in me. And I kind of then pull that from myself if I'm around mothers and they start talking about something. I go into *me* and I know somehow it's in me already.

Maslow: Supposing you had a baby on the table.

Carole: How would I feel towards the baby? I—well, I know. I have felt this way. I have a friend who is older than I am and who has a baby, and although she is a good friend of mine and I like her tremendously, I'm jealous of her that she has a child. There's no question that I have this feeling. It's not the kind of envy that she has something that I'll never have. It's a very minor sort of jealousy. But there's no question that she has something *now*—that I wouldn't *want* now for myself. I'm not ready to have a baby.

Maslow: How do you react to her baby?

Carole: You want to touch, you want to hold. Last time you were asking about kissing. I don't feel anything about kissing a child. I just want to hold it close, play with it.

Maslow: Could you express the kind of holding, for instance?

Carole: Yes, holding it up close, holding it against you.

Maslow: Is there an impulse to squeeze?

Carole: I fight this because I can recall aunts who came up to me and squeezed. I have a desire to do it but I also know children don't like that; they are being hurt—and I react against it.

Maslow: Can you add anything to that? Imagine a baby right here, a real baby, this cute little baby all nice and clean and dressed, gurgling, smiling. David Levy has a whole scale of the appeal of a baby from the most appealing—a smiling, clean baby who's gurgling and who holds its arms out, is absolutely irresistible. [*General laughter*] Nobody can resist them. There's no woman in the whole study; in fact, no man either, probably. And then it can go on down being less and less attractive. What would happen—perhaps I can ask you— supposing this baby were a sick baby, had jaundice and you could see it was yellow and it was crying?

Carole: It was physically ugly?

Maslow: It was yellow; it's frightening.

Carole: Oh, I don't know . . .

Maslow: It's not a pretty child; it's not cute, and it cries, whines. It's a sick child.

Carole: If there were someone else there, like his mother, I would certainly prefer the mother to pick the child up. Considering it is ugly, I would be upset by it. But if I were there alone, I would have to, because it's my responsibility.

Maslow: You would have to? This has nothing to with causes or determinants or the history of, or the relationship to, or anything. Just the feeling itself.

Jayne: I figure if it belonged to you or someone you knew you'd be more apt to feel pity for it, do something for it, than if it belonged to someone else; then you'd probably be more repulsed by it.

Clara: I feel completely the opposite. If the child was uncomfortable, the main thing that I would want to do is make it better no matter who's in the room. Even if the mother was there—I would still feel an obligation, even a desire, to help the child, to make it comfortable.

Sharon: I came to kind of a horrible realization last week. Before I had my own children I felt this tremendous yearning and hunger to be a mother and have children. Since I've had my own children, they are the only ones I've really felt this for. I've stopped feeling this way toward all—I mean, I didn't feel *cold* toward other children. I was just much more diffident about other people's children. This is kind of a big, horrible thing to learn about myself. It's just sheer ego gratification for my own children. This was what happened. I feel it's kind of a thing where you were satisfied with something that you wanted and you feel this before you have your children, because you don't have it in the absence of a Platonic kind of a deal. You yearn for what you don't have. Now I feel that I would want to tend to a child, to do something about it, but I wouldn't feel that same—what I would have identified as "maternal"—feeling before I had my own children.

By the way I resented it last week, as a matter of fact. It seemed to me we were proposing a "how little girls should feel toward children" kind of idea by trying to explore these maternal feelings, by trying perhaps to make people feel inadequate because they don't have these feelings.

Melissa: If there were a baby on that table now, I know what I'd do.

I'd smile at it, and I'd smile not because I was smiling *at* the baby so much, but because a tremendous feeling of happiness and "yes-ness" wells up in you. If you can't touch it or hold it, all you want to do is smile.

The same thing just happened to me yesterday. I was in my room on the second floor studying and some children were below and they were laughing and it just sounded so good, and I went to the window smiling. I looked and waved at them and one little boy turned around and said: "Look up there, there's a girl waving at us!" And then I was smiling because they were just being so direct and the response was so honest. And I thought if *I* were down there and someone up there were waving at me, I probably wouldn't think, you know, "Look! See up there, someone's waving to you—let's wave back!" So maybe this is one of the reasons that children make me feel so happy. It's a directness.

Maslow: There is obviously much to be learned there. You know what we're doing now has never been done. Nobody has ever investigated this as research, running around asking people, "What do you feel when you see a child?" I am very curious simply because I don't know. We've heard from the women about these feelings. Could I ask the men to respond? Do men feel the same way? Does this sound like what you would feel, or is it different? I don't know. *Man*kind doesn't know. There's no what we would call "scientific" or "reliable" knowledge.

Paul: I find myself preferring to *play* with a little older child—even a girl—of five, six or seven, rather than showing much affection by hugging or kissing. And also, about this ugly child versus pretty child. I know one thing—downstairs from where I live, there are three children. The middle child in this family is the most neglected and shy and I find myself showing much more warmth to her.

Maslow: Did that click? Do you have any yearning for children? Do you feel this in yourself, spoken of by others?

Paul: Yes. But I think I would tend to agree even now, not having children, that I would still be more gratified with children of my own rather than with just children in general. I respond to a little girl cousin of mine more than just any little girl.

[*Pause*]

Maslow: Gentlemen?

Mike: I would just like to comment on something you said last week about—a statement about not being able to feel what a woman goes through in childbirth. I found that I felt very antagonistic about what you said. My sister-in-law is pregnant now and I see a tremendous difference in my brother and the way he swelled up [*group laughter*] and I know that somehow he feels this. He swelled up inside; he is so much more complete. I can't explain exactly what I have seen in him, but it is quite different than it was, and they have been married four years, and it's quite different now. And also, I feel that as a man who's taking part in creation, *that* compensates enough to know the feeling. The feeling couldn't be there without his participation, and . . . I don't know.

Maslow: If you were describing your feelings as a father—a potential father—or his feelings as a father, do the feelings differ? This is my question: Are the feelings different from the feelings of the mother?

Mike: I guess just because he is not having the baby, they would have to be. But there are feelings of emotions, not just the physical thing.

Maslow: We don't have any . . . we don't honestly know.

Mike: I don't think I can accept that, saying that I couldn't feel.

Herb: You seem to be asking for experiential reports. I can recall many times when holding a baby I have a feeling of real inadequacy. I don't mean *maternal* inadequacy, which I should have; I mean, there's no reason I should feel any qualms about that; the bond is with the mother. But I feel awkward when I'm holding a baby. I don't really have the feeling that I do know how it should be held or what kind of treatment it should be given. I have the feeling that I have to be overly gentle with it. It's almost like I have a fear of crushing it or squeezing it too hard because I don't have an intuitive sense of how the baby should be treated. I expect that it's there when there is a sense of kinship, which I have never felt for a baby yet. I have never had a child so it makes a big difference, I assume. When I do, I am sure it will evoke a whole range of feelings which I am simply incapable of feeling now. But I just haven't felt those things.

Maslow: We're going to break up in a minute. I want to report to you Laski's comments. She noticed that there was no single incidence of ecstasy by fathers; that is, a father-love on having a baby or anything like that. It just simply wasn't reported. And I don't remember any in my own research—I guess I better check before I say that[17]—but she checked her data and makes the report: there are no ecstasies that came from the father. And then she's the one who made that comment, "Why is it we take for granted mother-love when we don't even have any word for father-love? It's a special thing."

Doug: This summer a gentleman mentioned to me the feeling of being ecstatically involved with his wife while watching the operation of his wife's giving birth. He witnessed the operation. He said, "I wanted to feel something so this is the only thing I could do. I felt it wasn't my baby; it was an attachment." He did this and he said he did feel a whole, just—

Maslow: Natural childbirth people are putting this in as part of their program of having the father in the delivery room, being there while the whole business is going on. It would be interesting for you to try introspecting on that and whether you approve of that. Do you feel it's a good thing or a bad thing—you men especially, whether you would like that or not. Their feeling is that the sense of participation makes a stronger bond between the father and the baby than is now the case. And it may possibly be that the bond between mothers and babies— which we take to be stronger, generally—may be partially an "imprinting," or just simply they are more intimately involved with the baby, with childbirth. Maybe. It's something to think about.

For next time I would like to turn to the report of these desolation experiences and peak-experiences. I would like you to think about that before we meet for our third hour next Monday. And I think from then on I won't bother directing it. There are some things I would like to put you in, I'd like to exercise you with. For next time would you think about that?

NOVEMBER 4, 1963

Lecture

Maslow: I suppose already my impression is—I may be wrong—that there's some differentiation between those of you who seem to be quite serious about what we're doing, caught up with it, sweating at it, working, and others who aren't. Now since I like to make life more easy, for the former group rather than the others I'm going to try not to put on reserve those books which might be better at home. So before we get into psychedelic drugs, I want to make a couple of recommendations about readings, for the aficionados, now. For seniors, rather than freshman, you might say. These are two Jungian books. One of them is a very, very wonderful book; it's a great book, even. It's very difficult. I don't recommend that you read it during the semester, during the school year. It's just too involving. It's a little like being analyzed. Save it for a summer, I would think would be the best time. *Archetypal Patterns in Poetry*,[1] by Maud Bodkin.[2] Bodkin herself is a marvelous literary scholar and has read C. G. Jung very carefully, very well. And Jung is very difficult—it is three-quarters crap and the other one-quarter is so wonderful. It's a difficult thing to know how to handle Jung. Well, she handles it as well as I've ever seen anyone else handle it, far better than Jung himself. I think she's more respect-worthy than he is about some things. You can buy it and put it aside for when you feel strong, healthy and vigorous and ready to work at it. It's so condensed that you may have to read a page or two or three at a time to take it seriously. I remember when I read it, my notes—my reactions to it—were almost longer than the text itself. But it's a good, clean book—no contamination, no phoniness, no crap, no besmirchment, no poison, no trivialities, no meaninglessness—it doesn't happen very often. It's worthy of your very best effort.

The other book is *Experiment in Depth*,[3] by P. W. Martin.[4] I'm less impressed with it and yet it can be useful to those few of you who—after this semester is over and after you have done the various types of readings that I want you to do—are still interested in self-analysis and want to continue with it. This would be one of the books you could read and get something out of. The book is an effort at self-analysis in the Jungian style, resting to some extent also on T. S. Eliot[5] and Arnold Toynbee.[6] Primarily Jung. The leitmotif of the book is the "withdrawal and return," which Jung would call the "death and rebirth" motif or schema. It is the giving up of something, the dying to something, in order to be reborn in a different and better style.

We needn't get too fancy or classy about that, by the way, because this death and rebirth schema will hold exactly for improving your tennis or swimming, or whatever. Say you would like to improve your swimming, for instance. A good teacher will examine you and say: "You're breathing in the wrong way. Let's start all over again from the beginning." And then as you start and get half-drowned—you can't swim at all for a little while. Death, rebirth. We needn't get too fancy about this. You can improve, and you do this for many areas.

The book I really respect more is Bodkin's, which I think will win your esteem. It's not recommended around very much, but I think in spite of that fact it's just a great book, simply because it demands so much—it's so difficult but it's more serious.

So we can have this master list of books to which we can add these two. It's a very, very good bibliography for this area of thought. You can keep it around, and I'm sure a few of you will remain interested in this. Or you may recover your interest seven years from now, and I'd like you to have this around so you can have a good place to start.

Other books I want to add to this list have to do with case histories of psychotherapy under LSD. One of them is the Constance Newland[7] book, *Myself and I*[8] and the other is Jane Dunlap,[9] *Exploring Inner Space*.[10] I think those are both pseudonyms. I know the Newland is a pseudonym. I must tell you frankly that I don't really care for these books. I get suspicious somehow as I read through them—both of them seem very far out, the experiences. Dunlap has hallucinations, and so on, and I'm not sure that they would be a good model or a good exemplar for you to base yourself on, or to identify with. Everything there is too nutty for models. You can use them without buying them. I'd recommend them with this caution I make, that I feel suspicious and uneasy, as if they were too hysterical somehow and maybe fake too. I don't get that nice feeling of cleanliness that I do with Bodkin's. There is a slight phoniness in the air there someplace; it may be made up. They themselves may be actresses a little bit. They may be in the strict, clinical sense of the word "hystericals," who dramatize too much, who are over-enthusiastic, over-emotional, over-black-and-white and the like. That's the feeling I get from both of them. They go into "transports" when it's not quite necessary.

I'm going to use one of the clinical histories from Constance Newland—maybe next time—and you'll see for yourself. It's pretty wild, and it just doesn't *happen* that way; it's an extreme instance in psychoanalysis which just does not happen that way very often— maybe one in five hundred would be that, you know, atomic explosions and earthquakes and so on. Usually, psychoanalysis and the working through of peak-experiences and B-cognition is more like walking through mud. It's not like flying so much. There may be the moment of flying, but then comes the working-through process, which takes such a long time and is just plain sweaty work—like hiking with a forty-pound pack on your back. And these dames are too much—as if they were on Pegasus. And yet they are useful, especially since there are so few reports of this kind.

It may be that we have a situation here of volunteer error, the same thing that we found in the sexual studies by Kinsey.[11] For instance, when Kinsey asked for volunteers for his study, in one study I was able to test these volunteers and found that they were statistically significantly higher in dominance feeling or self-esteem; that is to say, they were simply stronger people.[12] Now, stronger people are much more pagan about sex, much more experimental, much more efflourescent, much more trying everything out. And therefore, Kinsey's figures are contaminated by volunteer error. There are not nearly enough virgins in his figures, for instance. There are not nearly enough non-masturbators, monogamous people, shy and modest people in his study. His figures are disturbed by the fact that those people who are apt to volunteer when they are asked are much more free about talking about sex. The people who are free about talking about sex are also free about sexing about sex. Now, the same thing here—it may very well be that we have volunteer error with the reports of psychotherapy. What I've just said about these two people I have to say about every single reported case history that I know about. Of the big ones: *The Story of My Psychoanalysis*[13] by John Knight[14], who is on your list; Lucy Freeman,[15] *Fight Against Fears*,[16] the story of her analysis. If you make a list of a dozen such cases, they seem all like Ms. Dunlap and Newland—too hysterical, too exhibitionistic, too trying-to-make-an-impression.

I wish we could get some of these stories from more troubled people, more sober, more serious, more shy and modest. I have the same feeling about Alan Watts[17] too—by the way, this is all in confidence, for we are now in "clinical privacy"—a little bit showy-offy perhaps, a little bit prancing in public, exhibitionistic perhaps, like acting sort of thing. But that's in a certain sense. Besides, these are the only full-length stories that I have, so I'm using them. They will be good for you—you can read them and talk about them—if you keep in mind my suspicions so that you don't buy it completely.

Let me start this off by reading some of this stuff from Alan Watts. You should all know him. The best book of his that I recommend is *Nature, Man and Woman,*[18] where he was most sober. It's probably the best single introduction for Westerners to Zen Buddhism and Taoism, that kind of thing, comparatively. It also adds another angle of mystic experience, from the Eastern point of view. The book I have chosen today is *The Joyous Cosmology.*[19] I get a little uneasy about it, the way I do about others. That's my personal feeling. I may be wrong, but I'm simply reporting my personal feeling; it may be just a slight incompatibility of some sort. Watts has reported often enough on peak-experiences and has in fact written one of the best accounts in *This Is It*.[20] The title essay in the book is an account of how his peak-experiences felt. Since he is so intelligent and so good with words, it's one of the really good accounts, even though I might have my private suspicions about it—how much is words, how much emotion and so on.

The Joyous Cosmology, subtitled *Adventures in the Chemistry of Consciousness*, is a report about his own LSD experiences. There are some things that he has put very well and I can recommend the book as a whole. Again, just be aware of my suspicions, my uneasiness, and see for yourself as a reader with a certain reserve. Some intellectual things have been said very well at first:

> Science pursues the common-sense assumption that the natural world is a multiplicity of individual things and events by attempting to describe these units as accurately and minutely as possible. Because science is above all *analytic*—

Take that word seriously: "analyzing" means breaking down, pulling apart.

> —in its way of describing things, it seems at first to disconnect them more than ever. Its experiments are the study of carefully isolated situations, designed to exclude influences that cannot be measured and controlled . . .[21]

Good statement. And it's embedded in the context in which he says he's trying to do different, and that this whole report—which I would say, for my money, is perfectly respectable scientific datum, scientific material, as any good introspective reports are; as a matter of fact, they are the *basic* scientific data, I would say—he contrasts it with this other kind of thinking. Another statement:

> The transformation of consciousness undertaken in Taoism and Zen is more like the correction of faulty perception or the curing of a disease.

Very good.

> It is not an acquisitive process of learning more and more facts or greater and greater skills, but rather an unlearning of wrong habits and opinions.[22]

Now this is a very, very nice condensed statement of what I've been trying to write myself, as the validity of the knowledge gained in peak-experiences and mystic experiences. I call it B-knowledge, the knowledge of being. I wound up saying something of the sort, only not as well as this. It is what Martin calls "psychoperception" or "psyche-perception," as I want to call it—inner perception, the inner happening. This is not so much as if suddenly you had your eyes opened after having been congenitally blind. It's not like seeing something which simply didn't exist before, like seeing a rabbit pulled out of a hat or something come out of invisibility. It's not like that at all so much as it is a change in attitude, a change in attention, a change in your gestalt perceptions, your perceptions of relationships, of depth, of the abstract Platonic essence that lies behind the trivialities and the irrelevances and so forth. Now I'll be talking a lot about that, but I couldn't resist this very, very nice and very condensed statement here. I'll repeat that; I'd like you to have it in your notes:

> The transformation of consciousness undertaken in Taoism and Zen—

And I would say that happens in the LSD and the psilocybin experiments under good circumstances, in peak-experiences, mystic experiences and also in B-cognition generally.

> —is more like the correction of faulty perception or the curing of a disease.

It's like getting good lenses, a good pair of spectacles when you didn't realize you had astigmatism, or presbyopia, or something of the sort. And we must give up in our context, in this room, the paradigm of learning as the acquisition of facts and the acquisition of skills. Rather it's new ways of seeing old things. New habits of attention, perhaps. Different attitudes toward what has been around you all the time. Another statement:

> Consciousness-changing drugs—

"Psychedelic" drugs is the word that everybody has agreed on. We can also use the term "psychedelic" because it means consciousness-expanding, consciousness-enriching, which is exactly what we are trying to do also, and it has nothing to do with drugs necessarily.

> —are popularly associated with the evocation of bizarre and fantastic images, but in my own experience this happens only with closed eyes.

You will have hallucinations and bizarre feelings and the walls will melt and so on, but they're not important as it happens.

> Otherwise, it is simply that the natural world is endowed with a richness of grace, color, significance, and, sometimes, humor, for which our normal adjectives are insufficient.[23]

Of more interest to me:

> . . . one's transformed impression of the natural world.[24]

The world that he has seen all the time, but now sees in a different way, more vividly: the colors are brighter, more colorful, the outlines are sharper, the "suchness" of things becomes more "such-y"; chairs become more "chair-y," tables become more "table-y," and stuff like that. There is no other way of saying it. And this is what he's talking about with the "transformed impression of the natural world" itself. It is not that you see a chair where you didn't see a chair before. You see the same chair, only now you see how much a chair it is and how miraculous this fact is. It all sounds beautiful—don't you agree?—and how cosmically humorous also, which is another part of the story.

Now for his own introspections:

To begin with, this world has a different kind of time.

This is under LSD, and he also had psilocybin—it seems to make no difference for him.

> It is the time of biological rhythm, not of the clock and all that goes with the clock. There is no hurry. Our sense of time is notoriously subjective and thus dependent upon the quality of our attention, whether of interest or boredom, and upon the alignment of our behavior in terms of routines, goals, and deadlines.

Calendars, clocks and the like.

> Here the present is self-sufficient . . .

That is, the here-now experience that we talked about before. I won't say anything more about it.

> but it is not a static present. It is a dancing present—

"Dancing" is the here-now—here-now and alive.

> —the unfolding of a pattern which has no specific destination in the future but is simply its own point.

That's an excellent way of saying "it's not going any place; it just is." This is why the words "being," "isness" and "suchness" so frequently come up; people will come back to that in sort of a helpless way and say, "Well, there is no better way of saying it!"

> It leaves and arrives simultaneously, and the seed is as much the goal as the flower. There is therefore time to perceive every detail of the movement with infinitely greater richness of articulation.[25]

Now this is under drugs and not so much in peak-experiences, which tend toward ecstasies, or in those desolation experiences, which tend to be passive rather than climactic, you might say. Let's say like the sexual orgasm, as a model: coming to a peak, and then passing. This is one difference with the drugs; it's as if this peak were not a passing peak, not a climax, but simply going up to a plateau and staying there. Come to think of it, that's reported as a kind of orgasm by women, not by men. Men are climactic in their sexual responses.

Some women, rather few of course, report this sexual plateau that they get up on and stay there for a time. Not a climactic orgasm but a plateau orgasm, you might say. That would be the difference in general between the descriptions that I've tried to make. I've spoken of peak-experiences, most of them, and so have Laski and most other people, as climactic, more or less; it's a matter of seconds, or minutes. The plateau kind of experience is relatively rare under these natural circumstances. Now, I've seen it; it happens. The love delirium could be a plateau; that is, it's possible to be in love and be nuts altogether and to be "peaky"' day after day and week after week. It doesn't happen very often, but it can happen.

Experientially these drugs and the peak-experiences are not very different. That is, I could use Watts; he is talking about LSD, and yet I could use him here to describe B-cognition; that is, the cognition of the world in the peak-experiences. We can use the same words, same content but with one difference: he is talking about plateaus and I've been talking about climaxes.

A footnote is that I really don't know what to make of it yet. We'll certainly have to puzzle over it together.

There are, after all, after-effects of peak-experiences. There is the occasional perception of something, or the realization of something you hadn't noticed before. Perhaps it will happen to you as we play our games here. One experiment that I'd like you to do and probably you've never really done in your life, is really to look at another person's face with care. Now very funny things happen: piety, holiness, religious feelings and all sorts of feelings. I don't know if we can do it. I've never tried that as an experiment with whole groups before, only with single people. I don't know if we can do it, but we can try.

Many of these feelings are irreversible. That is, you can discover by examining another human being with great care—*caritas*; that's Latin—in the old biblical sense, implying a kind of love, "loving care." Then you'll observe, for instance, how fantastically beautiful a face can be. You know, you've been sitting around, walking, talking, passing by, having all sorts of dealings with people. Sometimes this stays with you—that is, you notice that the face is beautiful, the person is beautiful, and then forever after it's fixed with you. You hadn't noticed it until some Thursday afternoon at 2:15, and then for the rest of your life there it is. Well, what shall we call that? We can't call it a peak-experience because it's not in ecstasy, it's not thereafter in the great emotion, but it's more serene, it's more calm. It doesn't come and go, it's not climactic, it just sticks with you. It's a new way of seeing, simply.

Just in the same way—if your experiences with music, let's say, are the same way as mine—you listen and listen to something and then it breaks through. That's the way it was with me anyway. For instance, I can remember the first time I ever really heard *Firebird* by Stravinsky. I had listened to it before a couple of times, but one time it clicked and broke through. That was a peak-experience. I still remember it. And then I must have listened to it a hundred times. I drove everybody nuts around my home just listening to it and listening to it. [*Pause*]

But it wasn't always a peak-experience again. There wasn't this first delirium, this first ecstasy. It was now just a new perceiving, a new correction of vision—a new perceiving of something that was there all the time, only I hadn't been able to see it; I wasn't a good enough perceiver. Well, what shall we call that? I have been groping for names—"serene B-cognition," rather than ecstatic or emotional. Let me call it that for the time being—serene B-cognition. B-cognition, you know what I mean by that. I've asked you to read about that in my chapter on the "Cognition of Being in the Peak Experiences."[26] I don't have much data on that—on keeping it forever, keeping it available so that you can turn it on and off when you like. Nor do I have data, except my own introspections, which one day I would like to do more with, about what happens to the *Firebird* after I've heard it three hundred times. Now, for myself it's a sad thing. One of the sad things I find about aging is that all these pieces of music . . . It's almost as if they're equal to an old sweetheart. The fires may be gone, the ecstasies may be gone, the peak-experiences may be gone, and yet there is a love for each piece of music in the standard repertory.

Each piece came through to me like that. I can remember the circumstances of Brahms' First Symphony; that was on the stairs, going up, just halfway up the stairs it clicked as I heard it playing. I can place every one of the whole repertoire, yet it's all gone in a certain sense. They'll be playing on the radio or the phonograph and I'll be reading the newspaper. I can recover the memory—there is certainly some kind of perception of something very wonderful and beautiful—but the ecstatic feelings are gone. Well, is that B-cognition? I can recover them perhaps by listening very carefully again. I don't even know any more if that's just a memory of something. [*Maslow chuckles*] Remember that joke, Red Skelton's joke on television?[27] He is saying: "I'm not so old, I still chase after girls. I just don't remember why." [*General laughter*]

What is the feeling? Well, you see, we're in a puzzle there about this B-cognition, this plateau kind of perceptiveness. Let's call it for the time being—you might as well use my word unless you have a better one—*serene* B-cognition.

Now there's a difference: one thing about the serene B-cognition is that you have time, which you don't have in the ecstasy itself—in the great moment when the tendency is to be paralyzed or to be hushed, not to move, not to want to do anything, just to absorb the whole experience. It may be that perpetual peak-experiences would simply kill us; they're just too wearing. That much emotion would be more than a human being could stand. Maybe the heart can't stand it, who knows? [*Pause*]

I continue with Watts now:

> Normally we do not so much look at things as overlook them.

See, the guy is a very good phrasemaker. He manages to pin the feeling down very nicely. That's an excellent sentence.

> The eye sees types and classes—flower, leaf, rock, bird, fire—mental pictures of things rather than things, rough outlines filled with flat color, always a little dusty and dim.

> But here the depth of light and structure in a bursting bud go on forever.

Now he's talking about that feeling of eternity which we will get in these transcendent experiences.

> There is time to see them, time for the whole intricacy of veins and capillaries to develop in consciousness, time to see down and down into the shape of greenness, which is not green at all, but a whole spectrum generalizing itself as green—purple, gold, the sunlit turquoise of the ocean, the intense luminescence of the emerald. I cannot decide where shape ends and color begins.

That's very true when you really look at something with care, with love.

> The bud has opened and the fresh leaves fan out, and curve back with a gesture which is unmistakably communicative but does not say anything except, "Thus!" And somehow that is quite satisfactory, even startlingly clear. The meaning is transparent in the same way that the color and the texture are transparent, with light which does not seem to fall upon surfaces from above or from outside but to be right inside the structure and color.[28]

To go on, this is another experience:

> At the same time everyone and everything around me takes on the feeling of having been there always, and then forgotten, and then remembered again.

Very characteristic.

> We are sitting in a garden, surrounded in every direction by uncultivated hills, a garden of fuchsias and hummingbirds in a valley that leads down to the

> westernmost ocean, and where the gulls take refuge in
> storms.

He lives near San Francisco. It's the Pacific Coast.

> At some time in the middle of the twentieth century,
> upon an afternoon in the summer, we are sitting around
> a table on the terrace, eating dark homemade bread and
> drinking white wine. And yet we seem to have been
> there forever. . .

Does that click with you at all? Do you remember feelings like that—
timelessness, eternity? It's associated with nature. It comes often with
love experience. Do you remember? Try to remember. As a matter of
fact, let me ask you if you remember. Write it down and put it in your
notebook, try to remember for yourself, to recover. Sweat a little bit
with it, recover these experiences of timelessness. That's a big,
abstract word, but maybe Watts's phrases will help you get the feeling
for it, and then you can recover them from your memories.

> . . . we seem to have been there forever, for the people
> with me are no longer the humdrum and harassed little
> personalities with names, addresses, and social security
> numbers, the specifically dated mortals we are all
> pretending to be.[29]

That word "pretense" does so frequently come up. As if in
B-cognition, you were seeing through the persons, through the masks,
through the pretensions. Tim Leary[30] calls it the game—the game of
being what you are. From this eternal point of view, how ridiculous
we look, because we are all embedded in a moment in history in a
particular culture. For instance, look how ridiculously I'm tricked out.
Look at this particular thing [*fiddling with his necktie*] I have stuck
around my neck here. [*General laughter*] It's very peculiar from the
point of view of Mars: this dopey thing around my neck. This peculiar
thing of cutting my hair in a particular way. You know, if this were
the fifteenth century, I wouldn't have done this. Where are my nice
curls, my ringlets, and so on, and why did I cut them off? You have a
very peculiar outfit. What's this in here—this lapel—what does it do,

why does it exist?

It is quite peculiar if you look at it from the point of view of other cultures, other times—even your own time, even your own past if you live long enough. Look at those uniforms and the games you are playing, and those peculiar things that you wear—as a matter of fact, *are* wearing. Why do you wear those things at all? Why do you cover your nakedness? And these funny things that you have done with your hair, look around you and see all the peculiar things that have been done with hair here.

Well, back to the present. [*General laughter*]

"These specifically dated mortals we are all pretending to be." Well, I know who clicked that off. It was my wife, who was running through these big piles of pictures and photographs and trying to classify and organize our old family pictures. Then she found a picture of me as a baby—a child of two—and a picture of her at two years old. It's another century, almost: clothes are different, the little boots that the boy wore are quite different from what they would be today. Then the style of hair was very different: I had ringlets and I was blond, of all things. Well, where are my lost ringlets? Anyway, that brings it up.

> They appear rather as immortal archetypes of themselves without, however, losing their humanity.[31]

Does that make any sense to you? Again, that feeling of timelessness. We are going to try exercises of it: just try to think of a person not just in himself but as standing for something—not that particular guy who is in 1963, in a particular place, in a particular uniform, playing a particular game, and talking with particular formulas, but rather "man" with a capital "M" and with roots that go back three thousand, five thousand, seven thousand years, and going on into the future—we all hope another seven thousand years— standing in a long line. You can get this feeling of timelessness perhaps more with nature as you watch the recurrence of the seasons than you can with a person, but you can do it with a person too, any person.

Well, I think of Thomas Huxley[32]: "A hen is nature's peculiar way of carrying on eggs." In the same manner, any person is just as "peculiar" from the point of view of Huxley. He is just a sort of carrier for his great-grandchildren, his great-great-grandchildren, great-great-great-grandchildren. He can be placed in timelessness in a Platonic way. You'll find in the Martin book, for instance, one very good discussion of the archetypes—the particular archetypes of the wise old man, which is a kind of self-actualizing, abstract ideal for man. And for women, Magna Mater, the Great Mother, you might say, as the cliché, as the stereotype, as a Platonic form, which *lives,* which *exists,* which every woman has as a model, the ideal, something which she is moving towards. It's a kind of an Aristotelian *telos*, the final cause there, something which she has identified with, and is moving towards and modeling herself on. Well, we can take each other in that way. I know that I have had the feeling that Watts is talking about.

I remember once very vividly in one of the academic processions here at the commencement a couple of years ago. Normally I would be the, you know, 1963 sophisticated man, quite aware of the ridiculousness of the whole situation—the cap and gown—the medieval hangover with the University of Paris in 1300, 1400, and here I am, tricked out in these things which are like a vermiform appendix. And sometimes I feel very foolish with these things, in this gown and this idiotic cap with the thing dangling in front of my eyes. [*General laughter*]

Then at other times I can have the feeling of standing in a long line, clean back to 1300, and then get thrilled and awed a little bit and identify with the doctrine—the doctors of philosophy and how many there were. And I stand in a kind of parade which is not just this little parade but goes back 660 years and is going on into the future for a long time too. And one can get awed by the identification of oneself—not just me exactly, because the guy next to me with his cap and gown is just as much in this parade and just as much identified with the whole Platonic essence, with this eternal and timeless thing, as I am with my particular symbolic type of thing.

Well, I don't know where you'll get your feelings of timelessness from. I think that the basic things of life—childbirth certainly seems to produce it. Pregnancy, parturition, feeding the baby, that sort of thing. Even the worst sons-of-bitches—I'm thinking of one man, who was almost psychopathic, a real evil villain of a man—was touched with pregnancy and with his babies. This horrible person could be touched. If nothing else will touch you, however cast-iron a soul you have, *that* at least will do it. The ocean, the forest—people get struck into dumbness on a mountain view. You go pursue your own experiences. I don't know where they are for you—the experiences of timelessness, where everything sort of stands still; they don't move forward or backward in time, but where the past and the future seem somehow to be existing at this moment now. Watts says it very nicely:

> They appear rather as immortal archetypes of themselves.

You're not just a particular guy. You're a Man, a sacred man, a sacred *who*, the god, the goddess, the priestess and so on.

> It is just that their differing characters seem, like the priest's voice—

Religious people can get that feeling particularly about a priest. For the Catholics, the priest is clearly not one particular male person. He stands for something which is far beyond himself.

> —seem, like the priest's voice, to contain all history; they are at once unique and eternal, men and women but also gods and goddesses. For now that we have time to look at each other we become timeless. The human form becomes immeasurably precious and, as if to symbolize this, the eyes become intelligent jewels, the hair spun gold, and the flesh translucent ivory. Between those who enter this world together there is also a love which is distinctly eucharistic, an acceptance of each other's nature from the heights to the depths.
>
> Ella, who planted the garden, is a beneficent Circe—sorceress, daughter of the moon, familiar of cats and snakes, herbalist and healer—with the youngest old face one has ever seen, exquisitely

> wrinkled, silver-black hair rippled like flames. Robert is a manifestation of Pan, but a Pan of bulls instead of the Pan of goats, with frizzled short hair tufted into blunt horns—a man all sweating muscle and body, incarnation of exuberant glee.

Incarnation—a good word for this kind of thing. This happens to be sort of a "passing," the putting into flesh of a much better idea than he is, so to speak. Plato is very good at that.

> Beryl, his wife, is a nymph who has stepped out of the forest, a mermaid of the land with swinging hair and dancing body that seems to be naked even when clothed. It is her bread that we are eating—

And that could be a sacrament too.

> —and it tastes like the Original Bread of which mother's own bread was a bungled imitation. And then there is Mary, beloved in the usual, dusty world, but in this world an embodiment of light and gold, daughter of the sun, with eyes formed from the evening sky—a creature of all ages, baby, moppet, maid, matron, crone, and corpse, evoking love of all ages.

Mary is a little girl.

> I try to find words that will suggest the numinous,—

I want you to know that word. N-U-M-I-N-O-U-S. The Latin, "*numen*," meant a sort of god-like, supernatural creature, a god.

> —mythological quality of these people.

That's the kind of feeling, by the way, that you get from those Jungian books that I recommended—more than from Jung himself—this Bodkin book for instance, or the Martin book, I think. You get the archetypes in the Martin book very well, I think.

> Yet at the same time they are as familiar as if I had known them for centuries, or rather, as if I were

> recognizing them again as lost friends whom I knew at
> the beginning of time, from a country begotten before
> all worlds.[33]

Does that do anything to you? He is speaking for many, many people. That is a mouth speaking for many, many voices and many experiences through the centuries, through many different cultures and so on. Those feelings, if everyone had the literary talent to express it, they would be repeated thousands and thousands of millions of times. I choose Watts not because he is Watts, but because he is speaking for the whole species, simply because he speaks well—he is a good word-man.

Now, one thing that I'd like you to get and watch for is B-humor—a humor of a particular kind: self-actualizing humor, as I first called it. I don't know how else to do it except to give you example after example and hope that you can pick it out on your own. And if you get interested in what I say here, what Watts said, then the reference is the section on self-actualizing humor in my book, *Motivation and Personality*, the chapter on "Love in Self-Actualizing People."[34] There's a brief page or two description of this B-humor there. I did the best I could with it. The best example I could ever think of was Abraham Lincoln,[35] who seemed somehow not to have any other kind of humor. So reading his stories might help as my case example. Then in that same business of the B-cognition and the B-values, see if you can make sense out of what I myself can't make too much sense out of—humor as one of the B-values; that is, as one of the characteristics of the world when it is seen in its most Platonic form and when you are a most perspicuous seer—as in peak-experiences, perhaps—that somehow the world looks humorous in a way that's very hard to describe. You may have experienced this. It's characteristic of many people in ecstatic moments, or even in moments of just "high happiness," that there is a tendency to laugh, that you can see something very beautiful and laugh at it. This can be puzzling to other people, perhaps puzzling to you yourself. One can laugh with delight. It suddenly pops into my head—I remember one person who describes this very well is Thomas Moore,[36] describing the laugh of exaltation, the laugh of delight, the laugh of sheer delight with the world, with whatever it is that absorbs one particularly.

It's a very interesting exercise that I get—you can try it too. It struck me as I was struggling, wrestling with B-humor: why it is that there's practically no religion that has humor. Where is humor in religion? Most of the gods—the Jewish God, the Mohammedan God, the Christian God, the Buddhist god—most of them don't, I think.[37] There is no laughing, no giggling, none of the B-humor. Why is it then that we have created our gods so sober and humorless? If there were gods of that kind, obviously they would be humorous because our god-like people, that is, the best people we can find, like Abraham Lincoln, they all have B-humor—a particular kind of amused view of the world, delighted view of the world and everything in it. Does that click with you all?

Paul: The Jewish God is even suffering; he's not only just sober.

Maslow: Are there any jokes in the Bible any place? Any jokes in the Koran? I don't think so. It's one thought that I had once. It suddenly dawned on me that as we know more about the heights of human nature now, higher people will create higher gods too. And if you can conceive of a god with a sense of humor, a god with B-humor, then suddenly many old theological problems get solved. For instance, the creation of the world and the creation of mankind, it's easy—it was a joke, obviously. [*General laughter*]

I am reminded also—and this is personal. These are free associations that may help some of you to make things click. I'll toss out these things, maybe one out of three may push a button in you.

I think of two art shows which I saw. One was in Dallas or Houston. I was travelling and stopped in at the local museum of art as I was driving through town. And there was a big show, the biggest show I have ever seen of collages and assemblages—the best one I've ever seen, in the sense of breaking through. That was one moment in which it broke through, like that example of the music that I told you about. The collages of the Cubists, of Picasso and Braque and that gang, left me cold. I never got anything out of it. It's, in fact, silly to me. I certainly got no aesthetic pleasure from them.

Well, as I went through this big show—and in one other breakthrough of the same kind—suddenly I found myself laughing, and then I went through the whole show again as if I sort of got the idea. Of *course* that's what they were doing! This was B-humor—that's what it was. These huge assemblages of a lot of tarpaper, and old lathes, spools of cotton, and God knows what else, certainly had the effect on me. I had been looking for the aesthetic—I had already predefined aesthetic reaction in a particular way. This is not an aesthetic reaction that I got there, but something else, but it was at B-level very definitely. This was a cosmic humor. These guys were poking fun at human beings; that's what they were doing.

And then I got this even better. I would suggest this for you. This was at a show in New York City. I didn't want to go, but I was with a friend of mine, David Levy, the same guy that I was talking to you about. This was a show in a gallery right across the hall from his office. I wasn't interested; I thought it was nonsense. And he took me into it. It was a show of this little junk art, and some guy had put together old boilers and tin cans and stuff—you've seen that sort of thing. I had seen many of them and, if anything, got indignant, you know. As a matter of fact, I still get indignant at most of them. I think this is 57th Street *chic* mostly. But this guy had put together all these things into little engines and motors, and when we came in, everything was quiet. But this David Levy is a big art collector, and whenever I've gone to an art show with him, immediately everybody swings to attention and they start turning on lights and putting on things and so on. And whatever can be seen *is* seen. Well, when Levy walked into the place with me this guy pushed a button and suddenly all these things, a whole room of little engines, started working like mad. [*General laughter*] Shuffling back and forth, moving back and forth and whistling and doing things. And then again that reaction came about, the humor—how ridiculous human beings are. This was like within one room of all the big pyramids that have been built by human beings—great structures—and I think of Shelley's "Ozymandias," and so on and so on, and there were all these engines huffing and puffing so much and working so hard—sweating and straining, whistling and making noises and going absolutely no place and doing absolutely nothing, just going back and forth, running like mad down the track and then turning round and running like mad back. That was B-humor in the sense that I am trying to, and in the sense that Watts is trying to, get over.

Now if this clicks with you, then you have got something very existential. Bodkin has it in her book too—the relationship between the tragic and the comic is exemplified in such things. The assemblages which are at one and the same time death itself—busted old automobiles, torn chunks of tarpaper and broken bricks—which have yet been put together somehow. It's a little like the human being, like the ship going down with its flag flying. It's something like that, dying with amusement—I think that's the very nicest way. This is the way Rabelais[38] is reputed to have died—with amusement—or Gertrude Stein[39] did very, very nicely. You know that story about her—as she lay dying, Alice Toklas,[40] her companion, sidekick, whispered in her ear, "Well, Gertrude, what's the answer?" and Gertrude sort of smirked back and said, "What's the question?" and died. It's not a bad way to die; that's a good death.

Let me put it more intellectually, in a formula, that this kind of humor is a resolution of the existential dilemma between the tragic and the comic and between death and life, between the fact that we are god-like and most dignified and Shakespeare can write big things about us, and yet we are also absolutely ridiculous and weak and helpless. We have this soaring imagination and yet we die, and we know it, and we are scared of it. What I want to do is to add here, as one of the great integrating mechanisms, this B-humor, the solution of the existential dilemma, the solution of the human predicament, the fact that we are simultaneously big and small. Now you can get conflicted about that, or confused. We are sacred and yet we are stinkers too. Now against that background, listen to this—I think it should come through.

> Later that same afternoon, Robert takes us over to his barn from which he has been cleaning out junk and piling it into a big and battered Buick convertible, with all the stuffing coming out of the upholstery. The sight of trash poses two of the greatest questions of human life, "Where are we going to put it?" and "Who's going to clean up?" From one point of view living creatures are simply tubes, putting things in at one end and pushing them out at the other . . .[41]

Which is a thought that he has and which is a thought that many human beings have with this: on the one hand, the dignity of man, and on the other hand, this picture of the digestive tube, shoveling things in and taking care of the stuff that comes out.

> The problem is always where to put what is pushed out at the other end, especially when it begins to pile so high that the tubes are in danger of being crowded off the earth by their own refuse. And the questions have metaphysical overtones. "Where are we going to put it?" asks for the foundation upon which things ultimately rest—the First Cause, the Divine Ground, the bases of morality, the origin of action. "Who's going to clean up?" is asking where responsibility ultimately lies, or how to solve our ever-multiplying problems other than by passing the buck to the next generation.
>
> I contemplate the mystery of trash in its immediate manifestation:

Remember, he's drugged now—he's under LSD. Obviously one thing happens to you—you get very philosophical, very ultimate, very B-cognizant.

> Robert's car piled high, with only the driver's seat left unoccupied by broken door-frames, rusty stoves, tangles of chicken-wire, squashed cans, insides of ancient harmoniums, nameless enormities of cracked plastic, headless dolls, bicycles without wheels, torn cushions vomiting kapok, non-returnable bottles, busted dressmaker's dummies, rhomboid picture-frames, shattered bird cages, and inconceivable messes of string, electric wiring, orange peels, eggshells, potato skins, and light bulbs—all garnished with some ghastly-white chemical powder that we call "angel shit."

Which is not an accident, by the way. It's a fact of the transcending of obscenity. It's in the B-cognition: dirty words don't always appear dirty—actually they're Platonic, you might say.

> Tomorrow we shall escort this in a joyous convoy to
> the local dump. And then what? Can any melting and
> burning imaginable get rid of these ever-rising
> mountains of ruin—especially when the things we
> make and build are beginning to look more and more
> like rubbish even before they are thrown away? The
> only answer seems to be that of the present group. The
> sight of Robert's car has everyone helpless with
> hysterics.

That's the answer.

> The Divine Comedy. All things dissolve in laughter.
> And for Robert this huge heap of marvelously
> incongruous uselessness is a veritable creation, a
> masterpiece of nonsense. He slams it together and
> ropes it securely to the bulbous, low-slung wreck of
> the supposedly chic convertible, and then stands back
> to admire it as if it were a float for a carnival. Theme:
> the American way of life. But our laughter is without
> malice—

That's self-actualizing humor, it's like that.

> —for in this state of consciousness everything is the
> doing of gods.

Gods with a sense of humor.

> The culmination of civilization in monumental heaps
> of junk is seen, not as thoughtless ugliness, but as
> self-caricature—as the creation of phenomenally
> absurd collages and abstract sculptures in deliberate
> but kindly mockery of our own pretensions. For in this
> world nothing is wrong, nothing is even stupid.

Do you remember the discussion of that? Everybody reports in the
peak-experiences, or in any moments of B-cognition, the world is

accepted. There is no evil, so to speak. It's beyond evil. Nothing is wrong.

> The sense of wrong is simply failure to see where something fits into a pattern, to be confused as to the hierarchical level upon which an event belongs—a play which seems quite improper at level 28 may be exactly right at level 96.[42]

That's an old Buddhist way of looking at these things, in levels of perception. [*Pause*]

I don't have anything else to say about that as a professor would say, apart from all sorts of intellectual conclusions, generalizations and so on. Do you have any reactions? You've got about 10 minutes before we break up.

Sarah: Have you ever read Hermann Hesse's *Steppenwolf*?[43]

Maslow: That reminds me—*Steppenwolf* is on every reading list that the drug people have. I must confess that I read it and didn't like it. It was recommended to me by those people that I respect. I read it a long time ago—I wasn't ready for it then, I guess. I'm going to read it again. But this reminds me about a book by Hesse which I will recommend for fitting into the kind of talk that we are talking, *Magister Ludi*.[44] It's a most remarkable novel which isn't respected enough. Then I will recommend *Steppenwolf*, not out of my own knowledge and experience, but because so many other people have.

Do you have any comments on this humor business—on B-humor? You can make jokes, you know; there are hierarchies of jokes. I've been collecting some of them, some that are poignant—jokes where you could almost cry as easily as you could laugh. One story which comes to mind. This is a cosmic joke. An Abraham Lincoln-style joke. B-humor: funny, sad, cute. This was a cartoon in the *New Yorker* perhaps 10 years ago. It's a children's party—little kids sitting down at the table with their ice cream in front of them, with their funny hats on their heads and so on. They were two or three years old. One little boy is sitting next to a little girl and he turns to her and asks, "Can you talk yet?" [*No laughter*]

Now I'd say this was condensation of cuteness, of love, of

ludicrousness, of humor, of sadness. It's a mixture of a lot of things—existential humor, like Saul Steinburg's,[45] for instance.

Paul: I'm often under the impression that Charlie Chaplin[46] movies are a good deal of this kind of humor. His nothing machines and things of this sort, and even the situations he places himself in, seem to capitalize upon the general absurdity of the living situation itself. It's not with any kind of resentment, but with a sense sometimes of almost incomprehensible delight in the absurdity of the moment itself. I think this is partly why we laugh at him without realizing it.

Maslow: Do we have any humorists like that now? I don't think so. I think that business is sort of wise-cracking rather than a B-humor. You see, the thing about this other kind of humor is that nobody laughs. They get thoughtful, they smile—no belly laughs, no guffaws.

Jayne: What about Philip Wylie?[47]

Maslow: Wylie? Some of it. Well, he wouldn't be called a "professional" humorist like Bob Hope[48] or Jack Benny[49] or maybe Godfrey.[50]

Doug: Fernandel, the French comedian, does a lot of movies.

Maslow: Yes, you reminded me of a French movie—just as good as the Chaplin things—*My Uncle*. I forget the name of the guy who was in it.

Mark: Jacques Tati.[51]

Maslow: Yeah, that's it. Well, the one I'd recommend is I think a great existential humorist, Saul Steinberg—the cartoonist, if you want to call him that. I think he is a great artist, really. In the *New Yorker*, every issue or every third issue there is something by him. The book I'd recommend there is *The Labyrinth*,[52] a collection of his best stuff. I made slides out of much of this stuff for one of my classes. I wanted to teach them about this existential psychology. Have you seen these things? Maybe I should bring them in. Would you like that?

Jayne: Could we try?

Maslow: Could we manage here to show slides? I think we could. How many of you know Saul Steinberg? I think it's worth bringing them in. For what I've been saying and for what I've been reading here from Watts, Steinberg would be a very good illustration.[53]

There are a few things I wanted to say before we go. First of all, I'd like to give you a few assignments in this journal writing. Even though I've got very few of the things turned in to me, I still think it's a good idea. I don't want to press you on it. But where you do have reactions, turn them in to me without waiting for a long time. In any case, I have decided not to wait till the end of the semester with that notebook but to take two looks at it. One would be, let's say, right after the mid-semester. I'll ask you to turn these papers in to me—papers, notebooks and so on—and then I would like to see each of you individually and talk. And then again at the end of the semester.

Now, I'd like to give assignments every once in a while. I'd like you to write your reactions to my comments or my talking on conflict about **sex**.[54] What were your reactions to my comments last time?

Also, I must tell you that I was sort of disappointed with our last session. I don't know exactly why. I just felt sort of let down a little. Do you have any comments on that? I'd like you to write those to me.

Thirdly, there was the business about the expression of hostility. I know it's a difficult thing but I encouraged that you should have practice at being able to affirm yourself. A few of you have been able to do it when you feel bored, or when you feel something is wrong or something you disagree with—you just say it. Now with this writing, we can take the edge off; that is, make it less of a confrontation. You can write about your disagreements or grievances or whatever. It's easier than to just say them out to a crowd. And I think I would want you to do that in your notebook.

Also I would ask you to try to get to know each other. We're too big a group, it seems quite clear to me now, for the effort that we are making. In the future, we'll just make it smaller. I would like you to get to know each other to the extent that that's possible outside the class. If it were possible, I think, I would suggest meeting without me around, a fourth hour if you can manage that. I don't know whether you can or not; maybe we'll discuss that later. How many of you think such a thing could actually come to pass and work? [*A few hands go up*]

My experiences with this business is that it doesn't work. College students here at Brandeis and most other formal schools, classical schools—if the teacher isn't around nothing happens. Although in the progressive schools—Sarah Lawrence and Bennington and places like that—it does happen. It doesn't make much difference whether the teacher is there or not, which is a measure of the tangibility of the educational atmosphere, you might say. I could suggest a fourth hour, but I have a feeling that if I weren't here, very few people would come, and not much would happen. Maybe you can get to know each other better, feel more bound together. Let me make that suggestion a month from now and see how it sits with you.

Finally, you must take it upon yourself also, as I suggested last time, this business of the intellectualizing. Of course, now we are intellectualizing, we are in class and this is our proper job: to draw generalizations, abstractions, conclusions and so on. It's legitimate now, but in the third hour, if anybody does intellectualize, then I'd like you to point it out, make something of it. And the thing is, this must include me. Because I think this is perhaps what crapped up the third hour last time. I got off on a lecture about something. I'm an intellectual and you have to tone me down sometimes or the words will run away with me. I suggest that to you.

Okay, let me ask you, how interested are you in this drug stuff? I had brought in a lot of stuff. Shall we take the session next time to go over some of that stuff? What I was going to do is to say a little about the state of research, the state of knowledge, and then to express my own reactions, emotional and intellectual, and then throw the floor open to both the intellectual and emotional reactions to this whole business, because I think this too is a kind of a crowbar into the B-realm. The discussion of my reluctance, for instance, to take LSD—my own self-analysis of it has been very illuminating to me. Why is this so? It touches on many, many big issues around the being, you might say. It could have nothing to do with drugs themselves and they are very appropriate to the whole discussion of peak-experiences and B-cognition. I was going to do that. Now, do you want that, are you interested? [*Murmurs of agreement*]

Alright, we'll do that next time.

Melissa: Next time we don't have classes.

Maslow: No? What's up then?

Melissa: Armistice Day.

Maslow: That's to celebrate the passing of all hostilities of war. I think the whole joint is closed down, isn't it? Alright, we'll just pass it on to the following week, that's two weeks from today. I'll probably be around next week. That might be a good time for these individual consultations with you. I'd like to meet each of you alone. Supposing I take that time; I'll see that the door to the building is open. I'll be in my office from two to five, that is the time we're supposed to meet. Shall we make dates specifically or should I just be available?

Melissa: I like it better with appointments.

Maslow: Shall we make appointments? Alright, we can do it here. I'd like a good longish session rather than just a few minutes, and then we'll have more sessions later on for these appointments. [*Maslow makes an appointment schedule on the blackboard for students to sign up*] Our next meeting, two weeks from today, is the mid-semester exam time. We don't have to take the whole time. Supposing we take the first hour for writing the paper I've already given.[55] You can bring in any notes you want to, but don't bring in any books. And I want you to think the paper out as much as you can before you come here, but in this room I would like you to write on your own—not to have it prewritten. And we'll take no more than one hour.

Jayne: Can you repeat the assignment?

Maslow: I can't give you the exact words. It has to do with your impressions of William James' *The Varieties of Religious Experience* as of today. How good is it? What holds up? What needs correction? In the light of everything you've learned so far, especially of the [Aldous] Huxley[56] books, the peak-experience stuff, the papers that I passed out and the whole of the James book.[57] Anything else? I think that covers it.

Herb: I'm having real difficulty trying to correlate what we've been reading and doing in class with the James book for the simple reason that all of the experiences which he listed are terribly religious. That's all he wrote about, really—religious experiences. It involves some notion of deity whereas none of ours have.

Maslow: Well, let's see what you can make of it. It's your problem, and our problem.

<hr />

NOVEMBER 4, 1963

Laboratory for Self-Knowledge

Maslow: Would you shut the door behind you, please? Partly I'm thinking privacy. There are always some people who just sit there and listen. I don't know why—strangers of all sorts. I'm sure you don't want that either.

Clara: In painting class they do that too. They sit at the door and watch.

Maslow: That I can understand better than this. [*General laughter*] Okay. What I thought of suggesting here was to see what happens when you try to talk about your own peak-experiences and what they mean. The questions you have about them and so on. Do you want to try that? Let's see what happens. [*Long pause*]

Sharon: Will you begin with your own?

Maslow: No, I think this time I'll pass the ball. I don't like to push anyone yet. As a matter of fact, I suggest you not push yourselves either.

Paul: I'm just thinking of a specific situation that occurred last Tuesday. Some experiences I have, I don't doubt, are peaks; others I think would be classified as happy moments, and so on. But the feeling which I got in this particular experience—if I had to classify anything as a peak, I would put this in. I've been going to the Massachusetts Metropolitan State Hospital once a week to work with chronically ill mental patients there. Many of these people are incapable, for whatever reason, of engaging in any kind of genuine and meaningful communication. A sense of humor which is genuine, rather than laughter which is provoked in a kind of incomprehensible sort of way, is a rare thing. When I see it, it's more meaningful than it would be in a situation such as this, where we're all completely normal people sitting around a table.

I've been talking to one woman there. I understand that she has been completely hostile to all the volunteer workers who have gone to the hospital for more than a year now, and I know the past two times that I've been on the women's ward, she wouldn't let anyone approach her. She would yell at you to leave her alone. Her appearance is quite unique. She wears a big yellow bow in her hair and has heavily rouged cheeks. She must be about sixty years old and used to be some sort of a . . . This isn't the proper word, but a belly-dancer. At any rate, I'm just trying to give you a kind of idea of the type of person this is.

For some reason, the last time we went, not only was I able to engage in a very warm, brilliant, human and meaningful kind of conversation with her, but there was just a general feeling on my part that you can't always judge people simply in terms of the situation in which you find them and in terms of their appearance alone. And all of a sudden, after we had been talking, she made a remark—she let out a real big smile on her face to one of the other women patients who was sitting close by, who also has a superior mental faculty compared to most of the other women there. She said, "Doesn't he remind you of when you were young and foolish?" and this other woman shook her head and says "Yeah, yeah." And then she said: "And now you're old and foolish!" And we all laughed and it was a kind of laughter which was real laughter.

I hadn't experienced that in a mental hospital before and I hadn't really expected to either. There was just a general peak moment there and I got a tremendous feeling of satisfaction—to be able to overcome what I thought was a barrier which was almost impossible to surmount in the given conditions, and it was a very great feeling. I think the peak-experience is the best term to describe it, because I don't know how to describe the feelings themselves, experientially, other than to simply say it really was a peak-experience.

Maslow: Remind anybody else?

Jayne [*who has worked in the same hospital*]**:** I heard this going on, and then I heard them laughing. Suddenly I thought, that's real laughter. There's a number of laughs there, but most of them you can tell are not really laughing. But this just suddenly struck me, you know, somebody has got a sense of humor here. They were well enough to have a sense of humor. Which is good.

Maslow: How does it feel to put yourself into their not laughing and into their laughing.

Jayne: Well, I could laugh. When other people there laugh—just hysterical sometimes—it makes you sad, or it sounds kind of irritating. But when they were really laughing, it just made me feel like laughing.

[*Long pause*]

Maslow: Anybody else have anything to say?

Mike: I'm going to tell about something that I don't understand at all. It's a feeling I've had I would guess eight or ten times in two different situations. One is when I look in the mirror and I actually look at what's there, and the other is when I stand in a particular place on my farm at home, near the corner of a building. I don't know the explanation for it but somehow the wind always goes by just a certain way—there's always a breeze there. I can see our land that's on this farm. I can't induce the feeling; I mean, it just happens. I suddenly feel a tremendous duality—I feel like my body is here but that isn't where I am. I feel like I could imagine—I always think of being in my cousin's body, what it would be like to be him—he's had a high-school education, he's working in a garage. And I think I could be tortured or something and they couldn't really get at me, and I keep waiting, I keep thinking to myself: "Well, something else is going to happen; I am going to get an answer to something." I feel, you know, "What next?" and nothing ever happens. So I kind of avoid mirrors. When I shave or something, this doesn't happen. It's just sometimes I *really* look in the mirror. I don't know what that means. I wonder if anyone else has ever had any . . .

Maslow: Have any *feelings* about it? Guesses?

Mike: No, I just can't understand it at all. I just get this feeling of being above myself, looking and saying, "Well, that's strange." I feel incomplete—like there's a next step which doesn't happen.

Maslow: Well, keep going.

Mike: I don't know where to go. That's why I asked you about it.

Maslow: Keep babbling about it. If you think back—this is the way in which you can recover your ability to introspect, you know, to describe what goes on inside, simply by trying. If you try to reinstate, try to imagine yourself experiencing that again and then simply watch yourself. What happens, how do you feel, what do you feel like saying? And so on. There's no hurry about it.

Mike: I've never told anybody. I've never said anything to anyone about it before. I just kind of noted it and passed it on.

Maslow: Would it help you, are you interested in, do you have a sort of therapeutic interest—personal interest, you might say—to know how many in the population have that kind of feeling? If you want to, it's easy enough, just take a poll of hands. [*To the whole class*] Those of you who have had some kind of experience like that ever, would you raise your hands? [*Some hands go up*] It's not rare anyway. Do you want to try describing it some more?

Mike: Not really. I don't have anything else to say. It was just there. It happened.

Maslow: Do you have any associations to it when you're looking? Any thoughts come?

Mike: No. I often wonder if it's religious.

Maslow: Why do you wonder that?

Mike: Maybe because I've always wanted to bring more religion into my life. And I . . . I don't know whether it's . . . I can't say I feel *whole*. I feel very, very different.

Maslow: Can you describe the feeling? Do you have any body feelings, for instance? Does anything happen to your insides—your heartbeat or your skin?

Mike: No, nothing like that, except the body part of me feels empty, where the other part of me is outside watching.

Maslow: Where is the other part outside that's watching? Is that above, or at the same level or behind?

Mike: I never tried to guess.

Maslow: Just keep on trying. This is the kind of differentiation one could have made about the laughing, for instance, if it were pursued. I think we all have some feelings from what was said here about the difference between real laughing and the "Pagliacci"[1] kind of laughing and other kinds of laughing and so on. And you can go on trying to find the words to express this difference or to make a more vivid account. You would do this, I think, by just simply introspecting on it more and adding the way your body feels and the way you feel and what thoughts come out, the "as-if" feelings and so on. That's part of what we're trying to do—to use Martin's phrase—to become more "psyche-perceptive." He talks about the inner voice, the inner sounds, the inner visions and so on. He talks about the inner ear which is turned inward to hear what goes on there.[2]

Melissa: I'm not sure whether or not this comes under the heading of peak-experiences. In fact, it probably isn't a peak-experience in terms of big moments. Since I've been here there have been many, many moments of increased perceptions—things like instead of being cold outside, *feeling* cold—to the point of wanting to feel other things.

The other night, I was washing my hair and somehow or other the water got hotter without my turning it on. I was very, very much aware of it and it felt very strange and all of a sudden—hotness and water just swept over me, a whole feeling. I started fiddling with the dial on the shower and made it as hot as I could and then very, very cold, and it was a wonderful feeling.

And another time, walking back to the dorm, just listening to things and all of a sudden a deeper kind of thing—I heard crickets. And it occurred to me that this is probably the last night there will be crickets because it's getting to be too cold. These sorts of things. Or sometimes walking outside and all of a sudden everything will be blue and gold—just for a moment. And it will be incredibly beautiful and it's a feeling that sweeps over you. You don't even think about it— it's just there. And these aren't really peaks, I guess. They're little, maybe mild peaks.

Maslow: This is the *concreteness* that comes in peaks, you know, the kind of things that they try to do now in creative art education classes, especially with children and also with grown-ups. Apparently, this kind of feeling, or the actual experiencing of sensory things—hot and cold, smooth and soft and blue and so on and so on—is not as common as you might think. For instance, Victor D'Amico[3] started that kind of education in the Museum of Modern Art in New York. One of the things he did was simply to have kids experiencing all the sensory things that they possibly could. It's not only colors—he'd bring in all kinds of "feeling" things—sandpaper, fur, and so on. He'd actually have people focus and concentrate attention on them completely. And then he tried to do what I was suggesting you try to do: to make better describers, better "perspectors" or in his case, better painters and also better "sensors," let's say.

The trick that they have there—that you can possibly use for yourself but we can't do in class under our circumstances—is to try to *draw* the feeling, such as "to draw the smell of an onion." Do the best you can with that. Now, of course, for us we'd all get paralyzed a little bit. That would be a very, very difficult task, but they report that four-year-old kids, six-year-old kids—they don't bat an eyelash! "Let's draw the smell of an onion." Nobody makes any comment, they turn around and start drawing the smell of an onion—no trouble, no problem. And this kind of . . . shall we call it synesthetic, synesthesia, or physiognomic perception might be one way for us here to try to become better introspectors and better expressors.[4]

The sensing part of it—I'm now working up lists of exercises[5] for you and I think I'll have some like the ones from the Museum of Modern Art. It would be just as helpful if you could actually focus entirely, concentrate on the hotness of hot water, let's say, which most of us don't do. We just simply only half-experience everything because we're focused on other things passing by. But supposing you tried in your efforts to express your feelings? Supposing you tried going over into this physiognomic and synesthetic kind of statement—you can say "It's *like* something else."

It's the same way if I ask you, "How would you draw the smell of an onion?" One gambit that you have is "What is it like?" Or what does it *feel* like when you look in a mirror and you are sort of observing yourself there, as if you are sort of outside yourself and inside yourself at the same time. What is that like? Is there any figure of speech of any kind which would help you to express it? Or with the laughing that we were talking about before? It's another gambit, another way of approaching it. Shall I give you examples of this? Would it help? Because it seems to be kind of difficult. Supposing you play the game—maybe we should play it right now as a preliminary. Maybe it's more difficult to talk about peak experiences than it should be. You can make these synesthetic connections.

I remember one session that we had, everybody was clicking. It's a lot of fun when it works. I had some guests at my house and I brought out a lot of cheeses and a lot of liquor, brandies, wines, beers and half a dozen different kinds of bread. And it was a very nice, pleasant sort of thing—a smorgasbord, with all sorts of tidbits, and we had a fire going in the fireplace. It was all very pleasant, and everybody got into the mood. It was like a good basketball team—if you've ever been on one—they click together. And we played these games about what goes with what. It was about the cheeses: somebody picked up a glass of beer, for example, and then picked some cheese up. I remember this: "No, that cheese doesn't go with beer!" And it's true: some cheeses don't go with beer, some do. Well, you can play that game, if you want to. What cheese *does* go with beer? For instance, you take several things. Which cheese goes better with beer? Cheddar cheese or Roquefort cheese? And which cheese goes better with bread?

Melissa: Cheddar cheese goes better with beer.

Maslow: I think there's an old trick that . . . If you don't quite get this—this is the professor talking now—there's a book by Heinz Werner[6] coming out on this soon. His old book is available for what I'm talking about. It's the *Comparative Psychology of Mental Development*,[7] and this is one of the exercises, one of the little experiments that he did there. And there are many experiments like this that were done by the Clark University people in the psychology department. Now there's a whole big, fat book full of them which is in the press now. Heinz Werner and Bernard Kaplan,[8] *Symbol Formation*.[9] There are lots of such things. He made up nonsense words to go with these things and—supposing I ask you—one is: [*Writes and draws on the blackboard*[10]]

Nonsense Words	Figures
1) takete	
2) lumuma	

Now, which word goes with this thing? When you do try it, try it with your friends. If we had time, I'd have you write it out. Perhaps 90% of the people in this room—95, 98% maybe, if I pick my figures and words well enough—will agree that this goes with that, and this word goes with this. And then I ask you, well, why? Well, it's troublesome, and yet if you are good enough introspectors, you will give me something with isomorphic forms and structures—some are sharp and have sharp changes of direction or something of the sort.

But I might also ask, you know, "Which cheeses?" Or which composers—this is an easy one now—which of these [*hand-written music scores*] is Ravel and which is Bach?[11] [*samples shown, followed by a long pause*] I'm surprised that you look puzzled. Which is Ravel and which is Bach?

[*The students talk to one another, seemingly mildly amused and surprised that Maslow is puzzled they can't answer this. Some make guesses.*]

How many of you would say Ravel is the top one? How many of you would say Ravel is the bottom one? [*polls taken*] I meant it to be Ravel and Bach. [*Indicates samples; some general laughter and comments from class*] Maybe I'm not picking very good examples. What Werner did was to actually try out his examples and pick those things which would get 90% agreement.

Max Wertheimer[12] used to play a game at parties—he'd sit down at the piano and improvise. If he were here now he'd go around the room and play a little thing to express you on the piano. The thing was, everybody always recognized who it was. One time we had a party and I remember recognizing everyone but one. There was one that puzzled me, and I noticed everybody was looking at me. [*General laughter*] Which itself is revealing too, isn't it?

Well, this kind of thing you would call synesthesia, which means the mixture of senses. If I asked you, you might find that for some of you, numbers may have character; let's say, five is blue for some people, and yellow is sharp. There would be these cross-sensory modality lines. My guess is that for mathematical people, numbers are synesthetic. For me I know they're not—numbers have no character at all. They just don't seem to have any different character the way people do. And for some of my friends they do. "Seven has a very 'seven-ish' quality," they'll say, "and that's so different from a six-ish quality. Sixes and sevens are extremely different. They have different characters; seven you like and six you're very suspicious about, you might say, and they'll go on and on. They have a kind of feeling in the same way I do for music—perhaps I chose the area where I feel more comfortable—where extremely different characters permeate for everybody, really.

For instance, Rudolf Arnheim[13] did one very simple experiment which you can try for yourself. For the people who knew music, he simply got photostats of the manuscript writing of Beethoven and Mozart and Bach, and then he asked people who knew their music,

"Which of these was written by which?" It came close to 100%; there was no problem at all—that's Bach, that's Mozart, that's Beethoven—no question about it. It was so characteristic and so, I would say, isomorphic of their music.

Well, try that kind of thing. It's alright in this room to say that something is like Roquefort cheese, or it's very much more like Tchaikovsky than it is like red wine.

By the way, that *Magister Ludi* book is based upon such language-isomorphic structures. The bead games that Hesse talked about is a kind of isomorphic structure game, just in the way that some people or characters will remind you of different figures.

Supposing I pressed you; couldn't you run around the room and look at everybody here and draw a kind of formless line? Try it; do it, for instance with one line. Make a nonsense figure like this. [*Maslow draws one*] Do me. Try it. What do I look like in meaningless curves or lines, or something like that? I used me because you all looked at me much more than you looked at each other. Just a line. [*Everybody giggles and doodles on paper*]

And then you could go on with this. Try your line and if it's too hard for you to do, then there's an inhibition; you should try practicing it at home. Think of the various people that you know. Try simply to express them in an expressive line of some sort and keep on doing it till you can do it freely. You should be able to. Then if you like, try to express it in terms of a style of music. How would you play it on the piano? How would you sing it? Or if it's too difficult about individuals, you can make it males and females. [*Shows two nonsense figures*] Now, that's easy—which of these is male and which is female? Any problem?

Another exercise which I am going to tell you about now is again to develop a skill which will help you in your expressiveness in picking figures of speech. For instance, supposing I ask you, as I will, to complete sentences; I'll say "As fast as . . ." and then you're supposed to complete it and you mustn't use a cliché. It's forbidden to say "as fast as lightning" or "as white as milk" or "as cold as ice." You have to be a little bit more original, a little more creative.

Now, in that same way you can learn to express the difference in the two kinds of laughter, the real laughter and the not-real laughter, by breaking out of conventional analytic language. It is the same way with that feeling of slight depersonalization—the feeling of standing outside yourself, which most of us have experienced and which also probably most of us understand whether we're conscious of it or not. This is called "poetic language" and is what a poet would be trying to do. And if this were a class in poetry, you would be having exactly these exercises. [*Pause*]

Melissa: I'm not certain, but I think that in having peak-experiences or having any kind of acute perceptive experiences, the bridges or the links that bring them are terribly important. If you're suggestible— I'm suggestible—they can be created fairly easily, very effectively. Sometimes a piece of music can always be a link back to a certain thing, or looking at a certain color or a certain fabric, or just reading something. And I wondered if you have records of people who can actually make themselves have peak-experiences by presenting themselves with the necessary links to them?

Maslow: Intellectual answer, data and so on and so on. No. Nobody can. No one has ever been reported to, throughout human history. All you can do is make them more likely. For instance, one of the exercises that I would like you to try, now that I'm reminded of it, is erotic music. I've got a pretty decent collection of it in my sex histories, from when I started asking about this. Practically everybody has some music which makes them feel romantic, sexy, available, excited and so on, and which I have encouraged. I've used these things—it's my original emphasis. I started working with pornography as an aphrodisiac because I was looking for aphrodisiacs. There are no clinical aphrodisiacs that are not dangerous. I was thinking about the erotic feelings in the marriages that I had been working with where there *weren't* enough of these feelings. Couldn't I, a Ph.D., a scientist, and so on, have some suggestion about this? Sure, if there are suggestions when you put them together. One simple one was finally, I would say to them, "Find out what music makes you feel sexy." And there is always something that does. Now, there are some standard pieces which are more sexy than others, to a large percentage, that the people could play. Some of this is obvious, the stuff that is actually the mimicking of the sexual act, sexual heightening, like the "Venusburg music" from Wagner's[14] *Venusburg*, or the "Liebestod." Wagner's full of it. Actually mimicking the sexual heightening. But there are others which are not like that; they're not strict mimicking—they're just . . . Ravel's *Valse* for some people, for instance. The repetition of the theme will be erotically stimulating.

Now I bring this up: in no case is there any *trigger*, erotic trigger, which works all the time for any person. It's only that they have a kind of repertoire; all married people tend to do this anyhow. If they know they are going to have a sexy evening and they prepare themselves for it, they've learned how to put themselves in the frame of mind, and they're partners. Every woman generally learns what stimulates her husband and will then dress herself or do whatever is necessary. If she wants a pleasant evening then it's a sensible thing to do, to be as stimulating as possible both for herself and for her husband *and* vice versa. All you can say is you hope it works, or it usually works. But there is nothing in the whole of all of my experiences with all of these things—with peak-experiences or sexual experiences—that works inevitably. Nothing. It just doesn't exist; you cannot push a button and make an experience. In fact it's not even true with the drugs, which are never 100%.

Supposing I present you with that problem. That's a good one to talk about because it's so infrequently talked about: why is it that music can be erotic? That's just like this exercise here. You know, leaving aside all the specific associations—something that just happened by accident to remind you of something because it was conditioned with something else.

John: Can you demonstrate any instance that there is any real stimulus in these things, where you cannot outline the line of association? For example, if you get five thousand people to draw squiggly lines representing you, will there be any similarity? I don't think so. I'm tempted to draw something which looks realistically like you rather than a mere line. There's no significance at all. I don't believe it.

Doug: I was able to draw a line which I felt a little bit satisfied with.

John: Would a line drawn on successive years have certain characteristics if they were drawings of him, for example?

Doug: I would say this: that among my friends I think, I could guess, that the lines would be the same for each one of us, over time.

John: I don't think that's so.

Maslow: I know what would be an easier thing. I've laid out the most difficult problem. But supposing you were asked how to draw two lines which would express us. Let's say, one line which would be him more than me and one line which would be me more than him—that might be easier to do. And the point is, it can be done—and the gestalt psychologists have done this—and they can get around more obvious things, such as soft sounds as over against soft lines. These isomorphisms are very, very difficult to express. You can get around any particular explanation you have for a particular parallel or a particular *isomorph*—isomorphism meaning a parallel structure or parallel form.

This business with the liquors or the wines—if I got back to that—anybody who likes wines will use a big vocabulary. They will say, one wine is "sort of impertinent." And you might think, "What do they mean by that? Are they showing off or something of the sort? Or "That's harsh." Well, that's easy to understand. And they've got a whole vocabulary of adjectives and adverbs to express these subtle differences—you can do this if you know wines well enough and are sensually aware of these differences. You might do the same if you like tea very much. If you are very sensitive about teas, then you can describe to another tea-lover the differences so that you are actually communicating. And this would be entirely at the metaphorical level—it couldn't be anything else.

John: Does this at all demonstrate it? A lot of people object to art criticism on just these grounds: the terms they use are really meaningless. If you say, "Here are five teas. One of these is expressive, moving, tangy in such and such a way. Now pick it out for me." I don't think it could be done off-hand.

Maslow: I think it can be—

John: If these terms are used. The example you gave about the beer and the cheeses was different because this is like, "What color goes with red?" in this instance—this is understandable. Which cheese goes with wine? You don't put vinegar in spaghetti sauce—you put something else, obviously.

Maslow: That's a good question. You may ask, why? Why? Why not? I don't want to pin myself to the art critics, by the way. I don't know any good art critics.

John: Exactly.

Maslow: It's nonsense—as far as I'm concerned. But with the wine-drinkers, tea-drinkers, the "aficionados"—*they* can communicate with each other. I tell you that they do. Now nobody's ever made an experiment—which I suppose somebody should—to see just whether it's really true or not, whether they're kidding each other. My impression is, yes, they do communicate. For one thing, I've been able to communicate with people who share my enthusiasms and we can play the game, and this is a lot of fun. If you are a cheese-lover or a wine-lover or a tea-lover or whatever, anything that happens to be your particular sensory enthusiasm, you'll find that the people in the world with whom you can communicate are the ones whom you assume have had the same experience you have. And the others just don't have the experience; you say they're blind.

John: The communication can be very successful in understandable terms, but what I object to is the possibility of its success in terms that don't make any sense.

Maslow: Well, I'm sorry that I just don't know. I haven't made enough piling up of instances. All I can tell you is that the experiences we've had in these games, which I've never taken seriously but which Heinz Werner has—I've seen them do it—every time you make a reasonable explanation of why a cheese and a beer should go together, then I'll gambit you by relating that same beer to a color. For people who know beers well and are sensitive enough to them, I'm sure that I could make a little spectrum of colors and they could say which one is more red, which is more purple and which is more blue, or which beer is more like which fabric.

John: Well, why don't we choose something that we don't know about and see if we can get a correlation?

Maslow: I have just given you a few of them.

John: There have been, for example, experiments done in this sort of thing with foreign languages, languages that people don't know. For example, I'll give you the words for "big" and "small" in Japanese and you tell me—

Maslow: The meaningfulness is definitely involved so that I wouldn't try to use it with other languages. This is not intrinsic in . . . it's intrinsic in the meaningfulness, in the penumbra of its meaningfulness. Well, in any case, you're absolutely justified in raising this as a research problem and asking for proof. Some proof you'll get in Werner. Some is also available in Rudolf Arnheim's book on gestalt psychology and art, or some such title.[15] He has examples of this sort, and he has records of his own tests.

Another one that occurs to me now, that you can read, is *The Expression of Personality* by Werner Wolff.[16] Until he died, he loved making games and experiments out of these, which he has written about and which he found very meaningful. For instance, he would give two colors and say: "Which is your mother and which is your father?" Since he had already had a lot of associations to those colors, he would then tell you what you thought about your mother and what you thought of your father at the unconscious level, even if you didn't know. This is a game you can play also: what color is your father, what color is your mother, each of your sisters, each of your brothers?

It's a meaningful question in a certain way.

The research stuff I'll pass aside now and make no references—we'll let it go. You seem to be having difficulty with your expressiveness. These are all possible aids in expressiveness. It's like a trick—it's to break out. Suppose you are trying to describe what are the qualities in me, which you supposedly stared at when you looked at me, and then you were supposed to put them into a line or into a little improvisation, or into meaningless words—describe me with meaningless words.

Or make these synesthetic parallels—which cheese am I like, which wine am I like, which brandy, which whiskey, which food? Which am I more like: do I remind you more of a steak, shellfish or spaghetti or what? They carry meaning, they actually carry meaning with types.[17] It will click with some of you as I go down the line: what kind of fabric should I wear, for instance? That's a meaningful question; we ask it all the time. And for you girls, by the way, don't you? Always particular fabrics are right for you and others are not. Particular colors are right, particular styles of clothes, particular shoes and hairstyles and so on. And you know darn well that you discuss this at great length, very seriously, and it's a meaningful thing. And then, when you women will be picking out clothes for your husbands, you will find that your husbands are less sensitive about these things than you are, generally, in our culture. And if you have any sense, you'll go help your husband pick his clothes. You'll find that some fabrics are right for some men, other fabrics are just plain wrong. Colors, vests. Is a brocaded vest right for me? [*General laughter*] Professor Frank Manuel likes these vests. It's sort of colored, sort of elaborate, baroque vests—they seem to fit him. [*General laughter*] My impression is that they are suitable for him and yet they wouldn't be for me—I don't want them. I'm not the baroque type.

Does this help in any way? For instance, about the laughter—could you break out of that bind that you were in, that you were trying to describe?

Jayne: It's really hard.

Maslow: Do you want to try? Try these tricks—the synesthesia, the physiognomic perceptions, metaphors and so on. See if you can say more expressively how it feels in some other realm of communication.

Jayne: It's like a vicious circle. If you try to communicate in another realm it's a very subjective thing, and what it may mean to you is going to be interpreted differently by another person. The taste of the cheese to one person may be quite different to somebody else, and you just seem to keep intellectualizing and getting further and further away from the actual sensation or emotion. I don't know. I find it can be very confusing.

Maslow: Sure, but you can learn to play the game. For instance, I think you gave me a good example—you have a sweet face. [*General laughter*] Try to figure that out in terms of lines. We use such expressions. Don't we use these words for people, such as harsh, or strong? What does the word "strong" mean? Powerful? Sweet? How would you compare that, since it's obviously not physiological and you don't get any feeling on your tongue there of that parallel. Yet there is something isomorphic between this sweet face and the sensation of sweetness, as we have shown. And you could, if I asked you to, you could look around the room and say which faces are sweet and which are not. It's a meaningful question.

Jayne: She's got a sour look, sour-puss.

Maslow: Sour-puss, sure. Sure you do. I was thinking of another one—when I had to work with self-esteem—high levels of self-esteem and low levels of self-esteem and so on. I remember that I had to make up whole lists of words to try to describe, to communicate. Well, how would you describe "strong," a strong person, in such physiognomic terms—strong character? One big distinction there was what I called "sweet" and "strong." In what sense are sweet and strong opposites of each other? [*Pause*]

Let's ask—let's have a little poll. For how many of you is this uncomfortable? You know, in that it doesn't click very much? Let me ask it the other way as well: How many people feel that they understand and feel what I'm talking about, and how many would be less so, or trying, or don't feel it? Or could you express that in the sense of being confused?

Jayne: I'm trying to understand the point of it all.

Maslow: Do you want to try? You can try. We're in the realm of psyche-perception now. It's a difficult thing. You can't talk about it with analytical language—the mathematical, physical, chemical, biological—you can't make any sense about it. As to the question— what's the sense in it at all? Do you want to try it?

Sharon: Well, I think it makes sense if you've had an experience that you can relate it to. Like if you have an association, if you remember a time when you saw somebody draw a line, or you saw somebody express something in a metaphor in these terms. And if you don't remember anybody ever saying something like that, then it doesn't mean anything.

Alice: Well, it seems to me that we know roundness because we come into contact with things that are round or soft, and therefore when we see a line that is round or soft we can somehow relate it back to that other experience, even if you don't remember it, because it's a whole series of related experiences that are like that. I agree that if you just said something's like something else and you told me so, I don't think that it will make sense. But if you keep saying, "It's like this and like that and like that," and they come back to you and say, "Oh, yes, do you mean like that, like that, like that?" then if you can click and you are able to feel *their* experience and they now know they are in touch with what you're referring to, then you are communicating.

John: You're suggesting that there is a logic, but it's just non-discernible. That when someone makes this connection, there *is* a logical connection; there is some sort of association that was once made, and this is why it's made now. Is this what you mean? Well, I think this sort of thing is really only useful if it makes absolutely no sense. I shouldn't say "can be understood" if it makes no sense—but is "acceptable." Because if it makes absolutely no sense, then it performs the same function as the Zen koan[18] does. And this is a very difficult thing to understand, because "understand" indicates logic and concrete understanding. It's something non-rational. I don't understand it. Accordingly, it seems the only way to get to it is through a non-rational process, or a process which destroys rationality in exactly the same way that the koan does. When you ask a Zen master, "What is Buddha?" and he whacks you over the head with a stick or says, "one flax," I think is the famous answer—Buddha's just a measure of flax. So, it seemed to me that it would be more important if it *didn't* make sense.

Maslow: I've just thought of something which is appropriate. There is a very famous, a very important study by Solomon Asch. I don't have the original reference, but it's reprinted in the book called *Documents of Gestalt Psychology*,[19] edited by Mary Henle.[20] And I wonder why I didn't think of it, because it is a brilliant piece of work, a beautiful experiment.

What he found was that in all the languages which he could investigate, the physical expressions of human personality tended to be about the same; it's universal across all the languages, the language groups. That is, where we talk about words like "sharp," "sweet" or "rough" as applying to personality. The physical meaning of that word, the roughness in the physical sense is parallel in every language group which he investigated. That is, the word which we use to describe roughness in personality, is physical roughness in all languages. So is sharpness, so is strength, or tallness, or straightness—a straight person in the sense of honest—now I remember that one. Straight is used for the word honest, for the honesty in the person in all language groups and all the specific languages he investigated.

The reason he did this was for the gestalt reason, the Wertheimer kind of reason—thinking of the species as a whole, and of trying to demonstrate, as the gestalists have again and again, that you're talking about a whole human species now—in some cases anyhow. That it's not just a matter of local associations but that these associations are so profound that they go through all cultures. Take a look at that and see how it applies, because obviously it can't apply altogether, since we do have some absolutely local associations.

The word "sweet," I think, is one of them. It's found in every language as a personality description just the way we use it; you know, the sweetness of sugar, the physical sweetness of sugar.

Paul: I would guess that there are some sensations which are universally and biologically pleasant to people, so that it's no wonder that in experiencing something pleasant in one realm, they would intuitively associate it to a pleasant experience in another realm, if they are asked to draw any kind of relationship between the two. It just seems natural somehow, rather than surprising.

Maslow: It might be. For myself it remains a puzzle. But in any case, so far as we are concerned, perhaps these things don't matter too much whether universal or not universal. We are exploring and trying to become more perspicuous, more perceptive of our own inner world—whatever it's like and wherever it comes from and without regard to the questions of determinants, causation, history and so on. Simply just to become more acutely sensitive to them. I think all of these things would apply whether you find them in Japan or not.

I'd like you to make an assignment out of this business. Think about it and if you have anything to say about it, write it in your notebooks. I'd like to look at them a week or two after that mid-semester exam. There will be a class two weeks from today and that will be that examination.

NOVEMBER 11, 1963

Armistice Day – No Class

Maslow's memo recorded on tape, Monday, November 11, 1963

On Monday, November 11th. It's a holiday, and I started interviewing the students individually. I hope to do each of them twice during the semester—once around the mid-semester time and once before the end of the semester. I spoke this time with five students for a half hour each. And I expressed what I wanted in a different way, a way that I don't think I did in the classroom. I asked them to consider themselves with me as co-investigators, as participant observers, all of us, in an investigation which we were all doing, all together. We would try out various things and then they as participants were supposed to report back what had happened or what had not happened. I urged them to get away from the model of the high school old teacher and young child, simply reporting in order to be graded or something of the sort, but rather to think of themselves as psychologists who are making an investigation of a Daniel Boone[1] sort; that is, without foreknowledge of what would happen. My impression was that they took this well. It helped, I think, that I stressed the scientific worth of a positive report. That is, I had urged them to tell if something failed to happen, or if something didn't happen, and a few of them were able to do this. Without this encouragement they might not have thought of this as a worthwhile result. I don't think I'll try to say what happened with each of them; I didn't take any notes. I doubt if I could remember very much anyhow.

Maybe I will hereafter keep a notebook by my side just to jot down that which is interesting.

NOVEMBER 18, 1963

Lecture

*The first hour of this session was taken up by the mid-term exam.
There was some grumbling about the exam among the students, and
Maslow begins the second hour with the following remarks
on writing as a means for self-actualization.*

[*The recording starts with Maslow in mid-sentence*]

Maslow: —saying to someone in a reassuring way that this is one way of learning to write easily—like talking or walking or doing things casually and easily. You could do it the way professional writers do it, which is a realistic situation. You're given one week to do such and such, or you have to knock out two thousand words by three o'clock in the afternoon. I assure you that anybody can learn to do it, neurotic blocks that are contrary notwithstanding. If you're put in a condition where you have to do it, you do it. And this is one neurotic block which is rather easily overcome apparently. I've seen it several times happen that way.

If you're jammed up on expressing yourself, either about talking or about writing, now here at least there's a simple solution: talk your head off or write your head off, one or the other. Just push yourself to it, force yourself to it, do it the way a professional writer would, make believe you have to earn your living that way. And this kind of assignment would be a normal assignment. The professional writers I know put a certain value on each hour. They have to—they have mortgages and children to support. So they must say "Well, I must earn so much in this hour; is it worth it?" If someone pays them, let's say, $100 for a thing, they figure, "Well, that's three hours' worth," or four, or whatever price they put on their time, and that's all they'll allow him. They'll do the best they can in that time. I would say that this is part of maturity. Responsible citizens have that kind of confrontation all the time—something you're supposed to get done by next Thursday or by this evening. So I will permit you to beef about that examination crap [*the mid-term exam that the students took in the previous hour*], but about the job itself, it's not bad and I suggest you even do it for yourselves. I haven't gone into it very strongly with that journal notebook that I have recommended for you, but perhaps now is not a bad moment to expatiate on that a little bit.

Part of growing up is the whole business of expression, of learning to express yourself and of being able to pin your thoughts down as they fly past and then to be able to express them in a satisfying form. This is one example of self-actualization on a small scale. If you have some vague thought through the middle of the night or some bright idea that comes to you sometime, if you let it go, if you throw it away, if you waste it so to speak—it's like throwing away your baby or your precious possession or something that you have created. It's like leaving it as an abortion, so to speak; it's like not growing it up to full term.

Expressing is part of the process of thinking, and mature thinking is expressed thinking, expressed saying, expressed writing. So I would recommend to all intellectual people, all people who have I.Q. enough for the job—and you all do—to learn to write. That is part of your normal equipment, just like being able to comb your own hair or eat with a knife and fork or walk with shoes on or whatever. And the way in which it's recommended—experience now is piled up—is simply to write. For the ones who take it very seriously, they allow themselves one hour per day, let's say, whatever the convenient hour—nine to ten in the morning. Professional writers like Somerset Maugham,[1] for instance, will write from nine to twelve—that's his day's work. He sits down at the table, he picks up a pencil or pen or whatever, or sits at his typewriter—I forget which—or whatever is his way, and by gosh, he sits there. If he has no thoughts in his head, he jiggles, he wiggles, he writes his name over a hundred times. He just writes, that's all.

S. I. Hayakawa[2] has published lessons on this. The standard procedure is: sit yourself down, get yourself in the situation—your chair, your table, your pencil, whatever slippers you like to wear or whatever it may be—get the right temperature and whatever other requirements are necessary. You sit down even if you haven't got a thing in your head—as Hayakawa was recommending—and make nonsense words. Just write as many words as you can. And the report from the writers—the expressers I might call them, or I would prefer to say, the thinkers—is that if you do this regularly, then finally it starts flowing. Inevitably it starts flowing. Thinking is not completed unless it's written or spoken.

Now, this is one of the things that we are having in our book on "self-therapy."[3] We're going to have a chapter on just this stuff—keeping the journal, a nineteenth-century Ralph Waldo Emerson-type journal, a Henry David Thoreau-type journal.[4] I've seen Thoreau's journals—bound notebooks—there's a whole chest full of them. It's a life's worth—about twenty, thirty notebooks that he filled in his brief life. That's normal. It's like having breakfast. It's a normal part of life for anybody with any brains. Now, in this chapter I know we're going to make warnings for people with brains and especially for women who always have such a temptation to be stupid. [*General laughter*] The whole world encourages them to be dopey all the time, even rewards them for it sometimes.

If you have brains but don't use them, then you're doing so at the cost of cancerous fatty degeneration, of regression, deterioration, just in the same way that your muscles will atrophy if you don't use them. So will your brains atrophy. Year by year you get less and less capable of sitting, of reading, of discussing, of writing, of thinking, until finally you become a self-loathing creature of the kind Betty Friedan[5] and other women writers were writing about. You've just got to do it; you've got no alternative. I warn you. The doctor, you know, is telling you: "If you don't have enough exercise then you might have a coronary, a heart attack" or something like that. And this is worse than a coronary. To be dead while you're alive—that's not so good. To be dead is bad enough, but the living death is no good.

Now, one thought for you people, and all of you are intelligent enough: obviously for this kind of continued growth, you must exercise your mental muscles. Under pain of regression. I would warn you that you must do it. There's no way out, whether you like it or you don't like it. Just like my recommendation, that you must have a certain amount of exercise—walking, swimming or whatever.

Ben: I remember reading somewhere a couple of years ago, some study of genius where the authors were trying to account for the fact that some of the greatest geniuses live to a very, very old age. And there was something about the enormous amount of juice running through the central nervous system that kept things going. Is there any tie?

Maslow: People think so, but it's not entirely proven. I've been collecting data on this whenever I run across it. It looks as if all desirable traits correlate positively. In general, that's my opinion. The positive inter-correlation of all desirable traits is—"to him that hath was given, and from him that hath not was taken away even that which he hath."[6] You know, it's that kind of thing. And I have all sorts of collections of data, determined data.

If you pick people with a high I.Q. and then test them for other things, you'll find they're superior in everything: the girls are prettier, the men are handsomer, the muscles are stronger, their teeth are better, they live longer, there are less neuroses, there are less psychoses and so on. In the Terman research with I.Q.'s of over 140[7]—you know, that famous one—the only inferiority, if you want to call it that, of maybe a thousand that he tested for . . . These kids were better at everything than the controlled population. The only thing at which they were worse was that more of them had to use spectacles, if you can call that "worse." Because they used their eyes. Apart from that, the liver is better, the kidney is better, the arches and the metatarsals and the carpals and the heart functions better.

John: All sorts of social reasons.

Maslow: That may be, but it's also possible to think in terms of constitutional reasons because there are studies on animals—chickens are like that too. A chicken who is selected out for being better at one job turns out to be better at half a dozen others.[8]

John: Probably social reasons are there too.

Maslow: No, not in this particular experiment. It looks as if the social reasons can account for about half of the variance there and the other half seems to be approximately constitutional or hereditary. Constitutional may mean, quite early in the lifespan—social, maybe—I'm not sure.

In any case, if you pick out any human being who is very, very exceptionally good at anything, then you can gamble on it—Las Vegas style—that kind of gambling is about the odds in the long run. You can lay 51-50, it's that kind of thing, that such a person is more likely to be good at anything else they choose in comparison with controls, average population.

What's being implied in this little sermon I was preaching a moment ago is that this "self-making of yourself good" should improve everything about you. For instance, if we had fine enough techniques for it—which we don't have—I would guess that a person who keeps a journal, if he does seriously, would thereby live longer, be more resistant to coronary heart disease, to cancer. He would have better teeth, be more resistant to cavities and his hair wouldn't fall out so fast and so on and so on. It sounds crazy but that's the way it looks; it adds up.[9]

John: Well, this doesn't seem real to me. For example, this contradicts all of Kurt Goldstein's[10] ideas in which the individual is going to express himself through those particular channels through which he, in some innate manner, is able to function best.

Maslow: The journal applies to you. I don't run around telling everybody the same thing. For instance, I had a feeble-minded man who came to our house to clean things and to do the handyman's work. I wouldn't recommend it to him. Why torture the poor man? He's not capable of it.

John: You mean it is for people just above a certain level—only true of people above a certain level but not true of others?

Maslow: Yes.

John: And this level is determined by what? It seems to me this level is determined by the fact that people are able to do lots of things well, which is what I.Q. is, for example, or supposedly. It's almost a tautology.

Maslow: Well, this is somewhat circular because we have already tried it at both angles, at both levels. There are data—crude data from both angles. You take intelligent people—intelligent, young people, then we have a fair amount of material showing that they deteriorate rather easily. You can deteriorate more easily than that poor, feeble-minded man. He's got no place to deteriorate to and you have.

And then we know, from Goldstein and from other people, that the process of deterioration is felt. This is a way of making intrinsic things—existential things. If you know that you're a smart person and yet you behave stupidly, or if you're a brave man and you behave cowardly—you'd stab yourself for it unconsciously, preconsciously, even consciously. I don't bother about the borderline cases because you are all very well within the extreme end of a simple I.Q. scale. You are selected here already—somebody else has done the selecting of this experimental group here. You are far beyond those limits of the borderline doubts. You are all exceptionally intelligent; you are a selected group. Now, you can also become exceptionally stupid if you don't watch out, and that's what I was talking about. [*Turns to John*] Is that what you were driving at or did I mesh with you there?

John: I'm not sure. I have a feeling . . .

Maslow: Try it again.

John: Just that . . . What you have said seems to be only an accurate measure among the people who by definition are good at lots of things. As Goldstein points out, there are these counting wizards who are feeble-minded and who are not good in anything but this one particular thing. Now it seems to me that this carries through in lots of other examples. Maybe I am statistically wrong, but these are the ones that come to mind—people like Galois[11], who didn't live long, who died before he was twenty and was without doubt a genius. People like the chess player Reshevsky[12] who's a brilliant chess player—but he's a bank clerk and can't do much else. It seems to me that there are lots of people like this.

Maslow: Oh, yes. I was talking—I still am—about Las Vegas odds, professional gambler's odds. It doesn't bother him a bit if somebody breaks the bank once. They are talking about long term odds and long term statistics—what do they call it there? The "edge for the house" or something like that. It's a very small edge that they have, but they don't need much to get wealthy. They'll set their machine so that it pays back. Let's say it pays back to the public maybe 99 cents out of the dollar that is tossed into it. There are lots of jackpots and so on; everybody is very happy about it apparently. That one percent is enough to make them all into millionaires. This is the way it is.

Now we can't make decent experiments with it, for we can't have a thousand Galoises. But Sorokin[13] has tried to make statistical researches with this sort of thing. He picked out amongst saints of all sorts. He found that the saints, by comparison with a control group, lived very much longer, had much more longevity, even not counting in the assassinations and the crucifixions and the burnings and so on.

Thorndike[14] did a lot of it. If you are interested in this, look it up—he's got a whole compendium of it. It's a big fat book called *Human Nature and the Social Order*[15] by E. L. Thorndike. And he reports there all these interrelations. For instance, one old study by a man named Woods,[16] in which he studied all the people from whom he had biographical material—the crown heads of Europe for the last five hundred years, for instance.[17] And he typed out the stuff and each of these crown heads got a rating—without the names on it—for intelligence on the one hand, and for virtue and goodness on the other, and it comes out positive. There are dozens of others, Francis Galton[18] for instance, who did that kind of work. It piles up.

If any of you are interested in doing a social service for the intellectual world, you could pile up this kind of stuff. I have—whenever I run across them I just toss them into my file. If I were interested enough I could put it together into, I think, a pretty convincing case. Positive qualities correlate—desirable qualities correlate with each other in the long run—maybe + 0.1, that's all. And maybe you need thousands of cases to see the trend. But every time anyone takes it seriously, the trend shows up.

So we sort of expect it to show up. We have had special cases of this—let's say this chess business, which seems to be more like a kind of a lunacy than . . . Well, in 1963, in the world that we live in, for anyone to devote his whole life to playing chess or bridge or golf, or whatever, is an insult to everybody who's ever been murdered.

There will always be moot cases in borderline issues. Those are the questions that would come up. But if you take the clean-cut, extreme instances, as Thorndike, Galton and Terman did, or as has been done with the chickens and white rats, or even with our own psychosomatic data which are coming in, the same trend is there.

For instance, Lawrence LeShan,[19] who is going to give a public lecture at Brandeis soon. Have you got the announcement of the lecture yet? I recommend it. I've rounded up LeShan, who has been doing psychosomatic work on cancer, of all things.[20] Everything we know indicates that cancer is a psychosomatic disease. Now, psychosomatic doesn't mean just psychic, but both somatic and appreciable psychic determinants. For instance, LeShan found out that for women the reproductive cancers—breast, uterine, vaginal cancers—come most frequently in widowed women. Well, it's the loss of love object—that's what he found. And he's got his tables there, which are very significant. And the woman who is living a normal life and a good life is more resistant to cancer. There are indications that I've seen, and if I were in this field, I would certainly want to try them out.

Breast cancer, which is a known killer for women, the prostatic cancer—cancer of the prostate which kills so many men—come from not using them well and completely. It's my impression that prostatic cancer correlates with not a full emptying of the prostate glands. That is, it would correlate with not a full sexuality. The male sexual climax varies a great deal. There are good and complete ones, as Wilhelm Reich[21] pointed out, if you're interested, and yet most men—as near as I can make out when I ask questions of them—don't know what a full orgasm is. They're quite content with any old ejaculation.

Something emerges and that's it—one is as good as another—in the Kinsey, machinist style. Well, in the full orgasm, in the full ejaculation, the prostate is just squeezed and emptied. And we know that in an incomplete orgasm the prostate can fill up with prostatic fluid—the spermatozoa swim in the prostatic fluid—and then this can become crystallized, and then you get a hard, enlarged prostate in which there is stasis. And it looks as if, in a general way, this stasis may be carcinogenic. So for the breast, it ought to be used well. [*General laughter*]

That type of visual image is immediate.

John: Do you recommend sex?

Maslow: In this case, no. What I was recommending was use by the baby, by the infant rather than by the husband. So far as we know, we have no data on the sexual use, the love use of the breast in this connection. But there are indications that the breast as a milk-producer, as a mammary gland—that this also is like the prostate. By gosh, if I remember my histology, histologically they're very similar to each other. I remember I couldn't tell the difference between mammary tissue and prostatic tissue under a microscope—that close. The breast gets too engorged and filled and has stasis. If the breast isn't emptied out, then this may be carcinogenic—I guess; I suspect.

Well, that's the good—that's self-actualization. Self-actualization is a big, nice abstract word that covers thousands of specific instances in the full expression and the full use of the capacity—that's what I mean by it. The breast, the mammary gland, the baby-feeding organ had better be well used, for anything that's not well used atrophies and makes trouble and becomes a center, apparently, maybe, for infection or whatever.

The prostate, and apparently—you can ask LeShan when he gives his public lecture; you are all very cordially invited—he's lecturing now on psychotherapy with dying cancer patients, which is itself a fascinating thing. Ask him about this female cancer business: why it is that a woman who has been widowed is more subject to uterine cancer? I don't know. How the husband uses the uterus exactly is hard to say. Not just sex here apparently, although that's involved—in a full female orgasm the uterus contracts. It has these contractions which are very much like the first stages of labor, just the same kind of thing. And it may be good for the uterus to contract like that. Maybe also there's some general kind of health that's involved in just being happy and normal and complete and so on. Maybe the uterus prospers under such circumstances, and I imagine everything else does too, kidneys also.

Well, that is all under the heading of self-actualization and, believe it or not, it's under the same rubric of what I started to talk about there with that expressing yourself in the journal. For instance, I have a suspicion that breast-feeding—I just have intuitions—seems a better thing to do if it's possible. I recommend it on insufficient grounds, maybe out of pure sentiment or something. But doesn't it seem right that an organ which is given to you ought to be used because we have so many other instances of atrophy among disorders?

Sarah: I usually distinguish between two kinds of cognition, as you do in your book, secondary and primary. Our exam that we had today was more secondary—we had been able to think about it, gather our ideas and so on. It was pretty well-organized, like most exams are. I wonder about our journal: is that supposed to be organized? Or is it—

Maslow: Both. I hope I've encouraged you sufficiently so you know I mean it about using informal modes of communication and expression and free association. For instance, those primary process, mythological, metaphorical, poetic, rhapsodical trends of communication can be used when that seems best, when it's right for what you have to express. Then also I would imagine you'll use formal modes of communication, since I've given you very professorial, academic exercises of various types—those would be more structured, more linear, A, B, C, D, more archetypal—but both modes are valid.

That reminds me of some assignments I want to make. I would like you to read two of my papers: one is "Rhapsodic, Isomorphic Communications"[22] and the other is "Some Dangers of B-cognition."[23] Now, that has to do with the discussion that I wanted to have—if we have time—for this drug business—the dangers of

LSD, psilocybin, marijuana, heroin. The danger of—if I could say it another way—artificial kicks. Also, I'm putting on reserve a mimeographed book of mine: *Summer Notes on Social Psychology*.[24] Is that on reserve, do you know? [*Several students indicate that it is*]

I would like to assign the section of that book, "Notes on unstructured groups at Lake Arrowhead." It's really comments on my first contact—the first contact of a psychoanalytically trained person with these T-groups. I'd never seen them before, and this was a confrontation of two worlds, of two ways of thought.

The book you're supposed to get, the one we'll work on next, is Fromm's[25] book on dreams, *The Forgotten Language*. I've thought and thought about it and finally I have chosen it partly because it's very good, partly also because it's a paperback and cheap, and partly because Freud's stuff, *Interpretation of Dreams,* is so complicated that I couldn't hope to manage it in a brief time.

And then for beyond that, the Horney[26] book on self-analysis, about which I have wavered and wavered. I've decided to order it. The price is not too big and it's really an excellent book. So I'm going to ask you to buy that now. It won't be in for a little while because I must order it today or tomorrow—*Self-Analysis*[27] by Karen Horney. The Fromm book you should get and start reading right away. Then I want you to have a paper by Kurt Wolff,[28] a paper on surrender.[29] I thought I had copies of it and I discovered I hadn't. Does anybody take any course with Kurt Wolff? [*Several students say he's not here this year*] He's not? Okay, no paper. It's a very good paper, but I may be able to think of something more accessible.

Oh, a little piece of business—I want to keep on trying to see you individually so that we can talk with each other. I'd like to see you all, whether you want to see me or not. [*General laughter*] So pick yourself a time this Wednesday afternoon, if you can manage that. Then I think we'll make dates for the following Wednesday afternoon also. Try to get together.

I've been reminded also, before I forget, of the spirit in which I want to discuss with you, and the spirit in which I would like to be more explicit henceforth, is as co-workers, collaborators, co-investigators in an investigation. This is not an experimental research designed in advance, on purpose; this is sort of a groping exploration into the unknown. We don't know where we're going. But I would like you to think of yourselves as not so much students who are beholden to a professor but rather as collaborators in an enterprise in which we all want to learn as much as we can so that we can pass this on to other people. I'm the professional here, so most of this communication will be done through me, but that doesn't prevent you from doing it, if you feel like it. I might be your mouthpiece to the world, so to speak, and it's through me that the lessons you learn will be taught to other people. But essentially we're partners in this, and that's the way I conceive it.

I'll ask you, and I have been asking these people that I've talked with, in this way: "What do you have to report about this whole business? How does it hit you? What happened? What's of interest for the records? What shall we pass on to those people in California[30] who are so interested in this?"

There are dozens of other people very much interested in this as an investigation both in mass self-knowledge techniques and also from the point of view of therapy, also from the point of view of educational reform. Can you think of it that way, please? That means your embarrassments and your privacies and so on are of less importance; you have professional duties to the world already, so to speak. You must offer yourself. That's the only way I could say it.

You are junior partners in this enterprise—not even research assistants. You're junior partners because you've got the data! I don't have it. I'm tossing out all sorts of seeds all over the place like an old-fashioned sower with wheat grains in every direction. I don't know which work and which don't and the only way I can ever find out is for you to tell me. And that means, by the way, one important thing—you must regard as exactly as valuable the failures as the successes. I may get very enthusiastic about something; I think it's a hot idea and yet it may not touch you—for instance, as I've already learned from several people about the William James book. I love the book! Everybody I know does. All psychologists love it, whereas several students reported one after another that it left them cold or they didn't like it or they couldn't get it. Well, this is something I learned and I'll pass that on. This is the scientific attitude that whatever the truth is, that's the truth—negative, desirable, good, disappointing, pacifying. [*Pause*]

Do you need a break? Well, let's break, not for a long time this time. I've got eight minutes to four. Let's break until four. That means don't go over to the snack bar. You won't have time for that. You can stretch and walk around.

[*Break*]

[*Note: The following is a fragment of a conversation picked up by chance by the recorder during the break. It is reproduced here as an example of informal conversations Maslow often had with students after the class. Maslow is discussing Aldous Huxley and psychedelics—the theme he is to elaborate on in the next hour. The beginning of the conversation is unintelligible because of the noise of the class breaking up. (HMC)*]

Maslow: —comparable experiences, perhaps even in some cases, more intense.

Carole: Which works of Huxley are you considering?

Maslow: Huxley? Well, Huxley is a very fine man. I don't think he *was*, judging by his early writings, but he *is* a very good example of self-actualization. What he told me was—I asked him this—he's very enthusiastic *still*, even more perhaps now about these drugs, for various good reasons that I want to mention.

Carole: It's just that in his writings he seems to be destroying or denying himself in order to have the experience.

Maslow: Well, that's one of the paradoxes that you have to get familiar with. I mean, it looks like a contradiction but it's actually not. [*Pause*] The data are mixed, still. Not all the data on psychedelics are in. We get reports—there are some reports which indicate really that the work must go on. There is no question about it because even the results just with the use of LSD in the treatment of alcoholism are so startlingly good. I want to talk about that next time. I'd like to pass on a kind of summary of the data and of the doubts and so on. This may be a personal question for all of you eventually—it may be right now,

I don't know—so that it would be better for you to be intellectual about it. Take the data, the pros and cons, make the judgment, clear decisions and so on.

NOVEMBER 18, 1963
Laboratory for Self-Knowledge

Male Student: I didn't like what he had said about human relations. Huxley.

Maslow: In these books? Huxley's changed a good deal. He certainly doesn't mean that. Not alone, anyway. If you read his *Perennial Philosophy*, for instance, or if you're interested in Huxley's contemporary thinking. Maybe you'll meet Huxley. He may come east, and we're supposed to get together, and maybe we can manage something, I don't know.[1] It would be good for you to know him. In the first place, the promise of growth—I think that he's a man who has just simply grown steadily. If you read his contemporary work and compare it with the early smart-aleck novels, and with this kind of, oh, *Brave New World* dystopia[2] sort of thing—and compare that with his most recent novel, then you'll know what I mean. His most recent novel, *Island*,[3] is a lousy novel but it's a very good essay. It's a very good . . . He's better at essays.[4]

Anyway, I have not taken these drugs, don't have first-hand experience, and I feel very suspicious and very reluctant about the whole business—I don't like it. All I can pass on are the pros and cons of whatever data we have. Frankly, what impresses me is the recommendations from people themselves. There are people whom I trust and people whom I don't trust and Huxley would be one of the people I'd trust. He just gives it a clean bill of health and says it's wonderful, it's marvelous, it's good—he's not afraid of anything.

So we'll talk about that in a little more detail next time. This may be one of the great paths to richer consciousness, to the enlargement of consciousness which may become quite common in our society. *If it turns out that psilocybin really is harmless as so many people claim, then you'll be giving that to your children probably, or something like it.*

Carole: What if it is harmful?

Maslow: Well, I think the issue will be solved in a couple of years, two, three, four years.

Doug: How will it be solved?

Maslow: Well, as we get to know more about the conditions under which it may be harmful, the conditions under which it's not harmful, whom it helps, and so on. We already know enough, for instance, that I can now make this recommendation to you. Some of you are going to become dipsomaniacs—alcoholics—in your thirties and forties—a few, a certain proportion. Although you can't tell today whether you will or you won't. For alcoholics, I now recommend either LSD or psilocybin without qualification. It's the best cure. The greatest chance of cure known to mankind today is the LSD cure for alcoholism. It will cure about 50% of the cases. Psychoanalysis is helpless, practically. So, that's what I mean—as the data come in.

Also, there is another thing which has just come up that I'm going to pass on to you. I've got a letter from R. E. L. Masters[5]. He's a sex fellow [*General laughter*]. Uh, a sexologist, I guess. A sex researcher. I don't know him except through correspondence. He's not one of the scientific people. He's written lots of books and they're not awfully sound and solid and yet they're interesting and useful. I just went through one book, but I can hardly recommend it to you. One thing I popped out of it is this one good portion, which is new. What Masters did was to get happily married couples—husbands and wives who really liked each other—to take mescaline before they had sexual intercourse. And the reports are pretty delirious. If mescaline did turn out to be harmless, as it appears to be—that seems to be the best guess—then this would be a way of having a honeymoon or something, or a second honeymoon. You can read his accounts. These are the introspective reports by the participants. He had about three or four couples. Now he wrote me a letter and said there have been more since. The only trouble is I don't know the guy and I don't know whether to trust him or not, but that's the way you deal with beginning data. I'm sure that there'll be research on this and if there is, it may affect you. The chances are mescaline is harmless. If it can enhance the sexual experience so very, very much, then that's a nice thing, of course. So there you are, hot off the press. This may actually affect us, if it is to be more widely used.

Doug: What are you going to do when people who are importing and manufacturing alcoholic beverages start some enormous campaign to discredit drugs, which is certainly possible, and the government pressure—

Maslow: It's very difficult to discredit the truth. Don't fall for the advertising stuff. They have always failed when they buck the truth. The only time they succeed is when the truth isn't known; for instance some claims about toothpaste that you can't check.

Doug: Well, nobody knows the truth.

Maslow: Well, that's why a campaign today might be effective. But as we get to know more, as we get more data, then there is little question about it. I'm not afraid of their advertising.

Doug: Also government pressures?

Maslow: That too will fold before the truth. The trouble is, we don't have enough truth now, we don't have enough facts, we don't have enough data. When we get clear, well…

[*An unidentified female student asks another question: "Can you explain how (unintelligible)]*

Maslow: Uh [*sighs*], I think we'd better let it go, because we have our third hour; let's be experiential instead of intellectualizing. You want to bring that up next time that we meet? I'm going to talk about it a little more systematically.

I had a thought since my request last class [*i.e., Lab, November 4*]. My suggestion for an exercise last time was talking about these peak-experiences and so on, and so few of you did. And several people have reported to me in private conversation that there are understandable blocks against that, and suggested to me in turn to make it less glossy, less high. I was going to suggest that you not just talk about peak-experiences but about simple, high, very happy experiences, which everybody has had, and there shouldn't be any showing off of any kind, and so shouldn't lead to these inhibitions or blocks.

But something occurred to me before: you've just gone through an experience which is symbolic of many others—this business of writing examinations and pulling yourself together. And I'm not sure how aware you are, how conscious you are of the kinds of ambivalences and ambiguities and aggressions and hostilities and happinesses and God-knows-what that come with that. If you'd like to play with that, it's a good thing to analyze—it's a good thing to play with—and I leave it to you.

I'd say that the floor was open for either the happy experiences, short of big peaks—which I think it's still good for you to try to say and try to express. And also, if you would like, the floor is open to any introspections on our experiential reports that might set things off about your feelings about taking exams or writing this paper.

Melody: I have a question. I wondered, at the beginning when we first came to talk about peak-experiences, I think, somebody asked if there could be a low peak-experience—one that wasn't happy, that's extreme depression.

Maslow: Desolation experience.[6]

Melody: I wonder if you could explain that?

Maslow: No, next time. Let's be experiential. [*Then, directing the question to Melody*] How about you? Have you had low peaks? That's a personal question probably, isn't it?

Melody: I was thinking of one; that's why I asked.

Maslow: You know that old story. All psychiatrists are so used to that—people come in and say, "I have a friend who . . ." [*General laughter*] An old joke among medical students is a man comes in and says, "I have a friend," and then describes the symptoms of gonorrhea. And the doctor listens very carefully and says, "Okay, drop your pants and I'll take a look." [*General laughter*] Well, if it's not too private, do you want to start off?

Melody: With a low peak? Well, I'm not really sure it's a peak-experience, it's just a feeling. After we had talked about peak-experiences it made me think perhaps this was just short of one.[7] I work in a nursery school and I established a real warm feeling, I thought, with most of the children, all of the children. And I felt a real closeness with them and all of them showed a great deal of affection, which I was giving back, and it was a good feeling. And then one day out of the clear, blue sky, one little girl said to me, "I don't like you." And you know just everything good seemed to go away, and it was just such a frustrating type of thing. I just thought maybe it was a low type of peak-experience because just everything that I'd been working for and everything I'd been doing and everything I thought I saw, I didn't really see.

Maslow: How did you feel? Keep trying.

Melody: I almost felt nothingness, numb. You know, I just couldn't believe it when she said it, I guess, I felt so bad. It was terrible.

Maslow: Did you feel like crying, for instance? Did you have any pain any place? Sometimes in such moments you get sort of pain around the heart. Did you feel anything like that?

Melody: I didn't feel anything physical, it was just a mental feeling. I just felt really, really bad.

Maslow: The technique is try to re-experience that if you can. Very vivid thought. Try to pull it back right into consciousness, as if you were living through it again, so that then you can look at yourself and see what feelings, what sensations, what emotions are going on.

Melody: Well, my first reaction was to say, "Why? I like you!" And then I thought, well, it will pass, but later on the same day she said it. We were in a group together and she said it again.

Paul: Why did you think it might be a low peak? Why peak at all?

Melody: Because I just couldn't get over how horrible this was. It was just . . . just for a second all the other kids in the room seemed to disappear and anything that I was doing just wasn't there, just this one little girl standing there, saying to me, "I don't like you." You know, that's all I could see.

Paul: But aren't peaks usually pleasant experiences?

Maslow: No, but it doesn't matter anyhow because what we're looking for here is just how you can describe this narrowing down. It's certainly very clear to me. Keep going, you're doing fine. [*Pause*] The technique is—just what you're doing—to try to re-experience as if you were trying to re-taste the food that you've eaten or something like that. Can you? [*Pause*]

Melody: I don't think that I really know any more about it. I just, you know, didn't get it. All I could see was her.

Maslow: How did she look?

Melody: She was so cute that I couldn't feel upset with her. [*General laughter*]

Maslow: Did she look different in any way than she had before she said it? Did you look different to yourself?

Melody: Yeah, because I had pictured myself as someone that was likeable to them and she didn't give me the impression that she liked me and so I thought, "What did I do?" But I hadn't done anything. It was just out of a clear, blue sky.

Maslow: I mean did you feel less attractive in any way? Uglier? You know that sort of thing—repulsive?

Melody: Well, I guess I just didn't like myself for the fact that she would say it. I didn't like myself for whatever it was that made her say it. I didn't know what it was, and I still don't.

Maslow: This might be one of the standard questions you could ask of yourself in such moments: "How do you look different to yourself, how do you feel different to yourself, in what respect has the self changed?" And the other question is: "How does the world look different?" And you describe "How did she look different?" Then the world looked different because it was now undone. You forgot about everything else—you just saw the little girl and yourself. [*Pause*]

See now, if you were alone, if you were doing this as an exercise at your home where you could be quiet and peaceful and lock your door, then you could just stick with it and wait and then things would come. You have free associations, things that may not seem to be related to that situation. Almost every situation is a repetition of former ones. If you are a good free associator, you must have been reminded of former situations which were like that, where somebody repulsed you. [*Pause*] Did you feel ashamed, embarrassed, guilty in any way?

Melody: Maybe guilty, but I didn't know why. I just felt that any closeness that I had thought was there wasn't really there. I mean when we were discussing in class the warmth that automatically a woman is going to feel for her children; I think I had such a real warmth towards her. Perhaps I felt guilty that she could feel the opposite towards me.

Maslow: It's a universal experience. [*To class*] Do you have any thoughts to suggest to her? Help along with enriching us?

Sophia: I guess a lot of times when things like that happen to us our first impulse is to step out of the framework that the terrible thing happens in. I don't know, maybe we'll say, "Oh, well it's just a little kid, you know. All adults certainly can't like all other adults and this really isn't anything." This, I suppose, all comes under the heading of defense mechanisms and things like that.

Did you stay in there? I guess it's pretty horrible to make yourself stay in a situation and face it on its own level rather than getting out of it into some sort of cosmic perspective or something like that.

Melody: Well, I think it was . . . You know, her attention changed and it was forgotten, at least in her mind, temporarily. And next week I went in and . . . I didn't want to avoid her, but I really couldn't help it—I was afraid of her.

Maslow: You didn't do any defensive things? See, that's a very profound question; that's the whole Freudian question.

Melody: Well, the next week when I came in at first I was avoiding her. I was afraid to go over to her, you know. I was afraid to make any advances, but then I decided it was just silly because doing that I wasn't going to find out why she had done this, and I wouldn't have been able to be myself with her unless—

Maslow: Did she still look cute?

Melody: Yes.

Maslow: You didn't make her into a repulsive, ugly thing, saying who cares whether she likes you not anyway, and so on? Do you see all the things that could have happened here? See what Freud thinks about defense in such situations—to devalue the little girl, maybe, or make some good reason for retaining your self-esteem. But you stayed right in it. Well, what happened?

Sharon: Did you try to rationalize in any way—that you were like her mother or that it didn't have anything to do with you at all, you just happened to be there?

Maslow: That you were just a symbol.

Melody: Yes, because she said it again.

Sharon: Once she sensed the effect?

Melody: She said it again. Well, I tried not to show the effect towards her. Because she said it again, and the teacher said, "Well, I like her," and then one of the other girls came over and kissed me and said, "Well, I like her," You know, and said, "And you like her too, don't you?" and she said, "Yes." And I felt this impression that she was just trying to test me, you know? Why is it that she can play with us and yet she can tell us what to do and that's why she'd say that—to see how I'd react.

Herb: Well, I had an experience with an older boy that I worked with last summer. At first he just told me that he hated me: "I can't stand you and I don't ever want to see you again." I took it personally and the first thing I thought of was—he's making a personal accusation, he was making a character judgment. And this is the first thing you have to overcome. And then I learned about things like—I was identifying with the boy too much and I was losing my sense of counsellor relationship and I needed a person to point it out to me. I guess you just need more experience with a child to show you. And then you have to rationalize, but you do go through this period of self-doubt right after the experience in question.

Maslow: Can you see how that experience is partly mixed up with abstractions there? You're perfectly correct of course, but the simple, experiential account of it, the simply permitting yourself to experience the whole business, which is to let flow without respect to words. What is going on and how you actually feel, and so on. And you can observe that this is such an easy way of discovering what your defenses are. I think that you wouldn't be aware what a huge proportion of the population, for instance in that situation, would have killed that kid, slapped her in the face. Of course, this is a pretty high-class group of people here and I doubt that anybody here would do that.

There would be milder defenses or maybe no defenses at all, as in this case—you are just simply confronting the situation naively, simply. So that I would ask you just to go back to the experiences—to ask simply: how did you feel, how did the boy look, what happened to your gut, did it get tied up? For instance, we each have our weak spots and it's a good thing to discover, too. One of mine, in a situation like that, is when there is a threat or a confrontation, my guts tie up—I can almost feel the tightening. The colon especially is spastic. It just tightens up, under a fluoroscope you can see it. Some people will report a pain around the heart, some people gasp, sort of lose their breath, as if they have been slapped with cold water.

Now that's the experience itself. That's what happens. Then what do you do about it? How do you react? How do you stand? Again there are many people in the population—after all 10% of our population is schizophrenic—who would react in a situation like that by saying, "My God, I must be smelly" or something, or, "I'm made of feces"—there are indeed fantasies of that sort—"I'm repulsive, I'm nothing." Well, for us I think it would be most desirable to learn first of all simply how to confront what happened—the truth, simply the truth. You felt very hurt or angry or the picture of the child suddenly changed; the child became loathsome, or you felt impulses, that you had to restrain, to smack the kid or whatever it might be. [*Pause*]

Carole: I . . .

Maslow: Do you want to question either of them?

Carole: I want to question Melody. You said you wanted to cry? Or you didn't want to?

Melody: I did. I felt like crying.

Carole: This is why I wonder because I know I do that too. Isn't that somehow not experiencing? We couldn't start crying in a group, obviously. How did you stop from crying? Because that would have been experiencing it even more fully, I should imagine.

Melody: I wanted to cry, but I don't think the tears really would have come. The first thing I said to her was "I love *you*"—you know, just like a shock and a reaction. And I think that when she said it again, I think the hurt was just too much to cry. Do you know what I mean?

Maslow [*turns to Herb*]: Did you have any impulse to cry that you were aware of? Prickling in the eyelids . . . ?

Herb: I guess I was on the spot. I felt conscious of the fact that I was being observed. I felt very inadequate; I felt I had failed somehow and

I was being confronted with it.

Maslow: Even there you can learn too. My footnote, professorial footnote—this is not experiencing but categorizing—you can watch in such a situation whether you feel intropunitive or extrapunitive. For instance, that's characteristically the intropunitive—you had failed somehow. Whereas the extrapunitive—the child has failed. "That dopey kid." WHACK! If you observe the experiential truth carefully then that's the kind of thing you can learn.

Sharon: I realize that we rationalize, but I was just thinking now how much more you'd stand to learn about yourself by being able to experience it.

Melody: I think that I didn't rationalize as well at first because I did take it as a personal affront. I thought this was a personal thing—she didn't like me as a person. But I think afterwards, when I think about it, I can take it less personally.

Herb: I find that when I'm rejected by people younger than me or people whom I might feel superior to, I sense a loss of power—like I become naked. On the other hand, people whom I see as superior to me, when they reject me, somehow I'm extrapunitive.

Maslow: Do you get angry?

Herb: No, it's sort of like the former really hits home and somehow is inexplicable.

Maslow: Can you think of a specific example, one in particular?

Herb: Well, I work with camps and youth groups, and this happens all the time—people rejecting me right and left. And the thing that bothers me is that I seem to hold such a high price on their acceptance of me, and this is something which I do learn in this experience. I know I rationalize and I put up my defenses, but I know that I don't believe in them at the moment really. It's sort of a ritual.

Maslow: Well, are you able to get further back there, for instance, and think in terms of how you feel or how you have changed? That is, how you feel differently from what you did two minutes before and also how the kid changes, and the world, and this and that and the other thing.

Herb: The kid always seems legitimate and he stays that way. He never changes, I think.

Maslow: How do you know that?

Herb: His rejection of me doesn't change, and what does change, I think, is my own sense of inferiority or loss of power. I think I can slowly gain it back, have more strength, but his legitimacy remains there.

Maslow: Well, you can feel yourself trying—this conscious trying to pull yourself together, trying to regain power, trying to feel strong?

Herb: I'm having difficulty with it. I can think of several experiences but one on my mind now is a poor example to pick out in the first place, just starting out. I can't think of other ones, you know. I don't remember. It was a long time ago. I think I did become very conscious of trying in this. It's not usually an unconscious type of thing. [*Pause*]

Maslow: Do you want to pursue this, any of you?

Saul: Not long ago I again had an experience of being rejected. I think I felt kind of a sour taste in my mouth and my heart was constricted—that was my feeling.

Maslow: That constriction of the heart is very often reported. What it means physiologically, God knows, but it's a pain around the heart or clutching, or people will describe it in various ways—it's very common.

Saul: It takes me some time to recover from this sort of bad feeling— inferiority feeling. I could stand a rejection by children better, but it's harder for me to cope with a rejection by other adults. It's my problem.

Maslow: Do any of you—I guess we've all experienced this of course—have the defensive reactions? See, that's the trouble—you're all too healthy a group to report these extreme reactions, but you must have some defensive reactions—milder ones.

Sarah: Well, I think it depends somewhat on our experience and somewhat on the child—like at camp this summer. I had a hypochondriac in my cabin, and when all at once—I wasn't in the cabin—she called my junior counsellor a liar, and it upset my junior counsellor so much that she ran out of the cabin and I sort of met her halfway, and she was crying like mad. And the minute I heard who said it, it seemed to me, "You shouldn't take it that way," because you sort of don't respect the value judgment of that girl in this case, because we sort of know what's wrong; we know this is the way she reacts. I think it depends, too, if it's just a child you feel there's something wrong with, you shouldn't trust her opinion, or if it's someone who you can't see why you wouldn't trust her.

Carole: I know that for me it depends upon the situation. If I'm in public or in a place—especially when I'm with children around—where I cannot react fully. I asked you about crying; this is one of the ways I interact fully, to get back to your burst [*commenting on Melody's experience*] and it's over with usually. But if I'm in private with my family or very close friends, then I can let loose. I can let the experience touch me fully at the moment, but in public I know I'm tense and I can feel myself so that I can't let it touch me. Of course it *is* touching me and I also know that later on I'm going to have to cope with having tensed up and not having let it touch me, which it obviously had. But there are other circumstances in which I could carry on without it being obvious what had happened.

Herb: I feel it depends really on what role I'm playing in a situation. I know that in situations when adults let me down, I'll tend to sulk. I won't be able to hide my feelings very well, but when I'm with kids I feel that I have to exhibit a certain stable influence, and show them that I'm more mature and I have only to maintain my role. I don't think it breaks down as much as when I'm a bit disappointed by older people. And I guess with peers I'm not more of either type.

Melody: I think if I was playing a role at the time it happened then maybe it wouldn't have affected me so much. Maybe the first time I was there I was playing a role, but by this time a few weeks had passed and I wasn't playing a role any longer. It was a part of me and I really felt the genuine closeness of the two of us, a real affection for her. This is why, it hurt so much more. And I think that when—

Maslow: Why does it hurt so much?

Melody: Because *it was me*; it wasn't anything I was acting. And I think that with a little child, there's a difference in the way you react. I think it hurts because you don't expect it from someone that young.

Maslow: Did you really like the kid? Can you use this—this is very nice—can you use this statement? This is a universal experience about which you are making self-reference now, about when you're most genuine, most sincere, most authentic, most open and understanding—that's when you're most vulnerable, of course.[8]

Now, can you think about that? In itself it is a defense, a very important defense—the inability to love, frigidity, sexual frigidity and so on—is a kind of defense in advance, you might say. It's a way of saying, "I don't want to get hurt in the future. I've been hurt in the past. I'm not going to stick my neck out. I'm not going to expose myself. I'm not going to be naked or open." Does that touch off anything? What she was talking about—did you notice that she said that just because she was open and sincere? She wasn't a persona; she wasn't an actress in a play of some sort. Somebody gets mad at a role in the play, you'd think "That's not personal." But supposing it's you, simply you, and then *that's* rejected. How about that?

Melissa [*addressing herself to Melody*]**:** I think that must be great. I know when things like that happen to me, my first defense is to negate it—just out of this world—negation. Someone that I care about makes a criticism and then it just doesn't exist. The person who says it doesn't exist, maybe. And even I don't exist, certainly not in that framework—it's just like stepping out. And I know that it works sometimes, for instance, in situations where you have to tell a lie. I've told lies and there's some sort of psychic shift-over as soon as I've told it, believed it—genuinely so—which is just a defense. You negate the truth and believe the lie and you save yourself that way. I'm just amazed that you wouldn't do it, and I think it's marvelous.

Maslow: Do you want to ask things of Melissa? That's off in other directions now—other kinds of experiences.

Carole: May I? I personally am very afraid of lying, mainly because I'm so afraid if it ever—well, I wonder just how you do that. Aren't you afraid that you're going to find out that this is not true and you're sort of like destroyed or something?

Melissa: No. It's easy for me to believe things, and I have a kind of close relation with all sorts of things that needn't be real, that can be pretend. It's a susceptibility, you know, and so things like that can be perfectly legitimate and it's not a matter of fooling yourself because I'll never find out.

Carole: What if you tell someone and he found out? What would you do?

Melissa: I'd negate that. It just wouldn't fit.

Jayne: The fact that you can tell yourself a lie and believe it, kind of implied to me that you didn't really believe it. You're very aware that you tell a lie, and maybe at the moment you're trying to tell yourself that you believe it. But we all tell white lies, and we like to call them white lies because we think we're preventing somebody else from getting knowledge that will only hurt them or perhaps change the image that they have of us. We're very aware of what we're doing, I think.

Also, this idea of negating something which somebody said when you really like the person—I find it works completely the opposite with me. When I really like somebody and they say something to me which I feel has been very critical, I take it very personally, and I find that I want to do something about it. I want to try to understand what they are saying and why they're saying it. I look to find out what's wrong with me because I want to be a better person to this particular person. In your situation, Melody, if I really did care for this person and I got this surprise, I would immediately start to rationalize; I don't think I would have internalized it as much as you did. I feel that you internalized it because you still seem to get very choked up to speak about it. I think my attitude in each situation is usually to rationalize immediately and say "Well, children are very erratic and I've seen so many kids, you know. One minute they love you and the next minute they hate you." And it's just surprising to me to find that we all have so many different reactions to this thing and it's so hard to begin to generalize.

Maslow: There is a prime question even about hurt, when someone rejects you and then you negate it. Does this imply that you don't feel hurt?

Melissa: No . . .

Maslow: Do you get more angry or . . .?

Melissa: It's the same thing. Not that you don't feel hurt and not that you don't know you're lying—you just remember them until you can get outside it. Certainly I do feel unsettled and I care who makes the criticisms. Certainly I think about it and I want to know why it happened, but not *then*.

Maslow: You said you think about it, you want to know why it happened and the prime question is: does it hurt?

Melissa: Sure, it hurts.

Maslow: How does that feel?

Melissa: Your throat tightens, and your stomach, and then you get outside of it and then you can talk again. I can.

Maslow: You seem to make a little denial of hurt here. At the beginning, anyway. Supposing I made a statement that anybody who gets rejected is hurt by it. No one's going to fight with me about that. They'll just assume it's true, and yet the fact is that frequently we may try to run away from that hurt. Part of what I would like to get you to do is simply to experience the fact that you are hurt and that it has particular feelings, it's defined experientially in a particular way for you. You've already seen the very different reactions: Saul has a sour taste in his mouth, I've reported a tightening of the guts, and there's a prickling in the eyelids as if you were about to cry—there can be all sorts of things.

Paul: What about headaches?

Maslow: That's common—a tensing of the muscles back here [*pointing*], "headache muscles" you might call them. Now again it's a matter of a simple question, which is a real confrontation of the whole damn culture. We agree that any place in the world, any human being who is rejected, is hurt. It holds by law for chimpanzees too—primate heritage. Is there anything wrong with that? Is there any reason for fighting or denying it? Why should we? Is there anything to be proud of in not being hurt when someone rejects you? Is it a desirable thing? Should we try to learn not to be hurt when some kid comes along and says "I hate you"?

Paul: There's a big difference, though, between being hurt and being smashed. And it is important that we regain our defenses.

Maslow: That is a good point. Let me pick it up from there again for you. I've been assuming this would be hurt—it can be a feeling of devastation altogether. If you commit yourself to feel these things, then this is your thermometer to tell you. For instance, if a child were to say to you in a nursery school, "I don't like you," and you just collapsed altogether, then this is a very important fact that you found out about yourself, just in the same way as if you eat strawberries and get a rash on your face. That's a particular sensitivity that you have, a particular weakness. That's your sore toe somehow.

In analysis or in self-analysis, it's a kind of thing that you learn to do after you have been analyzed, that you make use of—some rather extreme reaction. I hadn't even thought of this but if it is extreme then you jot it down in your mind there and go home and think about it. Don't let it slide, because that indicates, "My God, I've got a weak kidney or I've got a weak spot." Better find out about it, confront it, accept the truth of it. We could say—couldn't we?—that this talk about hurt under the impact of rejection is simply being truthful, accepting the truth. What is the case?

Now, I think you'll also agree on the one hand we are hurt when we're rejected. You'd have to be 70 years old and have a long lifetime and be a philosopher not to get even a little twinge of hurt from this kind of situation. It could happen. The saintly man, or let's say under moments of B-cognition, it could be so. Or a good psychiatrist learns to do that because he gets the experience again and again and again and again—the patients banging at him all the time, hostile, and this, that and the other thing. And then finally he can get saintly, you might say, and not react with hurt.

Well, this is almost like a recommendation: let it flow in upon you without fighting it so much. It's a human thing to be hurt in that situation, for most of us—especially for younger people who haven't yet worked up fifty years of philosophizing about it. Then I think you can see also—you can use it for that if you watch yourself, if you are a good self-observer, a good introspector. If you permit it to flood you, simply to be hurt just in the same way that it might be recommended if you are hurt physically: yell! That's all. Which means to permit it to happen, so to speak, to let it flood you, not to try to control it. To roll with the punch the way this kid did: as it always happens in the newspapers. The kid drops out of the window of a three-story building and comes down and hasn't bruised—where any adult would get all tight, would break half his bones, and he would probably be killed.

Then you could also observe—I think it's separable—the hurt, or maybe over-hurt, maybe being crushed, and also ask what are your responses to that? How do you feel about it? Do you tend to run away from it fast? Do you tend to negate it or rationalize it or any of these various things that we've been talking about?

Charlotte: Last year I had an argument with a friend, and it was the first argument I had every really had with any friend, ever. It really was the first rejection I had had, ever, I think. And I was completely crushed—completely, entirely. For two months, I couldn't study, I couldn't eat, I lost about twenty pounds. I just felt so completely hurt and so completely devastated that it bothered me every time I thought about it, even after I evaluated the situation. It bothers me now, and I feel . . . as much as I try to rationalize, as much as people have given me rationalizations to use, it's still impossible for me to overcome it.

Maslow: That was two months ago, you say?

Charlotte: Oh no, four or five months—five months now.

Maslow: And it still hurts?

Charlotte: Yes.

Maslow: What could we say to her, by the way, if we turn into professional psychologists? It would be the obvious things, wouldn't it? People would say, "Keep your chin up, pay no attention to it, turn away or get involved in something else"—whatever.

Melissa: Did you ever tell this person? Can you talk about it and get it off your chest?

Maslow: What kind of a guy is he anyway?

Charlotte: It's a her. [*General laughter*]

Maslow: It's a her? Well, what kind of a person is she?

Charlotte: Not feeling—not a very feeling person, and I am. It was a situation in which other people told me, and I tried to think of reasons, you know, jealousy. She wanted to get back at me for something perhaps I had done, or perhaps she had felt. She knew that she could hurt me deeply, you know, if she just acted this way. She knew she could do it.

Maslow: So you know you were vulnerable in a particular way. [*Turning to the class*] What can you say to her if you are a psychologist?

Saul: I don't know. Is it possible for you to say to your friend, "Do you like me?" You need courage or strength to do so.

Maslow: Do you?

Charlotte: Well, I never felt . . . I still like her and I would be friends with her. At the time she wouldn't talk to me at all for weeks. She'd turn her head the other way and wouldn't talk to me at all. I just didn't know what to do. I just was in tears half of the time. And at the time, I wanted her to be friendly, really; I made all the moves.

Maslow: Do you feel you know why this was so? Do you feel satisfied that you understand this situation?

Charlotte: Now I do.

Maslow: About her reaction.

Paul: May I ask you a question about it? Generally, the way the English language works I think it's an unfortunate thing that we don't usually use the term love to describe a relationship which takes place in an ordinary friendship. But recognizing that, if I were to ask you at this point whether you feel that when the friendship existed at its lowest point, did you feel a bond of genuine love in the sense of friendship? Would you say you did?

Charlotte: I do. And I do feel it disrupted . . .

Paul: She was giving up love?

Charlotte: She made a lot of accusations towards me and towards, well, my husband now. I just never had this happen to me before. I was never rejected, I had never been accused of anything, and it really completely destroyed my sense of balance.

[*The tape ends here, even though the session continues a little longer*]

DECEMBER 2, 1963

Lecture

Maslow: I was just asked about the exams, the grades, and I have a very peculiar little speech to make here. What I would like to suggest to you, which may finally turn out to be an order, I'm not sure, is to pay no attention to the damn exams and the grades—not to ask me for them. My suggestion is you not look for them, not try to find out what they're like because, especially in this instance, they turned out to be extremely poor indices of the worth of your papers.

On the whole, the papers were excellent as a group, better than I've had in years. There was only one poor grade in terms of grades but we've got into this funny position where I almost couldn't grade them. In the first place, I know about half of you—a little about you as a person—which immediately makes it impossible for me to put you on a continuum with anybody because I can't compare you. Some particular person would write a paper which was for her extremely good, and I felt pleased. I felt gratified as a teacher, knowing that something had clicked, something had developed, something had happened. But the end product of that might be not comparable with the end product from some other person who pleased me in a different way, let's say. So that I could say that I was pleased with the group of papers in general and found them impossible to grade—just impossible. I could have tossed coins, and the results would be approximately the same. If I put down A- for all of them or B—

should it be B- or B+? The whole grading system broke down entirely, put it that way.

I think what should be of importance to you, what should be of worth, if you are properly virtuous and sensible, is that they were very good papers. Now if somebody else comes along and grades them in some way, it means comparing you with each other as if you were racing. This is nonsense. In effect, what I am saying is that I assure you as a professional person that, by comparison with your own potentialities and capacities and so on, you've done well. You got the point. I could be proud of the papers as a group—that is, to let other people read them.

You're an insightful group of young people. You got different points which I couldn't compare. I really got into a sweat about the damn thing and it took me days—I spent a whole blasted week struggling with those stinking papers about grading. It's as if I had to judge you by running a hundred-yard dash—it would be just as wrong. So I've decided for myself that the grades are meaningless. I have to turn in grades in order not to lose my job [*general laughter*], which I don't care to lose over so trivial a matter; therefore there are grades, which are to please the registrar.

Paul: Are they all the same thing?

Maslow: Approximately the same grades, yes, which represents really a failure of the system rather than my own failure. Do you have any suggestions about this? My suggestion is that if you're wise, mature, if you are really interested in the expansion of your soul and your psyche and your character, in growing up and so on—make yourself independent of grades in the same way that I suggest you make yourself independent of, let's say, alcohol. Especially in this case, I tell you—it's broken down.

Now in a math exam, the grades really make much more sense. They tell you whether you've reached a certain level of capacity, but we're in another area of life. This capacity which you have reached is in terms of your own potentialities rather than, let's say, comparing one person with another person who is essentially not comparable. They sure aren't. I must give in grades. If by any accident you learn what they are, I suggest you transcend them.

Mike: Are we going to get our exams back?

Maslow: If I could really trust you to transcend grades, sure I'd give you your papers back. Maybe there I had better. You want to transcend yourself? That's your business. I can urge you to do it but then you've got to do it—I can't do it for you. Alright, I'll give you back your papers next time we meet. Did I write the grades on the papers? I think I did. But maybe I can erase them all, or something. But I'll see.

Now please take it very seriously. For instance, think of it this way—I found this to be a very effective anecdote. This was for a man who really loved education and who wanted to be educated. You may have heard this story about Upton Sinclair[1]—the way he educated himself free and got a college education for nothing. I think it was City College in New York, a long time ago. They had a rule there that if you flunked a course you wouldn't get credit for it and you had to take another course. But as he read the fine print someplace he found that you didn't have to pay for that other course—in those days it was possible. He flunked every course every semester for year after year before they caught up with him. [*General laughter*] Well, think about it.

It's serious. Most of our people with B.A.'s are uneducated people in this country. As a matter of fact, I have suggested—it's quite serious; it's not a pardox—that there are 30 or 40 schools in the country that I would spare. But there are approximately 2,000 colleges, and I suggested once, sort of three-quarters seriously, that it would be best to close down all but 30 or 40. It's perfectly true that some literacy would be lost. There would be some things lost— professional training skills and stuff like that. But the trouble with schools of the sort that I've visited so many of is that they give the students the delusion that they have an education, which they haven't. I mean they have been mal-educated. They have been destroyed, frequently, turned into anti-intellectual people, people who loathe books and so on. If you want data on this sort of thing, look up a book called *The American College*, edited by Nevitt Sanford.[2] There are very few schools in this country which don't harm the incoming freshmen by teaching them to despise the professors and intellectuals, books, courses and the like. [*Pause*]

I'll take back that business about returning the papers—I'll think about it. It might serve as a kind of spiritual exercise—to have the papers back maybe with the grades or without—I'll see which I think is best for you. You understand, I've got my own responsibilities here. It's in the same way, for instance, that I can't prevent you from smoking cigarettes, let's say, which I consider very harmful—at least I don't have to give them to you.

John: If you feel the way you do about grades, why don't you give all the papers A's? We would be able to transcend that very easily. [*General laughter*]

Maslow: For a spiritual exercise, in truth, it wouldn't work that way. Taking seriously what you say, that would be like indulging your neurosis, gratifying your neurosis. You can frame psychoanalysis as a *frustration* exercise, if you want to be serious about it. Walter Toman[3] has defined psychoanalysis as the only therapy which is *not* need-gratifying. And the very fact of *not* gratifying neurotic needs—which then brings up the anxieties and the hostilities and so on—that's the stuff that you work with in psychoanalysis. It is the emotional responses which then you can actually experience and which hopefully you can then self-observe and say, "Look, I'm being silly" or "I'm being childish" and then make use of it.

Gratifying neurotic need would be a way of punishing people. For instance, I wrote a little story once—this is a kind of Count of Monte Cristo thing. I was trying to make a point to a class once and wrote a little story. It's a little sketch and was one page long—about how I hated a lot of people—this Count of Monte Cristo business. Five people had done me great harm or injustice or something and I was very vengeful. How would I revenge myself upon them? And the worst revenge I could think of—I gave them each a million dollars. End of the story. You write the sequel.

Roslyn: Have you ever tried it?

Maslow: For myself?

Roslyn: No, giving a class all A's or something like that.

Maslow: No. I haven't tried giving my class opium either.

Roslyn: I've been in a class—it was in Antioch—where the professor told us at the beginning that we would all be given an A for the course, and I think it turned out very well. We all had our own consciences to wrestle with and we all did excellent work throughout the whole class.

Maslow: Well, if I could have my way I'd take all your automobiles away from you and let you walk. That's too easy. It happens by the way, and since I want to be realistic about it, I'd then get fired sooner or later if I gave everybody all A's. It's not done around here. I'd get the administration after me. And I don't care to be heroic about silly things.

Ben: It just seems to me that the way in which you're directing the heroism, from my point of view, is almost as silly in this sense. It's all very well to say to transcend grades, but when you're working within a system where your ability to continue with education and jobs and the whole business that we're working after here, is *dependent* on a thing like grades, then I think we have to come back to the practical reality. Now if you're working within a system where this business is to some extent abrogated, then I think it makes sense. But this is like saying "Why are you neurotic? Don't be neurotic." I think the grades—in the way they are done here—are an indication of a deep and very serious sickness, and I think as an indication of sickness it can't simply be transcended. What you suggest is the kind of thing which you might be able to do after a great deal of work and analysis of the subject of your investigation, but you certainly wouldn't be able to hit it immediately. And even if you could, it would do no good because there is this "higher power."[4]

Maslow: This anticipates a little one of the exercises I was going to talk about in a couple of weeks—the transcending of money.

Ben: That's easier to do. [*General laughter*]

Maslow: I think you'll understand better what I talk about today after I read some stuff I've got picked out. It's about the definition of what is real and what is practical and so on. Also again I will refer you to that book which has finally come into the library and which is almost like one big footnote to what I'm going to read today. This is a book by Lester Kirkendall[5] and it's called *Premarital Intercourse and Personality Characteristics.*[6]

I think I mentioned to you. This is the study of around 200 college males, but in a poor college—it makes quite a difference—out in Oregon, and of the levels of relationship that these men had to women. And perhaps I'll say something about it. The book is locked away there in our library. You have to go to that special service desk and you can say that Dr. Maslow *forced* you to read it. [*General laughter*] This takes care of all sorts of shyness and so on—you can blame it on me. You don't want to read it at all; I'm making you read it. And this has to do also with this business of what is real and what is not, and of the transcending kinds of reality that I want to start introducing you to today. I could do it with grades. I hadn't thought of it particularly. I was going to use money as one of the examples and sexual relationships as the other. But we can do it with the grades, I suppose. Especially since it parallels so nicely the money situation. It's very easy with the money situation to say, "After all you have to live and you need some money," which is perfectly true. And it's also perfectly true that there can be circumstances under which I can understand how it would be necessary to do something bad for the money. A situation I was reading about, for instance, for a woman to prostitute herself for money, or for men to prostitute themselves in various ways, all of which can happen and be understandable and forgivable. I can understand that in certain situations which have been outlined to me.

Yet on the whole there are some choices. That is, the necessity for remaining alive does not justify, for instance, the totally disgusting and nauseating situation in which, let's say, a fine actor like Edward G. Robinson[7] now will sell himself for some kind of advertising on the television.[8] It's a very disgusting thing. Undoubtedly the man would say "Well, you have to make a living, don't you?" Now this is a man who's one of the wealthiest men in the country. Apparently he gets a great deal of money for that—seventy-five thousand for a single week of "prostitution." That's pretty good pay—being a "call boy." And it could be understandable. Our job is not to look over the fence at the others, but I can understand for myself that there are certain circumstances in which I would have to do that. I can imagine. And yet this is a circumstance in which it definitely was *not* necessary to do it. This was a matter of temptation, giving in, corruption and weakness. Furthermore, it would result in the loss of respect, undoubtedly, of most of the people who know the guy. It's a matter of giving up his friends, and so on. For instance, to make an example there, it just happens I know Edward G. Robinson lived across the way there from this David M. Levy, whom I mentioned to you several times and who is a very respect-worthy man. I don't know how close they were, but anyway they knew each other. But I cannot conceive a virtuous man like Levy having anything to do with a son-of-a-bitch who could do anything like that. Therefore, this stupid man has given up not only his own self-respect undoubtedly—because this is an intelligent man—for just simple yet unnecessary temptation, but undoubtedly he has also given up a lot of friends too. Well, it's a question in that case about what is realistic. What are the realities in that situation? Is the $75,000 more real somehow than David Levy's friendship or my disrespect, which must be multiplied by ten million? It's not nice to be despised; it doesn't feel good. Is that less real—the contempt of half the population, of all the highbrows, the intellectuals, the aesthetically sensitive people, just the people that this man likes to hang out with, likes to be friends with? It's a question.

Now with the grades, the same kind of talk is possible. There is absolutely no question about the fact that, the way things are set up in our reality now, it *is* true: you have to have a bachelor's degree for all sorts of jobs. For any male not to have a bachelor's degree dooms him in this country, the way things are. It cuts him out of all the professions. It cuts him out of a good life very quickly. Therefore my advice to anyone is to get a B.A. If you can't get it in a good school, I suppose you'll have to get it in a bad school. Try to enjoy it; if you can't enjoy it, do it without enjoyment, if you have to. It's a matter of circumstance and bad fortune or good fortune, but there still are *choices* possible.

For instance, if you have a choice between a good and meaningful B.A. and one that's not, then I suggest that you take the meaningful one. I would suggest you take the one that really stands for an education in just the same way that I would suggest that if somebody makes a mistake and offers you a Congressional Medal of Honor for bravery and it really belongs to somebody else, *don't* take it. The clinician tells you that because you'd have so much guilt and lowered self-esteem and conflict within yourself for the rest of your life, it just doesn't pay. It doesn't pay to feel like a crook. It doesn't pay to feel like a coward. It doesn't pay to feel mean and trivial and small and so on. Anything that makes you feel that way is very, very expensive. Extremely expensive.

Now, if you want to put prices on it, that at least will help—it's an exercise. For instance, I know that this has saved me from stupid temptations of all sorts. I have never been paid enough in my life; I probably never will be. One time I figured I've never been paid up to 20% of what I could have earned by being the psychotherapist which I started out to be. Well, then it's a temptation if somebody offers me a job which carries $2,000 or $3,000 a year more than I'm getting. It's a meaningful sum, it's a meaningful increment to a professor, where it might not be to a man who's making $100,000 a year.

Well, it's very easy to be tempted by the $2,000 or $3,000, and I learned that I had to safeguard myself against this by putting money values on the intangibles so I could add them up. For instance, I have good friends here and I'd put a money value on each friend. How much would I take to go someplace far away and to never see my very nice colleagues again—how much would that be worth? Well, if I put a money value on each of them and it adds up—it's a great deal of money. Then how much would I take for leaving the place I'm familiar with and the school I'm familiar with and the students I'm familiar with and so on? I put money values on each of those. If I went to another school then I would be green—I wouldn't know anyone. I'd have to make friends all over again. And at my age that's not so easy and not so pleasant any more. In any case, the three-thousand-dollar increment that was offered to me in one job was three thousand dollars more than I was paid here. It turned out to be a swindle because I would have lost seven thousand dollars in psychological money if I'd taken it. [*General laughter*] That's the way I figure it, and it was easy to resist it, of course.

About the grades. It is true that you need grades—some of you much more than others, the males much more than the females. The females generally don't need a degree at all, many of them, although if they can get it easily and pleasantly and without much waste, it pays to get it since it's kind of an insurance again about this business of getting jobs and so on, in case you get to be a widow or something. It's not as desperate an urgency as it is for men. That would be one point—there are differences there.[9] Now another thing is that at Sarah Lawrence College and Bennington College[10] the grades are given to the students for each of their courses, but the grades are kept secret. That is, the grades are not given to the students themselves; they're kept on some record and they are used there in case the girl has to transfer to another school—advance grades. So they have got grade equivalents and it's a feasible and practical and practicable thing to do.

And one last point. I'm trying to cover a lot of waterfront here with a very few points, and you can talk about this endlessly, but one last and big point is the *transcendent* point. That is, from the point of view of B-analysis which I'm going to talk about now, from the point of view of Being psychology, from the point of view of ontological psychology, or from the point of view of ends-rather-than-the-instrumental-means things—it happens that the best way to get good grades anyway is to forget about it. That is, the best way to get good grades, it still turns out, is to be a very well-educated person; that is, to know your subject better. This is the proper end. I mean the gain there, if you're keeping your eyes on the ball, the thing to do is to learn your chemistry, math, French history or whatever it is that you're supposed to be trying to get a grade for. If you can focus your eye on the end—the proper end there, which is the knowledge, information or whatever—and if you analyze it, if you want to work that through, you'll find that this is the best way to get good grades, which will then come as a by-product of your knowledge, and which will then make your behavior in general more efficient because then you will bend your efforts to the proper goal rather than to the false goal or to the means to the goal. Do I make myself clear now? Do you want to pursue that?

David: Back to this Robinson thing, I don't think—

Maslow: Can I stop you for a moment? This conversation that we're going to have is under the head of Being-analysis or B-analysis—so you can take note of that, because I want to pursue this into other areas later on—and which can be defined for the moment in terms of concentration on the *ends* rather than the means. It's a very therapeutic kind of thing to do if you can learn to do it—things like keeping your eye on the ball instead of going off after red herrings.

David: It doesn't seem that his [Edward G. Robinson's] despicable act is so important in light of his friendships. In other words, I don't think that friends are so judgmental as you are. For instance, you say "the son-of-a-bitch." I agree with you, but friends don't judge or cut off or totally reject you because of one rotten apple. Most people don't give up their friends like this.

Maslow: You make a very good point there—once you're hooked on to somebody, it's . . . But if you're not hooked, and supposing you're sort of an acquaintance, as I'm not hooked, for instance? I'm sure his wife won't give him up for that, or his daughter won't cease to love him, but it would probably shake them a little bit.[11]

Sharon: Are you assuming that David M. Levy no longer associates with him or do you know that for a fact?

Maslow: No, I don't know it. I'll ask him next time. But I chose him as an example because he happens to live there. It's true—if we were to go really deeply into this, this business of the judgmental quality—it's a very moot kind of thing. Our culture really hasn't worked it out well enough yet. I'd predict that as we become more conscious—inevitably we will—of the difference between the B- and D-, between the transcendent and the factual or some such dichotomy, that we'll have to re-evaluate the business of judgment and being judgmental and being compassionate and so on.

Now it's perfectly true that any therapeutic or helping roles—the psychotherapists, the child psychologists, the teachers, the nurse, the physician—must professionally be *not* judgmental, at least in their professional lives. They must accept everybody, must have this "unconditional positive regard," or in the religious language, "Everyone is the child of God equally and everyone is a brother." We also know that there are professions in which we *must* be judgmental: a policeman, a detective, a judge and so on. And we have these two worlds in which we live. I can't think of good names for those but I call them the B-realm and the D-realm. One of the things that's implied in what I've just been talking about is somehow to learn to live gracefully and well and realistically in both the B-realm and the D-realm.

It's true you have to live in the world of policemen and laws and judgmental qualities. And as a psychologist, which many of you will be, you have to learn on the one hand to deal compassionately with, let's say, a psychopath or a paranoid person and on the other hand, to be absolutely ruthless—or what looks ruthless—also. It would be another kind of realism which is just as necessary. For instance, you must learn not to lend money to a psychopath, not to lend your rent money. If you want to give some, that would be alright; but you must learn to be—in that sense—realistic, which means judgmental. Furthermore if your daughter falls in love with a psychopath and wants to marry him then you must immediately lock her up in a jail cell someplace and say "no"; forbid her, and shoot him if necessary. [*General laughter*] And then he would say, "Well, who are you to judge?" And you would answer, "I am me; these are my judgments and I stand by them."

You will have to make judgments in just about the same way I was pushed into a judgmental position—being forced by the milieu in which I have to give you grades. I have to give grades and I may have to give them back to you. But I am trying to step aside from it and be independent of it as much as possible. I have learned, for instance, not to worry about pleasing the registrar on this matter. I just barely do as much as necessary in order for me to keep my job, which I don't want to lose. Or at least I'll lose it when I want to lose it, deliberately, not through some stupidity.

Well, keep in mind too about this B-realm and D-realm.[12] For the moment it means that I ask you not to dichotomize. This is one of the things you must learn—the transcending of dichotomies, polarities, of oppositions, of the "either-or," "A—not A" type of thing, the "black-white" kind of opposition. One of the things that we can learn from this transcendent psychology is that most of the choices into which we think we are forced we are *not* really forced, as we can have both. We can have the B-realm and the D-realm; you don't have to be always judgmental and you don't have to be always non-judgmental—it depends on the situation. When life forces you to be judgmental, then you damn well better be able to do it and do it strongly and without doubt and without a weak arm.

I got so impassioned in this little sermon here that I have forgotten what the original point was. I take this stuff very seriously, so don't mind if I get all absorbed in it. [*Turning to David*] You take over again, I've forgotten what you started to talk about.

David: No, I've nothing else to say. The only point was that by such an act one doesn't lose his friends because that's the situation in which you would be living in the B-realm. Friends are not so judgmental.

Maslow: That's true. On the other hand, as a psychologist you must recognize that friends and lovers, sweethearts, husbands, wives, parents, are far less judgmental than other people, but ultimately they may have to be. I'm thinking of two divorces that I was involved in recently—two men with paranoid wives. And two men with children. My advice and everybody's advice to these reluctant men was to forget that they loved their wives, had loved them, and that something was still there. They finally divorced their wives. Our advice might have been a little different if they had no children.

It's very difficult to love a paranoid person; it's very difficult to love, in the long run, a psychopathic person. They hurt you too much. There's one blow after another until finally the love disappears. It's very difficult to love a chronic alcoholic, as some of you will very tragically learn. There are enough of them so that's part of your fate— for a few of you—to marry an alcoholic or the other equivalents. The compulsive gambler—it's very difficult to keep your love for the compulsive gambler—and so on and so on. So your point is true, up to a point.

Sharon: I think you can still . . . There may not be any complete rejection, but there's probably disappointment. Even if it's not really great, you'd still maintain a strong friendship and there'd be a little disappointment, regardless of anything [*unintelligible*].

Maslow: Do you want to say anything about the grades?

David: Do you have any comments on the exams?

Maslow: I finally gave up printing them. The first paper I read seemed so good to me so I wrote on it "very good" and remarked on some things, and the next paper I wrote "very good." I kept on writing "very good" and finally gave up. As a group, the papers were very good. There was one paper that I finally, in order to spread these things out almost artificially, by compulsion I gave a rather poor grade. But even that I felt pleased with, for the particular person.

John: You would suggest that we as a group are not capable of both B-type and D-type work or satisfaction at the same time, because if we were, we'd be able to use the grades, and that this wouldn't matter—this would give us our D-satisfaction, and it wouldn't have any effect on our work in the other realm. Is this right?

Maslow: I would think that I would say more cautiously that I don't know you well enough to know that. That's a pretty deep judgment about a person, about how big he can be, how much above small things. I don't know you well enough. I am sure some of you cannot.

John: What I'm trying to get at is, I have the feeling that you're attempting to teach—or rather preach—a moral point of view and this is a peculiar change in the course. I mean, up to here we've been talking about the validity of religious experiences, say. Now you are preaching and telling us what morality is, and, well, I don't like it.

Maslow: True, true. Let me get off here perhaps to this start, where I had intended to start. By the way, one of the dichotomies that's going to disappear as we keep learning more about values, and about value problems is that the line between teaching and preaching is going to disappear by the year 2000. I'm pretty sure of that, at least in all the value sciences—what we now call psychological and social sciences—maybe the others as well. I would make the differentiation that my preaching—and that *was*; I feel very strong about this, *impassioned* almost, you might say—is that the thing is that I can support it empirically. It's the one difference between my preaching and the preaching out of some vision or sacred book or some tradition. And that's what I would like to start to do now.[13]

Ben: Just one more question I think you may be able to answer rather quickly. I was thinking this morning about those two ways of judging someone: judging someone arbitrarily against a standard of other people in the organization, or judging him against his own capabilities. And it came down to the point of asking myself, "Well, what does it really mean to 'judge him against himself'?" In other words, what is this new definition of "heroism"? And the only thing I could come down to was the idea of sheer will, where when the person knew what the difficulties were, he would work as hard as he could to escape from them, to transcend them in some way. I don't know what your criteria are. I wonder if you could explain them.

Maslow: I can't put it on the same continuum. I think of one student who is not here. I don't want to talk about anyone here at Brandeis who might possibly be identifiable. I'm thinking of a young girl who just entered college—this is her freshman year. She's a very vulgar little girl. Her makeup is crazy, you know, with eight different kinds of things on her eyes and these great structures; her hair is dyed, her heels are too high. For a 17-year-old girl, she's picked up all sorts of prostitute ways. It wasn't becoming for a 17-year-old girl to flirt with a 55-year-old man. There's kind of a vulgarity in the atmosphere generally. She had learned to be seductive with any man who came along, whether suitable or not suitable.

She lived in a rich suburb and her values were all wrong generally. She isn't conceivably capable of picking a good husband and she's going to make a lousy marriage. It's unlikely that she can be a good mother because her values are wrong in the sense of being very competitive in a suburban sense. She'll be, I think, one of the people who show off and make their children compete with everybody else. The kid will have to get grades or else, for instance. She'll have to go to dancing school or riding school or whatever the blasted school is that happens to be fashionable in that particular area. She has no conception of ends and she lives in a world of means. She tends already to judge people by their money. For instance—a 17-year-old kid talking about "that boy is rich, that boy has a red convertible, that boy only has something else," and so on—and tends to be seduced and seducible by any young man who either has wealth or who can fake wealth one way or another, such as with flashy cars. She gets bedazzled by uniforms and by status and so on.

I'm a friend of this family and I've been around. Suddenly this kid starts taking *me* seriously and starts nestling up to me a little bit. She saw my name in a book. Now for me this is an extremely insulting kind of thing. Can you understand that paradoxical kind of thing? As if I didn't count for anything, and as if what was before her eyes was worthless. But somebody there in the Walter Winchell[14] column, or the intellectual equivalent—somebody else said that I amounted to something and therefore suddenly she looks at me differently. Well, what shall I think of her in her judgmental state? We know about mentions in books and mentions in columns and so on—you can buy that, if you like. I could get a public relations man anywhere and you could—you can get your names in all sorts of books and be quoted, if you like—it's easy. Well, she mistook the means for the ends, let's put it that way.

Then she chose a very poor school to go to. Her parents had asked me to talk to her about schools, but she rejected my recommendation. She picked a lousy school—it's one of those huge places with social prestige, where there are sororities and fraternities. She's joining a sorority, which is really doom altogether in most of these places, such as a state university in Mississippi—which means she gets put into the hands of a social committee. I don't know if you girls are aware of how these places work. I've done field work in these subcultures—they're corrupt little societies generally. Not all of them—there are some good ones. But the chances are, if you're tossing dice, that they will corrupt this girl even further. Now she's already corrupted, but she is also corruptible even further.

Her mother tells me now, this girl is getting straight A's. I know the girl has as little use for her studies as she has for Indian wampum. [*General laughter*] That's the way you do things, is you get good grades. She studies, works very, very hard, but my impression is that it doesn't touch her any more than water does a duck. The grades mean nothing to her and they shouldn't mean anything to her mother because the question is: is this girl getting educated?

I'm thinking of girls like that on this campus. I'm very pleased and very happy if I can get some such girl as that, with that kind of background, to show some awareness of serious things. I'm tempted, you know, to sound drums and blare trumpets and so on. There should be a great ceremony about this because this is the taking of a different fork in the road, just going in a different direction altogether. I could say this in a clinical way but we can say it more simply. It is becoming—just becoming a more serious person, a decent person, a person who will work for proper values, a person who is less likely to become a Nazi, a John Birch-er,[15] for instance. And that's not just a matter of taste either, because it's a matter of being correct or incorrect, it's about truth and fact.

Well, that's progress for such a girl—I see this here in my students, and I like it when it happens. But there are also students whom I've had here where I tried to make this kind of progress and it didn't happen. I've had the personological studies of a particular type: very self-satisfied, no psychiatric symptoms—you see, so that the psychiatrists would say, "Oh, this is a very healthy person"—but with totally incorrect values in terms which we as psychologists will start to take for granted as factual. That, for example, making a bad marriage, in the psychological sense is a very tragic type of thing. It's a very real thing. And to choose the wrong person to marry and to choose the wrong model for motherhood in her case, and to choose the wrong way of using her brains, which means it's this kind of person who deteriorates intellectually almost inevitably.

She'll stay in school, but my guess is she won't finish it. She'll get married soon, as that's the fashion now. Whatever is the fashion, that's what she'll do: be married at the age of eighteen, be pregnant and giving birth at the age of nineteen and then play dolls with her own children for the next decade. She can't possibly make a decent wife. Her husband hasn't yet shown up, but I think we can predict her husband is going to be sleeping with other women about seven, eight, nine years from now. It's not a good basis for marriage. She's going to be miserable, and then the chances of her becoming an alcoholic at the age of forty are very considerably greater than if she were really to get excited about Kierkegaard all of a sudden, and take it seriously. Just getting excited about Kierkegaard or Nietzsche or anybody; just getting impassioned about a book would immediately cut her chances for alcoholism or drug addiction or compulsive promiscuity or essential hypertension or a lot of other psychosomatic illnesses. It would lengthen her life, would make her life happier and so on. These are among the ultimate criteria by which I'm judging means and ends.

Now for someone else who already is a serious person—in the sense of being aware of the difference between means and ends, who knows what money is for and doesn't get tangled up with it for its own sake, who can use it well or who can use grades and education well—such a person's paper is a different kind of thing. What would be a good paper for one person would be a very different kind of paper than for the first one. So I'd really grade them on different continuums, using different bases altogether.

I must confess that I'll grade men differently than women. Men have different values, different lives, different fates, different destinies. There are different things that I would want them to learn; there are different demands that I have for men and women. I'm more apt to demand manliness of the men than of the women for instance, on the grounds that their lives are in jeopardy. A man who isn't manly is in real trouble and a woman who isn't manly can get along without it.[16]

Sharon: I may have missed the point, but I still don't understand how you justify giving a rather poor grade to a paper which you were pleased with.

Maslow: Because the grades are . . . I get into a tangle there. Partly I'm trying to see through other people's eyes when I give those grades.

Sharon: But they're not going to see the papers.

Maslow: Well, the point is that I was shoved into the grading situation. Suppose I was shoved into being a judge in a law court. I've got my own opinions on juvenile delinquency for instance. The laws say such and such, I might condemn somebody because I was interpreting the law even though I disagreed with the law. So partly when I give grades I have to see through the eyes of the administration, through the eyes of our faculty rather than through my own. I'm an officer of the court so to speak. I'm a member of the society.

Sharon: Can't you transcend that as long as you're getting the grades in?

Maslow: I can transcend it, yes. I do.

Sharon: It seems like here is the ideal opportunity to do that.

Maslow: Transcending doesn't necessarily mean acting in a particular way. You can transcend death too, all you have to do is spit in its eye, but that doesn't say you don't die. Read Victor Frankl on the subject if you are interested by the way. Victor Frankl in his *From Death-Camp to Existentialism.*[17]

Sharon: From what?

Maslow: *From Death-Camp to Existentialism.* You'll see what I mean there—even death can be transcended. You can die in a dignified way or you can die like a pig. And to some extent this is within your own power even in a concentration camp, as Frankl found out. He gives you illustrations of it and so on. This is within your own power.

I think I'm being misunderstood to some extent. Let me start as a professor and start from what I had planned in a more organized way. It's about this B- and D- stuff. I've chosen one example; that's the relationship between men and women. The clinical and scientific research that we have is not truly adequate, but it puts the whole thing on an empirical basis. It happens that the best single thing I have run across is this Kirkendall book, and that's my main reference for you to check this stuff with.

Also, there is no really good book on love yet, but I think I can recommend a few on these levels of love, the B-love and the

D-love—uncomfortable names which I hope to find better words for. For one thing, in my book *Toward a Psychology of Being*, there are in a few places brief discussions of B-love and D-love, and I would like you to look for it.[18]

[*Maslow then picks up a manuscript he has been working on*] This is what I'm talking about—the title of this thing is "An Example of B-Analysis—the unitive perception of the B-woman and the D-woman, of the B-man and the D-man."[19] Please don't mind that gawky vocabulary. "Any woman can be seen under the aspect of eternity"—at will, I would say—"in her capacity as a symbol, as a goddess, a priestess, a sibyl, as mother earth, as the eternal flowing breasts"—the symbolic breasts—"as the uterus from which life comes, and as the life-giver, the life-creator" and so on.[20]

This reminds me again of a good book by Mircea Eliade,[21] *The Sacred and the Profane*.[22] It's much better than the Jungian stuff on this general point about the B-woman and the D-woman, about the sacralization, the way in which various cultures made sacred the biological things of life, the male and female and so on. I won't recommend the Jungian stuff at this point—it's very confused and mixed up and so on. It's very good if you're willing to spend a year studying it, but Eliade will do just as well.

> This can also be seen operationally in terms of the Jungian archetypes which can be recovered in several ways.

I rewrote this essentially for psychologists.

> I have managed to get it in good introspectors simply by asking them directly to free associate to a particular symbol.[23]

This is for older women, older men. If I tell them what I'm looking for and sort of push the button and tell them to introspect, they can go on, and if they get into this primary process kind of free-association state, then these archetypes come up very easily—the symbols come up.

Actually, of course we can get it in dreams all the time, too. Now, we have new techniques turning up on the horizon—one which hasn't been published yet and which I'm going to inspect probably in a few weeks in New York City. We will soon be able to do experimental work with dreams directly because there's a new Witkin technique. Herman Witkin,[24] a well-known experimental psychologist, has discovered that if you put people to sleep—that is, you get them as they're going off to sleep and then use this old technique that other people have used of waking them up when they are dreaming . . . We now know when a person is dreaming because of the eye movements. This can even be done electronically, automatically. You put a little gadget on the eye, and whenever you dream they start moving in all directions. You're looking at what you're dreaming at, so to speak. The eyeball is not circular, so that the bump in the cornea in the front will set off the little gadget, which can in turn set off anything that you want to set off.

Now what they've been doing is, they have a kind of tape-recorder microphone which hangs right over the sleeper, and when he's dreaming they wake him up. And he's learned—you can all learn this—to talk right into the mic, so to speak, without fully waking up. And it has been discovered that in this way you remember your dreams. You know, for us most of the time, by the time we wake up in the morning they slip through our fingers and we've forgotten most of them.

What Witkin has just discovered by accident is that if you start this from the beginning—that is, you start a person free-associating while he's going off to sleep—in effect you finally have a sleeper talking of his dreams. He just talks as he goes into sleep. And these are very profound Freudian-level dreams—very "deep," as the Freudian would say. "Come along and we'll get your dreams for you if you want," and I'll have the possibility of having my own dreams tape-recorded for me so that I can go and listen to them. It's like listening to my own unconscious, and without twenty-five bucks an hour. It's quite a thing. So it looks as if at that level we are going to be able to work rather easily within the next decade with these archetypes—the Jungian kind—of the witch mother and the good mother and so on.[25]

> Practically every deep case history will report such
> symbolic, archaic ways of viewing the woman, both in
> her good aspects and her bad aspects.[26]

If you read the psychoanalytic literature—the Freudian or the Jungian
literature particularly—you get lots of this stuff. If you want to read
some of these case histories that I have mentioned about the LSD
reports—I think I mentioned a few of them—you'll also get under
LSD this kind of B-realm and D-realm kind of differentiation. The
woman or the man seen not just as what's concretely before your
eyes, but seen also as a symbol.

For instance—again, if you're interested—read the literature on
transference and counter-transference. This is B-analytic literature—
using my vocabulary here. That is, the therapist, as you well know
from your reading, tends almost automatically in the frustrating
situation, in the mirror-style Freudian situation, to become not himself
any more but a symbol, a myth, an archetype. The patient will get him
all mixed up with her father, and with authorities, and with old
teachers, and with policemen, judges and all sorts of authorities,
soldiers and the like—even with gods. That, I think, you are familiar
with, no? It can also be seen the other way about:
counter-transference is the same kind of non-rational viewing of the
patient by the therapist, so that the patient can then be seen as a child,
for instance.

Of course this is all transcending the concrete—where this person,
this patient, might be the scummiest kind of character you could
imagine in terms of the concrete, in terms of the judgmental, in the
D-realm. One of the most pathetic examples is the book *In the Life*[27]
by Rubin,[28] which is a kind of an attempt to analyze a prostitute, and
it's very good. For one thing I would say it is even prophylactic these
days when everybody seems to tend to want to sentimentalize the
prostitutes, as in movies: generally poor, miserable creatures, totally
miserable and unhappy, destroyed and diminished and so on. That
would show it. He couldn't get very far at that superficial level, but
even there there is a transcendence of the concrete. You could see
very clearly that for this psychoanalyst there is eventually affection,
compassion and even sacralization; that is, the woman even becomes

sacred. The Melanie Klein[29] people in England also go in heavily for this kind of symbolization.

Another way of getting at this is in terms of the artificial dreams suggested under hypnosis; we have good literature on that. See, what I'm trying to do now—I'm trying to be an academic, the professor, the empiricist, not only the preacher. So I recommend you here to, let's say, David Rapaport's[30] book, *Organization and Pathology of Thought*.[31] There's a whole section of classical experiments by Pötzl,[32] Silberer[33] and several other people on the dream suggested under hypnosis—that is, the trance dream. And then you get these symbols that I'm trying to talk about now, and they are empirical things. They are things you can experiment with, you can produce them in the laboratory, you can work with them, you can count them, you can do anything you please with them.

If I can give you one example here—it was a simple experiment by Medard Boss,[34] who is a Swiss psychiatrist. What he did was to hypnotize three neurotic women patients and three healthy or normal women, and suggested that they dream that night the following thing: that a man whom each woman knew very, very well and liked would, in the dream, approach her—the dreamer—naked, and with sex in his eyes, with sexual purposes, and then she must report the dream. You can get these dreams more easily if you then put the person back into trance. I found in my own experiments that memory for dreams under trance was better than waking memory.

The normal women had dreams which were straight wish fulfillment you might say, straight undisguised, unsacralized sexual dreams as the man approached them. They each chose some man, according to the instructions, someone whom they liked, that they were attracted to, and then they had this straight sexual dream. By the way, these were all married women. The man approached them sexually and swept them off their feet and so on and so on, and then they had sexual intercourse and it was enjoyable. The reports were that this was a sexual wish fulfillment.[35]

The neurotic women had these standard, classical dreams. In one case, as I remember it, the man approached with a threatening face and with a gun in his hand and shot the woman as she cowered and quivered and begged for mercy. What penises mean, and sex and sexual intercourse, and what a woman means to the dreamer and her picture of what happens to the woman in sex is obvious enough. The other one was some variant of that. I think she was cut with a dagger or something of the sort and blood flowed and he wanted to kill her, such things. If you want to look this up, this is in Medard Boss' little book *The Meaning of Sexual Perversion*.[36]

Now that kind of empirical stuff is available for you. Any of you who want to do such work in the future can do it. This is not the esoteric type of thing. For instance, several of our graduate students have learned to do just this sort of thing. They have learned hypnosis—it's easy enough. It can also be investigated by spontaneous drawings of the sort that the art therapist uses—there's a whole school of art therapy now.

Still another possibility is the George Klein[37] technique, which I think I've mentioned. Do you remember that, where the two cards succeed each other very rapidly in the tachistoscope so that you see the symbol, so to speak? [*Pause*] Well, I'd better report that briefly, because this is a good technique which again you may want to use in your own researches, if you become psychologists.[38]

The tachistoscope is a machine for making very rapid exposures, down to one-hundredth of a second, of anything that you want—card or picture or something of the sort. Now it's possible to set this up in such a way that you have two exposures, one after the other. You can put in card A for one-hundredth of a second, and then a delay of one-hundredth of a second, and then card B exposed for one-hundredth of a second. Phenomenologically, subjectively, it has been discovered again and again: consciously you perceive only card B. That's all you remember. You don't remember card A; you never saw it consciously. But it has also been discovered that card A has its effects on the memory of card B and what you consciously perceive is a sort of fusion of card A and B.

In the first and famous experiment, card B was a line drawing by Mrs. Klein, who was an artist. It was a line drawing of a head and shoulders of a rather hermaphroditic kind of person—you couldn't tell whether it was male or female exactly. Card A was—variously, in the experiments—could be either a line drawing of the actual genitals—male or female genitals—or a symbolic version of the male and female genitals. The symbolic version of male was the "Trylon and Perisphere"—you know the business of the circle with the long, thin phallic line. The symbol of the female genitals is the delta, which is traditionally the upside-down triangle—the shape of the pubis, the pubic hair.

It was found by George Klein and by Gilbert Smith,[39] and a lot of other people since—we've checked this—that it made no difference whether you showed the actual picture of a penis, for instance, or this Trylon and Persisphere thing as card A. In either case, card B—the reproductive drawing of card B—turned out to be shifted toward the male. If you want to look this up, you can, in George Klein's papers—he has done a whole series of researches. Is that clear? This hermaphrodite person was now drawn as a male, with more blocky muscles and a shorter haircut and so on.

If card A was either the picture of the female genitals or that symbol of the female genitals—it made no difference—the hair of this hermaphrodite was made more curly, the hair was longer and he was rounded, his shoulders were more rounded and so on. He was shaped more towards the female—he became more female. So the effect upon the final drawing is indiscriminate, whether this was an actual concrete picture or a symbolic picture. Understood? You can see why psychologists will take these symbols very, very seriously. And this went on to all sorts of other experiments; it needn't be just a symbol.

For instance, in one experiment, card A was a printed word in block letters—"HAPPY"—and the other one—"UNHAPPY." They didn't see the word "HAPPY" in card A; they simply made the drawing of a face smile more and look more pleasant. If the previous word was "UNHAPPY," then they made the picture sort of less happy. The word had its non-conscious effect upon conscious perception and was embedded somehow, was fused into it, melted into it. That's still another technique for studying just what I'm talking about.

Any person who has been psychoanalyzed—that's easy. Any person who has been through an analysis can fairly easily fall into such symbolic thinking, metaphorical thinking. Any decent poet, of course, does it all the time, in his dreams or free-associations or fantasies or reveries. Furthermore, it's possible for you too, if you want to. I'm going to suggest all sorts of exercises in this: to recover your ability to fantasize at will about this, or even to look out consciously at the world and to see in this B- aspect or in this Platonic aspect or the sacred or the eternal or whatever you want to call it— symbolic, metaphorical.

> It is possible then to see the woman under the aspect of her Being.

In this transcendental way.

> Another way of saying this is that she is to be seen in her sacred, rather than the profane, aspects; or under the holy or pious aspects—

Of course, in the non-religious sense.

> —or from the point of view of eternity or infinity; from the point of view of perfection—

From the point of view of her potentialities, of what she could have been or could become.

> —from the point of view of the ideal end-goal; from the point of view of what in principle any little female baby born into the world could have become.

In principle, in theory—even though we know darn well most of them cannot, in fact.

> This fits in with the self-actualization theory that any new-born baby in principle has the capacity to become perfect or healthy or virtuous although we know very well that in actuality most of them won't.
>   On the other hand, the woman seen in her D-aspect, in the world of deficiencies—

Of deficits, of D-needs, D-motivations, deficiency motivations and the like.

—of worries and bills and anxieties and wars and fears and pains—

Judgments and the like.

> —is profane rather than sacred, momentary rather than eternal, local rather than infinite, etc. Here we see in women what is equally true: they can be bitches, they can be selfish, empty-headed, stupid, catty, trivial, foolish, boring, mean, whorish, and so on. The D-aspect and the B-aspect are equally true.
> The general point is—

For living with women, that is, for getting all the gravy that's possible to get, for getting all that's available in the experience.

> —we must try to see both, or else bad things can happen psychologically.

Remember, I can use very tough-minded language here equally well. I say "bad things"; I could speak in terms of clinical consequences and so on.

> For one thing, if the woman is seen only as a goddess, as the Madonna, as unearthly beauty—

As the Platonic idea of Woman with a capital "W."

> —on a pedestal, as in the sky or in Heaven of some sort, then she becomes inaccessible to the male—she can't be played with, she can't be made love to. She isn't earthy or fleshy enough.[40]

As a matter of fact, such a woman—by the way, we know this clinically—reduces erections rather than creates them. If you read the literature about the Madonna-prostitute complex, which you'll find in most Western cultures, rather commonly you'll find that there are many men who can't sleep with a woman that they respect. The woman that they respect becomes holy, pious, beautiful and so on, and since they think of sex as dirty then they cannot profane the woman. It gets all tangled up on analysis with incest fantasies and with sleeping with the mother and stuff like that, which they can't do. And all the defenses against incest. I think all sorts of religious defenses would go into action so that the man would simply become impotent. He is unable to have sex with a goddess, if she is only a goddess, seen only in the B-aspect.

> In the critical situations in which this actually happens with men, they often become sexually impotent and find it impossible to have sexual intercourse with such a woman. This is good neither for his pleasure nor for her pleasure either.

She may say, "Please don't do me any favors, take me off this pedestal. I'd like to be a wife and not a goddess."

> Especially since making Madonnas out of some women goes along with making prostitutes out of other women.

That is, these are the same men who then find that they can be potent sexually only with "dirty" women, only with women they despise, only with women who are nasty or whom they don't respect, put it that way. Now in the Kirkendall book we have a whole set of case histories of this, all laid out from these verbatim interviews with the men, of the way in which they feel about these women. And also something indirectly about the psychology of women who do this, who stand for this sort of thing—which is not our point at the moment.

> And then the whole Madonna-prostitute complex which is so familiar to the clinician comes up . . . Somehow it is therefore necessary to be able to see the B-woman, the actually noble and wonderful goddess-woman—

Which every woman is, *in potentiâ*.

> —and also the D-woman—[41]

As a child certainly—the three-year-old little girl, the four-year-old little girl, the five-year-old little girl—it's very easy to see what they could become if the world were nice and everything were lucky and so on and so on. They seem so clean and beautiful and charming and sweet and everything that's good. It is possible to get sad about it because you know damn well that most of them will turn out to be average women. "Average" means they've renounced most of their good possibilities—

Ben: Spiritual possibilities, or—? I mean, genetic characteristics have something to do with this.

Maslow: No, not so very much. Genetically speaking, practically all women and practically all men can, and to some extent do, what I'm coming to later. That is, to some extent we are all B-women and B-men, we are all D-women and D-men, and what I would like to teach is the ability to perceive the difference. I'll be talking on and on and on here with one example after another and hope that you can manage—you must tell me whether it works or not—I hope that you can manage to perceive both of these aspects.

Something comes into mind. This is something I've heard about more recently—a case history. It's rather commonly reported that young men who are awed by women—as every young man probably is, sometimes anyhow—will fight against it. Well, one good way of fighting against it, especially which you'll find in lower class men—this is also reported in the Kirkendall book—is to desacralize women. You can desacralize the authority, the god-man and so on, by remembering all sorts of nasty things about them. For instance, in one of these cases, the man may try to get a vision of this woman defecating, sitting on the toilet: she stinks, she smells.

For the Madonna-prostitute kind of man this is incompatible—well, the fact that she menstruates for instance is almost a test case. Is menstruation perceived as a dirty thing or is it perceived in the symbolic way? It's not dirty at all. It's something quite awe-inspiring instead, which it also is. To some extent you can *choose* how to perceive it.

Well, this is a kind of game: remember she's made up just of gristle and bone and flesh, and remember she'll die one day and rot, or remember. . . This is the way these people will try to desacralize the woman, to make her into just a piece of flesh. Because to some extent they are disarmed by their respect for the woman. The man who cannot sleep with the woman that he respects must, if he wants to sleep with her, de-respect her so to speak. These are techniques for de-respecting her, for taking away her B-value, this aspect of Being.

Or to cite an example, one which I've used as a symbolic example in some of my writing and thinking—so much so that I don't even remember whether I made it up or read it, or where, or what. This is of the medieval man seeking to join with God and meditating and praying in the chapel, and working himself up into this holy state, fixing his eyes on the stained-glass window with Christ on it. In this atmosphere where he prayed and prayed, he felt himself rising to God, rising to this holy and religious feeling—and then he had to go to the toilet.

This can be true—I've read many such things in the literature of the Middle Ages. If you've touched that literature at all you know that this was a torture for these people. They scourged their bodies; they tried to master their bodies; they tried to make nothing of them— ascetics who would almost deliberately torture themselves. Plenty of them tried to rise above defecation simply by not eating anything for long periods of time because they saw defecation as an absolute contradiction and mutual exclusiveness with what they were trying to do, with higher thoughts and higher impulses.

All right now, the D-woman and the D-man—they defecate and they have halitosis and they snore and they lose their hair, and they— make up your own things; you can add all the ills and frailties of mankind, put them together and imagine this, if you like.

Aldous Huxley just died a week ago, the same day President Kennedy[42] did. He died of cancer. I don't know what kind it was, but in many cancers you stink as you die. You smell bad and the room smells horrible; it's a terrible thing, not to mention all the agonies and tortures which are possible in some cancers. Well, the question is, are you able to put that together? Is it possible to respect Aldous Huxley while he's stinking, and perhaps in terrible pain, perspiring, turning and twisting and so on? Aldous Huxley's character structure didn't change at all, I'm sure, at his death.[43] He's a very remarkable man, a very wonderful man. Can you put those together? That's the job for us.

> Somehow it is necessary to be able to see the B-woman, the actually noble and wonderful goddess-woman, and also the D-woman—

—the deficiency woman—

> who sometimes sweats and stinks and who gets belly aches, and with whom one can go to bed.

Excuse me; if one is a man. [*General laughter*] It's obviously a male writing this.

> On the other hand, we have very considerable clinical information about what happens when men can see women only in their D-aspect and are unable to see them as beautiful and noble and virtuous and wonderful as well. This breeds what Kirkendall in his book on sex has called the exploitative relationship. It can get very ugly both for men and for women.

Ugly in a way that I doubt that any of you know. You've probably lived in good sub-societies and I doubt that any of you, except by accident almost, would get the kind of thing for instance that Kirkendall reports, about the ugliness of sex with a man at his exploitative level. We have the real dirtiness of it and the hurtfulness of people, you might say psychopathologizing each other. Now one thing:

> Certainly it can be deprive them of all the love pleasures which means also most of the major sex pleasures.[44]

It's my strong impression from the bits of data that I have—I haven't done much work with the exploitation kind of relationship, or with the lower-class male, but reading the whole literature and so on, it's pretty clear that sexual—

[*TAPE CHANGE*]

—also if I question them about the subjective quality of this. I'll bet if I ask them to describe the sexual act or the sexual pleasure, the descriptions come out differently than when I ask somebody to describe the sexual relation with somebody he loves very much. They just come out differently—the look in the eye, the look on the face, the tone of the whole conversation is different. My strong impression is that the sexual pleasure itself is very much reduced in the D-sex relationship, and it's just not much fun. When people speak at that level, there's a common word they use: they talk about relief—sexual relief. In the Romeo and Juliet situation nobody talks about relief; it's not getting *rid* of something. An act of love is not a relief—getting rid of something—it's more described like the peak-experiences that you've read about.

Furthermore, even the relief doesn't matter a hell of a lot sometimes in situations like that—especially for women. A very large proportion of women don't have sexual climax in these situations, and yet the woman who loves her husband very much can, without a climax, report very beautiful experiences—very nice, very high, let's say. [*Pause*]

I don't get very far with this, do I? It's about time to quit. But I guess I'd better go on with this because I want to go into detail, as much detail as I'm able to, with this mixing of the clinical-philosophical and the empirical-experimental—at least in this one thing which I've worked at very carefully. I spent a lot of time putting together as much of the evidence as I know about to serve as an example.

Thereafter, we can take for granted this vocabulary—B- and D- and transcending and stuff like that—no matter what we apply it to, whether grades or money or any other area of life. So I'd like to, if you would be patient with me about it . . . I think I'll hold off questions and interruptions and rebuttals and so_on until I'm finished. We'll do this next time. For now we'll break for 15 minutes.

[*Noises of the class breaking up*]

May I have your attention for a moment?

I've been a little uncertain about those notebooks of yours. I thought at the beginning of the semester it would be better if I saw them before the end of the semester. I think it might be a good idea because if you're off on the wrong foot or something, it just gives me a chance to talk to you about it. Yes, I think yes. Could you turn in your notebooks to me, today if you have them, or next time, or during the week sometime? I promise again to guard them with my life, so to speak. I promise to keep them as private as humanly possible. Nobody else will see them.

Melissa: Will we get them back at all?

Maslow: You'll get them back.

[*Intermission*]

DECEMBER 2, 1963
Laboratory for Self-Knowledge

Maslow: In talking with most of you now, individually, the question has come up about procedure here, and since I have not set on any one way of doing things, I'd like to raise this question. Some people feel quite definitely that the business of going round and round should have been continued because it takes away the onus or the stigma, I might say, for starting things or offering things and so on, which for American college students is a very difficult problem. There are others who felt just as strongly that it would be better not to have any pushing or expectations of that kind and who prefer rather to leave the thing open, as it has been in the last few sessions, to whatever happens to come up and whatever we happen to pursue. I'd like to get some impression from you, by a show of hands, about how you feel about this. I didn't start thinking about this, so I have no statistics.

Ben: Well, I don't think those are realistic alternatives because what seems to have been happening, at least as I've observed it, is either we go around the room as we first did, or you start a question which is always directed in your own terms and, as far as I can tell, with no consideration of the feeling of the day, place, time, what's happening—and then when there is silence you begin talking and you keep talking. Now I—

Maslow: Yeah. I've been told that by practically everybody. [*General* *laughter*]

Ben: I for one am very annoyed at this. I can't say anything else, and I wish you wouldn't do it.

Maslow: You speak for many.

Ben: I don't see any reason to do it. I think if people don't have anything to say, they shouldn't say it. I think if there's going to be silence here for a whole hour, there should be silence here, but I don't think that you should talk, and I don't think that you should structure it in one direction. To give an example: a thing came up several weeks ago, a month and a half ago, about the qualities of femininity: do you like to have babies? It occurred to me when I was going over the notes afterwards that there was only one possible response to this. In other words, women being the way they are, if they didn't have these reactions to babies they were simply going to shut up; they weren't going to say anything. And I think it ought to be left as loose as possible. I think there ought to be a clear division made between your speaking, instructing, preaching or whatever, and what's going on with us, because I think we've wasted an awful lot of time that could have been well spent.

John: Why do you object to his speaking in lieu of silence when you said that you'd rather be silent? The only thing that bothers most people is that he speaks when they want to speak.

Ben: Well, that too, but that's something different. [*General laughter*] I was thinking of a different way of looking at what I think is the same problem. I think it's only a question of time before someone does speak if there's silence.

Maslow: I should say that several people have been able to say this— I gather it's more than several. And also, I should say I'm quite used to it—my wife has told me about it all. [*General laughter*] I'm a talker alright; you can see that. Well, that's easy because I regard that as a failure also. I'll try. All you have to do is to remind me if I start blabbering—just tell me to shut up. That's the way we do it in my family. [*General laughter*]

But another point separate from that, that I would like you to consider, is don't go too much by the models that you have in your mind, because these models are about therapy, you know, about spontaneity, about "be silent until someone wants to speak" and so on. The purpose of this third hour which was set at the very beginning [October 14], is to try to figure out, to try to discover by actually participating for a new purpose. We have no guidelines for what we're doing—not therapy in the ordinary sense, but rather of this recovery of experience, the recovery of self-knowledge in that sense.

If it turns out that silence works well, rather than talking, okay. If it turns out not—well, I don't care what turns out, but I'm interested in trying everything that will . . . By the way, I'm as much interested in negative experiments as in positive—as interested in bad results as in good results. Of course, you're not, because you have a different purpose than mine. So we must try to keep these together. Just don't guide yourself only by the therapy model—group therapy model—as some people have in their conversations with me.

John: You say this although you spend a lot of time justifying what *you* do in this course—using therapy as a reason. For example, it seems that you justify your withholding of the grades on therapeutic grounds entirely.

Maslow: Well, to be more technical, this would be on "psychogogic" grounds, which is the only lousy word. It's funny we don't have a good vocabulary. I used the word "therapy" in lieu of a good word to describe the stress on growth and self-actualization, the discovery of one's positive potentials, the recovery of positive capacities. The word "therapy" I want to use, as in the dictionary, is for the removal of symptoms—and we're not doing that. I tell you that we can't do that. It just won't work very well. The purpose here, as set from the very beginning, by the boss, was not therapy in the sense of attempting to remove symptoms or to remove illness but rather therapy or some future word which we need—"psychogogic" was one that was offered by one person—to mean the positive improvement of already normal or healthy people. *That's* the point here.

Now it may be that many of the therapeutic techniques—group therapy, individual therapy, psychoanalytic experiences of the various schools and so on—are really the only main models of the real paradigms we have to go by. And to some extent, I've been trying those out, see what develops there, what happens.

My own impression is that what I had planned to do is to use this going round and round in a circle because I've tried it in the past and it worked. I stopped doing it here because my impression was that various people—those more vocal people—wanted to do something else instead. It doesn't matter to me much what we do because I want to try all these experiments to see which will work. So I think I'll still put it to you. I've got no special irons in the fire here and I'm perfectly happy to try whatever the sense of the group is. How many of you feel that some variation of that going round in a circle . . . ?

Paul: The thing that we've been doing lately has meant the need of your acting as a moderator—you know, the people raising their hand to you. Could we just make the alternative that we have a free discussion, with no raising hands?

Maslow: Yeah; I was going to suggest that. That was one suggestion I was going to make too. Let me say that it's become more clear in my own mind—which is already one result—is that I saw my function partly as—without having planned it that way—correcting intellectualizing when I saw it. That is, of trying to make a point, trying to label the intellectualizing where I saw it, in favor of more experiential talk. Perhaps you should do that. You remember I asked you to, but if you don't then I'm going to continue stopping intellectualizing where I see it, because I think that's off on the wrong foot.

Paul: I'd like to make a suggestion—not just pass judgment—about one procedure we could use in the future. I'd be curious to know how the group reacts to it. I'd like to suggest first of all that you truly keep out of the discussion at all points except where necessary—not just say so, and not constantly explain why you're interrupting, but truly do this. At the beginning of this third hour we immediately begin without anything being said on your part, without even suggesting what we're going to talk about so that we can really start to attain group spontaneity, whatever that may mean.

Maslow: We're not trying to attain group spontaneity.

Paul: Well, I . . .

Maslow: We're trying to attain experiencing rather than intellectualizing. That's the purpose of gathering here.[1]

Paul: I understand that. What I meant is that you'll not have said something which will tend to direct the discussion from the start, plus the fact that you won't perhaps spend 10 or 15 minutes talking to us—using up our third hour for whatever reason. I'd also like to suggest that we should respect silence much more. I second this a great deal. I think it's almost wrong to consider a few moments of silence a failure, somehow, on the part of the experiment. This is the kind of endeavor that I think in a way requires silence or meditation in order to really come up with the things that we're striving for.

Maslow: My intention, after talking with other people, was to keep much more quiet and interrupt less—except for this one point where I will continue to interrupt because I think there's too much intellectualizing. I'll try not to explain it, because it's true we have less time.

Now without further discussion could I ask for a kind of show of hands on this one question which I raised. How many of you think that it would work better, or that you would be more free, or something of the sort, if we had this going around in a circle, one after the other business? What do you feel on that? How many of you prefer not to do it that way?

[Polls taken—the majority favor a non-structured approach]

Well, that's clear enough. I'll make the suggestion that you use as a basis for discussion—it doesn't matter what you start with or what anybody wants to start with—keep in mind this experiencing business and the ability to report, and to express well, that experiencing. You can use any of the stuff that we have been talking about in previous sessions where I've been lecturing mostly.[2]

[Silence for approximately one and a half minutes]

Clara: I'd like to make a comment about what we're doing. I think we're confusing the course called "Group Process" with this last hour here. We should be talking about experiences; we should have some kind of experiences to start out with instead of just expecting the whole group to react like they do in that course. Rather we should have some sort of direction for creating some kind of topic that we can begin discussing.

Paul: It seems to me that a topic is much less likely to drift off into intellectualizing if there is some central theme.

John: Why don't you suggest one?

Paul: How about reactions to President Kennedy's death?[3] At least that's something we have all experienced one way or another. It's common grounds for experiential comparison with anyone.

Herb: At Kennedy's death I had an experience related to extreme guilt. I think it's very interesting. At the apartment which I live in, our landlords are devout Catholics. My wife and I asked our landlady whether we could come down and watch the funeral on television and she said yes. We were down there and we were watching when they went to the rotunda, and the whole business, and we were talking away, just chatting, and then came the Mass. We were watching the Mass, and before we knew it our landlady had asked her children very quickly to go get their rosaries, and before we knew it they were down on the floor. And I was standing there with my wife watching the Mass and I felt—first of all I just had a reaction to just watching the Mass. I hadn't seen one for years. I thought it was just horrible. It's just ritualization of ritual and the most impersonal and cold experience.

So in my mind already I wasn't thinking much of the whole experience, and yet when they got down holding their rosaries I felt very guilty and I stared ahead, I just wouldn't look, I wouldn't turn my head to the side to look at them. And I immediately had thoughts in my mind—she must be very upset that we were here because she's going to have to explain to her children why we are not holding rosaries too, or something like that.

So the funny thing is that from an experience like the Mass which I was deprecating in my mind as I was watching it, I turned around and had fantastic guilt feelings about it. I just fantasized that a person who had always been very warm to us and very close to us, you know, just all of a sudden disliked us intensely because somehow we were interfering in this moment.

[*Silence for approximately thirty seconds*]

Doug: Many people expressed disbelief; radio announcers all over were saying "I don't believe this." I believed it. I would like to know about the rest of you. Well, I can say a little more—my wife called me on the phone and said he had been shot, so I immediately assumed that this was some wound that he would recover from. He probably wasn't even hurt too badly. And then I went up to the newsstand to see if it was in the newspaper, because I didn't know it had only been within the hour—I thought it might have been earlier in the morning. And the guy selling the newspaper said, "The president is dead," and so all the other people were saying it to each other and I didn't believe—well, I reserved judgment. You know, I thought, "He has no real direct connection with any good source of information probably," and so I went driving off in the car and had the radio on and then the two priests that were with him made statements that he was dead when they administered the last rites to him, and then the radio announcer came on and said he was dead, and so on, and I believed it. [*Pause*] A great deal of grief.

[*Silence for approximately ten seconds*[4]]

John: Well, what use are all these particular descriptions of reactions to the events to our understanding of personality?

Doug: Well, don't you think that the way people feel has anything to do with the understanding of personality?

John: Sure, but this is not something which is suddenly available to us here for the first time. I think that everyone understands the way people react to events and the variety and gamut of human emotion which is possible at such a thing. I think what's better is—given this particular set of information that I think we all have—to produce something. Say, since we feel this, where are there similarities? What results are there? And I don't think the third hour ought to be spent doing this either, this sort of anecdotal type of affair. And even if there are things which are difficult to say in front of other people.

Doug: What is it that you suggest?

John: I'm not sure I have a suggestion. My comment is sort of only destructive.

Sharon: Why don't you make it?

John: What?

Sharon: You said you have some feelings that are destructive?

John: I said the comment was.

[General laughter]

Sharon: I thought you said—

John: Yours is a projection. My comments were almost entirely destructive, I didn't say they were invalid because of that. It's possible to get rid of enough things that we don't like and then something might arise. I don't necessarily feel that I can only say something that's bad if I can offer something good in its place.

Charlotte: John, was there anything in your particular situation which surprised you? You say that we all know how people will react in most situations. Were you not surprised at your own reactions to this particular event or at the reactions of your friends? Or did you take everything that happened quite for granted? I mean this is—

John: I didn't take the event for granted. My surprise was not at the reactions. My surprise was at the events, and I think that's a difference. I certainly didn't take the event for granted. There was certainly a great deal of shock in my reaction. But the types of reactions were, I guess, what I did take for granted. After all, nobody expressed surprise after the president was killed when they saw people walking around and expressing various things, acting in strange ways which weren't normal—nobody was surprised at this.[5]

Doug: I talked to a girl who was surprised, as a matter of fact; she was surprised at her own grief. She said she had read about the nation being in grief when Lincoln was killed but it just sort of passed her by. But now she actually felt it and it was surprising to her.

John: That lots of people were in grief—is this a psychological surprise? It doesn't seem to me that it is.

Maslow: You are talking about other people and not about yourself. You can't experience other people's experiences; you can experience only your own experiences.

Paul: I had an experience this weekend which had nothing to do with the Kennedy assassination, except that I think of it right now. It was a unique experience to me and I came to realize I was doing something and I had to fight myself to prevent myself from doing it.

I was in New York this weekend at an institute for "reconstructionist Judaism." This is a relatively small body of people who have discarded pretty much of the supernaturalism which surrounds the religious concepts of traditional Judaism, and yet it retains traditional Judaism itself in practice. I was curious to see what it was all about, and I found the theology of it highly intriguing. At any rate, I arrived there after a difficult trip traveling and I had mixed feelings about being there. It wasn't the kind of thing that I was looking forward to. I really had gone to find out what it was rather than with any kind of positive expectations. Mixed emotions.

At any rate, the first person with whom I was confronted when I got to this thing was a rabbi. His name was Rabbi S—. He was a very stimulating, very dynamic, highly intelligent man, but I was immediately taken aback by his tremendous outward air of pomposity and arrogance and complete lack of humility. I was so taken aback by it as I listened to him and watched him, because his gestures were as much indicative of this whole spirit of his as his words themselves in his way of expressing himself. He would roll his head like this [*showing head motion*] with his eyes shut. He had all kinds of gestures which almost gave you the impression that he was talking only for the sake of giving you the privilege of hearing his analysis of the situation, but at the same time was looking upon you completely contemptuously because he had no expectation that you could really understand him. And if you disagreed with him, it was because you were inferior to him and hadn't had proper experiences or something of this sort. And I didn't only get this impression from simply listening to him; I got it from hearing his answers to certain questions which were posed to him, which really seemed to imply this kind of thing.

Well, the reason I am describing him to you is because of what went on inside me when I was confronted with this, which is I felt a very strong drive—I literally had to fight myself in order to resist it—to actually fight his views, his intellectual views—with which I had very much in common—out of spite for his own personality. And to put this into words isn't to really describe the experiential effect of this. It was really a powerful desire on my part. It was as though I wanted to attack him intellectually just out of pure spite for him. I have never reacted to anyone in a position such as his before in this way. I found it impossible to have any respect for his brilliant analysis of reality, from his own point of view and even from mine, because of an inner reaction which was taking place in me, to him personally. And this has never happened to me before, that I can recall.

Herb: It seems like you thought of him defecating or something?

Paul: Quite possibly. If I ever felt like ascribing terms of that sort to people, not necessarily in a verbal manner, but in terms of feelings, I guess that you could say that. I was very much taken aback. I found it very revolting.

Herb: I've known that it can occur because I know that same person—I have the same feelings.

Paul: Oh, you know that man? [*General laughter*] That's interesting. Can you concur with my experience or reaction?

Herb: Yes. But why? The question is why? I find this with other reconstructionists. You know, I completely agree so much with what they say and I find the men so despicable. But I don't know why I do.

[Silence for approximately ten seconds]

Sharon: Someone I know judges people, or his own self, by saying that you have to learn to accept truth from a drunk, and I can't do it. It seems like it influences me and I think perhaps it needs a very strong person that can.

Herb: Do you know what?

Sharon: What? This is just a metaphoric way of saying the same kind of thing: that regardless of how miserable or despicable somebody is, that if they are speaking the truth then...

Herb: Do you know why you can't accept the truth from—?

Sharon: Well, I've never tried to. I mean when somebody is presenting the truth, it seems like it has to be framed in just the right way to be acceptable, which in this person's estimation is bad; you should be able to accept it no matter how it's presented.

Melissa: Maybe one difficulty in that is that truth is such a relative, flexible thing. A truth from one person isn't a truth from another—at least it isn't a truth as you can receive it or work with it at all.

Sharon: Well, you're talking about something which you know is applicable to you.

Melissa: I'm not speaking of the kind of truth like "the sun is in the sky." It's pretty easy to accept that sort of truth from anyone. I'm speaking of a more abstract feeling.

John: Very intellectual. *[Gentle laughter from the group]*

Charlotte: Can you say how you felt about this rabbi? Did you feel as if he was trying to be better than you or trying to tell you how you were to act, that he should be more humble? Why was he supposed to be humble? Because he was a rabbi? How did you really feel?

Paul: I can answer that without much evidence. Uh, the very fact that he is a rabbi, by definition, implied to me that he somehow represents the spirit of the Jewish tradition, outwardly as well as inwardly. Simply professing to have the title of rabbi is enough to do this. One of the things which I've always cherished about the Jewish spirit is humility. Probably nothing has capsulized my whole impression of what the religious spirit is trying to achieve than the words of Micah: "Of what thou the Lord requires, be only to love justice, to seek justice, to love mercy and to walk humbly with thy God." Somehow to me this is the epitome of the image for which the religious person is striving in his own life, and he didn't fulfill this for me in any genuine sense, from what I can perceive. So that I didn't feel that he had the right to claim that there were religious overtones in what he was doing. He was a brilliant philosopher, perhaps a brilliant theologian, but I didn't consider him a rabbi in the sense that I feel a rabbi should be.

Charlotte: Was he fooling you? Was he trying to trick you?

Paul: Oh, this isn't a question of deception. I was disgusted by him because he was, to me, degrading something which I felt to be somewhat sacred. [*Pause*] And I use "sacred" in the secular sense.

John: You give an immense amount of value to his mannerisms, it seems.

Paul: Yes.

John: Well, I wonder about this. It surprises me.

Paul: I often feel that a person expresses himself equally, if not more, in his facial expressions and gestures and the tones in his voice as he does in what he's saying simply as if you were looking at it on paper. I can say this very well by saying that when you read a man's books, you haven't met that man. I would probably have read *his* books— and he's written a good deal—and I've been very impressed with the writing, but somehow meeting the man shows me the context out of which his experiential reality goes.

John: What you suggest is that you should get the same impression from looking at the man as from reading his book, because you say that the expressions and mannerisms are true indications of what the man is.

Paul: Yes, but his words aren't.

John: Oh, his words aren't?

Paul: No, that's just it. I would say that if I did get the same impression after reading the book and meeting the man that they were one and the same, and that you could equally well read one into the other.

John: Can't one control one's mannerisms as skillfully as one controls one's words?

Paul: Possibly, but I don't think people—

Sharon: Do you feel he's a phony?

Paul: Perhaps to himself, I think—not a phony in the sense that he's trying to fool *me*. I think he's a very, very, brutally honest person, but I don't think his type of honesty—and that was what I reacted against—his type of honesty is *not* the kind of honesty which belongs under a title which exemplifies something which is precisely the contrary of the philosophy which he's preaching. Because it seemed apparent to me as I listened to him, and as I watched him, that the religious medium in which he was living was only a means to power gratification on his part.

He was one of the nine rabbis who went down to Birmingham, Alabama, and spoke in that church a few days before five little girls were blown up in a bombing. I posed the possibility to him that possibly he was partially responsible for the growing tension down South which ultimately lead to the blasting that took place there, that in some sense he had a burden of guilt to bear as a result of that bombing, in spite of the fact that he went down there for what he felt to be a moral obligation on his part, so it justified it. He couldn't see that at all; he absolutely refused to consider that possibility. And to me this isn't a question of phoniness. It's just using causes in an invalid way to validate motivations which just don't belong. In this sense it's phony.

Maslow: You've spent most of your time talking about other people.

[*Pause*]

Saul: I think I would like to talk about my feelings that day when Kennedy died. It was so untimely in the sense that the day before we had a baby girl—it was an extremely happy moment. But the following day Kennedy died. I felt kind of a sudden plunge from the top to the bottom. I knew there was death for every person, but it now became a reality and it was very hard for me to take it. That day my heart was pained all day.

Maslow: Did it feel like crying?

Saul: Not really, not crying.

Maslow: Any of you? Did any of you feel grief?

Mike: Yes.

Maslow: Is that a common reaction? Did any of you behave queerly in the way somebody mentioned about behaving? Again, the tendency is to talk about other people. You talk about other people behaving queerly but nobody has reported themselves in this way. Did any of you do any peculiar things which surprised you yourself, or feel in a way that surprised you yourself, so that you saw something in yourself that you've never seen before?

Ben: Well, I found a couple of things that I could have predicted and some that I couldn't. I could have predicted my own reaction in the sense of not reacting emotionally for about three days, until I started to visualize that really pathetic scene—Jackie Kennedy with a bloody stocking and all that business—which really moved me after a while. But the thing was immediately after the event I had a tremendous feeling of being extremely young. I mean like young, fair and debonair, like a Pepsi-Cola type of thing. Why? And I don't think I felt that way for years in quite the same way. Not quantitatively but qualitatively the same way. I had a feeling of being extremely sexual in the sense of "the only way to counter this death is by creating a child" or something. It's a strange sort of fatherly feeling. It wasn't of the regular variety, and it was at least as political as it was sexual in a strange way which I wasn't able to account for.

Sharon: I'd like to ask John a question. Do you feel this kind of thing comes under the realm of relating anecdotes? And trying to recover experience that you felt at the moment this was going on, and your own soul-searching about topics which you might not have thought about—about death, about what kind of a civilization we're living in, about how you cope with reality and whatnot? Does this come under your heading of trading anecdotes?

John: Well, I, uh, you're not quite clear.

Sharon: Or shall I say, do you feel there's any benefit from this kind of thing?

John: What you say and what happened are two different kinds of things. I feel that when people sit around and say "This happened to me at this particular time," that this is of no use to us as a class.

Sharon: Not even how we felt?

John: This would be of use to them. Unless we're all pretty unimaginative and also pretty naive I think that we can visualize these things happening. Now this may definitely be of use to the individual who tells it, but I'm told by Dr. Maslow that this is not a therapeutic session and I also assume that that's so.[6]

Sharon: You don't feel it helps you recover anything in your own experience by hearing some of these other things?

Doug: I couldn't have visualized this [*referring to Ben's experience*].

Sharon: I couldn't have either.

John: And . . . well . . . this is slightly aside from my point, which is—I don't say that I'm not interested or that what he says is not worthwhile, or that it shouldn't be said to other people. My only objection is that it's said here. What I'd like to know is what use it has to this particular class. How does it apply? How do we learn from it? Because we are obviously here to learn.

David: Suppose it helps you understand your own experience more?

John: What? Someone else said he's had an experience. That's all he said. How can that help one understand one's own experiences? [*Everyone talks at once*] Does the fact that someone else had a similar experience make you understand the experience you have?

Melody: It brings back memories. It brings back feelings to us. It brings back feelings to *me*, at least. Listening to what another person has to say I can remember the same feeling in myself.

John: And therefore you have some sort of simpatico ego-boosting which makes you feel good.

Sharon: I don't think so. I think you recover your own feelings a lot more that way. Maybe you don't, in which case you shouldn't be here.

John: Do you know why I'm here?

Sharon: Why?

John: Because of that grade which was being held up above my head like the sword of Damascus, and I have to stay until the end of the term to get it.

Sharon: But this hour has nothing to do with the grade, I presume.

John: I'm not sure about that. If you'd like to make that a subject it's another interesting point.

Sharon: I feel last time our session on rejection was very, very provocative, soul-searching in helping us find out our own feelings and stuff. Did you feel completely removed from that, when everybody was telling about rejection experience?

John: I didn't come.

Sharon: Oh, you weren't here.

Ben: It was very elementary. There was nothing we couldn't have learned on the outside.

Sharon: Even if it wasn't—

Ben: It was a good discussion, but it really wasn't very instructive in that sense.

Sharon: Sure, maybe so, but maybe everything doesn't have to be instructive that dynamically.

David: It wasn't instructive to you.

Sharon: It was instructive to me.

Ben: Naturally, I can't speak for you.

Sharon: I discovered how I felt about some things. That's all that matters to me, naturally, of course. I found out how I discovered about rejection listening to Melody talk about her feelings of rejection. So, to me it was valuable.

Paul: The element of instruction which I felt in these discussions has been in the realm of hearing people verbalize non-verbal experiences which I hadn't generally tended to concentrate on. Somehow, something which has been a part of me all along, suddenly became conscious. It's there and I could recall it if I thought about it, but I've never thought about it before. In this sense, it was educational. And in a similar sense I've also heard people speak of experiences which I've *never* had. This is also educational to me. I think I'm benefiting from that somewhere along the line.

John: Well I would suggest, at the risk which I guess I have to take of being very insulting, that the people who *do* learn in this fashion are ignorant of the culture, because I am convinced that in the culture there exists the understanding of all these particular things.

Sharon: Maybe this will help the people to learn how to take advantage of this.

John: This is something else. Now you've brought in something else. You see, now you're saying something else again, which is different. Now first we were talking about learning, which is a very good point, that this helps one become aware of, or bring our attention to particular things in our experiences which we haven't been able to. Now this is something aside from making *use* of that once we have it, and that's not the same point that was a made a minute ago.

Sharon: You said the people who could not learn this in the outside were ignorant of their culture—right? Did you say that?

John: Well, I'm saying that they didn't . . . that it simply—[*abruptly*] yes, okay.

Sharon: So would you feel that it would be beneficial if they could perhaps learn to do this a little more so that they would not be ignorant of their culture as a result of going through this kind of thing in class?

John: But the point is—

Sharon: Suppose you're right: they are ignorant of their culture. Can this help?[7]

John: Oh, okay, yeah, I suppose so. What I'm complaining about—and I have to get down here to what Dr. Maslow suggests, that we talk about ourselves—is that I don't want to be here.

Sharon [*rather coolly*]: Go.

John: Okay, fine, go. But I try not to separate the third hour from the other two because, as Dr. Maslow suggests, they have a certain amount of meaning as a result of each other. And I took the risk of insulting everybody because I don't think people here are so naive. I don't think there are people here who don't understand differences which this course suggests that they don't understand.

Paul: How could I understand how a woman feels when she observes a child?

John: You never will.

Paul: How can I even be aware of how she feels when she observes the child from my culture itself?

John: How can you be aware from any other way? My point is that—

Paul: A woman can tell me, and that's why—

John: Okay, your culture can tell you. Your culture can tell you if it has been there and if you've read what are called, let's say, the "great books" of this culture. You should know that. You should also know a great deal about the kinds of feelings people can have in reactions to different things. What you can't know, and what you never will know, is what each individual's subtle difference is, and this, it seems to me, is what is being brought forth here—the minute iota of difference that one person has as a response to any given stimulus. This is just sort of a random process, if that's what you're trying to get. It doesn't accomplish much. But the other, the actual, the genuine feelings which are known to exist and which some people don't appreciate or just have not yet become aware of, are elsewhere. They're in books. This is also a type of communication, and it's not so different from the anecdotal type.

Paul: Does the fact that they're elsewhere invalidate this kind of educational experience?

John: No, it doesn't invalidate it. It doesn't invalidate it at all—it just makes me want something else. What I look for are the kinds of things that I can't get so easily elsewhere.

Sharon: Like what?

John: Well, the type of particular insight that one gets out of good intellectual discussion for example and—

Maslow: That's not the purpose of this class?[8]

John: The purpose of this class? I thought it was to understand more about the personality.

Maslow: No, it's not. It's to make a point that there are two different kinds of knowledge. Much of the discussion has been about the kind of knowledge which you've got for fifteen years. There's another kind of knowledge which you probably haven't heard of much and which consists of the opposite of what you talk about. I want you to become naive instead of avoiding naiveté. I would like you to be simple and sensory. I would like you also—it's one of my purposes here—to be able to express—it's not simply . . . I think you've missed my purpose in part if you don't recognize our suspicion—the suspicion of the psychologists, the intellectuals in general—of purely intellectual knowledge, of the kind of knowledge that you get in a book, a verbal knowledge, instead of the actual recovery of experiencing. Now, that kind of thing can be helped by expressing, especially expressing in public.

For instance, you passed it by rather easily when I asked the questions about weeping, the impulse to weep. A very large proportion of our population are not conscious of that, especially the male population—they fight it like mad. It's not just suppression; it's probably repression altogether, so that not only are they not even aware of it, they are not even able to [cry] anymore, after a time. This is a kind of freezing process.

I would like to explore the possibility of recovering *that* kind of knowledge, in contrast to what Bertrand Russell[9] refers to as "knowledge by acquaintance," for instance. I would prefer to say were are concerned with "knowledge by experiencing" and "knowledge about"—

John: This is being done here, not in the sense of knowledge *about* but in the sense of knowledge *of*—

Maslow: I'd like you to feel, so that you could describe to me what it feels like to have an impulse to cry. You probably don't know. You probably couldn't express it. You might read it in a poem someplace or you might read what somebody else has to say about it, but I can assure you that your impulses or *your* whole sensory feelings might be quite different. Is it, for instance, a prickle in the upper eyelid? For some people, it is a prickle—that's the way they describe it—a feeling of prickling in the upper eyelid and from behind, from in-out.

Now the point of this operation, this experiment is: can all this saying, talking and the group encouragement help? The fact that other people can report these things has been found to help other people to be able to say them. And being able to say them has been found to help people to be able to experience them, actually to feel it—to feel a prickle in your eyelid which you've not been able to before. There are two levels or two kinds of knowledge: the knowledge by acquaintance versus the knowledge from within, the knowledge of actually going through it. [*Pause*] Poor professor Harry R. is now in the hospital. He has just had his gallbladder operated on, yanked out, and something else pulled out and so on. The poor guy lies there. I *know* because I've gone through it—he's absolutely *miserable*, totally miserable. I know how he feels; you don't.

John: Is there any way that through discussion you can tell me how it feels?

Maslow: *That's* what we want to find out. Now about gallbladders, I won't go that far. But about crying? *Yes*. Or about an impulse for the kind of things that are possible, for the kinds of things that I expect you have experienced, in a crude way.

John: What experience is comparable to a gallbladder operation in the sense of being something we haven't experienced? I can't think of one thing that has been brought up, offhand, that I haven't been able to experience, and I'm not so completely unrepressed. So I just don't understand the—

[*Everybody talks at once*]

Sharon: In other words, you don't feel there's any point to it.

John: I'm just wondering: what are these experiences that I'm supposed to have—

[*Everybody talks at once*]

Sharon: Maybe if you go through the ones that you did experience, maybe we'll hit some that you didn't.

John: I'd like to find those.

Mike: I want to know how real physical pain feels—wounds and things like that. I've never had any real serious injuries. I want to know what that is like.

John: Do you feel, Dr. Maslow, that you could tell us how it feels to have your gallbladder removed?

Maslow: Yes, some, some.

John: Well then, how is our knowledge any different from the intellectual knowledge of that?

Maslow: It might be nothing more than that. But there are other things where . . . I've been very much impressed by the fact that when I described peak-experiences—this may be one of the reasons why I wanted to run this, this semester—that if I can describe peak-experiences in a very vivid way, it seems to fan to life the rather mild, little sparks in other people. That is, if we could compare notes on experiences which we've both had, perhaps which I've had more vividly than you or you've had more vividly than me . . . The kind of thing, for instance, the kind of conversations that perhaps you've had with an artist who can see things. You can see them *too*, but he has to point them out to you—then you see them more clearly—like the colors of the shadows or the outlines and so on. Yes, I think we can learn from each other. I'm not sure how *much* and I'm not sure what the limits are, but I'd like to try it. [*Pause*]

Something—I interrupt as the professor here—which I want to say is that expressing is a form of knowledge, that when you're able to say something this is already a kind of finalizing. It's really a more vivid, more concretizing of what you felt. You'll be able to recognize it more easily again. For instance, I'd like to try this with anxiety, which we've all felt, or the desolations, the tragedies, which we have all felt, by saying them.[10] Maybe the whole thing is a waste of time. I'm not certain—at least I don't think so, but maybe it will be, or maybe it will be for some and not for others. But if we could focus on something which we have all experienced in differing degrees of vividness, in differing degrees of repression and intellectualization, rationalization and defensiveness, and so on, then possibly we could not only be able to express our feelings—which is already something that you get in the group therapy situation; it's a valuable sort of thing just to be able to speak more freely, without hiding—but even, I suspect, actually to permit to come into consciousness, to permit actually to experience. Maybe if we talked about weeping enough here you'd be more likely to feel an inchoate impulse to weep, and I guess you'd actually be able to weep more freely, more easily, which would be a very desirable thing. [*Pause*]

Little notes I wrote here about this: I want you to become naive— that was a good reaction to what you said there. I want to make the point about this as a kind of naiveté, sort of simplicity, honesty, authenticity. And then this expressing in public has its virtues—I would make an expert guess. It would be very hard to prove these things, but I think they will be proved. Being able to say something in a group is itself an achievement in some respects. We know that it creates certain social changes, that we should start seeing people differently in the long run. In this group you should feel more intimate, friendly, close and so on—relax, take off your shoes, as we can with our good friends, intimate friends. And then finally I want to know, if you can manage to say these things, does this increase the possibility of the conscious happening—of the thing happening; let's say, this weeping?

Sharon: Can I ask Ben one question before we go? Suppose you have experienced a great many things and are able to express them and so that this may be all very boring, you know, in that—

Ben: I don't think they are—

Sharon: What I'm saying, if this were the case, would you be willing to go along with being a part of the group in the sense that maybe you could help other people recover their experiences even though it might not be very meaningful for you? Maybe I could ask the same question of John, perhaps?

Ben: I think that puts us in a slightly different position. That puts us in the position of being in a sense, teachers.

Sharon: No, not exactly; it's sharing, I think.

Ben: Because there's no dialogue in this hypothetical situation.

Sharon: But, you see, if you're bored by everybody experiencing these things which to you are perhaps old-hat—

Ben: Wait a minute; that is one of the most loaded sentences I've ever heard. [*General laughter*] You're saying this is true or—?

Sharon: No, I'm saying if you *were* to be bored then it would be hard to participate.

Ben: First of all, let me say this—I find it very difficult to be bored with any particular situation, because if there isn't something interesting going on, I'll invent it. [*General laughter*]

Sharon: You look kind of bored—

Ben: But now if we're stripping this down—we're saying we have to stick to the point—and there's no dialogue going on, there's only one way. What are you asking?

Sharon: I'm asking: are you willing to go along with other people discovering things which you may have already discovered?

Ben: Sure, 'cause there's always—

John: Why should he take the course? If this is a course for the people who are still discovering?

Sharon: Right. Are you willing to go along with the people who are still discovering or is it just too much of a waste of time?

John: It's not too much of a waste of time at all and this is done very frequently in the course of love, but not in the course of a class.

Sharon: Do you feel it's a waste of time for you?

John: If I were in love with you I'd be delighted to spend lots of time [*general laughter*] there while you discovered things.

Sharon: You're not enough of an altruist to help the rest of the class discover things you've discovered?

John: Not on class time [*chuckles*].

[*General laughter*]

Paul: Are there any of us who are not still discovering stuff?

John: Of course there aren't, but that's not the point.

Paul: There is no possibility of discovering that?

Sharon: If he feels it's a waste of time for him, it's a waste of time for him.

Ben: I think that the question is of classification. I think we've been looking at this in a sense as a vanguard action, when in a certain sense it's a rearguard action—you know? I'm not sure where it is, it's sort of floating around up there in my mind now. In a certain sense it's very much in the front ground but in terms of what we're trying to achieve, in this particular sense that we have been discussing it today, it's somewhere more towards the rear in a way.

David: Do you think maybe that's because people are not wanting to talk about their experiences, their realities?

Ben: Well, partially it's that, but partially because I don't think there are very many people—I'm not a fascist but I'm going to say this anyhow—I don't think there are a great number of people that are interesting, especially because the peak-experiences which people have had are, in the end point, ineffable. If there were enough and a great number of varied peak-experiences that could be related, they would be tremendously valuable, but we come up with the same words to describe them.

Sharon: Am I so wrong to say that you seem bored, then?

Ben: No! That's not bored.

Sharon: That the experiences are not interesting?

Ben: No, that's not the same thing as my being uninterested.

David: I'm not sure if I understand you completely here. Is it that most people, almost all, are not interesting, or most are not but some are very interesting?

Maslow [*after looking at his watch*]**:** Let's stop for a moment. Some people have to go, I know. Those of you who have to, go, and the rest of us can stay on if we want to.

> [*Class time is over but nobody leaves, and the discussion resumes immediately*]

Ben: One thing—for example, when I was first studying this a little bit—the idea that you could really understand someone by how he got his kicks, was amazingly enlightening to me. I really thought it was very valuable, and I took it into myself and tried to work with it, and did for quite a while and opened up a lot. And it made me much more able to understand people as themselves and stop demanding, stop imposing my own preconceptions and needs on them.

But I tried to work out of this and I found myself stymied by the "peakness" of the peaks here—because you can't go over something which transcends, something which is transcendent to something else. I think we have to go out in some other direction now. I don't know what it is. That's what sort of bothers me and I wish someone could help me.

Paul: Some other experiences—other than peak-experiences?

Ben: Maybe, I don't know.

Paul: I think there's another direction that involves becoming interested in the people as well as the peak-experiences. I may be wrong, but I actually don't find the peak-experiences themselves especially interesting.

[*Everyone starts talking*]

Ben: We have no reference to individual psychology here, do we?

Sharon: But the rejection experience was very interesting.

Paul: That depends on how you treat the course, I think.

Ben: Well, it's not treated in terms which would permit us inside the individual personality, necessarily. It's too large and we have no time, so we have no recourse in that direction.

Paul: I think this is a failure. It's a limitation which is very seriously felt.

Ben: It seems crippling, to me, in the terms that you put it.

Paul: But I think that's the direction we go in around here.

Ben: Perhaps. I don't know.

Paul: And you were right that time when you said it is to involve some aspect of love—it's really one and the same thing. You can love your friends; you don't necessarily have to love only the person you marry.

John: All you said was you can. I agree with this. But you don't have to love everyone in a class of thirty-five.

Paul: No. But I say, when peak-experiences *do* become interesting is when some element of love is involved at the same time—if only on a friendship level.

Ben: You want to hope that there's love involved there even when one's not discussing peaks.

John: In other words, you would suggest that there were two kinds of communication. One is Dr. Maslow's intellectualizing which doesn't involve love and the other kind which involves love—the kind of knowledge one gets via love. And then the only other way to get knowledge aside from the intellectual way would have to involve this love, and—okay, I tend to agree and say that that's impossible in this situation.[11]

Maslow: It may be relevant to point out to you—I know of no good phenomenological description of how it feels to love. There are all sorts of books about it. I've written some myself, you know, descriptions from the outside.[12] Now my thought is that it is possible by helping each other—by dredging up whatever we've got to offer about our own experiences. For instance, what you said touched off something in me. Now it may be that I'm more professionally experienced—that is, a person who has been analyzed, for instance, goes through this endlessly. But your unusual experience about the Kennedy death—it was certainly unusual, at least it was for me—and something happened here. [*Referring to Ben's comment about his feelings the day Kennedy was killed*]

Now if we could pool our experiences in this love thing. We've all had experiences of some sort, experiences that we called love or felt love or thought were love or whatever—put that label on. The question is, is it possible to come to a kind of fuller consciousness of what this feels like? Therefore, whenever you get it in an inchoate form the tendency is to build it up—right? That is, to encourage that rather than this, in the same way that we have done with the peak-experiences—where my impression is that everybody is a little more conscious of them and is a little more able to say, "Well this might be," or "This is a weak peak-experience and it could be built up, or I could understand it better or feel it better."

What I want to do is to interrupt whenever the talk is about love with a capital "L" and the theories of love and so on. I would rather talk about how you *feel* when you think you love someone.

John: But that's a theory of love. The minute it's said it becomes a theory of love.

Maslow: No. If you want—I think that the words—they call it experiential theory, if you like, as over against abstract theory. The words don't matter. But people come to me here on the campus as an older man, also as a psychologist, also a teacher, professor and so on, and it comes up again and again: "How do I know? I think I'm in love with this guy. He wants me to marry him. How can I tell?" Then I start asking an awful lot of questions. I think sometimes I can tell—not always. Sometimes I can tell from those questions about these kinds of experiences which the youngster—the boy, the girl—hasn't asked himself.

Maybe we could learn about such experiences a little more, about how to spot in ourselves whether we're loving or not loving or what kind that is, or to tie the experiences together with a particular label. I talked earlier about B-love and D-love—that's what you call abstraction. Now what subjective blood can we put into those words—*that's* the thing. And this is what I'll always look for. I think this last conversation has been the theory of love in abstract capital "L", capital "O", capital "V", capital "E".

John: Whatever happens when someone tells you about their love? This is subjective for them but it's not for the listener. For the listener it comes from without, it's someone talking, using words, which are the symbols of intellectual communication. And they are describing, then, what they felt like.

Maslow: There are different kinds of symbols, and if you become a psychologist, as you may, then this question is going to be put to you seven years from today and you ought to be able to make some answer to it. I've sort of improvised in each of these situations but by now, maybe, I know a little more—in a professional sense of being able to ask questions to draw out the presence or the absence of particular experiences and then to be able to make some judgment, which I'm asked to do.

For instance, I studied people who did love each other and who then reported to me. I remember one of the questions is, "If something good has happened to you, do you have an impulse to share this?" "Do you feel sad when you're having a good time with a beautiful sunset but your sweetheart isn't with you? Or do you jot it down some way in your head so that you can pass it on?" This eagerness to share, or the fact that the experience itself is poverty-stricken unless your sweetheart is with you—that makes it good somehow, that makes it better somehow—there we're talking about experience. That's what people have reported, even though they don't know how to say it very well.

John: That is somehow different from the theory of love? If you say that that the absence of the loved one makes the experiences less than full?

Maslow: That's the generalization of a lot of the specific experiential statements.

John: How is that different from theory?

Maslow: How is the Oedipus complex different from reading Calvin Hall's[13] *Outline of Psychoanalysis*, which I think is an abomination and a curse? Abolish all the textbooks on psychoanalysis. Plus, it's not the experience. People run around talking words and they haven't got the slightest conception of what this means in terms of the kind of things which would *happen* to you if you actually laid on a psychoanalytic couch and struggled your way through two years of talking. The psychoanalyst would keep telling you, "Don't intellectualize! Don't intellectualize!" It'd bother you like hell, and then, piquant: "What do you *feel*? What is it you fear?"

John: You know, this is a perfect therapy, it sounds like a great therapy. Is this a therapy?

Sharon: This seems kind of pointless that you're trying to convince him of something that you think he might feel but he won't. John, do you have an open enough mind to suspend judgment and just see what happens in this class? Write it off. You're not going to learn anything intellectual or anything you didn't know. Are you open enough to just see whether you *do* learn anything? That would be a good experiment.

John [*rather meekly*]: What does this have to do with me? I've been sitting here, I've been listening, I haven't— [*General laughter*]

Sharon: A lot of us *do* feel that we are gaining something by this kind of thing and you are claiming that you're not gaining anything in particular by this kind of thing, that it's irrelevant and intellectual. Can you just suspend your judgment while we're in the class period in this hour to see whether you *do* learn anything about yourself? If you don't, then we have some empirical proof.

John: Well, it depends; I have to make up my mind whether this is the same sort of thing that goes on in a church or the type of thing that I think goes on in the classroom.

Sharon: Why do you have to make up your mind?

John: What?

Sharon: Why don't you just say either "I'll participate" or "I won't participate."

John: Because I can't. I'm not in a position of free choice. Because if I were able to make that choice I simply might not have come anymore.

Sharon: Well, you *do* have the choice of not coming.

John: I don't have the choice. I have to get a *grade* in the course.

Sharon: Didn't he beg people not to come if they didn't want to be here?

John: It seems to me you're making too much of a division between this and the other two hours of the class. They're under the same heading: this is the third hour of such and such a class, and there's supposed to be some sort of relevant connection. Believe me, after the first two hours, if there's some hope of finding out what's going on in the third hour, I'll come. But what I'm still trying to find out is [*unintelligible*].

Maslow: I must run but you can stay. One of the things that came into my head while you were talking was the possibility of having the group meet without me for various reasons. Perhaps you'll think about that and we'll bring that up next time. I want to see also how that works and what happens when this is tried out. I suggest now—I have to go, but many of you don't—I suggest you stay and see what you can make out of this. This is one intellectual discussion which I think is useful because it sharpens the contrast—the very contrast I've wanted to make—between the abstracting and the experiencing. See if you can work it out more. I may not have said it very well. Just play, you know, and pluck that same string. I'm trying to say that there are two levels of knowing, two kinds of thinking, two kinds of knowledge. For one of them we don't have very good words. Experiencing in contrast to the abstracting. Perhaps you can play with that too—try to work out "what does that mean?" and so on.

| DECEMBER 9, 1963 |
| Lecture |

Maslow: There are a few announcements I want to make. First of all, I have this article by Bugental[1] and Tannenbaum[2] called "Sensitivity Training and Being Motivation"[3] and it's on reserve for you. I recommend it. The two people who wrote it are among the leaders in this T-group wave, "sensitivity training," or various other names that they call it. [4]

Here's a new name that they're calling it; I just got this leaflet from the University of California. For some reason, up in California all these things seem to . . . [*pause*] I don't want to imply that they're nuts. [*General laughter*] No, these are good people. Here [*showing a brochure*], this thing is called *Education of the Imagination*. Everybody's running around looking for good names for these enterprises and nobody has found a good one yet. This is a leaflet on a course that they're going to run, it's called *Education of the Imagination*—"a human relations and creativity workshop to discover the excitement of personal growth." These same people are involved; they are the UCLA department of—well, the therapists there, the clinical psychologists, the School of Business Administration, and a lot of other people are involved. It's a great center for research, development and experiments of all kinds. Some of the experiments are just plain nutty and some of them have worked very, very badly, so that the scandal goes out and there are all sorts of stories about crazy groups of people. But some of them have worked very well. These two authors for this paper are from UCLA. One is a clinical psychologist, a psychotherapist, and the other is in the School of Business Administration. "Sensitivity Training and Being Motivation" is the paper I've run across. If I had to pick one paper, that seems to be the best one I've seen, so that's among your assignments.

About the Kurt Wolff paper, I've decided not to bother, especially since we're all jammed up anyway till the end of the semester. I recommend that when Kurt Wolff of the Sociology Department comes back, you ask him for a copy of his paper yourself. He's away now—I don't know for how long. The name of the paper is "Surrender as a Response to Our Crisis," which is in the *Journal of Humanistic Psychology*.[5] [*Pause*] It's with all of this stuff, it always teeters on the edge of the ludicrous. And I think it's all right. You're permitted to laugh; there is a slight ridiculous quality about the whole business, too. It's a little like the ballet for instance—it's always on the edge of the ridiculous but it can also be very serious, very beautiful too. I guess the best attitude toward the whole thing is to take it seriously and lightly at the same time—or, let's say, be amused but work at it.

[*Picking up a paper*] Wolff has written a series of papers on surrender, and I think he's preparing a book. One of the papers—I forget which one—is in *The Journal of Humanistic Psychology*, which is in our library, so that's available for you.

Then I would like you to—and this is a paper that I had wanted you to read but I didn't want to get started on that mimeographing business—but it just appeared yesterday in this *MANAS* magazine that I've spoken to you about, which prints so many very good things. I'll recommend again that you subscribe. The author of the article is Walter Weisskopf,[6] who's one of our great intellects in this country and whom, therefore, you've never heard of, and nobody else has. He's a professor of economics at Roosevelt University in Chicago but he's also a very, very fine psychologist and psychoanalyst. Since the economics professors can't understand such a combination, he's just an isolated man, and only connoisseurs like *MANAS* would pick him up—absolutely first-rate brain.

Come to think of it, he was here about a year ago—I invited him to lecture. Were any of you here? [*Pause, no response*] Well, that's also normal. [*General laughter*] If he comes again, he's worth walking ten miles for. The name of this is "Existential Crisis and the Unconscious."[7] Now here's a man who has soaked in, of all things, this combination of Freud—he knows Freud very, very well—and classical economics, which he's destroying and which is really a lot of nonsense, as any psychology student should know. Tillich,[8] who's the representative for him of this whole existential business—Max Weber,[9] Marx[10] and so on—Weisskopf is putting them all together. It's a very, very sophisticated mix, and this is as good as anything he's done, and you can have it for fifteen cents.

I checked on our calendar and we're all jammed up. We have only four more meetings after this one. I always get astonished by this—caught by surprise. Well, next week, Dr. Richard Abell,[11] who I mentioned—he called me up—he can come. That will be next Monday. He's bringing these two video tapes on group analysis that I spoke of. Did I not? [*Pause*] He's a psychoanalyst himself who's specializing mostly in group psychoanalysis. Now my impression is that he's one of the best of them; that's why I asked him to come. My suggestion is that you use him well. He'll be here for the whole afternoon, from two to five. We'll simply take the whole time as long as we have him. Look through the Beukenkamp[12] book again for whatever jots you may have made about questions and so on.[13] He's the best of the people I've run across in this field—so right from the horse's mouth you can get the goods. Also, he's quite experienced, which few people are now.

Then for the time following—since I'm getting jammed up—what I'd like to do is simply read to you or talk, lecture at you about these various suggestions about exercises that have been piling up in my notes from one source and another. Perhaps we'll discuss each one—not in any order. I've tried to put them in some kind of structured order and it doesn't work. It's just a collection of suggestions from here, there and elsewhere, and we'll try them out and talk about them, perhaps some of them we can even play. Maybe in our third hour we can play some of these games. [*Pause*]

My intention is mostly to have you write these things down and then at your own will, your own wish, at your leisure, to try them out since most of them are pretty private things, I would guess, and then to report on them in your notebook. I doubt that we'll have any time to discuss them at any length anyway.

That's what I've planned for next time. Then I'd like to try some of these other things, going over into techniques of meditation and this and that and the other thing. Some stuff that I've been able to extract out of the literature of the past on meditation and contemplation and the various religious orders and from the Eastern literatures. Most of it I think is useless for our purposes here. It's one of those recipes, like the Hermann Hesse affair[14]—find yourself a cave and go there for ten years. You know, that kind of thing. These recipes I think are for us not very practical. I've waved aside those suggestions as not feasible for us, and I've picked out those which are usable and which presumably some of you, if not all of you, could actually put to use—and maybe to *good* use.

One of the things I'd like to suggest, if you can manage to get it— this would be after the holidays—is an article in *The Journal of Nervous and Mental Disease* for April, 1963. It's by Arthur Deikman[15] and of all things the name of the it is "Experiential Meditation."[16] It's really fantastic. And who is this guy? He's a psychoanalyst, of all things, from the Austin Riggs Foundation out here in Stockbridge, Massachusetts. What I suggest is that those of you who find this an interesting thought, write to him, send him a postcard and ask for a reprint. Remember, I told you, everybody's flattered by that—write for a reprint.

It's the first of its kind that I've ever seen. It's one of these auguries of this new era that's coming in, I think, of tough-minded, hard-nosed, skeptical in the western scientific tradition, rigorous, careful, measuring approaches to this kind of meditation—contemplation—which has usually been in the hands of mystics and priests. And it's of great interest to me that Deikman is in a certain sense saying nothing new—most of the mystics would say this is not new, we've known it all the time—but I would say it is new because he doesn't take it on faith. He has actually tried it out with various people. There's specific data—the reports, the verbatim protocols—and he tells you how many people he used it with, who failed, who didn't. This is in the natural world now. It's in the realm of human cognition, not faith or exhortation. You don't have to believe him. He's got this set up in such a fashion that each of you can try it for yourselves and see what it's like. And that means that's different. It's in the broadest sense *scientific*, which it never has been before. So I consider this an extremely important paper.

Paul: I wonder if you have the time for something you promised to talk about several weeks ago but never got to. We were talking about psychedelic drugs, and you mentioned your reluctance to actually engage in using them. You never told us why; you said you would tell us.

Maslow: Well, I pushed that aside because we were in such a jam. I know you're interested. May I condense it? I'm not trying to duck anything. [*Pause*]

Let's say it this way. I've been just talking to a man who has gone through a new kind of mystical experience that I've never had reported before, with all of these things we've talked about and described under the peak-experiences. This was after an operation. So then I talked with several surgeons and they say, "Oh, yes, this is very common." It's a confrontation with death, you know? The sense of relief and exhilaration after they wake up and find they are alive. And then come all sorts of mystic experiences and visions.[17] The surgeons I talked with were very casual about it. "Oh, yes, Demerol, morphine" or something of this sort, which is absolute nonsense because with some of the patients their lives changed—like this guy giving up his job. He said, "I saw it was all a lot of crap and I'm not going to live that way for the rest of my life." Now that's not Demerol. I asked this guy, "This was wonderful, would you like to do this again?" He says, "No, I wouldn't like it."

And I've looked up Paul Bergman,[18] who has published this description of his own LSD experience in a new journal.[19] He's one of our great analysts. He had this perfect ecstasy, the most beautiful moment in his whole life. But he's never taken the drug again. He doesn't want to. Well, the answers that I've got, and the answer I feel also, is that the experience is too sacred. It doesn't belong in the five-and-ten cent store. You know, every afternoon at four o'clock with a cocktail or something like that. I get the fear of devaluating the experience. It's just too wonderful. We have an example of that with great music. We have devalued, most of us, great music for ourselves because it's playing all the time. It's around, it's in the background—you get into an elevator and they play Beethoven's Fifth Symphony. I don't know for you younger people, but music is lost for me, much of it. I don't get the peaks out of it that I used to when I was your age. It's just too common.[20]

We also know this from sex. The sexual history of mankind indicates that when sex becomes too free, the pleasure is lost, let alone the rapture, ecstasy, beauty, and so on. That's the experience of many, many cultures. Sex must not be too readily available, too easy; it must be worked for, so to speak.

That brings me to my second point. One is that it is too sacred and could be devalued by being experienced too easily and too often. The other is that it ought to be deserved, I feel. Well, that sex business, for instance. One of the clinical findings—not experimental—is that men who use prostitutes—for instance, in Mexico, where most young men start their sexual lives with prostitutes, or in our own—here—as described in this Kirkendall book I mentioned to you. Having the sexual act with prostitutes, where a man has simply bought someone and she obeys his orders. Her pleasure or her thoughts or her wishes are simply not involved. The clinical experiences show that such men become poorer lovers with their wives. That is—any way I say it, it sounds funny—they don't try to earn it, they learn not to court, not to woo, not to deserve it, so to speak, since the prostitution experience is obviously not a romantic experience. They become poorer husbands. Put it that way. I got very passionate about this once, I remember. It was a sort of speech—we were having a debate—and I remember saying something like, "Would you want to take an escalator to the top of Mount Everest?" [*Pause, and some laughter*] I think it's a very good question, and it makes a certain sense and expresses what I feel.

Saul: You mean, they tend to make an easy short-cut.

John: I may take an escalator up there if I wasn't sure the top of the mountain existed.

Maslow: Yes, well, that's a very good point. And you might ask on the one hand, "Why do I feel so skeptical and reserved and conservative about this whole business?" and I could say on the other hand, that's why am I absolutely determined about pressing the research in this field. I was just talking to Professor Morant,[21] and we keep on talking. Professors Morant, Rand[22] and I some years ago thought we'd like to start this research going. This is just on the side of caution, conservatism.

Yes, there's no question whatsoever, in my opinion, that these psychedelic drugs have already proven their usefulness beyond a shadow of a doubt. As with alcoholics or non-peakers in general. For instance, I would like to use them for drug addicts. I would like to use psychedelic drugs as an anti-suicide therapy, prophylaxis. I would like to use it for homosexuals—at least the homosexuals that I've met. There's still a lot of debate about normal, healthy, happy homosexuals, but I haven't met any happy homosexuals.[23] The people that I've met were generally unhappy people, miserable and so on, and maybe they fit in this whole realm of the non-peakers. Now it's quite clear that through psychedelic drugs the non-peakers can often get something like a peak-experience, and there's no question that it's a good thing to try. I think it shouldn't be made a chronic, you know, Thursday afternoon jag regularly—for these other reasons about cheapening the whole thing and losing the heights, losing the great ecstatic quality.

So, this is what I was going to say in two hours with lots of footnotes. On the one hand, I want to justify trying to present to you the data that are available, which I've got piled up, which indicate very clearly that psychedelic drugs must be used for research—it's criminal to close them off. All that can be reasonably asked is conservatism and caution because it's quite clear that they do and can and have hurt some people. I'm willing to take the chance on the hurt just as I am with experiments with cancer, because this is, I think, even more important than cancer. Some people may be hurt and I'm willing to risk it; I'm willing to take the chance myself too. It's worth the danger, but to *deny* the danger is kid's stuff. If we do this here on campus, we do it quite carefully. You might be asked to be a subject but you shouldn't be sold a bill of goods. I think it's very nice that people would be willing to take a little risk for the sake of mankind. But we're not going to lie to anyone about this being a beautiful thing, about it's being always wonderful, about there being no danger, no harm. There is danger—slight.

And then this other point—that would be one side of it, is to try to document. And the other is: why is it that so many people don't like the darn things and feel reserved, cautious? I think I've expressed that, at least some of the main aspects of it. I'd say the point about devaluating the experience by cheapening it, by making it too easily accessible, too inexpensive, you might say. There are others too. For instance, I would be afraid of the whole blasted culture breaking down if these were available, you know, as little pills in slot machines. These are real involvements.

Paul: On the other hand, didn't you say you hadn't taken it yourself?

Maslow: I haven't but I probably will sometime, as a good citizen, not because I have any great eagerness for it. I should try it; it's a professional responsibility. The only trouble is that if I go in with that approach, I don't know what will happen. [*General laughter*] But I can't—I don't want to discuss this, so I want to go on to other things. This is my credo, without documentation, because we don't have the time for it. I'd suggest to you, if I had to give you one reference, the best book is probably that one by Harold A. Abramson,[24] *The Use of LSD in Psychotherapy*.[25] It's a little old now—it's about 1958, I think—and many things have happened since. That's on reserve, so you can take a look at it. For more contemporary stuff you can look at the *Psychedelic Review*, which has just started. But I warn you that this doesn't seem to be critical or cautious enough—this is only the positive stuff. These are aficionados who are selling this. They think it's a wonderful thing. Well, it *is* a wonderful thing but they think it's a wonderful thing *only*. It's not just wonderful, there are also cautions and so on. [*Pause*]

Oh, another thing. I'm going to bring in, probably two meetings from now, the Saul Steinberg slides that I think I mentioned once which I would like you to introspect and meditate upon, to try to play with. It's primary process stuff and I want to use it for that purpose— they are good for exercises. Now I think it would help—it would do no harm certainly—if you got hold of Saul Steinberg's drawings. He has a book called *The Labyrinth*.[26] It's from that book that I took ten or twelve of these drawings. If you're interested, as you must be, I took one of them as a sort of a book-plate for myself. It's a kind of a leitmotif, you might say. Maybe I'll bring that along too. Since we've had all sorts of arguments and so on. I'm not quite sure that I've ever expressed myself perfectly and I'm sure that you're curious in some instances. If I had to present myself and my psychology and the kinds of things I'm interested in and how I look at them and so on, I think better than any words would be this one cartoon by Saul Steinberg which I have in my office. I'll bring that along. [*Pause*]

Okay, now I want to finish this B-psychology, this B-woman and B-man thing, and I'm not sure I said it well enough last time. What I am trying to do here comes under several different headings. The one that you might find in the older literature—especially in the medieval Christian mystical literature—was called the "unitive consciousness." This also has been very well expressed by the Zen people—D. T. Suzuki,[27] Alan Watts.

Remember the examples I gave you of the separation, the way in which people tend to dichotomize—meaning to make mutually exclusive, to cut off from each other altogether—the body on the one hand and the spirit, the soul, the higher nature or whatever you want to call it on the other hand. The unitive consciousness consists of being able to fuse them. Well, in the religious phrasings, it was always to perceive this particular person as God himself. It is to perceive simultaneously this person as the person with failings and whatever he was, with all the differentiae which make him different from anybody else, but also as the child of God, the brother of God or, in the pantheistic way, in a kind of Spinozistic[28] way, as the local manifestation of God. Also some of them have phrased this in terms of being able to see Heaven through the temporal, to be able to see the eternal through the temporal, to be able to see the universal through the momentary, to be able to have the *satori* experience.[29]

There's that very famous example in the Zen literature which is used again and again of the great Zen master who was asked, "Supposing you had a satori experience, a peak-experience; supposing you had an ecstasy while you were chopping wood, what would you do?" And the answer was, "Well, of course I'd continue chopping wood."[30] And the exegesis generally implies that anything can be made sacred, that chopping wood is sacred too, if only you take that angle, if you can see it. If you are able to perceive it, then chopping wood is sacred.

In the same way, perhaps for us the better example would be the one I used of bottle washing in the lab, dishwashing in the kitchen or, even better than that, *diaper washing*. You can make your distinctions so very, very clearly. If you are reduced to the concrete; if you can see only in this scotomatic way, as they say; if you can see only in this narrow, tunneled vision; if you can see only what's before your nose in this case, then it's just simply a dirty thing. It's just dirty and ugly and stinky and smelly and so on. On the other hand, it is possible— and it happens all the time—to see this in a unitive fashion, not to be reduced to the concrete and the narrow, the scotoma and the tunnel, but to see this in terms of what it symbolizes and what it means in terms of what else is involved, what it stands for. This might be a very hard test [*ripples of laughter from the group*]—a harder test than chopping wood—but I'm sure that it's possible to maintain and I'm sure that some talented mystics have been able to do that: to maintain the satori, the peak-experience, the rapture or the beauty that's involved, while washing the diapers.

Of course, that's an extremely hard test, and fortunately for most of us we have easier tests to make. I spoke last time of this business of, well, you know, here's somebody whom you see as very normal, beautiful, wonderful or something of the sort, then you can imagine all the intestines working inside that person. And this is a way of *devaluing*, you might say, of bringing them down. [*Pause*]

This is a good example here. In the exploitative sexual relationship—that is, in the kind of relationship which is endemic in the West in the lower classes, the less-educated people—it's a characteristic defense against being impressed—young men or old men for that matter—being impressed by a woman, who after all can represent, if you let yourself go, everything true and beautiful and good and virtuous and godly and religious and sacred and holy and so on. The young man, trying to be tough and feeling himself to be like Samson and Delilah—his locks are going to be shorn and his power—

well, he fears that he's going to be castrated. He's going to be made tender where he's trying to be tough. Such a person will fight against the woman and all her "tenderizing" influences.

One characteristic way in which young men, especially of the uneducated classes will do this is, "She ought to be raped." In these exploitative relationships, sex is dominant-ized anyway—that is, it's made into a dominance relationship. The woman is not being made love to by this man, but she is being used, she's being dominated. All the slang words express that. The slang words for the sexual relationship are simultaneously used for the sexual relationship and for the domination relationship, exploitation and so on. Well, I'd recommend the Kirkendall book again, because there you have clear layering of these levels. He starts in with the lowest level, with the most exploitative, the most dominating, what we might call the dirtiest relationship, the most obscene relationship between men and women, and then goes on up to the love relationship, which can be a very beautiful thing. [*Pause*]

Okay, that's what this is all for. It's this kind of trying to put together into a fusion the sacred and the profane or the B- and D- or the eternal and the momentary, or the high and the low, the high human nature and the low human nature. Or, if you want to say, the spiritual with the animal, the dirty with the ethereal and so on. Through history you have these lines of literature in which it has been demonstrated that they can go together, they can meld. It has taken very unusual and talented people to do that. Now it begins to appear that we have data to begin to indicate—not experimental data yet, but personological and clinical, you might call it—that this can be done. It can be done rather easily, almost casually, it's possible to learn.

Carole: I don't understand one thing. If a person thinks of the natural as low and dirty, can he then fuse it with the high? Once you label them that way, they're already mutually exclusive.

Maslow: If they stay that way, yes. But the question is, "Can it be taught, can it be learned?" Can the young man who comes into the therapeutic situation with this kind of dichotomy, or with this Madonna-prostitute business, learn? It's widespread through our culture. I think you can perceive this in yourselves, if I can ask you to introspect. Maybe it's still with you, in any case you're not too far away from it.

The young man or young woman in our society—the new, the adolescent, the-coming-into-puberty person—almost always cannot conceive of his mother and father having sexual intercourse. Or let's say, the eight-year-old or the nine-year-old—you may remember for yourself that this was an inconceivable thought. I don't know at what age you got initiated into this sort of stuff, perhaps hearing about it on the street corner somewhere—it was certainly that way in my time.

I think the first time we ever heard of sex in general was around the age of seven or eight or nine. It was definitely on the street corners—older people never spoke about it. There were no books about it so you couldn't look up anything. It sounds like the seventeenth century, doesn't it? [*General laughter*] Then, the instructions were from older boys. The girls didn't get any instructions at all until they came to college, for instance. They knew nothing of sex, nothing whatsoever in that time. I mean *nothing*, because in some of the sexological studies that were done at that time there were married couples who came in to a man I was working with once—Robert Dickenson.[31] Married couples came in and wondered why they didn't have any babies and the wives were found to be absolutely virgin. They had never heard of sexual intercourse; nobody told them about it. They thought babies came from kissing or whatever fantasies they had. That's only about fifty years ago, forty-five years ago.

It was very, very clear that sex was always presented as dirty, and that's the way it started. Then later on somebody would say, "How about your mother and father? Do you know where babies come from?" And then this would be renounced and you'd punch him in the nose for making such a dirty, rotten suggestion about your mommy and daddy. [*General laughter*]

That's what we're talking about. That's the Madonna-prostitute complex. That's what we mean by it. And if you look within yourselves you'll find it's still there in many of you—a little bit anyway.

It's hard to conceive. Let me put this as an exercise for you. See how difficult it is for you youngsters, for instance, to conceive sexuality at the age of 70. Now it happens, and we know it happens—there are all sorts of studies now. One of the reasons for old-age clubs now—you know these societies in which the old people get together—is that *there* they can flirt. It's possible for this old man of 75 to pinch the behind of this chick of 65 [*general laughter*] and his grandchildren aren't around to get absolutely shocked and traumatized by it—the dirty old man. These old-age clubs are hot-hives of sex. [*Roars of laughter*]

The percentages of marriages there are fantastic. It's a lot of fun in a way, because the nurses and the doctors are always having trouble about people sneaking into each other's dormitories. Remember, by the time you're in your sixties or seventies, you're shameless, and this is what goes on. Now these people cannot do it when there are young people around because the young people get absolutely horrified and shocked, even traumatized. That too is part of this making sex dirty, and this is one reason why so many old ladies are so miserable. The old men can manage somehow. But the old ladies in whom the sex keeps climbing and climbing and climbing are generally very unhappy. They can't even get sympathy from anybody; they can't talk with anybody about this thing because it would seem so funny—or dirty; one or the other.

Carole: Except that in unitive consciousness, if one is still considering it dirty then you don't really have the unity. I mean it would seem you have to stop thinking of it as dirty and start thinking of it as ethereal in order to have the unity.

Maslow: No, that's not the way to say it. You have to stop thinking of it as dirty, and it must become normal or natural or taken for granted—accepted is perhaps the best technical word there. Accepted in the sense of not needing any defenses against it.[32] [*Pause*]

I remember one of the first cases I ever had as a psychologist, was a young instructor in chemistry who, after a long romance and a lot of trouble, finally managed to get married. This was during the Depression and they took their courage in their hands. They loved each other so much, got married and even raised enough money to have a honeymoon for one night. They went to a hotel someplace, in a nice place. Then the guy showed up the next day for psychotherapy.

He had been absolutely impotent on his marriage night. Why?

It turned out as we got free associating that this was his first intimacy with his sweetheart. She took her shoes off and he saw a hole in her stocking and became impotent. Now you can figure what kind of visions he would have had of femaleness and so on. He couldn't take that much; what would happen, for instance, if she urinated in front of him? He would have collapsed altogether. [*General laughter*]

This was a very intelligent man and it worked very nicely and they lived happily ever after. Simply talking about this sex business and the Madonna-prostitute thing made him very conscious of what this implied: What did he expect of his wife anyway? What did he think she was made of? Was she constructed differently inside? Did she have some different kind of plumbing of some sort? And we talked in this way and he was able to assimilate all of it. He had to get rid of this "dirty" notion; it had to be normal and accepted. A woman had to be obviously somebody who could be dirty with holes in her stockings, and more serious things, and still he would be able to love her and to see her as an adorable woman. He was able to.

John: If through the unitive consciousness the commonplace can provide the source for good experiences which combine the profane and divine, does this in any sense devaluate art? Because it is almost an assumption in our civilization that art is the only way—or perhaps religion also—that this special thing is attained, and the unitive consciousness in a sense makes art lose all value. You don't need art, in a sense, if you are possessed with the unitive consciousness.

Maslow: There's a very important point in what you say but I think you've overstated it just a little. Now that's a very important thing. [*Pause*]

John: I overstated purposely for exaggeration. I'm just wondering, does this follow or not?

Maslow: Well, supposing I counter-argue, as I have, that this makes art *all* important because it aestheticizes the whole of life, in principle. I mean we can't run around having raptures all the time, but in principle it's possible to see anything as beautiful—some things more easily than others, including art. You might have said that this kind of talking, this kind of thinking is also a theory of art in the technical sense; that is, there is such a thing as unitive art.

For instance, the kind I like, and the only kind I like—and I don't care for other kinds—well, perhaps you could see it. I could recommend to you an art show that I just saw, the show on Newbury St. in the Swetzoff Gallery by Kepes.[33] If you want to argue with me about it. I consider him a great artist. He's a unitive artist. It's totally non-representational and yet manages very, very well to get a kind of fusion of the B- and D- stuff—the satori in the midst of the wood-chopping, you might say. That's the way it looks to me. You try it out and see how you feel about it.

It certainly takes away the special quality from art. Just in the same way, by the way, that it takes away the special quality from religion as the carrier of all values, with Sunday being, you know— that's sort of a religious day, which means the other six days are not. As the mystic religionists would agree—that's what they wanted all the time—that life itself was sacred or could be sacred all the time, anytime. They felt very badly in general, when they were able to speak about it at all, about religion being confined to a particular building or to particular words or to a particular day or particular food or something like that, which the mystics have united in regarding as anti-religious. So, for art, yes: art as it stands now is our only carrier of beauty. Well, it shouldn't be, or it needn't be.

Ben: When you speak about all life being sacred—

Maslow: It may be, it can be.

Ben: The terms I can't quite get clear—when you speak of all life to be sacred, we would assume, I think that—

Maslow: Please. It's not all life is to be sacred—it can't be. We'd all die inside of three days if we were all in this perpetual ecstasy.

Ben: No, I didn't mean the ecstasy. I meant the underlying idea of it. This implies that a great number of people have this ability to see life as sacred. But I can't quite take the terms in, because if those people did have this characteristic of being able to see things that way, then the way we look at the problem would be so changed that we wouldn't even know whether the unity of consciousness could be spoken about in the same terms. This is what sort of bothers me—talking about anything which is utopian.

Maslow: See, this is utopian only in a certain sense. If I now put on my robe as the scientific reporter rather than the preacher, almost, then I would report to you that this unitive consciousness is characteristic of people that I call self-actualizing. It's just simply one of the characteristics that you would describe. And presumably if you picked subjects in the same selective way, then you would find the same thing—or anybody would. So that this is not something that I'm propounding because I like it. You have to accept the fact that it exists, that this is way it is. Now, it's not only in this group of people which can be selected in our society in the West in this particular way, which I've described, but also there have been other people who have been described in such a way. So, it is just so; it just *is* like that.

Ben: Among individuals I can understand it very simply, but what I'm trying to understand is what happens if we put this in sort of a wide-range perspective. Supposing the entire population of the country, not just self-actualizing people, were able to achieve unitive consciousness in the terms in which we would speak about it? I'm not a philosopher and I don't know how this works out, but I just have the feeling that our orientation would be so shifted that, you know, it's like seeing around a corner now.

Maslow: Yeah.

Ben: We really can't predict accurately, or we have to compensate in some way which is not being done at the moment. I don't know if you could elucidate that a little further.[34]

Maslow: If you say it that way, I'd have to agree with you. Well, the truth is, we don't know what would happen. Many people have the feeling that some great revolution of some sort may be dangerous—possibly dangerous, possibly not so desirable—we don't know. **Huxley** tried it in his novel *Island*—not a very good job but, I mean, it was an effort, it was a try. I've tried making cautions against it in this chapter of mine that I've asked you to read, "Some Dangers of Being-Cognition" in *Toward a Psychology of Being*. I asked you to read this chapter and try to recognize some of the possible dangers which exist.[35]

Well, it's best to say we just don't know. Isn't this possibly dangerous? Should you be skeptical? Yes, I think it's perfectly fair to be. And I think that it's obviously called for—about being very cautious about these things, just in the same way that we are about the psychedelic drugs, for instance. Just take it easy, go little by little.

I think I'll try to finish this, as much of this as we can. [*Pause*] About this sexual thing—I'll recommend you to the Kirkendall book, as I have. Also, I don't know if I mentioned my own paper[36] on this, which is good for this purpose also, of showing the confusion between sex and dominance. That is, showing the way in which the sexual act can become a dominance act and the way in which sexuality can use dominance as a channel, and vice versa—that they can get all mixed up.

You can say, from the Freudian point of view, that practically every woman who comes into therapy in this society is a castrating woman and has penis envy. In one or another sense and at one or another level, there's some resentment of men and some treating of men's lovemaking as if it were an attempt at domination. So, women protecting their personhood and protecting the self and protecting their freedom and so on are apt to fight against being swallowed up by men. On the other hand, one way in which this is done is to resent men and try to cut them down in various ways that the Freudians would call the castration techniques—to belittle them, to humiliate them, to make fun of them—as so many wives do.

Then, on the male side, there would be, again rather characteristically, the confusion of sex with dominance, the confusion of the male thinking of himself secretly, unconsciously, as a dominator and of the sexual act as a kind of submission to him. He would think in various ways that go along with this, which I've already described; let's say, the penis as a murderous instrument, as dangerous, as destroying and so on.

A good outcome in psychotherapy is to transcend this and to

separate sex and dominance. I have described in this paper the case of a male relating to his male boss as if it were a homosexual relationship, as if every time his boss gave him an order that he was raping him, or assaulting him sexually. That's a very common kind of a dream that men will have, and I've collected a lot of them in this paper. This is the way in which the male with castration anxieties—which includes practically all young males in this culture, in our society—will transform into a Freudian dream some slight insult, perhaps by another man, or by a woman for that matter, and make it into a kind of visual presentation, the way we do in a dream, of an assault of some sort, frequently of a rectal penetration. It's a common dream.

Well, part of it, as one of the psychoanalysts said, is to teach, to try to separate out. The penis is a penis; it's not a murderous instrument. It doesn't kill or destroy. Or in the case of the men with these rectal fantasies or anal fantasies and so on: the anus, the rectum, is for defecation purposes, not for making love or for showing who's boss or anything of the sort. It's to separate out, to "uncompound," you might say. My simple formula here is to separate the sex from the dominance—that's the easy way of putting it.[37]

If you become conscious of the dirty tendencies in yourself, which we all have I think, then it's possible for you to de-dirty, to de-contaminate it and de-toxify it and finally to become accepting, to have it become natural, normal, as you become conscious of it. This is simple insight therapy. This is the model that psychoanalysis proceeds on. Here too, I would like you to become aware, as an exercise, of your own tendencies to contaminate sex and dominance, and to make the sexual act into a kind of ceremony or ritual in which one person is destroying another or dominating another or hurting another.

For both males and females, there is the tendency to depersonalize the woman. There's so much slang, for instance, that makes her into only a sexual object; she's not a person. There are different kinds. Some of it is very obscene, where the women are called by some slang synonym for the vagina, or for a sexual object—or a skirt. Now to talk about a woman as a skirt is a depersonalizing of the woman. One skirt's equal to any other skirt. It takes away individuality and selfhood and personhood and personality and the like. That would be good to become conscious of, if you hope to overcome it.

Now, one point here. You say this is obviously bad for her—talking about this depersonalizing by the slang, by these exploitative phrasings. But in a more subtle way it's also very bad for him in the sense that every exploiter is damaged by his being an exploiter, so that you'll find in our young men in psychoanalysis that they feel guilty about this. For instance, any man who has this notion of the sexual act and of lovemaking in general—as if he were somehow taking advantage of a poor, defenseless, helpless woman who's afraid of him and upon whom he forces his attentions—if he then goes ahead and has sexual intercourse with his wife, an inevitable consequence is guilt and a feeling of "Well, I'm a dirty person. I couldn't control myself. I'm not nice, I've done harm to my wife." So that even the exploiter is harmed here. The possibility of friendship across such lines is practically impossible.

Now, to sum this up. It means that there are horrors—pragmatically bad consequences—in seeing the woman only in the B-way; that is, only as the Madonna. And there are pragmatically bad consequences in seeing her only in the D-way—only as an object to be used sexually and not good for anything else. And clearly the psychologically healthy goal is for these to be combined, or to alternate, or to be fused in some way.

Now, seeing the man in a B-way means seeing him also in his ultimate, ideal possibilities. I'm quoting here the best stuff I know on this—two books by Marion Milner[38] that I've recommended.[39] She had to make her peace in her self-analysis with her ambivalences toward the male and the equivalent of the incest barriers—you know, the male as the father and as the powerful god and so on. I think her writing on the subject is the best that I've seen.

Seeing a man in the B-way means seeing him also in his ultimate, ideal possibilities—as in Milner's case—as God the Father, as all powerful, as the one who created the world and who rules the world of things—the world outside, the world of nature—and who changes it and masters it and conquers it.

Also, at this deep level, Milner, and many other women as well, surely, will identify the noble man, the B-man, as the spirit of rationality. Now this—the spirit of intelligence, and so on—also tends to come out in deep analysis. It's a common reaction: the spirit of intelligence, of probing, of exploring in mathematics and science and the like. The male as a father image at this level—semiconscious, unconscious, maybe conscious to some extent—is strong and capable, fearless, noble, clean. Not small; that is, not trivial. A protector of the weak and the innocent, of children and orphans; the hunter and the bringer of food. [*Some giggles from the class*]

These are—remember, I'm not playing games here—the reported fantasies, both from the Freudian and Jungian type of probe. Jung would call these the archetypes of the man as the hunter, as the spirit of rationality, or the woman as the ever-flowing breast. He can also be seen archaically as the master and the conqueror of nature—the engineer, the carpenter, the builder—which the woman is generally not. She rarely fantasizes herself in this way; very few women even at a deep, deep level find any desire to build bridges, for instance.[40] It is quite probable that women, when they get into the eternal mood or into the B-attitude or the unitive attitude, must see men in this ideal way, even if they can't see their own particular man in this way.

The very fact that a woman is dissatisfied with her own man may also be an indication that she has some other model or ideal in mind to which he doesn't measure up. I think that an investigation would show this idea—as Milner expressed it, or as John Rosen[41] finds it in his direct analysis of schizophrenics. There's very, very good stuff there on this B- and D-realm in the book by John Rosen, *Direct Analysis*. Clearly any woman who could not see her man or some man, anyhow, in this way, could not use men well. She would have to disrespect them. She might need a man in a D-world—life insurance policies and so on—but deep down she would be contemptuous of him because he didn't measure up to the B-realm.

In any industrialized society or in any colonial society or in any exploited minority, I'm afraid this is very, very widespread. For instance, Negroes are now becoming quite conscious of this. They are taken for granted, but the Negro woman is less destroyed by exploitation than the Negro man, who must be admired by his children—especially his son—and he has to be admired by his wife a little bit or else she simply can't live with him in any but a second-class way. So that the question is of dignity, and in a deep sense, the pressure is that the Negro man wants to be a man and his woman wants him to be this kind of B-male, B-man. Someone she can look up to, someone who's dignified, someone who doesn't get shoved off the sidewalk into the street and so on.

The D-man in the world of trivialities and the world of striving and the world of exploitation and so on may not be able to induce the B-attitude in his woman, which again is, unfortunately, very common. But this seems to be a necessity if she is to be able to love a man fully. At this deep level, it is necessary for her to be able even to adore a man—it has some element of a very deep level of worship—to look up to him as once she looked up to her father. It has something of that same feeling. To be able to lean on him, to be able to trust him, to feel him to be reliable. To feel him to be strong enough also—this I imagine must come close to your consciousness—so that she can feel precious and delicate and dainty and small, protected, so that she can trustfully snuggle down on his lap and let him take care of her. You get such fantasies easily enough close to consciousness, I think. My guess is that every woman in this room will recognize sometime how nice it is to not feel six feet tall. It's kind of rough for a very tall woman, for instance. She finds it very hard to feel dainty, and to feel precious in this sense of being something that the man will feel very protective of and awed by, something very, very beautiful. Another thing too is this feeling of being Oedipal—but maybe I better not go into it . . .[42] [*Pause and a few laughs from the group*]

Now this is especially so when she's pregnant—you get the dreams of the pregnant woman, for instance, as described by Therese Benedek[43] in *The Psycho-sexual Life of the Woman*. She is a psychoanalyst working with a histologist, and they found that in the course of the menstrual cycle the women's psyche changes, at the unconscious level. In the progesterone phase, women tend to have such dreams—very passive, very narcissistic. They want to feel beautiful; they don't want to do anything; they want somebody else to do it for them. They will be fed, for instance, rather than feeding themselves in these progesterone dreams or pregnancy dreams. Whereas in the estrogen phase, the estrogen part of the cycle, the non-pregnant—but rather, you might say, actively sexual, even predatory phase—the dreams are extremely different. She's quite an active woman who rolls up her sleeves and goes out hunting for someone, and they feel quite different from this other pregnancy fantasy of wanting to be taken care of, wanting to be admired and loved, wanting to be passive. [*Pause*]

Well, surrendering gets especially complicated here. It's quite possible that full sexual happiness for a woman is impossible without surrendering. *Maybe*. There's a lot of speculating by psychoanalysts. The Freudians generally believe this, and the classic book here is *The Psychology of Women* by Helene Deutsch.[44] And most other psychologists—Horney, Fromm and so on—would simply want to rephrase this, to simply say it in another way. They don't want to make it instinctual, they want to make it something else, and also they'll pick nicer words which are less insulting to the woman than "normal masochism," "normal narcissism" and the like. But I think they and the depth psychologists will all agree.

Now if the woman can have toward men only a D-attitude, then the woman has a hopeless future as far as fullest happiness is concerned. And the women who do have such an attitude are in fact not very happy; they simply can't make good marriages. She can have only a half-life, something like the men who can see women in only the D-way. She can have no relationship with a man except to exploit him, to use him, and this will make for the expected consequences of unconscious enmity and hatred, hostility and so on. If the woman can see her man only as a B-man, then she also cannot sleep with him, or at least not be able to enjoy him, because this would be like sleeping with her own father or with a god. He must be sufficiently down-to-earth so that she isn't too awed by him. He must be homey, so to speak. He must be part of the actual world and not some ethereal and angelic figure who will never have an erection, for instance. An erection has to go with the conception of the male.

Now, it sounds funny, but it's not if you think of—well, the Schweitzer[45] image, for instance. It's a little hard for women to think of Albert Schweitzer having an erection.

[*Pause*] I don't know my own mouth. [*General laughter*]

Let's assume of men in general that the Schweitzer type, the adored persons, the ones who are seen almost as holy figures—and some who *have* been, the saints, for instance, or the priests, closer to home; the ones who have become celibate by choice—these men must also be seen as sexual animals who have renounced sex, or who are trying to control it. They cannot be seen as sexless, for they have all the same machinery that any other man has, and it responds in about the same way.

Now for the woman who tends to see the male in this Albert Schweitzer or Abraham Lincoln way, in this godlike way, then play—sexual play or any other kind of play—would be rather difficult. Now she may make a good arrangement with a male, but on a very profound level she would be deprived. Another point is that inevitably she's going to castrate her son if she thinks of sex as somehow an exploitation and so on.

Characteristically such women tend to fall out of love with their husbands and fall in love with their sons, which starts a whole mess for a long time, and which has as a very common consequence the demasculinization of the son.[46] Why? Because he mustn't be sexual, because that means he's just like her husband—that old goat. And she wants to turn out somebody who fits with the unconscious fantasies. It gets very complicated, very complex. This kind of woman is apt to be horrified by any signs of ordinary masculinity in her boy. Well, since she has so much power over him, especially if he thinks she loves him very much so he can't get mad at her, then it's not good.

Paul: Have you read or seen *Who's Afraid of Virginia Woolf?*[47] by Edward Albee?[48] This couple created a son purely out of their own fantasy because of their need for one in various ways, and the husband accused the wife of having done all kinds of sexually perverted things to their son. And they're very much related to the kinds of things you've been talking about. I was intrigued when I read it but I didn't understand the significance then, but felt there was some.

Maslow: Well, I think for us, at our level, you can start doing the technical things. The best place to find the documentation for what I'm talking about is the psychoanalytic literature; that is, the case studies and case reports. If you browse through the psychoanalytic journals, you'll get this thing coming up again and again and again, and if you read enough of them you'll get some picture of the model case. If I've read God knows how many thousands of cases, then their perceptive mass forms. This is the documentation for my saying that practically all young women in our society who come into psychoanalysis—I have to specify that—do have something called penis envy or something that could be called that, or masculine protest or whatever word you want to make out of it. Then I could say, "Most wives are castrating women." That is, most wives occasionally will cut their husbands out of envy, humiliation, resentment and so on. They'll use different techniques for it, but to find a woman who openly admires her husband, you might wait thirty years to see that. If you travel around a lot, going to parties and so on, you just don't see it.

It may be that part of our cultural stereotype is that tenderness is too corny, that the woman is supposed to—well, in the same way that we have in the greeting cards. You know the greeting card stores? They're all "sick" cards. You love somebody very much—your wife, let's say, just had an operation and you're scared to death that she'd die. Maybe it was cancer. You send a card about "I'm glad you're dead, you rascal" or something like this. [*General laughter*] Do you know what I mean?—the sick cards. Just run through a greeting card store and you'll see what I mean—most of them are like that. It's a defense against any honest sentiment, against any emotion. They don't dare say, "I was scared that you might die and I'm so happy that you didn't." Did you ever see a greeting card like that?

John: Yeah.

Maslow: I haven't.

John: I used to sell them and they're there. The only trouble is they're way on the other side with the soppy, sentimental stuff. There's nothing in the middle. There are really vicious studio cards, and then there's the stuff with the little pink stuff that falls off. [*General laughter*]

Maslow: I just got interested in this since—

John: There's no middle. I don't know why.

Sarah: You have to write your own, don't you?

Maslow: Well, the whole greeting card business altogether—

John: I guess it would be unbelievable?

Maslow: Well, I went over to the antique show in Boston Saturday, trailing after my wife [*general laughter*], and I was wandering around there and I pick up a lot of these old Victorian postcards, greeting cards. They're just so unabashedly sentimental and they just . . . we couldn't do them. I just didn't realize how far we had got from this open expression of sentiment. It's impossible! We'd all blush to say such things, and then I remembered—I haven't thought to check since—in the greeting card stores it seems to me all you can see are insults which turn out to be "humorous" in quotes. I haven't seen these other things.

John: They're there; they're sold mostly to older people.

Maslow: Well, I want to get some of these. I'm curious now about it. [*Pause*]

The good man for the woman and the good woman for the man—and for herself or for himself—is a combination of the B- and D-. Now this means—see you have to start drawing consequences that these sick cards wouldn't permit—she must be able to be partly a Madonna. That whole archetype must be assumed—she must do it almost consciously. She must not be abashed to be adored, for instance, to be worshipped a little bit. She must be able to feel without blushing—like the Jungian archetype or the religious thinker or the goddess or the priestess or something of the sort.

We don't have many ceremonies of this sort. Well, baking bread, let's say, is still kind of a ceremonial thing. Or at least baking bread can be seen in the unitive way. You understand what I mean? If I could suggest it as an exercise, I would: just go and bake bread. For instance, I suggest this to the girls here, however you feel about it, because I assure you that your menfolk will enjoy it very much. The children will enjoy it. They feel somehow this is an intensification of the act of cooking and serving, which can also be a symbolic act. The baking of bread somehow has a longer history than anything else I can think of, and in many cultures it has this special character. Well, to be able to feel like the priestess in such a situation seems to be a necessity for the fullest development of womanliness, womanhood or the selfhood of a woman, or self-actualization in any female. She must be able to unabashedly, unashamedly feel like that in one respect or another.

Now, I've implied that she must be able to take the sexual act in such a way as a highly symbolic, ceremonial ritual. Let's say, like the Tantric—one sect of the Buddhists for whom the sexual act is the equivalent of the Mass. It's the holiest act that there is—the sexual act—and there are all sorts of prayers, statements and sayings and this and that and the other thing that can go along with it. I know very little about it because I simply can't trace it down. I guess it would be regarded as obscene or pornographic or something of the sort, so I have no good account of the Tantric sect. But the little I have got about it indicates that it's possible to take this as a rite, as a ceremony, as a ritual.[49]

Well, that would be one exercise. And the opposite of course for the males would be to feel again eternal, to feel themselves to be in a long line back to the cavemen and so on and so on, standing in the same line and repeating the same ceremonies and seeing things in approximately the same way. [*Pause*]

About these specific exercises or efforts to perceive, if it weren't embarrassing I would ask you to look around at each other, but try it when people are not aware that you're doing it. Would it be possible to do—as Francis Galton once did; it's a true exercise—he took a wooden figure that was supposed to be a god from an African tribe and he tried to throw himself into the framework of adoration. He reports that he finally he got the feeling somehow. Now, if we could pick somebody here—we just can't get away with this sort of thing, of course, but supposing we could—pick a male and female and just try to look at them in this way. Try to look at the woman as a goddess, as a priestess, as holy, as the eternal mother, try to see through to the miracle of the uterus, for instance—

[*TAPE CHANGE*]

—and so on. Protectiveness and the like. It's possible to do one exercise that I've tried to do for myself—or I guess I stumbled across it. Thinking of the pathos, in Mexico particularly, of a nice man in an industrial society with all the same impulses that the Neanderthal man had and with about the same id. The same unconscious, as nearly as we can make out; the unconscious has been untouched by history, it looks like. Here is this man. He loved this woman. He wanted to have children. And then, out of this perfectly beautiful impulse, he winds up sitting behind a thing in the bank all day long. He's punching up the totals on the checks. Five, six hours a day, just sitting at that thing. There's a check, punch it into the machine, there's another check— and he's been doing that for sixty years maybe. It's a sad thing. You might say that he was sucked into this. If he had no sense of responsibility, if he didn't have love for a woman, if he didn't want children and if he weren't male in the sense of enjoying responsibility and wanting to protect and to care for and defend and so on. He can be seen not as a ludicrous figure or as the Thoreau kind of quiet desperation; you can see him as a hero if you want, simply because he is so quietly accepting all of this business for the sake of his children. He can be seen in that way, and as it happens this is partly the truer way—*partly*, because some of it's just plain habit. But partly this is the truth at the unconscious level. He is a hero. In *fact*. I'm not saying, "Let's make believe," but from the point of view of all the things that he could give up. Especially in Mexico, where most males simply desert their families—that's the standard thing to do.[50] If you get a guy who hasn't deserted his family and he sits there behind a thing in the bank there and spends a whole damn lifetime doing this miserable work in order to take care of the kids who he fathered—takes responsibility—I'd say this can factually be called something "heroic"—if you don't like that word, you can call it "responsible." It can be seen in capital letters, you might say—symbolically. Now it's hard—it's much easier to see some guy on a horse as the hero—but at least symbolically it's the same thing. In principle it's the same thing.

Carole: I agree with you for our culture. I just wonder, though, can this be true for cross-cultures? In Mexico, you say, all the other males are deserting their families. Is it then that he's really acting as a male?

Maslow: This is a combination. This guy whom I talked about, I don't know. I just saw him there all the time when I came to the bank and I couldn't help thinking, "My God, if I had to sit there until I died, punching totals into a calculating machine and adding them up!" Now, I'm thinking of someone else whom I did know very well and who did deliberately, voluntarily—he was a fine man and took on these burdens and responsibilities.

Carole: My question is whether it's also part of what a man's supposed to do and what a female is supposed to do, determined by the culture that one lives in, and if the culture has a different view of what a man's expected to do and what a female's expected to do, then would you say if people don't do that are they being male?

Maslow: Well, I've just given you an example—a true example. No culture is absolutely univocal about everything. Let's say, four men out of five desert their families below the middle-class level.

Carole: Is it more universal?

Maslow: Well, it's a force, a cultural force. But overcoming the force makes one more of a hero.

Carole: The maleness, though, is universal?

Maslow: It can, yes, it can be seen as universal. There's no culture without an enduring family. Remember that: no viable culture. Maybe in the past, but no culture which exists today, which is known to the ethnologists, doesn't have a family structure.

Doug: Isn't responsibility an entirely arbitrary criteria for the definition of a hero, with the consideration of the bank teller being a hero?

Maslow: Yes, I wouldn't want to be too serious about that. That's certainly one part of it. Let me take it simply as symbolic, as one aspect.

No, I'd say, *sine qua non*. In our culture certainly and in most of the cultures I know, the male who doesn't take responsibility is not a man—he's not mature, he's not grown up. The man who gets paralyzed, for instance, is afraid of getting married because he has to take care of his wife, to get a job. Or the one who collapses when his wife gets pregnant, thrown into fear altogether instead of trusting his own brawn, his own shoulders and also liking it, too, rather enjoying being the captain of the ship—that would be one; there must be more.

Well, let's see if I can find any other exercises in our last three minutes here for this time before I leave it. [*Pause*]

Oh, the nursing—the nurse can be seen also as an archetype, and every woman ought to be able to be a nurse because it's demanded of her. That's the way men want her to be in the archetypal sense, just as she ought to be able to be a mother—I mean, motherly. For instance, Freud pointed out an awfully long time ago—it's one thing we learn fast—a woman who can't be motherly cannot make a good wife. And he's not talking about babies, infants, that is. He's talking about husbands. Well, this nursing, especially the wounded solider kind of thing. A woman setting out dinner on the table for her family can be seen as a ceremony.

If you want to do it in the Freudian way, they talk a lot about giving the breast. Well, you can see it that way, certainly giving the breast to the infant is obviously as basic as you can get in this sense— which is one reason, by the way, for breastfeeding that nobody talks about. The transcendent value or the semi-religious value of breast-feeding rather than bottle-feeding. This is seen by Freudians as a kind of paradigm, as a kind of model for a lot of other activities, and it takes it back to its symbolic precursors, you might say.

So also with this kind of sensitizing, should it become possible for us to see the man coming home with his paycheck—which he may have got from punching this calculator—as acting out an ancient ritual of bringing home a food animal he has killed in a hunt and which he tosses down with a lordly air for his wife and children and dependents while they look on with admiration because they can't do it and he can. This is the sort of thing you'll get in your pre-literate cultures quite openly, obviously. Now, it is certainly true that it is harder to see the B-man in this aspect of hunter and provider in the man who's actually a bookkeeper in an office with three thousand other bookkeepers. Yet the fact remains that he can be seen so, and should be, in some cases at least. [*Pause while Maslow flips through the pages of his notes*]

And then I have a suggestion about the re-evaluation of menstruation, for instance, as an exercise which we don't have time for but which I think is obvious enough. This can be seen as endocrinologists see it—they generally get awed by the whole mechanism as a very remarkable thing, very poetic, you might say. Well, their standard joke they'll put in a B-way: menstruation is the weeping of a disappointed uterus. This is the standard joke and they mean—well, the obvious. Try seeing it from that point of view and you can play games of a kind that should again widen your perception.

And I think I'll make this the last one—I'm speaking here about a cartoon which I hunted for and couldn't find but I remember—James Thurber's cartoon, which I may have mentioned. There is no caption underneath it, but it is simply a picture of a woman who's walking in one direction with four children strung out behind her. And then she passes, going the other way, a dog mother with four little puppies behind her, going on down, and the two females turn around and look at each other in such an understanding way. [*General laughter*] And this again puts them both in the same long evolutionary line, and it's a very poignant, very touching thing. Well, I'll let it go at that. Let's take about ten minutes off.

[Break]

Note: The following are snatches of a conversation picked up by the tape recorder that was left on during the break. It becomes indistinguishable from the background noise as students return from the break.

Maslow: I'd like to make a collection of these cards. I hate to spend money on them, so if any of you get sent these cards—you know the ones which are either directly sentimental or the ones which are counter-sentimental, anti-sentimental—instead of throwing them away I'd appreciate them. I have a lot of Victorian postcards. That's what I bought in San Francisco, and I'd like to pick up some of those sick cards too.

Carole: Sometimes those—what you call sick cards—they're not too awful. They're really funny because they're not true. I mean, if you are sending it to someone who really does understand, it's the same as a nice one; you're saying how you feel.

Maslow: The question is, is this the only way of expressing this? When I see the greeting cards in the store, all of them are kind of nasty—witty, sometimes very funny, but only in this hostile wit, you might say, this ambivalent wit. The truth is we are ambivalent much of the time, but shouldn't be all the time. Sometimes we want to say, you know, "Happy Birthday! I hope you have an awful lot more of them."

Carole: But personally, for myself, I prefer to get one that's witty . . .

Maslow: Well, it depends on . . . In our family we never buy a card of any kind. If we want to send something, we make it. I'd say that is a social phenomenon. The fact that up to 1960 they were practically all of the other kind . . .

DECEMBER 9, 1963

Laboratory for Self-Knowledge

Maslow: I've just been told that the Horney book has arrived at the bookstore. We'll have to talk about that. Would you remind me to make that announcement again next time we meet, since several people have gone already?[1] I'm not sure how much time we'll be able to spend with those books, so I may simply ask you to read them and then write about them for the final examination, whether we have discussion of them or not.

Doug: Is this *Self-Analysis*?

Maslow: This is *Self-Analysis* by Horney, and the Fromm book is *The Forgotten Language*. I doubt that I'll make any other assignments, especially since I'm recommending these two books so strongly, that you read them very intensively, very carefully. If I do assign anything else, it will be something short or small, and it would have to be especially good to warrant it. [*Pause*]

Well, I would like to be more active this time in view of the fact that we only have three of these hours left. I want to try out some of these experiments, and one of them I'd like you to use the time for is just what we've been talking about in this meeting and the meeting before. I would like you to respond to these suggestions I gave. What clicks? What did it do? Did it touch off anything? Now, I'm going to read a few more exercises that I have here, just a few, and then I want to leave it to you entirely, to your responses to this kind of thing. I hope you can be honest, forthright. We may take these up again more carefully, but for now, just to set the tone, these are the unitive exercises. I'll repeat these next time, perhaps, for your notes, because half the people aren't here. Now, just for atmosphere, and just to serve as stimulus:

> Imagine a person in the room here as a hero, as a saint, having saintly qualities—look for them, they're there. Or let's say as a big shot, a United States senator. Now, let's do it. Well, the truth is that the Senate will poke at people like you, for-the-love-of-Pete. There may in fact be somebody here who, if he likes politics well enough, might be a senator. It's an exercise; you can try it to see that it's a possibility, to see it existing now as a possibility for the future.

> Or as a famous intellectual, which certainly some of you will become. Let's say a famous philosopher.

> Or as a murderer, since everybody here is potentially a murderer. Try to see that if you can, the possibility of it—everybody has the impulse. I think you could say that our controls are strong enough so that it's very, very unlikely, but the impulse is what I'm talking about—that's universal.

> Or try to see someone in this room—across the sex lines now—as your lover.

Clara: Couldn't we get someone from out in the halls? [*General laughter*]

Maslow [*continues without pause*]:

> Or as a parent, as some of you actually are. But try to see the males as fathers and the females as mothers.

> Imagine this person to be your employee or boss.

It's difficult, but this is all real possibility, of course: think of some person here—use me as a target if you like—as dying of cancer. God knows maybe I am, it's possible. Imagine that we are all going to die in two, three, or four months. We're doomed. And since it's possible, it's also possible to look at another person in that way as potentially dying.

Well, another exercise here—this is also useful—imagine being locked in a jail cell with this person forever; such things have happened.

Or this desert island fantasy: pick someone to be on a desert island with you forever.

See someone here as your psychoanalyst; that is, someone to whom you would confess and someone before whom you would expose yourself.

Imagine the whole roomful of people here naked; this is a nudist camp. Can you see people in a different way in any sense?

If we have the time for it, to go around the table, in what respect can you see the greatness of each person?

Those are some I've written down, I'd like you to take off from there.

[*Pause*]

Paul [*arriving late*]: What are we supposed to do this hour?

Maslow [*to Paul*]: I had hoped—you came in a little late—I had hoped to have you use the hour with my discussions of today and last week as a stimulus, that is, to narrow down the responses. I'd like you to think about it, get into the mood for a little while and looking about, see if you can experience this, if you can see people in a different way. What occurs to you? Did anything that I said or any example that I said make anything click in your own experience already? What's wrong with it? Is it not possible? This is what I would like to use as your stimulus and then to go in that direction. Give yourselves a couple of minutes to think it over.

[*Silence for approximately forty-five seconds*]

Maslow: Is it difficult to talk about each other in this way?

Sarah: It's just so hard to do it just by looking at someone. You have to really know a lot about them. And although we know something about them, we don't know enough to make it specific, you know, or to even have feeling about them.

Maslow: Any woman has a uterus—make it that specific. You x-ray on through to the meaning of that.

Carole: I found that just in growing up, to an extent we do this all the time. You know, whenever you talk to a girl, you talk in a different way from when you talk to a boy. There is no question that one is aware so some extent of all these potentials that you speak of. But I have the feeling that when we do it here—which is very unnatural, I think—that you are offering yourself up to an intimate situation. Certainly when you talk about people being undressed it's very intimate, and we must have barriers to these things so we can live in society. I have a girlfriend who's in the theatre and she was explaining to me one of the problems in playing the promiscuous relationship in the theatre, that when you play a love scene with a male, he *is* a male; it's hard to forget, then, because you must open yourself up to the audience you see. And I think here when you ask us to do that, you're asking us to some extent to break some of society's established beliefs.

Maslow: That's what I just realized as I started meditating myself. [*General laughter*] Some I think we can duck, but there are some that are safe for us without getting too embarrassed. For one thing, what is the difference in our feelings towards a little girl and a little boy? Certainly we get them. I'm sure I have—I know I have. They somehow have different potentialities. I see them in different ways and I respond to them in different ways too.

Then, also the question that I would ask, which is personal and which needn't be embarrassing? For the girls: when do you feel the most feminine—when do you feel most like a woman—and when do you feel least feminine—least like a woman? For the males, the same thing: when do you feel the most masculine—when do you feel most manly—and when do you feel least masculine—when has this been taken away from you? I think we can use these—here we're dealing with universals again.[2]

Sharon: Why are you asking us to do this in the first place?

Maslow: To see if it is possible by words, by lectures and so on, to teach, to encourage, to enlarge this unitive consciousness, this fusion of B-cognition with D-cognition. That's the point.

Melissa: I just was thinking in terms of the analyst or the confessor. Is there anyone here, to whom in a one-to-one relationship I would say something of a confessional nature? And right away I ran into the problem of defense mechanisms. People all through our third hour are saying things, you know, that are biased, or they show their own defenses or the way they work. As I went around, you know, certain things about each person popped into my head, and just knowing this made it very difficult. All my defenses rose up, saying, "No, I'm not going to be judged by *that*." So there's a real difficulty right there.

Maslow: May I respond to that? The truth is that some people here are going to be psychotherapists. They are going to listen. Can you see this as a potentiality? I can. I think I can pick out let's say the half of the people in this class who would make good psychoanalysts, better than the other half. Maybe that's a way of saying it, maybe that will help you.

What I'm asking you to do is to be conscious of potentialities, let's say, in the same way that—well, most of you don't have children and therefore seeing you as mothers and fathers is a witnessing of your potentialities. Normally we take each other too much at face value for this moment and not enough as what we might become. Now it would be difficult to see you as a grandmother, but it's possible. Try to imagine what would you look like, for instance, at the age of seventy. Take that particular face and see wrinkles and add some grey hairs and this and that and the other thing—what would it look like?

Well, maybe I can turn it a little bit that way as looking at the potentialities, that's part of it. I guess I was thinking of each of us as a symbol. For me I think it's easy—you must be able to see me as the professor in a general sense and certainly standing in the long line of other professors and intellectuals and so on and so on, and I don't suppose I have to put my cap and gown on for that to happen. That might encourage it, so that suddenly you might be clicked into gear, even if we were intimate, friendly, if we knew each other well and so on. It's happened to me, I know when I see someone in a ceremonial situation, suddenly he's no longer my friend exactly—he's a symbol. You know what I mean there? [*Pause*] With me it should be easy— use me as a spirit of intellect or something of this sort.

John: I can understand how you can look at people and visualize them being either mothers or fathers, because they all really have this potentiality. But how do you go about looking at us and deciding which half are likely to become psychotherapists and which half are not? It seems to me that's something else again.

Maslow: Well, I don't want to become too personal because that gets invidious, but it's part of my job to see the possibilities for you, for instance. It is almost that I'm paid to see you as of ten years hence, twenty years hence, thirty years hence, and see what you can become and what your potentialities are. We give advice all the time, don't we? You would say to the person, "You should go to graduate school in psychology." For instance, if he said, "I want to become a dentist," you'd say "No!" Now, what am I responding to there but potentialities, the future, *witnessed* things in you?

John: It would be fun!

Maslow: We'll try it alone sometime. [*General laughter*] I think I can see things in you that you can't see for yourself. It's been safe enough. For instance, I can ask a standard question. Let me say it this way: I know, without knowing any better, that you *do* have, along with other fantasies you may have repressed—I might ask the question: what are your fantasies of greatness which you hide like mad from everybody and all the world? I know they're there, and I can make guesses in terms of the skills that I can see, intelligence and so on. I doubt that your great fantasy is to be a great baseball player—it doesn't go with the I.Q.—so you can start narrowing it down a little bit. If I knew you better I might start making guesses about these fantasies of greatness and also the fears of failure, because everyone here has that too. Or what don't you like about yourself? That too is a good way of judging others. In general, what you don't like about someone else, it's safe to say he doesn't like in himself either. He may be defending against it. He may not be fully conscious of it. He may be hiding it. He may build up all sorts of elaborations, reaction formations and so on. But in general he perceives it too. Well, that's penetrating through the defenses and responding to potential.

[Silence for approximately fifteen seconds]

Sharon: Can I give some more defenses? I think the ones Melissa brought up were very good. I find for my own self, the other thing which makes this difficult is that this is exactly the kind of thing that I find I try not to do. It has brought disastrous results. That is, trying to react, to form a one-to-one relationship on the basis of potential, often brings very disastrous results. Especially if you start judging people as a result of your own fantasy of their potential. This also sometimes brings very unfortunate results. So I have all kinds of reasons why not to do this.[3]

Maslow: Now what are the reasons to *do* it? While there may be harms, what are the advantages? I've made a very challenging statement: if you cannot do this to some extent, you are crippled forever, for the rest of your life. If you want to make it an extreme, read Kurt Goldstein on "the reduction to the concrete," and read in my book—I have a good, hot passage there someplace paralleling Goldstein on what I call "reduction to the abstract." That is, the inability to be concrete at all.[4] Your job is to be *both,* or else you're crippled, you're sick; you've lost something just as surely as if somebody had cut a leg off. As a matter of fact, cutting your leg off is a smaller loss.

Now that's perfectly true that we know about impulses and we know about defenses and the like. What I'm suggesting is treading out on thin ice, but you've got to do it. Now, look within yourselves. If you can't do it, you're an intellectualizer—that means someone who is reduced to the abstract. That means he can't get concrete enough. It means you're too generalizing, too abstracting, not able to see the particular person for the generalities—as in the standard story of the Victorian lady by one of the Victorian writers, Dickens[5] maybe. There are lots of people like this in Dickens. The woman who went in to see the play and wept so copiously, and showed her tender heart at the poor suffering people on the stage and came out to find her coachmen frozen. She had ordered them to sit in the snow all night. That kind of thing. I mean, I'm really talking about being a fake. [*Pause*]

Alright, are you going to try, let's say, this thing? It's about the least embarrassing thing I can think of here is to talk about these last two things I suggested. Can you feel, or pin down, the differences in your reactions to little boys and little girls, where you clearly talk about potential; or this other one about your own feelings of masculinity, femininity, high or low.

[*Silence for approximately thirty seconds*]

Melissa: Well, we all like to see children, and we all like to approach children, but since little boys and little girls have different potentialities—masculine and feminine potentialities—I think in little girls we like to look for feminine potentialities like playing with a doll or making bread in a toy oven instead of throwing a baseball or demanding a choo-choo train. And after a point I don't think we like to see little boys with dolls as much as we'd like to see them with a teddy, to feel like daddy or something like that. I think our whole approach to little boys is putting them in the framework of what they're going to be, or what they *have* to be. You know, as they grow up.

Melody: I think sometimes we react to children with ambivalent feelings based upon our own ambivalent feeling as to what should be expected. For example, I'm thinking of a man—most women will look at men as the people who do the least bit of crying in our lives.

And it's always a sign of de-masculinity if a man cries too much. But then again, most people realize that it's a very important thing for a man to do. I would say in a class like this, we find that expressing ourselves would be much better than holding it in. And somehow or other I feel that this conflict, as to knowing where the limits are set for a man, would cause him to have ambivalent feelings were he to see a little boy of ten years old cry because somebody took his bat. Instead of fighting, say the child ran to his mother crying or the child just sat there in tears. I don't know what the reaction is to this. Anybody else?

Paul: I have a reaction and I hope you won't stop me too quickly if I appear to be intellectualizing. [*General laughter*] My reaction is one which is *felt*, in spite of the fact that I have developed some conclusions as a result of the feelings themselves. I have the feeling that any show of affection between men is somehow thought of as having negative connotations in our society itself. Here I'm generalizing and yet I'm speaking of a very specific feeling which takes place within *me*. I feel a tremendous sense of gratification, perhaps the feeling that I'm loved for what I am, the feeling that I have a very specific identity—however you want to put it—when I engage occasionally, after an absence from home for a long period of time, in a very warm embrace with my father. And yet I'm well aware that this kind of action, this kind of physical show of affection, is very much frowned upon in our society in general. It's not openly engaged in, and when it is, it's done so with a sense of hesitation.

I think possibly the very regard for homosexuality in our society, or fear of it, has a great deal to do with our reactions, and I think this even carries over to crying, to showing any kinds of tendencies which in any way are considered effeminate. I have continued, and my family continues, in spite of the fact that I've grown up at this point—I still kiss my father regularly and my whole family has made what I realize is a conscious attempt to maintain this physical rapport and affection because of the emotional value which underlies it. It's very meaningful to me, and the feelings which take place inside me as a result of the sheer symbolic value of a display of physical affection are very significant. I think, therefore, the negative reactions against these things which I see all around me—the great hesitancy for men to be effeminate, and the word effeminate is a very un-carefully defined word—

Maslow: Is this what you're driving at?

Paul: This fear is so strong that I think we've become sick, in a sense. We've become inhibited to ourselves in a way in which we're cheating ourselves of something which could be very precious in our lives. This is just my general reaction to it on the basis of experience itself. I resent the fact that—I have a feeling that I want to shout out at the world sometimes that if they'd just let themselves go a little bit and overcome these fears so that people can really be with themselves and with one another what they really *want* to be, rather than simply accepting the mold into which society has placed them, with all of its restrictions against genuine communication between two people.

The word "love" itself is one which is rarely used between two men. The idea that one man can love another in a genuine sense of love—as it's generally used to describe the emotional relationship which takes place between a man and a woman—it's practically unthought of today. It's what is called "close friendship," and probably the only way in which we have accepted the usage of the word "love" towards a man from another man is love for one's father or love for one's brother. But if I were to say, "I love you," and mean specifically *you* now [*gesturing to another male student*], as a result of the fact that I have established a close friendship with you, this sounds corny. It sounds trite. I only picked you as a specific example only to avoid generalizing, not because there's any specific relationship which has taken place. I could point to any one of you and make this same statement, but the very ability to be able to say to a person, or to hear that statement, "I love you," makes the whole sense of respect and ability to appreciate one another in a friendship a very different thing. I think it's unfortunate that we're so inhibited in this sense.

[*Silence for approximately ten seconds*]

Ben [*talking rather hesitantly*]**:** Maybe it's sort of like the . . . what we were talking about before about drugs and sex, not getting too close . . . You don't find that too often, just as you said, but they have another name for it. It's not a "thing between men that you don't find between women." Now I don't know whether the "don't find between women" part holds, but this is called "love." You're quite right about that as far as I'm concerned. I've seen it time and time again. In other words, there are friends whom occasionally I would feel quite correct in "loving." In saying, "I love you." I wouldn't find it difficult but it might, somehow, abstract the poetic quality out of it. It's like—the only thing I can think of, the only corollary I can make—is women's underwear. At the turn of the century they had all these petticoats and corsets and stuff, and now we have this obscene *New York Times Sunday Magazine* with these brassiere advertisements facing the White House on the next page. [*General laughter*] It takes something away and it's only *that* quality—I can't put it in any other terms—just that describing all the hooks and the garters and stuff.

Paul: You know what I'm talking about isn't even going so far as to have to express this. The sheer act of thinking in those terms, which doesn't destroy the poetic quality, because you define it as you wish—but the sheer act of thinking in these terms makes your whole potential in the relationship on a much higher plane. Your whole ability to appreciate it.

Ben: No, I don't think so.

Paul: If you're completely inhibited to the point that you're unable to admit the possibility of it, that it *is* possible for you to love a male.

Ben: Do you know people who have loved and had not known they were able to?

Paul: Sure, but this experience isn't quite the same if they have not been able to recognize this.

Ben: I didn't say it wasn't different. I said it wasn't anything less.

Maslow: There are three words for love in Greek.[6] There are three kinds of love and we have, I notice here, just been using that one word for whole sets of connotations that we use. I wonder, does anybody know Spanish well enough? The Latin Americans who embrace each other when they greet have a word for it—"abrazo." Do they have different words for love, does anybody know? Different kinds of "love" words? The Greeks talked about *philia*. If we had some way of saying the love between men like "agapian" love, I think we could accept it very easily, without any trouble.

Paul: There are too many sexual connotations involved in the word itself.

Melissa: That's saying that the physical connotation is sexual. Aren't there certain physical relationships that aren't sexual? I know I have good friends at home—girlfriends that I think that I love, that I've had since I was very, very young. When I see them when I come home from school I kiss them. This isn't a sexual relationship—it's one of just affection.

Paul: You probably don't hesitate to embrace them either. And yet two men in the same position would have inhibitions about that.

Melissa: Maybe this is different with females.

Carole: I don't think it's different because I'm probably more inhibited that way—I don't kiss my girlfriends. I have certain people that I kiss and certain people that I don't kiss. [*General laughter*] Although we're extremely close in my family, we only embrace and kiss when something big happens, except maybe I would embrace my mother, certainly more than I would embrace my father. But when I came back to school after Thanksgiving all the girls came running out kissing each other, and I thought, Holy Mackerel! [*General laughter*] It's not that I'm not aware that there's a love between girls. Certainly this love can become sexual, and I think when you kiss a girl, it *is* sexual. I don't see why you want to deny that—kissing is sexual.

Ben: It reminds me of these two freshmen—one starts off at one end and they run towards each other [*general laughter*], almost knock each other over. It seems totally unreal, like they're just putting it on for each other—not for anyone else. It doesn't seem like it's a real expression.

Paul: I think you have to redefine the word "sexual" rather than just using it loosely. The Freudian concept of sex, which we have come to accept, includes almost all physical interaction between two people. So let me attempt right now to redefine it in terms of what I'm trying to say. I would redefine a sexual interest in someone else as some kind of genital interest.

Maslow: If I can take it there, keeping in mind also this experiential psychology business. What we're trying to do really is to go under the word, to differentiate out the feelings which deserve different words, like this love thing. If we have an experiential psychology of any kind—since you'll be carrying this load—you'll have to make up these words like this "*philia*," the "*eros*," the "*agape*," at least, and maybe for the sexual things too. Maybe we'll have to make different words.

See, what you started to do is like the professor who would start with "What is it?" and "How are things right now?" You know, try to make a definition with it. Whereas part of our job is rather to make some experiential differentiation between these feelings and then, if we *can* differentiate, to put different labels on them. For example, right now I've seen several publications in the last few months admitting for the first time the erotic feelings in the psychotherapeutic relationship and so on. It's possible, for instance, for the male psychoanalyst with a beautiful woman to have some erotic feelings, and it needn't be denied altogether as it has been. It simply has to be controlled, managed; that's all. Erotic feelings [*chuckles*]—you'll see what I mean from this story. It was supposed to be during the war—the standard question is, "Are you troubled by erotic feelings?" and this young man thought and thought and said, "No, I rather enjoy them." [*General laughter*]

Well, this I'd suggest is our job here—the trying to differentiate out. Clearly the erotic feelings that we were talking about there were different from what you have for a sweetheart. What I'm saying is that the experiences come before the words, and then maybe we can put the words to it, rather than starting with the words, then the experiences. Erotic feelings, if you want to take that for the first part [*meaning the experiential part*] of it—the Freudians would accept this. They have learned to accept, in this very broad sense, all sorts of feelings as erotic. They speak casually of them—the parents' erotic reactions to their own children, babies and the like. They're not frightened at all by this, but clearly this would be of a different sort than actually preparing themselves for a sexual act. [*Pause*]

We still don't have a phenomenology of erotic feelings—nobody's gone into this, nobody knows how it feels. For instance, no man could conceivably know from books what a female, a woman, feels like when she feels erotic. Unless you've worked in that field, talked to her and so on, you'll never know. I can't recommend, I can't refer the men here to anything like that; I can't refer the women to any good description of how male eroticism feels to the male himself. There's no description.

John: Well, I think that the inhibition is also for the relationship between the man and the woman. Aside from the specific single love relationship which is allowed in our culture, there is definitely I think, a difference in the type of erotic feeling one has for the man or the woman. The desire to have physical contact with a man by a man is submerged. It's different in nature, in that when you get to know a woman, you, I think, envisage—maybe not directly and concretely—further physical contact eventually culminating in sexual intercourse. I don't think this happens when you meet a man, even if you love the man as we say. I think that one desires a very different "surface" contact, a superficial contact. But what happens, I wonder, aside from the particular woman who you're allowed to kiss at a particular moment by society—what happens to all the other women, you know, whom you'd like to kiss and do God-know-what-else with? I think it happens, and this seems also not to be allowed, and shouldn't be allowed, necessarily.

Doug: We might have a situation now where it can be us who decides, rather than society, whether it should be allowed. You can decide your own fate, say, after you're married. My impression is that the opportunities are there.

John: For what?

Doug: For doing God-knows-what-else [*General laughter*] with these other women besides your wife or besides the one that you are committed to. It's a very real problem, I think.

John: We feel definitely here that what is almost desirous is the ability to somehow extend experience, to be able to see things in other ways. But what happens in this particular situation: suppose I'm married and there is this other woman I know. Now I can't do this naturally because my wife is going to object, possibly, and this may not be because of her cultural situation only; it may be a very natural, unconscious thing—the type of the unconscious which is not affected by civilization—that one doesn't want one's mate going around being too intimate with other people of the other sex. Under these circumstances, it's almost easier to be intimate with members of your own sex, at least among, let's say, above a certain education level where they are not so much affected by the fear of homosexuality.

Doug: Do you feel that the objections would come mainly from your wife, or do you think from you yourself?

John: Well, off-hand, I think we all have the feeling about these general things we'd like to do. For example, I've never been as intimate with my father as I would have liked to. But I think of it as a general feeling. It is really complex—what are the deterrents in any single case? In other words, I suppose I'd like to be more intimate with lots of women—aside from the adolescent promiscuity, which is a different thing. I think the only point I have, if I have any, is that all these things may not be so good to be universal. It may not be so good to be absolutely uninhibited, which is a label we give to all these things. I'm not sure that it would be ideal if we could be just as intimate with our female friends as we could with our wives.

Paul: That's what I was referring to before, though, when I said that you don't necessarily have to do those things in order to think in these terms. I think that the sheer act of thinking this way gives you a whole different orientation towards your relationships. You can experience a woman with whom you—according to social rules—cannot possibly touch, in two different ways.

One is to simply recognize the fact that there's a barrier there which, by its sheer imposition upon you, is unshakable, that it's simply foolhardy to even think of the possibility of these thoughts having any kind of realistic fulfillment. In fact the tendency with this kind of thinking is to chastise yourself somewhat for even having the thoughts.

There's another way of thinking which can make that experience a very valuable one even for your friendship. You can recognize that the desire exists, you can recognize that the limitations exist too, because society has put them there. But the fact that you are not simply accepting those limitations because they exist, but because you recognize there is a certain pragmatic value to their existence, means you aren't going to pass off these feelings as being necessarily evil, being harmful to your relationship, or being limiting in your own appreciation of the potential friendship which is there, which has never been fulfilled.

John: Well, I think the problem which you pass over lightly is just that phrase about the pragmatic things, the decisions that one will make, and it's just that we don't know. After all, there's some discussion right now as to whether what society has dictated about the relationship between men is any good or not. And we're possibly going to come to the conclusion that it's not, and that a great deal more intimacy should be allowed, and therefore we as individuals are going to ignore that particular rule.

Paul: That's possible, and I didn't say just now that society is always right in its rules. I didn't mean to say that.

Maslow: May I phrase this in a different way? Because it serves as a kind of support of the whole enterprise. What you're trying to do, or what we're trying to do now is in a certain sense new in human history, because always it has been assumed that the best way to control dangerous behavior is to deny it or to repress the thought. Following Freud now, we've simply turned from going north back to going south, in order to control behavior which is dangerous, because it's best to be conscious of it rather than to be unconscious of it.

Certainly awareness or conscious acceptance *doesn't* mean acting on it—that we had better be careful about. But you might say even that . . . For instance, if it's dangerous, as everybody agrees in every culture, to have just plain promiscuity—it doesn't work well—then, the best way to avoid promiscuity is apparently to talk as we are talking now, for men and women to be aware across the sex lines of how they feel, and so on and so on. The implication being that the more conscious you are of this, the better you can control it, the more free you are to make a wise decision about what to do.

I guess in our talking it would probably be best for us to be as uncensored as we wish with our own impulses or thoughts or whatever. But I thought, as you were speaking, that this might also be one of the benefits of this kind of course, workshop—this free talking around the table—because it just occurred to me that what you had said there, probably every man in the room would agree with and no woman in the room would.

Females [*simultaneously*]: What?

Maslow: This business about . . . A therapist would say, for every man every woman is a potential sexual object. That is, he'll speculate a little bit . . .

[*Giggles and voices of protests from girls*]

Sharon: We'd like to take a show of hands—those who disagree raise their hand.

Maslow: I won't take your hands in this case.

[*A burst of laughter in class to the double meaning of the phrase*]

What I'm trying to say across the generations here is that on the psychoanalytic couch ultimately most women patients will turn up as not sexually speculating on men, but rather matrimonially or amorously or whatever. But not simply as sexual objects—just as interest in sexual objects—where for men this is very, very widespread. It may be universal, I don't know. It's anyway very common.

Let's assume that I'm right and not argue about it, because I'm using it only as an example. If we could be phenomenological and co-educational: supposing it were possible for a group of men to expose their masculine thoughts, you might say—that is, to keep talking and talking and talking—and for the women to do the same thing—differentiating out what is different in their inner lives and the difference in the impulses and the judgments and desires and so on. That would be kind of a good byproduct, I would suppose, of this experiencing out loud, with feeling. Well, this would be your major constitutional difference in males and females, but it would also hold for the people of different body types, for people of different levels of intelligence or education or desire or capacity or skill. I want to jot that down as a finding, you might say, as a datum.

For instance, if we were doing that specifically, it might be smart to check how the other men in this room and how the women, one by one, react to that. Do they take that for granted? Do they feel the same way themselves, perhaps, or how many do or don't? I think we can profit from that. It's like permitting ourselves to look into each other's heads without behaving—just expressing an experience.

Sharon: Maybe this information about women hasn't been readily available until now. I think that maybe times have changed and you'll be hearing more of it than you have in the last few years.

Maslow: You mean about the women reacting in that same way? Well, this is why I said that I wouldn't pay any attention to it, because in the psychotherapeutic experience it's perfectly true that many women will, in the first hour, talk in this way and slowly, slowly, slowly, as you get into more profoundly felt feelings, they reject that and they talk in another way.

Here's another example which indicates our estrangement from our own experience in a mass way. Hysteria in the old sense has disappeared—all the practicing psychiatrists say that. The hysteria that started Freud off—the whole of psychoanalysis is built on hysteria—has disappeared. Except with your women patients who hang around for three or four months; then the hysterical character structure, the hysterical *Weltanschauung*, the hysterical impulses, experiences, feelings are all there, by gosh!

What has disappeared is just cultural behavior—culturally determined behavior. The hysterical girls who used to be "pernicious virgins," they used to call them, who were afraid of sex and stayed afraid of sex, now these same girls may sleep with every man around the place quite easily and feel, "Oh, how sophisticated" they now are. The soul remains different—they're still afraid of sex. They may have pushed themselves or forced themselves or felt this was the right thing to do or it's good for me or it's not good for me or whatever it might be. Behavior is not a good guide to experience, to experiencing, to feeling in this sense.[7]

Sharon: May I just interject the possibility that a woman may—you say they end up talking about a different realm. It might very well be that since psychiatrists are mostly oriented toward showing how sex is *used* for different things other than just sex, you know, and translating it into different needs and desires, that they're almost, shall we say, brainwashed or influenced to *make* it be that way. This is a possibility I just wanted to raise.

Maslow: It's a possibility but we have enough data to reject it.[8] I mean we have all this tape-recorded data. You can do it yourself, remember. You can take tapes or records which have been taken of therapeutic hours. It has been done both by the psychoanalysts and the Rogerians,[9] who have done most of this, but there have been others too. And increasingly it's now being done, and you can analyze out just how much suggestion there is.

Good psychotherapy, ideal psychotherapy, is still "uncovering," non-interfering psychotherapy. It is *not* suggestion—it is the opposite of it. And under such circumstances—which I've tried to do for instance myself—I would say that there are many more virginal females than they're aware of. I mean there are rather few technically—the number of actual physical virgin females decreases year by year. The first sexual experience starts younger and younger. But if you're talking about the virginal *spirit*, you know, there are plenty of them. Or you could say it another way: in terms of values, there are plenty of girls who should be virgins even if they're not.[10]

Carole: Just because in psychoanalysis they found out that hysterical women usually were afraid of sex, and today there's promiscuous girls who should be virgins are also afraid of sex—does that mean *all* women are afraid of sex?

Maslow: No!

Carole: Then, I don't understand what it is that women couldn't understand—

Maslow: That's a horrible thought.

Carole: Yes, I know. [*General laughter*] I just don't understand what you mean—that women couldn't understand those statements.

Maslow: It's that behavior is not an awfully good index to what's going on in your gut, not *awfully* good. That part of our job here is to try to strike below the words, the categories which were ready-made for us. We can also try to strike below the behavior which is only partially determined by our insides, our deepest impulses and thoughts, ambitions and so on. It's also partly determined by cultural expectations, by opportunity, by law and a lot of other things. This is all I was trying to say. If you want, I have research on this, on the pagan attitude toward sex and virginal attitude toward sex.[11]

Well, it correlates to some extent with actual sex behavior, but not terribly much. There are plenty of pagan attitudes where without opportunity or with—it depends on where you live and what's possible and so on—there are plenty of virginal pagans, you might say. On the other hand, there are also plenty of women who are not really ready for sex and who don't enjoy it when it comes and yet who will act it out. Now it would be good for them to know, in an experiential sense, "What do you really want? What do you really enjoy? What do you really feel?" For many women and for many men in many areas of life, they don't know what they want. You find very frequently that people will behave in a way in which they then deny when you get to deeper levels—in the same way which I think I have reported to you. I was friends with a guy for so long and it wasn't until after a year of analysis I found I hated the son-of-a-bitch. I didn't know it, but I discovered it through, as it happened, a dream—and it was some dream!

Carole: I still don't understand what it is that you say women—

Maslow: Let me generalize it in the abstract, in professorial terms: don't trust behavior to be a good index of experience, of feeling, etcetera. We chose this example of sex because it happens to be, among psychologists, a byword. I would expect among college people, for instance—well, I don't care whether the college girls sleep with boys there in the dorms or not. I feel that the *impulse* to **sexuality**, the real impulse to it, the ability to enjoy it, the ability to make much of it, is what counts. I don't care about their sexual histories—I've learned that doesn't tell me much. I want to ask other questions rather than "did you sleep or did you not sleep?"—it's not a very good index.

Sharon: Is this any different for men?

Maslow: Yes.[12]

Jayne: Well, I see a difference in just the orientation today of women, although it's changing slightly. In the average middle-class-values family, you have this training of the girl to accept sex only after marriage. It's kind of linked up: the person you marry is the person you're going to sleep with. Now, a lot of this is changing and therefore the concept—

Maslow: You could say it just the other way: the person you sleep with is the one you're going to marry. [*General laughter*]

Jayne: And, well, the concept of virginity is changing. You look at a person first to see whether he is good marriage material and it actually links up with the same thing as what you are saying about a man looking at a woman.[13] I mean it links up with this physical attractiveness too. Do you see what I mean? I think this is what you're saying, to some extent. Am I right, or—?

Sharon: How about after they're married? Then what?

Jayne: Well, then it has a great deal to do with how your marriage works out, I think.

Sharon: But see, then, are you looking for someone who's good marriage material?

Jayne: Yeah, but that's a different thing. I mean one thing is a physical attractiveness, and then you want something further than this in marriage.

Carole: Every boy you go out with, though, you think is a potential— I mean, you can't look at a male as not marriageable? I don't know, I think I can. [*General laughter*] I don't know about the other girls in the room, but I think I can look at a man—

Jayne: No, I don't think that's true. I think if you find someone who's not physically attractive, this is a part of it, and I think it's foolish to deny this.

Sharon: It's not a part of what?

Jayne: A part of desiring to marry someone. [*A brief, unintelligible exchange between Jayne and Sharon takes place, with both of them chuckling*] Oh, and someone brought up the topic of virginity and, I don't know, I think it's exactly what people are coping with today: which is more the virgin—the female who will just have these desires to sleep with many men, these physical desires, but who will force herself to wait until she's married and will be kind of flighty; *or* the female who has a very strong relationship with one individual though they're not married. Which is more the virgin? And I think this is exactly what the problem is today, because there is so much premarital intercourse we're all reconsidering what virginity is actually.

Sharon: Unfortunately the sex urge is not monogamous. I think that's the big problem.

Maslow: I report that it is.

Sharon: The statistics prove it's not.

Maslow: These are not statistics; these are long investigations.

Sharon: Shall I say not *only* monogamous?

Maslow: No, they're not.

John: Is there a correlate between that and health?

Maslow: That would be another story. Yes, there is some correlation between heath and the tendency to monogamy, in later years at least. I think that would be about as far as our data go. Any psychiatrist, psychoanalyst, psychologist, psychotherapist, any dynamic psychologist who found a person let's say past the age of thirty or thirty-five, who was married and who was promiscuous, we would say that guy needs therapy, he's a sick man or a sick woman. We simply assume that on the basis of experience—not on *a priori* morality of any kind. And this sort of thing gets *cured*. Promiscuity earlier in life seems to be compatible with health and so forth. As for the polygamous tendencies, the monogamous tendencies, there's a wide range of variation in women. This has been described, and it's available. There are different moralities, you might say, and different constitutions of women.

If I had to make recommendations or something of the sort, or if I had to think in terms of pragmatic results, there are clearly women who had best remain virginal. It is simply less trouble for them, a better life and so on and so on. And there are other women who just can't remain virginal and there's no sense in recommending it to them either. In the first place, they would pay no attention to the recommendations anyway. [*General laughter*] Here again we have the data for these women of the non-virginal, of the pagan types: in the first place, they have a lot of sex anyway, and in the second place you can't—I couldn't anyhow—see any harm in it. I couldn't see any bad consequences of any kind, nor has anybody ever turned them up. Kinsey, so on . . .

On the other hand, each of us has the kind of experience with women of the virginal type and who then get promiscuous—and you see all sorts of destruction and ruin. It's bad for them, and you say to them, "You should never have popped into that guy's bed; you shouldn't have done it—it's no good for you." This is not a general statement about virginity; it's for her, for that particular woman that we can make the differentiation—test for it, if you want.

With men, as things stand now, there probably are some men with particular kinds of bringing up to whom it would best be said also, "You'd better remain virgin, at least conventionally. Don't break the conventions; you'll pay too much for it; it won't give you enough plusses and it will give you too many minuses." You can say that too.

It's about the fantasies, however; that was what I started talking about, to differentiate them from the behavior. Let's say everybody here has been through six months of normal psychoanalytic therapy, and we're talking about what is conscious then—not at the beginning. Then you would find—

[*TAPE CHANGE*]

—is the way they're brought up. I myself don't think so. Practically none of the Freudians thinks so. They just assume that these are constitutional, especially endocrine differences, and there's a *little* evidence for that—animals and so on.

And then there are the different age levels. What's suitable for age 20, 18, 25, 35 and so on. For instance, the man who doesn't get married by the age of 35, let's say—every psychologist is suspicious of him. Now we're not so suspicious about the woman of 35 because she may not have been asked. Let's say it's in his power to get married, but if it's not always in her power to get married then you can't make the same conclusion and then you go from there to all sorts of guesses and so on and so on. Promiscuity, at least in our psychological experience, in our society—I have nothing to say about any other—promiscuity here past the age of 30, 35, 40 in either male or female is just regarded as plain sickness. It is also found generally that the desirable results of "uncovering" psychotherapy—classical therapy which tends not to interfere with the person—narrow down more towards exclusive relationships. It is also possible to be in love with more than one person at the same time, it appears, from the same experience, too, either for men or for women, but not with 30 people.

The sexual relations that we call promiscuous at this age are generally joyless anyway. They're just not much fun; they're not much pleasure. Also, generally, they tend to be regretted in terms of guilt and so on; they just don't pan out so well.

Do you want another line of evidence altogether, empirical stuff? You want to collect peak-experiences from sex, from love and so on? This comes to particular kinds of people which are implied in everything I've said. It's more likely to come to someone who's very,

very much in love with somebody and where the sexual act is a love act. I hope you like that consequence, but know that nobody is responsible for it. The management takes no responsibility in scientific research for what is discovered. [*General laughter*] It might have been something else, but that's the way it happens to look at this time. Everybody remember now, science is wonderful. Anybody who doesn't believe this could go out and discover it.

[*Sounds of class breaking up*]

Do you have any more of these notebooks for me? I'll try to get them back by our next meeting.

DECEMBER 16, 1963

Guest Speaker: Richard G. Abell, M.D.

Richard G. Abell, M.D., Psychiatrist and Lecturer in Mental Hygiene at Barnard College, visited the class with two videotapes (equal to two episodes) of the television program Road to Reality.[1] *This was an American daytime show featuring dramatized group therapy sessions based on actual sessions conducted by Abell. (More details emerge in the discussion below). The entire three-hour session of class was set aside for viewing and discussing the videotapes.*

Maslow: This is Dr. Richard Abell of New York City. He's just been telling me that he has the usual private psychoanalytic practice and that he's also still running some groups in analysis. And I've learned that he's doing just what some of us have talked and argued about. He is now giving a series of lectures at Barnard College—perhaps I'll ask Dr. Abell to say a word about that. It's twelve lectures, and then the same question comes up that comes for us, that I've confronted you with and you've bounced back at me. Taking advantage of a second-best situation, supposing you do have twelve hours and supposing you do have a youth squadron of—how many?

Abell: One hundred and eighty-six.

Maslow: One hundred and eighty-six girls to talk at. No individual contact is possible.[2] How do you use your time? How possible is it to communicate in words through the television series, through the lectures, through the radio and all the developed psychodynamics that are useable? To remind you again, this was the goal; this was the problem that I had in mind. We must recognize that this is a very difficult thing to do, that it's never as good as the ideal situation, let's say, of the personal analysis and so on, and that we're improvising. I'm glad to hear that Dr. Abell is in that same position. This is in addition to that television series that I mentioned to you, his *Road to Reality*. We've got two samples here that we're going to see. Which I guess was before its time.

Abell: Two years.

Maslow: How many of you have seen the psychiatric series, *The Breaking Point*[3] on Monday evening and *The Eleventh Hour*[4] on Wednesday? We were chatting about that a little. Well, the series that Dr. Abell worked up or guided or something—what was it? You were . . . ?

Abell: Well, I was the psychoanalyst for a group of six people, and I made tapes of the psychoanalytic process, of group psychoanalysis, and from these tapes we made scripts. The scripts were actually what the patients really said, with certain disguises introduced. The parts of the patients were played by actors, and my part was played by an actor. So, I'm the analyst you'll see in this film, but I don't look like me. I had a very interesting reaction when I saw the first one because I thought, well, now, I can find out how to be an analyst. [*General laughter*] It was very interesting—I couldn't recognize my own productions in this thing initially, but I gradually got to be familiar with it.

But that's what the program consisted of. The program consisted of a series of psychoanalytic group sessions in which these people were being analyzed for their various problems in group therapy. The program itself went on every day in the week for half an hour, 2:30 to 3:00 p.m. We had very strong competition—we had Loretta Young[5] on the opposite show on this time, which was very hard on us. But it showed the progress of a group over a course of about three years, I would think, with particular sessions picked out and filmed and acted out by the actors and put on video tape and then broadcasted. I see what Dr. Maslow has done is turned the floor right over to me. Shall I just go right on now?

Maslow: Yeah, I was going to run into the comparison of your series with these contemporary one-hour shows [*i.e.,* The Breaking Point *and* The Eleventh Hour].

Abell: I wish you would do that right now.

Maslow: Should we? Well, I'll pass on to you the conversation we had at lunch. You haven't seen very many of them, have you?

Abell: No, just one.

Maslow: I think I've seen most of them. Well, in my opinion, these two psychiatric films, or whatever you'd call them [*i.e.,* The Breaking Point *and* The Eleventh Hour] . . . It's a story, a one-hour story—a condensation of a whole case history into a single hour. And the one main criticism that I had was that they're not careful enough about showing that this is over the course of months, perhaps. It may give the very false impression to people that, you know, the huge insight and then suddenly life changes and so on. That's bad, even dangerous as a matter of fact, because people might expect big miracles instead of this slogging, trudging through mud and working your way up the hill kind of thing which is the usual, the real thing.

On the other hand, it was my opinion that, so far as psychodynamic truth is concerned, both of these programs are very good, increasingly good. That is, at the very beginning, the ones I saw in the very beginning were too formal; they were over-dramatic. But somebody's got after them and they've calmed down and they're more real, with this one exception that it's perhaps six months or twelve months condensed into a single presentation.

The truth of the matter is much more honestly presented by the kind of series that Dr. Abell worked out, where there's the spreading out in time and the clear impression of how much work this is, how much sweat the patients have to put into it. It is something that must be learned, so I would say that if we have any programs in the future, they had better take this format Dr. Abell set up rather than this one-hour shot kind of thing. I think we both agree on this.

Abell: Yes, I would say the same thing. The difficulty, of course, of doing more than one shot is that it's a very expensive thing to do, and unless they have sponsors and people who are interested in doing it, it might be somewhat difficult to carry out. We had sponsors for it, much to my surprise—we had chewing gum, we had every cleaning fluid, we had Johnson's wax—we had everybody sponsoring this show which ABC had, and the show itself cost about a million-and-a-half dollars to put on. I think the only problem would be one of sponsorship, and I certainly think that, technically speaking, it would be much better to give a series of programs to show development and change rather than just one program in which it was condensed.

But Dr. Maslow said to me just a short time ago that he thought the shows nevertheless were extremely well done, because when you think of having to present a show to a very large and uneducated mass of people, it has really to have dramatic interest. Perhaps we can forgive the producers for introducing some quick, sudden changes like—the man is about to stab the girl and one of the other patients grabs his hand in mid-stream and holds it—and everybody's attention is centered there. It doesn't generally of course happen that way. Did you want to say something else about that?

Maslow: That's all right.

Abell: Dr. Maslow said that I taught at Barnard College, which is true. I've been teaching there for three years now, and we have a required course in hygiene. It's divided into two parts: one is physical hygiene, which is given by Dr. Nelson, who's head of the health services; the other is mental hygiene, and I give the mental hygiene course. Now, I have found that giving a required course has certain liabilities. Students rebel against required courses, and they have in a certain sense rebelled at times against being forced to take a course. However, if you talk to them and try to get them to understand, they cooperate. I think the rebellion is part of, really, an adolescent finding oneself, which, if handled properly, becomes a matter of self-understanding. At any rate, one of the things I do is talk a lot about Dr. Maslow. Our chief book is *Motivation and Personality*.

As a matter of fact we start out by defining psychological health according to the criteria which Dr. Maslow has worked out for the self-actualizing person. So everybody in the freshman class knows about self-actualizing people and about Dr. Maslow. When I go back, I'm going to give your greetings to them; I'm sure they'll appreciate it.

The next thing that we take up is motivation. We discuss needs—why people do the things they do, and the best organized system of needs that I've discovered is Dr. Maslow's in his book *Motivation and Personality*. So, I present this, and then I take up the origin of the self, the concept of the self.

This would be directly related to what is going to appear in the film, so may I say a few words about that?

The concept of the self is a very strange one initially. I was surprised, when I first began to study this kind of thing, that the infant is born without any sense of self. I always thought that when a child was born it *was* itself, and it *had* a self. But I no longer think it does have a self. I think it has potentialities for growth but I don't think it thinks anything about its self at all. It doesn't even in fact recognize its own boundaries, where it begins or where it stops or where its mother begins or where she stops. And the sense of self really begins as a result of how the infant and the child, early in life, is treated by its parents—especially the mother.

The Barnard girls always like me to say there are other important people too, like the father—they don't want to take all the responsibility I suppose—but it's the appraisals of these parents of the infant that really determine what it thinks about itself. And the infant and child concentrate more and more upon what pleases or displeases the parents, so that the sense of self or the self-concept or the self-dynamism comes to consist of what the infant and the child feels will be approved by its parents.

Now, if the parents are perfectly normal, healthy people, this is fine, and the child comes to think well of itself and to have a positive sense of self and to be able then to grow from that point on through to the various stages in personality development of childhood, the juvenile period, pre-adolescence, adolescence, and finally maturity without any difficulty.

But, if the parents—as so many parents are—are neurotic, if they have problems; if they are over-anxious; if they tend to derogate the child unduly and unjustly, as many parents do in taking out their own anxieties on their children, the child pretty soon begins to have a feeling that it itself is the cause for the derogation, that it essentially is bad. It does not, as you might suppose, think that its parents are bad. The tendency of the infant and child is to think the parents are good, but if he, the child, is in the early stages mistreated, he thinks there is something wrong with him, and so he develops a negative sense of self.

Once this negative sense of self is established, it does various unfortunate things to the growth process. For instance, after the period of childhood, when the child becomes a juvenile in the pre-school and early school years, the characteristic need is for the child to belong to a group of peers with whom he will discuss what his parents say and what goes on in his home, and to get some validation with other children about what goes on in their homes. So some broadening of self-concept appears or develops. But in the case of the child with the negative self-image that was begun in this way, the child tends to withdraw from being in a group out of shyness or out of fear of being criticized by the peer group and tends to be on the outside; therefore it never has the experience of sharing. It doesn't have the consensual validation, that is to say, recognition that "this peer thinks the same way as I do about this thing," which other children have. It doesn't learn competition and compromise the way people do in peer groups at that stage.

Also, in the next stage—which is the pre-adolescent stage in the way I present personality development—such a child going on doesn't generally have the normal experience of the chum. You know what a "chum" is and how, in this stage of from about 8 to 12 years, a person has a friend of the same sex and learns to really care about the chum very much, and in fact learns to love—in the sense of non-sexual love—through this initial experience. But the child with the negative sense of self is afraid to make a chum or is afraid to be sufficiently confidential with a chum to really air all of her feelings or his feelings and get to have the feeling of really communicating everything, of presenting to the other person his own feelings, having them understood and learning to really care deeply about another person, which is what occurs in this particular stage.

And then in adolescence also, in the next stage, such people usually fail to have adequate relations with a member of the opposite sex, which is one of the big new needs that emerges in adolescence. In consequence his personality is warped; it doesn't develop adequately. Although such a person may want a girlfriend or boyfriend, it is very difficult for him to have one and to have this experience.

Well, people who are neurotic—and I would say that all the people that you are going to see in this film are in this category—have negative self-images. They have been thwarted in one way or another in their development by this early experience of negative feelings about themselves, and they have also developed patterns of behaving which were based on their original parents. Now, take for instance a child whose father is very derogating, who beats him too much, who punishes him too much. You can imagine the kind of reaction patterns this child is going to have toward male figures. He will be afraid of them; he will tend to withdraw from them, stay in an inconspicuous position, try to please them and so on, and when he grows up he will have the same fear of authority figures, or other figures, that he had toward his original parents or father. Harry Stack Sullivan[6] has called this a "parataxic distortion." People tend to see people in the present not as they are but as some original, significant, important figure in their background, and this blocks them from seeing reality.

Now, in this film you will see the people reacting to each other, and the way they react to each other is determined to some extent by the way they reacted toward their own parents in their own background. And you will see, or I will try to point out at times, the kinds of distortions that arise and the kinds of relations which in consequence develop. Dr. Maslow was talking about reality and its importance at lunch, and the narrowing of the area for seeing reality which occurs in people who are extremely anxious, and I think this is one way in which this occurs: the not seeing of other people as they are but the seeing of them as if they were like some other person from the past.

Now I think we might show the first film. I'll say about the first film that this is the fourth session in the group therapy that these people had, so that their method of relating is fairly superficial. They're talking particularly about a raincoat and what one of the members of the group, Vic, thought about his girlfriend wearing an old beat-up raincoat. He wanted her to wear something nice, something that she would look nice in, but she insisted upon wearing this raincoat. And you see the reactions of various members of the group to his production about this in relation to his girl.

Maslow: The second film, as I remember, is one much later on, isn't it?

Abell: Yes. Now, the second film is the forty-ninth session, which is quite a long period on, maybe a year or a year and a half after the first one. And in the second session, Lee, one of the members, expresses his very great resentment against his mother. You will see in this second film the kind of thing I was talking about—with the derogating and overanxious mother and what this has done in blocking the development of Lee's ego to a normal strength. He's struggling with this and in fact he's still in therapy and he's still struggling with it, and I'll say something about it later.

[**Film 1**] *Because of copyright issues, the videotapes have not been transcribed. Instead, brief summaries of the main events in each of the two films are provided.*[7]

Film #1—4th episode in the original television series

　　In this film a group of eight "patients" discusses various personal problems with the help of a psychoanalyst. This particular session focuses on Vic, a patient experiencing some conflict about the male-female relationship, and in particular the question of whether or not a man should feel superior to a woman. Vic is a bank employee afraid of marriage. He has, at the age of 31, fallen in love for the first time. As the session begins he tells the group about a recent quarrel he has been having with his girlfriend, Dori. The major issue is Dori's insistence upon wearing what Vic describes as a "beat-up old raincoat." He has been urging her to get rid of the coat for some time, but she refuses. He relates how on one occasion he snatched the coat away from Dori with the intention of replacing it with a fancier new one of his choice, but in the end he was forced to return the old one. He tells the other group members how he feels: "You see, I'm fighting for it . . . I've got to win, I've got to be a man, I've got to be dominant . . ."

The other patients in the group include:

Joan, a dental assistant, whose "parents' early domination has made her tense and frightened of people." Margaret is an older suburban wife dealing with a "need to control others" that is damaging her life and relationships. Harry is the manager of a department store whose "overbearing manner threatens his home." Lee is a management engineer harboring "great anger." Susan is a young housewife dealing with "periods of great despair and sudden outbursts of violent temper." These five members react to Vic and one another in such a way that reveals much of their personalities and in due course also their own emotional difficulties.

Discussion of Film 1

Paul: Does free association have any part to play in this group psychoanalysis?

Abell: This is a good question and a moot point. Free association *does* play a part, but it plays a part in group analytic work which is somewhat different from individual psychoanalysis. In individual psychoanalysis, the person sits in a chair or lies on a couch and his mind is perfectly free of distractions so he can describe what goes through it. But in a group you can't be free from distractions; therefore your associations, although they occur, tend to be determined somewhat by what's going on around you.

Now, when Lee attacks Vic, this in a sense is a free association, but it's acted out. It's an acting-out process; the thoughts that come to mind are frequently immediately acted out on the other people. You might think that because this is so then you can't free associate and therefore the process of therapy would be slower, but the fact is, it isn't. The fact is that, when the thing is acted out, the person gets a chance to see it and see its significance, and then, when it's pointed out, it has more meaning for him.

Paul: I wouldn't think the process would be slower but it seems to be a very different practice.

Abell: It is, in this respect. Yes, it is different in the respect that people in the group have a chance to test their reactions in a test tube, so to speak, in front of the analyst, instead of talking about them. Now, in the analytic session, the person can talk about what he did with his girlfriend or how he was afraid of going out or any number of things, but in the group you really see it right there as a living process.

Paul: Can I ask you another question?

Abell: Yes.

Paul: Does the insight take place while the person is engaged in this tension itself in the group, or does it take place when you ask him to examine his real motivation in reacting as he does?

Abell: Yes, it takes place in both places. Initially, the insight is developed as a response generally of the analyst's interpretations of the person's behavior, because the behavior goes on unconsciously and is acted out unconsciously; the person doesn't really know its significance. He's just reacting in the parataxic mode, as he would have reacted toward other people in the past without realizing that he's not really in touch with reality. But after he begins to understand this process and see the meaning of it, he becomes alert to looking for it, and then begins to pick up and say something like, "Well, you know, maybe the reason I'm doing this is because my brother used to beat me up and it frightened me very much."

Now, for instance, Vic, you could see, was somewhat threatened by Lee when Lee was so loud in his criticism of Vic's response about the raincoat. Vic was really threatened by this because it pressed the bell of his other fear of his brother. But as time went on, he began to get an understanding of this and to be able to react differently toward Lee, so that although Lee kind of shouted him down in the beginning, as therapy went on he saw he didn't really have to be afraid of Lee.

He could see Lee more down-to-size, and he began to yell back at him. After a while he was yelling louder than Lee, and Lee subsided, which was really quite amusing, and Vic became much stronger. This was a very important thing in Vic's coming to recognize that he could really behave differently. Are there any other questions about this?

Mike: In your opinion, is the effectiveness of group therapy very much dependent upon the validity of the concept of self that you just gave at the beginning of the hour? You gave this concept of social self, you know. . .

Abell: Yes, certainly.

Mike: Because otherwise what function does the group play for the individual in it? Obviously there are many different theories of the origin of self and the development of self. Can they find a place in the theory of group therapy or can only this concept that you have adopted be the sole determinant?

Abell: Well, what I would say is that any concept of self at all would fit into the actual process of what goes on, because they all have a certain validity. My own thinking is oriented around the one that I've presented so I would tend to think in that direction, but someone else might think in another direction and, for instance, might use Freudian terminology. He might think of Vic, the one with the raincoat, as being an oral personality somewhat dependent and passive.

And you could talk about it this way, but it wouldn't change the actual process itself; it wouldn't change what Vic is really doing. It might change the interpretation somewhat but my experience is that a great part of the curative process in analytic work is related to the relation of the doctor to the patient anyway, in terms of what kind it is: is it a good one? Is it a friendly one? Is it an accepting one? Does it respect the patient's integrity? And so on. And if the doctor does all these things, I don't think it makes very much difference, or not *all* the difference, as to what his particular orientation is.

Are there any other questions about this film?

Melissa: As a therapist you acted as a control during most of the session, but at the very end of the session you offered Vic a suggestion as to possible motivation for his behavior. Is that part of your role too? When you sense a breakthrough or insight that perhaps you get?

Abell: Yes.

Melissa: If this is so, when you give a suggestion, wouldn't he be much more likely to say, "Yeah, you know, maybe that's it, maybe that's me." Is this a good idea?

Abell: Well, now, I would like to explain about this—you pick it up very aptly. In dealing with a program to be presented to a large number of people on T.V., you have to do some things somewhat differently. Now, for instance, we were concerned in the program about how the analyst could make a contact with the audience. How can the audience feel a personal relationship to the analyst, so they don't feel isolated?

We decided that what we would do was to have the analyst talk to the audience first. And you saw the analyst here telling the audience something about what was going to happen in order to make a contact with the audience. And I noticed the cameramen have a trick—they start you out small and make you bigger as time goes on. You could see it in the film, and this is a kind of "I'm getting close to you" idea—making some contact. I don't know if that's a good contact or not, but that's why it's done. I would never make a speech like that in conducting a group session. Also, we decided that since the process of personality reorganization is so complicated and so slow that it was very difficult for a person who tuned in and didn't know anything about the process to understand what was going on. So, in order to pull it together at the end, the analyst would make a summary of what happened. Now I would never make a summary of what happened in my groups, but I would point out what happened at the time it happened, and the significance of it, and this is the way it should be done in the therapy. Are there any other questions about that? [*Pause*]

Well, I would point out a couple of things then. Do you remember in this film where Joan suddenly yelled out, "Shut up!"? Now, that wouldn't have any significance to you if you didn't know something about how Joan had been behaving in the group so far. Joan tended to withdraw; she tended to say very little, and she was gradually developing a feeling of not liking it. It was disfavorable to withdraw, but this was her basic character, her type of relating. But she became discontented as therapy went ahead and in this session finally the resentment breaks out and she yells, "Shut up!" and from that time on, she began to talk more. At first gradually, but more as time went on. So I think this was really a breakthrough for Joan. She began to see that she had the right to speak out and the others shouldn't take up so much time. But this is a frequent problem with patients in groups—they have to learn that they have got a right to do it. They don't learn this until the resentment for being quiet builds up to a point where they're going to break out with it, and she broke out with it right there. There's another—

Maslow: Excuse me, could you make some estimate of time there. Is this the fourth session for Joan?

Abell: Yes, this was the fourth session. This was a little more than the fourth session actually—it was the fourth taped session.

Maslow: Well, what's your experience generally? What would you expect with your ordinarily withdrawn and quiet, retiring person?

Abell: Before this happened?

Maslow: Before this happened.

Abell: Oh, I expect it might be about seven months or a year actually before she developed enough ego strength to really come out with it.

Maslow: You see, we'll be discussing this too, in relationship to our particular group and the strategy. This is the problem—

Abell: Yes.

Maslow: —of many people, of people who talk easily and people who don't. The question of what you would do if you have twelve hours, twelve weekly hours, rather than seven months.

Abell: Yes, of course.

Maslow [*turning to the class*]: We'll have to discuss that. I'd like to call your attention to it at this point.

Abell: I'll tell you one interesting thing about Joan. Joan was the prettiest girl, the one that I think is the prettiest that you saw on this screen—you know, with the hairdo. Joan got married during the program and she got pregnant. Now, she kept swelling up and this was quite embarrassing, and the producer was asking, "What can we do with Joan so she can stay in the film?

Maslow: The actress Joan?

Abell: Right, the actress Joan got pregnant. [*General laughter*] No, she wouldn't duplicate that, for that purpose. But, anyway it was a big problem. Joan was a big investment to the company and what could they do about it? So they kept lifting the camera up and after a while they had nothing but her face in there. And afterwards when she was having the baby, she was replaced. I'll show you the girl who replaced her, who's on the next film. Should we go on to that film now?

Film #2—49th episode in the original television series

This session is centered mainly on Lee, another of the male patients. Lee is struggling with a handicap he has had since very early childhood, a limp resulting from polio, and his resentment toward his mother, who has also suffered because of her child's illness. Lee is very bitter about her treatment of him during his growing up years, and this bitterness is still very much with him in this session and in his day-to-day struggles with life in general. Lee begins the session by saying: "I'd like to talk about . . . my mother. I blame her for many things." Lee does not feel that his relationship with his 68-year-old mother is improving. He comments that while he won't "be happy when she dies," neither will he be sad.

On the whole the group is very supportive of Lee, gently asking questions of him, showing concern and understanding of the difficulty he has experienced with his mother up to the present time.

Discussion of Film 2

Paul: Is it possible to treat secondary symptoms of compulsive symbolic neurosis with this kind of therapy?

Abell: Well, what do you mean by the secondary symptoms?

Paul: Well, sometimes the neurosis is recognized by the patient. The very thing which makes him the person he is an habitual action which is irrational, which he goes through, which symbolically—I hope I'm expressing this properly—which symbolically releases for him certain tensions which build up inside of him around a certain situation which has greater affective values. He doesn't have to confront the situation itself in order to release these tensions but can do it symbolically through these repetitive actions. But these people don't seem to be suffering from this kind of neurosis. None of them do.

Abell: Could you give me an example?

Paul: Well, [*pause*] uh, compulsive nose-picking or something like that could be considered such a symptom.

Abell: I see, yes.

Paul: There are many different kinds of things which fit into that category.

Abell: I see. Now ask your question again.

Paul: Can this kind of group therapy treat symptoms of this sort successfully or can it cure them in any sense?

Abell: Yes, I would certainly say that. The treatment of a symptom like that, just to use it as an example, which is caused by anxiety, which is a way really of releasing anxiety by doing some compulsive thing that makes the person feel more secure because he's doing it or he feels himself or something like that. It is basically caused by feelings of inadequacy and anxiety inside himself which go back to the original causes, the earlier difficult and traumatic experiences in childhood. These then cause the anxiety that is occurring in the present situation. The way to treat this is not to treat the symptom itself; the way to treat this is to treat the underlying difficulty.

Now the underlying difficulty in a case like that would be the self-esteem, the feeling about the person's self, whether he feels satisfactory. The treatment would be to build up his self-esteem so that he no longer had anxieties, to help him understand what happens so that he would no longer be afraid, and then I think the nose-picking would go away by itself, just as any symptom does. You never treat a symptom. You may reassure a patient about a symptom, like people who have phobias about their hearts. When their heart beats fast they think they're going to die so they run to a doctor and the doctor examines the heart and finds it perfectly all right; there's nothing wrong with it. Then the next day the patient is walking up a hill and his heart beats hard; he runs to the same doctor, the doctors examine it, there's nothing wrong with it. He reassures him about it and the next week he's climbing the stairs and his heart beats hard and he runs to the same doctor. The doctor is getting disgusted and he says, "What's the matter with you, anyway? I've examined your heart twice; there's nothing wrong with your heart." And he says: "Well doctor I just want you to find out for me." The way to treat this—he could keep on going to that doctor for the next twenty years and his doctor's reassurance wouldn't help him at all. What he really has to do is to have his self-esteem increased to the point where he is no longer so anxious about things, and then the symptom goes away by itself. Does that answer your question?

Paul: Fine.

Mike: How do you select a group like this? Do you have personal interviews with each patient? Do you envision the beautiful transference situations which are going to work out?

Abell: Well I'm not quite that grandiose but I know it's going to happen anyway. In the selection of members for a group there are certain criteria that you follow. One is, if you have too disturbed a paranoid schizophrenic, you wouldn't take him in because he might actually act out his hostility by hitting somebody or something like that, so you would rule out the very disturbed paranoid. You would accept for therapy anybody who can relate satisfactorily to some degree without acting out violently. That is, if they have enough social capacity to be in a group without doing things which would be contraindicated, then I take them in. This includes schizophrenics; it includes all types of neuroses.

Maslow: Have you ever tried psychopaths?

Abell: No, and I'm not going to. I don't want any psychopaths. I've had some experience with psychopaths but not in a group. I remember a friend of mine—

[TAPE CHANGE]

Abell: Are there any other questions?

Herb: I think that question should be pursued further, about how you pick your group, like how you distribute the sexes. Do you envision beforehand that you'll have a mother figure in the group, or a father figure? You know something about your patients' histories.

Abell: Yes, that's a good question. Well I would like to have diverse groups and I would like to have a mother figure and father figure, and then I would like a group very much like this group—younger people and both sexes. I try to have the sexes equal in number—preferably four men and four women. I try to have some variations in age so that the different problems of each one will be brought out by the other. For instance, take Lee, who was so hostile toward mother figures in this group. Margaret as a mother figure would help him to be able to bring out and become aware of the hostility he had. And he would express it toward her and it would resonate hostility in himself and he would ventilate it, and this would help him begin to deal with it better.

Herb: Is there a danger to . . . call this "structured therapy" or "design therapy" or something? I mean, in a way you go even further than a simple rule that you might apply in every situation where you had an equal number of sexes. For instance, you knew about Lee beforehand, and that you would make sure you had a mother figure in the group.

Do you feel it's okay to design things this way?

Abell: Well, you don't really go that far. You just put people together and you find that the problems come out when they're together. They're bound to come out because they act them out in their living, so they're bound to act them out with the people that they're with in the group, and it doesn't really matter so much whether you know ahead of time whether they have that particular problem or not. Whatever problems they have will come out and then you deal with it, is what I would say.

Carole: What about intelligence?

Abell: As long as a person isn't feeble-minded—that is, as long as they have intelligence which is normal—then I would say they'd be satisfactory. It is not in general such a good idea to put people of average or less-than-average intelligence with a group of very superior people because it merely reinforces the inadequacies they feel already, and then they will only get worse. But anybody in this room would be alright [*general laughter*] providing you could be persuaded. Does that answer your question? Any other questions?

Charlotte: There's something that I question and I'm not sure whether it's valid at all, but as the group is progressing they're supposed to feel free to be able to express themselves—

Abell: Right, anything at all.

Charlotte: —and I just wonder, they also tend to become very analytical, and they also seem to have more insight.

Abell: That's true. That's correct.

Charlotte: I was wondering if this in some way would hinder the process in that the people become so aware that everyone is ready to pounce on everything that in a way their defenses are working unconsciously. I just felt this way in his case because I felt that Lee did not have a very strong self-image, which he at no time actually said; he at no time admitted everything was the way his mother felt about him and that he embarrassed his mother. Now I would imagine that he should have been able to get to a point where he could say that he himself finally got to the point where he felt that he was useless or something of this nature. And he never said it. Is it possible that somehow the defenses are beginning to work against them all over again?

Abell: Well, I would say that everybody gets defensive and they tend to protect their anxiety-producing spots. However, in therapy the person, at one time or another, uncovers their defenses, does away with the defenses and finally faces himself the way he is. This is sometimes a very devastating experience, when a person finally realizes that he feels like nothing at all. But when that is true it is a very crucial thing for the person to finally realize, because if he goes around pretending he's something when he really isn't, he's all the time feeling inadequate and upset and he doesn't know why. But if he finally admits, "I am nothing," then he can begin to see why. And then he can begin to rebuild in ways that the analyst can help a person discover his own worth.

Lee, in this film, is not ready to face this yet. He hasn't come to the therapeutic point. Now he wouldn't come to that in one session. This would take many, many, many sessions before he finally could come to say, "Well, I'll have to face myself and do something about it and stop blaming mother." But you can see that he's not there yet; but it has got to happen. However, I would say in answer to your question, the defenses are ultimately broken down in the therapeutic process. Although they're erected, they are repeatedly undermined and so, gradually, they diminish.

Charlotte: Can I just ask you one more thing?

Abell: Yes.

Charlotte: A lot of this seems to have elements of psychodramatics. Have you ever used any psychodrama in the group process?

Abell: I haven't, no. We have never set up situations in which we play roles.

Charlotte: Because it seems to be falling into . . . at certain moments it just seems that way.

Abell: It comes out naturally.

Charlotte: Yes.

Abell: I prefer to have it come out naturally rather than set it up artificially.

Sharon: Could you give us some kind of a bird's-eye synopsis of how it all turned out and what happened in the end? Could you maybe give the highlights of the few people we saw, what developed in the course of the therapy?

Abell: Yes, certainly. I can tell you about each one. Take Lee, for instance, and his struggle with his mother. This was about a year and a half ago and he's still struggling with his mother. This is such a deep and pervasive threat to his security and he's hurt so much about it that he's still struggling. Now there's one other thing in that he has in fact a deformity and this bothers him a great deal. It's hard for him to forget that he has a deformity, and every time he's aware of the deformity he thinks about his mother, and then he thinks, "My mother was ashamed of me." And then he gets very bad feelings about his mother, and it's very hard for him to give it up.

But I think he's just about coming to the point where he's beginning to be willing to give it up because it's interfering with his whole life. For instance, he's a professional man and he's in a big office doing important enough work, but in an unobtrusive way, if you know what I mean. He tends to withdraw; he's afraid of his partners, so instead of talking to them, letting them see he's a capable person—he's a very capable person—he holds back. He's threatened if they make suggestions to him and so on, and this is really keeping him down from advancing. Now he begins to see, after many years in fact, that he's acting out his hostility against his mother and he's expecting others to treat him hostilely and is withdrawing on this account, and that it's blocking his own goal. Now he's beginning to mobilize some resources to overcome it, but he hasn't gotten to the point yet where he's quite free. Now in the case of Vic—

Maslow: Before you run off from Lee, was it intentional—did you design it in the film—that he couldn't use the word "cripple"? He says, "I'm a . . . I'm a . . . I'm a . . ." and never says it. Was this his improvising or what?

Abell: This is a very interesting point. I never thought of it. No, what is there was not improvised or anything. It's just what he said on the tape, so I would assume that this was his real—

Maslow: Can he accept the handicap too? Can he say, "I'm a cripple?"

Abell: He can't accept it. He wants to be perfect. He can't accept it. So that he always feels bad about it. Now in the case of Vic—he's the one with the raincoat. He's the one who was afraid of women. Well, at any rate, he got over his fear of women. He met his girlfriend—it happened to be the girlfriend with the raincoat—fell in love with her, married her. He's doing extremely well and he's very happy, but unfortunately the program ended before this happened; we wish it could have been longer here.

Carole: Does the group still continue on, the same group?

Abell: Some of the group does, yes, but most of the people have finished by now.

Maslow: Very fascinated to hear this. My wife and I have speculated a million times about what happened.

Abell: Oh, did you?

Maslow: And I meant to ask you when I saw you. We followed these films for a whole year and I think saw perhaps two-thirds of them.

Abell: I'm complimented.

Carole: As people go out of the group do you put new people in? I mean, doesn't that somehow unbalance the group? You know, new people there with people who have been expressing themselves for a period of time?

Abell: No, I'll come to that in a moment. I'll deal with that point. Margaret is the older woman, the mother. Margaret had been very threatened when she came into the group. She got very much better—by the way, Margaret was a real person on the program, of course, but nobody knew her because her part was played by an actress. We introduced disguises so the people couldn't be recognized, but it didn't interfere with the basic thing. A couple of interesting things happened during the program. One of them was that a friend of hers broke her leg so she began to look at T.V. all the time, and she came in and she was watching this program. Well this friend said to Margaret, "By the way, Margaret, have you watched this program *Road to Reality*? It's wonderful. There's especially one woman in there that I like." Well Margaret was on pins and needles. "Who's that?" [*General laughter*] "That's Margaret, she's great and she's so intelligent." And Margaret was just reveling. [*General laughter*] It made her feel very good.

Maslow: Was that therapeutic?

Abell: It was therapeutic.

Maslow: In a deep sense?

Abell: In a deep sense. An ego-building thing. Now she also had another experience. She began to get proud of being on the program, and although each person was urged not to let anyone know they were on the program, with the exception of husbands and wives, Margaret finally got to the point where she wanted her son to see the program. So one afternoon she got her son; they were looking, and this program came on—her son didn't know that she was in this program—and then she remembered that in this program there was a very identifying thing which happened in relation to a windbreaker that he had on, and he was discussed in this particular shot. She was quite threatened by this, but we had disguised it and we had changed the windbreaker to a sweater and there was no connection at all that could have been recognized there. She came on and the son said, "What's she on the program for? She looks fine," and Margaret was very much pleased again. [*General laughter*] It was a real ego-building thing for her.

Well, she got a job—she had been afraid to—and she did writing for a medical house, and she did really very excellent work. She was very happy, and she's feeling very well. She's not with the group anymore.

Melody: What were the patients' initial reactions about having the therapy sessions televised?

Abell: Televised? Well, they of course were invited to be in this. This is not the kind of thing you could do. I mean, you couldn't take a group and then put it on the air without telling them. This was a big thing in which each one was invited to be a part and came into it as something they wanted to do as a public service, and also they got their therapy free. The network paid for the therapy, but it wouldn't pay them. We tried to get the network to pay them, but they thought that that would interfere with the therapy.

Sharon: So they knew this was going to be on television as they were going?

Abell: Yes, they knew it.

Doug: Did this cause problems of control on your part?

Abell: It didn't cause any problems because the patients said, "We'll do it, but we won't do it if it's going to affect the therapy on me and we're just going to behave the way we feel like behaving"—which was great. And we put the microphone out there in the middle of the room and they didn't seem to mind it at all; they would just talk along. But when the program went off the air we still had the same group and finally we stopped taping. *Then* they felt terrible. [*General laughter*] That microphone had been there and they had been talking; everything they said was recorded, and I think that was an ego boost to them.

Maslow: We had a discussion like this about our tape recorder. [*October 28 class*]

Abell: Oh, did you? [*Pause*] Any other questions?

Sharon: What about Harry? He didn't look very sick at the time.

Abell: Well, you wouldn't know that Harry needed therapy at all; he didn't really look sick. And the man in here, by the way, looks quite a bit like Harry. Well, Harry's marriage was just about breaking up when he came in. He used to yell at his wife. I don't know if you could tell in this session, but sometimes he would get real dominating and he would yell. But during the process of therapy, people jumped on him for it and he began to see that he did it, and he began to give it up. He also yelled at his daughter, which was a great distress to her and to his wife also. His wife came in one time and told me that she was going to leave him if he didn't change, and I said, "Wait another session. We'll see how it is." But he got over it, and she told me after the thing was over she was so pleased that he was a far different person, and they're very happy now.

Sharon: I know we can't follow all of those but could you just give an idea of the relationship between Lee and Margaret—how that worked out at the end?

Abell: Yes, the relationship between Lee and Margaret—well, Lee was a very sarcastic person initially. He got over a lot of this sarcasm so he began to relate to Margaret much better. But I don't think he ever got to the point where he could really be perfectly relaxed with her, and he's got to go some distance before this happens.

David: Are the transferences generally as rigid as they seem to be? In other words, this person reminded him of his brother and therefore he reacted very much in accordance. Did this happen every time this person saw a figure such as this?

Abell: Yes, I think that transferences are of all degrees and of all variations. Some of them are very minor, but you wouldn't even pick them up, and some of them are very intense. I remember one you might be interested in. Margaret, the older woman, got threatened by loud voices because her father used to criticize her and yell at her. And one time Harry was yelling at her, or at least speaking in a loud voice which she thought was critical. And she was so upset that she got up, she walked out of the room, she went into the bathroom and vomited. And I was concerned; I went out to see if she was all right, and she did come back.

Maslow: Was she able to bring that material back into the group?

Abell: Yes, then she was thinking about why she did it, and she recalled her father and how he treated her. And I think this is one of the special virtues of a group—the situation is so dynamic and emotional, from the "gut," that at that time you can pick it out and trace it back and you really see the connection then.

Maslow: Right from the "gut."

Abell: I want to say, though, we had a showing of one of these films after the program was all over in the ABC studio, and Margaret was sitting next to Harry and she made the remark, "You know, as I sit here and look at you on the program you look like an awfully nice person, but I used to think you were a terrible person, but I don't think you are any more." And Harry turned around and kissed her on the cheek, which made her blush somewhat, but she really got over being threatened by this.

Roslyn: What happened to Joan in the series?

Abell: Joan? Joan is still in therapy; she is still in the group. She has made a lot of progress. You wouldn't know it, but she had homosexual tendencies when she began therapy; she's gotten over those. She is now head of her own department in a large hospital and is doing very well with it. She had been afraid of men and she had an affair with a doctor after the program went off the air, and she learned all about men from him. It turned out he wasn't the man for her and they broke up, but she feels much better about men now. So she's still in therapy but she has made a lot of advances.

Now who else is there whom I didn't mention. Susan! Oh, yes, Susan was the young housewife. I had a letter from Susan about three weeks ago, and she said she was so appreciative of having been in the group that she changed very much and their marriage was going very well. She used to yell at her children. She was an anxious mother and quite threatened if they went out alone and so on. She said she was feeling very much better and that she appreciated it and that maybe sometime she'd come back and see me, so I encouraged her to. I haven't heard from her since. Any other questions?

Herb: You mentioned that you don't use Freudian terminology. Do you use any particular orientation?

Abell: Yes, Harry Stack Sullivan's orientation. We use the terms negative *self-image*, *self-dynamism*, *parataxic distortion*, in helping patients to get some orientation, but other terminologies can equally well be used too.

Saul: I am interested in the comparison between group therapy and individual therapy. In your opinion, how many things that have happened in the group sessions could also happen in individual therapy?

Abell: Yes, well they could all happen. Well, not all of them; certainly, they couldn't react toward each other in individual therapy. They could all happen in a certain sense transferentially toward the doctor. That is, Vic could act out his feelings of passivity in the individual analytic session. He could tend to withdraw in the individual analytic session. You could pick it up and point it out, but it wouldn't have the same meaning or intenseness that it has when he acts it out in a group. The same with Lee. Lee can talk about his mother privately, but when Margaret is right there he experiences it in his present dealings with another person. He sees how it affects his life more. So there is a little different flavor to the group from the individual analytic, I would say. Does that answer it?

Saul: Yes, but could you explain a little more what the advantage of group therapy is over individual therapy?

Abell: Yes, I can do that. I want to say first of all, however, that I'm not out to prove that group is better than individual. As a matter of fact I do much more individual therapy than I do group. I only see groups twice a week. But I would say that groups have certain special advantages. One is that there are people there with whom the person can re-enact his original experiences, and with the analyst this is much more difficult to do. The patient *can* describe what goes on in his extracurricular life so to speak, but it's only his description of it. But in the group he really *acts* it out and it gives a depth, I think, to the experience that he doesn't really get in the individual work.

Another thing is that there are multiple transferences in the group, whereas in the individual session just one person, the analyst, that he transfers, for example, feelings of hostility toward authority figures or whatever. But in the group, you see, you have six to eight people, it calls out much more in the way of transference reactions, which is beneficial in my opinion. Also, there is a very interesting effect that occurs in the group. If the group members confront each other with what they really are as they see each other—now, for instance, if one person, like Lee, had a sarcastic way of sticking the knife in the back and twisting with little sarcastic remarks, the group would tell him about it over and over and over. They would confront him with what he actually did—which was beneficial. Now an analyst can do the same thing, but it doesn't have quite the same effect because, one, it may be threatening at times—but we have to do it anyway. But when it comes from a group of peers the person can take it more easily. Then, I think also that in the group, patients are encouraged when they see other patients improve. It gives them an idea that they can do it too and that's something that you can't get in an individual session.

And I would say another thing is that in the group you have both sexes. Now you can't have that in the individual analytic session. In the group you have a boy, you have a girl, you have a man, you have a woman, and they can react toward each other. But in the individual session, if you're analyzing a man you have only two men, and anything about females comes from outside, so I think this is really an advantage.

Those are some of the advantages. Now some of the advantages of individual work is that you can pursue a single thing farther and in a more concentrated way with the person, and at times this is very necessary to do.

Herb: Two questions: One, is it possible to say—do you have a basis in statistics—that individual therapy takes a shorter amount of time than group therapy? It seems to me that group therapy would be more of a long, drawn-out process because you as the analyst don't have the time to address yourself to the patients as much. I know usually these things are impossible to gauge, but from your own experience, what would you—?

Abell: It's very difficult. I wouldn't say group therapy takes much longer. I would say however that one session a week in a group is not equivalent to three private sessions. It would take longer if you did it once a week in a group, but if you did it three times a week in a group and three times a week privately I think it would be just as rapid.

Herb: The other question is the obvious question, our course question. What was the reaction, basically, on the part of the public with letters received and responses to the program—in other words, the mass therapeutic effect upon the T.V. audience?

Abell: Yes. Well we had thousands of letters from all over the country and the letters are—with the exception I think of two—very positive, very approving and very desirous of the program staying on. When the program went off we got other thousands of letters asking that it be continued. So there was a real contact and people were really following it. I would say it got across to the medium. They estimated about four-and-a-half million people looked at it every day. Any other questions?

Paul: I'm not—I hope I can get this across by phrasing it this way because I'm not quite sure what I'm asking—

Abell: Yes.

Paul: Why was there such a pronounced lack of verbal references to sexual conflicts or sexual relationships, general sexual problems? I didn't detect them at all in these films and I would suspect, with the little knowledge I have of psychoanalysis, that in anyone's life this would play a significant role.

Abell: Yes, it does indeed. This was just a matter of accident. **Sex** certainly did come up and was a very vital part of the analytic work, but it didn't happen to be in these two sessions. If I could show you some others you'd see the deep threat that Vic had about sex and his relations with girls, and tracing this back to his mother and other things which are important for him to know about. But we just don't have those films left. These are the only two we have left out of over a hundred. They wiped all the others free—we didn't know it—I didn't know it, anyway. Over a million dollars' worth of investment they just wiped off the films. They wanted to use them for another program when this program ended. I would have liked to have got hold of them.

Maslow: This was after I had written all over the place, to the networks.

Abell: Yes, you were very good about it. [*General laughter*]

Maslow: Before I was very good, I was writing for my classes; I wanted those films. The request was, "Could we borrow them? Could we buy them?" I knew nothing more about them than what I saw. I met Dr. Abell by the way in the course of trying to trace that down. I admired these things so much that when I went to a psychoanalytic meeting I remember asking, "Does anybody know about this marvelous film series that I saw?" He sort of got pink, [*general laughter*] and it turned out that he was the one in charge. No, I was just being selfish as a teacher trying to get hold of those things, and got all sorts of run-around letters; it was very difficult. They knew in any case that one school wanted those films. It was after I'd met you that I then started writing those letters about saving the program and trying to get some other people to do that too.

Abell: They did get the letters, anyway.

Maslow: I got the answers too, but they were also run-around answers.

Abell: Yes. What I would like to do, since in the program we really have recorded what goes on over a long period of time, would be to get this re-enacted again, maybe twelve significant episodes so you would have the beginning, the middle and finally the end of the thing.

Maslow: I think this may now be possible with the money that has come to the educational networks. They're looking for programs.

Abell: Really?

Maslow: Yes. It's possible that this might be worked out, and this would be without advertising, and of course this would be given to the world. There is a huge network within this country, and I believe there are international exchanges also.

Abell: I would like to know about it.

Maslow: Well, it's the educational television stations. I know the one here, but there must be one in New York City too.

Abell: There is one.

Sharon: I have two questions: Are you familiar with the book *Fortunate Strangers*?[8]

Abell: Yes, I am.

Sharon: I was just wondering, this is the only reference I have other than seeing those films, and my impression on first reading the book was that it sounded so dramatic. I thought it was fascinating but I wondered if it was a little overdone for dramatic effect in order to sell the book or something. Now I get the feeling from these that maybe it wasn't. Can you give any idea of how—?

Abell: I don't think that book was overdone. I think the analyst was dramatic himself, and I think he stimulated a lot of goings-on between his patients, and I think it was probably a fairly accurate description of what went on his groups. That was my impression.

Maslow: Do you want to pass on that reference that you started with?

Abell: Oh yes, there is a book, by the way, by Alexander Wolf[9] and Emanuel K. Schwartz,[10] which has just come out, and I think it's the best thing that has ever been written on group therapy. It's called *Psychoanalysis in Groups*.[11]

Carole: Could you repeat the first name, please?

Abell: Alexander Wolf and Emanuel K. Schwartz. It takes up all aspects of the group therapeutic process and presents them.

Sharon: Did you have a hand in casting? Were you allowed to cast, or to help cast?

Abell: No, nothing at all. No, that was done entirely by the casting director; I never saw the people.

Sharon: What did you think about it?

Abell: Oh, I thought it was great.

Sharon: Were there other reactions? Did people ever write in their reactions to the casting?

Abell: Yes, they did. Margaret, the older woman, had a big audience; they all wrote letters to the actress. She got thousands and thousands and thousands of letters, a lot of fan mail. They all got some fan mail.

Maslow: This was a daytime program.

Mark: With the soap operas in the afternoon.

Abell: Yes, that's right.

Sharon: What was the reaction to the psychiatrist?

Abell: I don't know, I never found out. I don't know if he got any.

Sharon: He didn't get any letters?

Melissa: Do you know if this affected the lives of the actors, if they got involved in the roles that they were playing?

Abell: They did, and I'm going to invite them all to a party and ask them. [*General laughter*] But one very unusual thing did happen, which is that after the program was over this group of actors got together every Wednesday for lunch and they had their own group session. That's been going on for two years now. [*General laughter*] I have never been down with them but sometime I'm going down and see what's going on. I should be taping it.

Now another interesting thing that came out of the program was that this offered to the patients who took part a chance to see themselves. Not their real selves, but they could see a person playing their part and saying what they actually said. And they did look at themselves, and I thought it would be interesting to collect information on tape about their reactions to seeing themselves, their parts played. They told me they felt they gained understanding of themselves much quicker by being able to really view themselves. Especially Margaret, who is very vociferous about how much she gained from watching the program, and Harry did, and Vic did, and I think if something like this could be done—

Maslow: We planned to do this for this course.

Abell: Did you? I'll tell you that it'll work. I think it has a real effect.

Maslow: There have been a few experimental studies. The auspices were not nearly as good. These were very experimental setups, you know. They would take a picture of people writing a letter—it was no more intense than that—and then confront them with the pictures. Or in one experiment . . . If you're interested, I'm talking about the Werner Wolff experiment on self-confrontation,[12] and then there was the recent work that was done over at Harvard in Murray's[13] lab. Nothing terribly much happened, although everybody—the people who saw the pictures of themselves—reported that they were very much interested, and so on. There were no huge consequences. There were no obvious consequences, and it seemed to me that the thing to do was to do something more emotionally involved.

Abell: Yes, I think so too. One of the many things I want to do—I would have done it if I hadn't been so busy, and maybe this Christmas vacation I thought I might do it—is to take videotapes of a group of maybe three people interacting and then right away play the videotape back where they see themselves and what they do and then tape their responses and see what happens.

Maslow: Yes, we tried this. We didn't have the money for this but one graduate student here tried it with a tape-recorder, which I was going to report to you later on. Simply took an hour to talk into a tape-recorder all by himself and then listen to it back.

Abell: Oh, really? And what did he find out?

Maslow: He thought this was very good. There was an objectifying effect. He was very pleased with it. He thought it was a good adjunct to therapy.

Abell: I certainly go along with it. I think it could be a valuable thing. Any other questions? [*Pause*] Well I very much enjoyed coming up and speaking to you, it has been a real pleasure.

Maslow: We're not finished yet. [*General laughter*] Let's try to use Dr. Abell on the—I've told him a little about what we are doing. It would be of interest to you, I should think, to get his angles on some of these things we've been trying—some that worked, some that didn't work—your approvals, disapprovals, guesses and so on and so on. Why don't you address him yourself?

John: Well, another question: Is it vital in group therapy that the individuals don't know each other, that they only know their first names? Of course, the type of thing we do is decidedly different, but in any case we all know something more about each other, and in some cases quite a bit.

Abell: Yes, certainly. Now I think that it's much easier if you don't know each other socially and if you don't know your last names, because you can then talk about the most intimate details of your lives without fear that this is going to be repeated or is going to have any effect on somebody who is important to you socially. Now, however, I must say that although in my groups people don't know their last names and they don't socialize as friends for the most part, once in a while they get so fond of each other they break out of this and they go out anyway, and once in a while they date. And I think one time one girl and one boy went to bed with each other. Anyway, they spent the night, I found out afterwards, and this has to be their choice of course, except when this happens it tends to interfere with therapy. They don't want to analyze it, or one of them wants to mention it and the other one doesn't. There you impose a block to the freedom of expression which is antagonistic to the therapeutic process.

So I don't encourage this. I would rather have it remain therapeutic, but some people have what they call alternate sessions, and in the alternate sessions the group meets without the analyst. Most analysts don't have enough room to supply a room for the group to meet in, so they meet in their own homes. So that obviously they get to know each other this way and they get to know each other's last names as well, so the anonymity is gone. They say that the therapy goes on swell anyway. I can't answer your question for sure; my feeling is kind of against it. Nevertheless, it is done, and the people who do it say that it's fine. What do you think?

John: Oh, well, offhand I'd say I feel that it should be just the other way around; ideally one should be able to work in a group in which one could talk about intimate things with people whom it very definitely might affect. In other words, the element of risk should be included. This is just an intuitive feeling.

Abell: I think your point is very good. I really think that it would be good if people could realize that their problems are really nothing to be ashamed of and they can really talk about them freely with friends—not with their friends but with their therapeutic friends, let's say, and not be threatened. I think this is one step further. Maybe *I'm* still threatened by this.

Paul: I reacted this way at the beginning of our sessions. I don't think the problem is one of knowing people socially. I think that the size of the group is a far more important factor. I know that the size of this group has hindered us in expressing ourselves openly with one another much more than our knowledge that we're taking a risk and that we know one another. It's simply that the more people you have, the greater the risk is, and it reaches a point of being too great a risk. Because every time you take a risk you're taking it on the basis of faith which you have placed in certain people. Well there are too many people to have genuine faith in.

Abell: That's correct. You can't really know them that well. That's right, I agree. I have found out also in connection with size that when I increase my groups above the level of nine they tend to be somewhat inhibited, or some people do. But I would be interested in seeing how big a group you can work with, and some people do work with bigger groups than that. Have you been doing group therapy, as a group here?

Paul: We decided not to call it that. [*General laughter*]

Maslow: You decided not to call it that because it wasn't that. [*General laughter*] The limitations that we have here—probably the most important one is simply the length of time. This artificial, semester-long—12 or 13 sessions or even less—put one limitation on it. Then the size of the groups here that are possible, is another very severe limitation. We had to see what we could do under the conditions which they impose.

Abell: What did you find you could do?

Maslow: We're in the process of finding that out now. I structured the situation from the beginning in a non-therapeutic fashion because I'd given up the hope of being that intimate and of being that patient also. I couldn't wait; I just simply didn't have time enough, for instance, for the non-talkers, which will always happen eventually, to revolt against the talkers. I didn't have time. You'd have to be too patient and it would take too long.

The question that I raised was: Is it possible in a larger situation to use dynamic knowledge—knowledge about psychodynamics and also other kinds of auxiliary knowledge from other fields—to increase or enhance or speed up the process of self-knowledge, particularly knowledge about the pre-conscious and unconscious—not about unconscious impulses but particularly about unconscious cognition, primary-process cognition, and so on: poetic, symbolic, metaphorical. Well I've learned a lot myself. I think the students—if I can judge from a good sampling of notebooks—it would be hard to summarize because they are so individually different from each other. On the whole I think the majority of the students would feel, so far as personal benefit is concerned, that this has not worked well. I think there is disappointment, in spite of my structuring at the beginning that this is not therapy. The therapeutic model—

Abell: —gets in there anyway.

Maslow: It's unshakable, almost, which I've found with a fair number of people. Well, that itself is certainly a lesson for me. I think I've learned something. I'm not sure that this group has had the same kind of nice feeling about being altruistic, about being used in teaching others. There are a few things that come to mind. I've got a lot of points written down that I want for us to discuss in our next meeting—pros and cons and so on of what's possible and what's not. Experimenters will always say, the main thing you learn from having done an experiment is how it should have been done. That is, how to do it better the next time, and we'll be discussing that. Supposing we had such an opportunity again, 13 weeks or so. How would we change it? How would we do it? And this would have to be done within practical bounds. It does no good to suggest that you have just groups of six; it's just simply financially impossible. What can we do if we have groups of 25? What is possible under those circumstances? Those are the things that come to mind.

Paul: Dr. Maslow, I think there is one very valuable thing that has come out of this endeavor that you can't very well be completely aware of—namely, what has taken place outside of the classroom situation as a result of it. You are probably somewhat aware of it through the notebooks, but they can only be a very partial indication of that. I know from my own experience, and it must have been duplicated by others in the classroom, that this very endeavor itself, in its very nature, both encouraged and enabled me to engage in discussions with the members of the class on a level that would never have taken place otherwise.

Maslow: Some people have reported that; I don't know how many. I'm going to ask for a more careful counting of how much of this has happened and how deep it has been possible to go in private conversations, or in groups of three. I've been checking on it.

Paul: That has been a very important thing to me, at any rate.

Maslow: Yes, this is the kind of information I want to get. Do you have any questions further about this? Of the group here? While you have them? Or vice versa? I'd like to stay out of this if I can.

Melissa: I have a question about beginnings. In our week we have two-hour sessions that are more of a lecture, a student-teacher relationship, and then we have our third hour. A couple of weeks ago, maybe the session before last, we tried to unstructure it a little bit more. You know, not, "Today we're going to talk about something," but more, "What should we talk about?" And we had certain difficulties in arriving at something to discuss, and after that certain difficulties in approaching it. It seemed we talked much more freely when given something to talk about. And in the movie you all kind of sat there, and whoever played you said, "Okay, what should we talk about today?" And some of them immediately came up with some really beautiful material. Does this usually happen in your groups?

Abell: Well it doesn't always happen, but it happens more times than it doesn't happen. Now the problem is considerably smaller in that kind of a group than I think it would be here because the subject is always, "What are your problems and how do you feel and where does your shoe pinch and tell us about it." And generally somebody's shoe is always pinching and he is frequently willing to talk about it, so there is always something to talk about. Now I think in the groups where the immediate aim is not to diminish personal anxiety this might be more difficult. One thing about the setup that the doctor really has is that there is always something to talk about, so you don't have in a sense the looking in your mind for something to talk about. It's in the dealing with what is talked about that a good deal of the therapeutic benefit comes about. It isn't always the depth of character of what is talked about, although we chide people who are superficial, but there is something there that you can work with.

Also, in a sense, about this matter of orientation that some of you have asked your questions about, although I think the orientation I use is—well, I started to say the orientation that I use is the best one, but I'll retract that. I would say the orientation that I use is one that I feel comfortable in. I would say that it doesn't make that much difference what my orientation is because I've got something to talk about. If I don't have any orientation I don't know what to say. Well I know what to say, because I know my thinking already, so I can make a comment about it. But it's in the character of the comment that a lot of the therapeutic work is done. That is, I respect the person I'm talking to, like him if he's likable; a lot gets over, and I have something to talk about. But somebody in the Horney group, say, which is very close to my own thinking, would have his own way of talking—like the "idealized image." But he'd have something to talk about then, and in the manner in which he dealt with the patient he would get at things. So I think this matter of something to say is really a useful one.

Maslow: Well what would you suggest? In the case of group therapy the main thing you talk about is personal problems.

Abell: Yes.

Maslow: And I come along here and renounce personal problems to talk about from the very beginning.

Abell: [*Laughs*] I think you're in a tough spot.

Maslow: Well, the thing was to try it out and see what would happen then.

Abell: Well—

Maslow: That's the easiest thing to talk about—it looks like. And there is no question that there are big empty gaps of time and so on. And then there's a great call for the leader's reacting and to come dashing in and supply things to talk and to structure things and so on.

Abell: Well what do you really do? Do you suggest a topic there? Do you have a general philosophy or formula, for it?

Maslow: Yeah. There's a very general philosophy, a general formula that really needs more working out for detail. The general formula is to try to experience rather than to intellectualize and to try to be able to get at that by expressing it in a group, and with me standing by and butting in, "Well that's intellectualizing." I think we need more than that, is my impression. I don't think that's enough.

Abell: I don't think that's enough either. Now what can you experience then, if you only have something to experience that you can center your attention on so that people can talk about it? I think it would be much easier than if you leave it completely unstructured so that nobody knows exactly what to say and wonders if it's the right thing.

Well I have one suggestion to make which is an attempt, when speaking, to be direct with the other person and to not withhold the person's *feelings*. For instance, if I were talking to you, say, if I had something to say I might hesitate to say it for fear that you wouldn't think that it was the right thing for me to say. To try to break through that and be direct, I think, would be a useful thing. In this way you wouldn't necessarily be exposing your problems. That is, the problem might be, if I exposed it directly, that my father used to beat me with a rubber hose, but I don't want you to know this. So I won't tell you, "I'm having trouble talking to you because my father used to beat me with a rubber hose, because I'm afraid you will, and so I'd better be careful what I say." But I will say to myself, "I am going to try to make a real attempt to be direct," and so then I say directly to you what I have in mind. Maybe that would be one hint.

This is the kind of thing that Erich Fromm talks about—direct communication. I think this is very useful. Or if you want to be direct in speaking to each other you might speak about, "You look to me as if you haven't any interest in what I'm saying at all. Is that right?" Which is a direct communication—you're saying something. And the other person could say, "Well, as a matter of fact, I am not interested." And then the other person might say, "Well, why not? I thought what I had to say was interesting." And the other person might say, "Well maybe it is. Tell me a little more about it," and try at least to communicate directly without going back to the deeper motivating factors.

Sarah: When you start a group for the first time, what do you do? Do you take a lead role and structure the group from the beginning, or do you just say, "Group, go ahead and somebody talk." What happens?

Abell: I'm going to tell you, but can I go ahead with this subject you were talking about for a minute further? How would it be if you assign something to read ahead of time, like, well maybe a poem or a play or something that you knew had some interesting things in it, and then came in and each person talked freely about this and there was an interchange of feeling? Would that help the process? I would think it might, Dr. Maslow.

Maslow: We're going to try a little experiment next time. I've made slides of some of Saul Steinberg's cartoons, which are very, very good, and we'll see what comes up. I don't know, I've never tried it before. The poem idea is certainly a good one.

Abell: Or if—

Maslow: I'd prepared a lot of materials which I've never used. I had started at the beginning to try the verbatim clinical materials. I was prepared to do that. Then I thought, well, I tried that about a year ago and I think I know how that works. That works very nicely. Let's say, if we had your tape recorder, run it for a minute then stop and pause and let yourself meditate, see what comes up and then perhaps to ventilate these.

Abell: That would be appropriate.

Maslow: I've tried that and it worked very nicely. So since I knew that it worked nicely and I wanted more information, I decided this semester to try something I wasn't sure would work nicely. There's a fair amount of such materials: phonograph records, tape recordings, verbatim transcripts of the literature, dreams . . . I've used other people's dreams as a basis for discussion, for instance, in a group such as this.

Abell: Yes. This is very interesting to me and I would think it might help each person in expressing himself directly and more freely. [*Turning to Sarah*] Would you mind asking your question again?

Sarah: I just wondered at the beginning of this session, do you have trouble getting people to start talking freely with one another? What do you do?

Abell: Yes. Did you ask me about the first group meeting?

Sarah: Yes.

Abell: Well actually there is only one time when there is a first group meeting and that is when the initial group begins. Now this group that you saw today was started about 12 years ago, and it has been going continuously ever since. I've picked certain people out of certain groups in order to compose this one group, but they had been in **group therapy** before.

But when they first come together, you get them together in a room like this and I say, "Well how do you feel about being here in a group? How about telling us your feelings?" And if nobody says anything at all—but usually somebody speaks up—I would say, "Would you tell me your feelings?" and then you might begin to tell me what your feelings are, and then somebody would begin to talk about her feelings, and pretty soon you have a group interchange going on, and then I would say: "I never have people in groups without having interviewed them first, so that I know a good deal about each one of you, and would you mind each telling the other what brought you to the group anyway, what your problems are?" But I never choose anyone. I try to leave the person to speak who wants to speak and generally somebody will begin to talk about himself, and this encourages another person, and pretty soon they've all begun to talk, and this is the beginning of group interchange. And then from that time on I would let them choose their own topics and interact. And from the character of the interactions, trace back the reasons for it and let insight come along as it came along. Now in the case of ongoing groups that don't ever stop—when one person finishes you fill in with another one—I would say to the person who comes in, "Just sit there and see how it goes, and when you feel like saying something, say it. Our primary rule is: whatever comes to your mind say it, no matter what it is, about me or about anybody." Then that person gradually works in.

Clara: Do you then not have individual therapy with people that you put into the groups?

Abell: Usually I *do* have. Yes, usually I do individual therapy and group therapy with people that are in groups. I see many people who aren't in groups at all, but when they are in groups I prefer them to be in therapy with me outside of the group, or with some other doctor outside. It doesn't have to be with me.

Clara: Concurrently?

Abell: Yes, concurrently. Because I don't think at times you can cover all the material you need to cover in one time a week, which is all we meet.

Maslow: All questioned out? [*Pause*] I guess it's about time to quit anyway. Thank you very, very much, Dr. Abell.

Abell: It was a pleasure, Dr. Maslow.

[*The actual class ends here, but Maslow continues on*]

Maslow: I'm trying to think if there is anything we could do now . . . Yes, perhaps even more than three years ago, in many parts of the country now the John Birch Society has suddenly got it into its head that mental health is a communist plot. [*General laughter*] This is true, and in smaller towns this kind of thing couldn't get shown on television, especially in the Southwest: Arizona, California—

Abell: I've heard about that.

Maslow: —Southern California, Arizona, and it's beginning here. There have been a few little sessions in Massachusetts where generally they have been beaten, but they've made a stir, made a fuss.

This sort of thing needs encouragement from the citizens. That is—there ought to be a call for it to start with. For instance, this Channel 2 we have—an educational channel—is extremely stuffy and conservative and cautious about everything. I suggested this to them, by the way: could they try to get those videotapes, and they never bothered. But I think in our capacity as citizens we could, on the one hand, kind of push or ask for this sort of thing and then when it comes, you darn well better be prepared to protect it, fight about it—you'll have to. We'll scatter out, you know, to many parts of the country, and if you live any place between the East Coast and the West Coast you're going to get into fights over this being a communist plot. Well it's true. It has happened, it happens right now. So I'd say that was something to place on your shoulders for the future. [*To Abell*] You haven't had any of this have you?

Abell: I haven't had any of this, but I've heard about it.

Maslow: In the last year or so.

Abell: In the last year or so. And I would say it shows the people who are doing this are really paranoid. They want something to fight with or they want somebody to attack.

Maslow: This is the group of so-called patriotic societies that we've been calling—this is the paranoid circuit. [*General laughter*] I hope that you'll be successful in managing to get the educational fellow at the television network to pick up on these. Perhaps redo the whole business.

Abell: Thank you very much.

Maslow [*to the class*]: I have these—some of these notebooks are to be returned. I'm not returning the ones that are not bound in a book. I'm keeping those because they're not necessary to return now. There are some of you who apparently have notebooks to give in to me. I'll be discussing these. I've made all sorts of notes on them for our next meeting. And meanwhile, if you'll excuse me. These are private and I want to pass them around. [*Passes out notebooks*] And for those of you who haven't turned them in to me, would you do that now, please, because we'll be running home in a little while?

JANUARY 6, 1964

Lecture

Maslow: I've got all sorts of other little announcements and bits of things that I want to talk about, and then I want to respond and give some comments on your papers. I think we'll spend most of our time on that.

First of all, on simply the mechanics. Insofar as this is a course, I'll give you a question for the final examination—it's actually a final paper, really. We'll do it the way we did the mid-semester: you can bring notes into the examination room, but you must write out the paper there. And it's something like this: What have you learned about human personality in general—and if you want to specify, I mean "theory of personality"—from each of the readings during the semester, the class discussions, the exercises and so on? From everything you've done this semester. That's the whole of the final examination.[1]

I doubt that we'll have time—we have only one more meeting after this one—for going over these books that I wanted you to read: the Eric Fromm stuff on dreams [*The Forgotten Language*]. I won't add any more to that. I had hoped that we could talk about some of the Freudian stuff or classical stuff and some of the Jungian stuff, but I guess that would be too much. In any case you are responsible for Fromm and also for the Horney *Self-Analysis* book, but that I know I won't have time to discuss. The things that I wanted to say about it

324 | PERSONALITY AND GROWTH

would be too lengthy. If we do have time our next meeting I think I prefer to go over the dream psychology.

You have this Aldous Huxley paper here,[2] which is, I think for you now, simple thought, but interesting, especially since Aldous Huxley represents a whole—well, I don't know how to say that. I just read the last few pages of Professor Frank Manuel's[3] paper. He's going off to Stanford to give a series of lectures—very hoity-toity lectures, some endowed, big-shot things there. The whole world of historians will be listening to him reading. It's on philosophies of history, and what he winds up with of all things is just what we've been talking about, trying to. He staggers around just as we have been staggering around, but what he winds up with there is what other historians of any stripe whatsoever—the Marxians, cynical, pessimistic, optimistic, imaginistic people—they all seem to wind up finally in the same corner or at the same end that—gosh, I don't even know how to say it. Toynbee called it *spiritualization*, and that's enough to make the flesh crawl for many people, but what he means is, in essence, the going into the self for the answers to the historical problems. That is, the finding within the limits of human nature itself.

Let me say it the way another historian, Franklin L. Baumer,[4] said it. I don't know if I recommended it to you, his book. It's far simpler—Manuel would be tougher to read and it's much more condensed. A simpler book by Baumer is called *Religion and the Rise of Skepticism*,[5] and the last two chapters are probably very much like Manuel's last lecture or two. On the one hand, the recognition that the human being has some need for values, understanding, meaning, or something of the sort. There isn't a good vocabulary yet, and it's all very vague and so on, although practically everybody is now agreed that there is *something* there. I can quote Dr. James Klee,[6] who said, "There's a much-needed gap here." Well, there's a much-needed "gap" in this area, and what many people will use different words for is the need for meaning or values, or the need for understanding, or for "a frame of devotion" as Fromm called it. There is this need, and then there's the recognition that all the social institutions, all the hopes, all the philosophies, that all the panaceas have failed.

All the thinkers seem to agree on this: that there is no recourse above and beyond nature—the supernatural explanations have certainly been a failure—that changing the society and giving everybody two bathtubs instead of one, and two chickens in every garage and that kind of thing, hasn't worked. The Marxian, socialistic, political things haven't worked. Nothing has worked. All of these people wind up with, finally, is something you could call the "going into the self" or the "going into human nature," perhaps you might call it—that is, within the bounds of human nature itself—to seek for the signposts and the finger pointers, however vague they might be, however subtle, however delicate, however difficult to bring into consciousness, and trying to look there for the clues as to the values by which people should live. As soon as you say it that way you are smacked with the unconscious and the pre-conscious and the primary processes, and this, that and the other thing, because the self, as hitherto defined—the rational, the surface, the conscious self—can almost be defined as a system of defenses against the unconscious and the pre-conscious.

Well, there's a guy like Manuel, who's as rough a thinker as there is in the country—as skeptical, as disbelieving. If you talk about the unbeliever, there he is. And we have this "hands across the sea" business. For instance, it could never have happened before—it struck me as very funny: Manuel and I will probably give a joint seminar next year—of all people, that's surely the meeting of the East and West, or something—on the psychology of religious experience.[7]

Here are two profound skeptics, atheists, humanists—whatever you want to call them—and they are dealing with the religious experience, or the spiritual experience or the transcendental experience or some damn thing. Part of our job will be to work out a vocabulary that won't make goose pimples on people who are sophisticated and knowledgeable.

Well, Aldous Huxley is in that group. It's such a sad thing that he died, because this is what he was trying to write about. If he had lived for another five years, I think we would have had our . . . the synthesis from this point-counterpoint thesis you know—really cynical, sophisticated, tough, values-rejecting, boy-scout rejecting, do-gooder rejecting kind of attitude, and then, over this, what you might call the thesis, the antithesis there over into Zen Buddhism and religion and mystical philosophy, then finally trying to work out some kind of approach which might be satisfactory, might be a synthesis in the old Hegelian[8] sense—of on the one hand, what has been called religious until now, and on the other hand, what has been called naturalistic, scientific, humanistic. Huxley was working something out. There's a hint of it here in this paper I just passed out to you. And there are others doing it—Lewis Mumford,[9] Stuart Chase,[10] for instance. You might say, publicists and general enumerators, writers of various stripes seem to be winding up in this final step.

The only thing that Manuel won't admit, that we would certainly argue about, is that I would consider that this step up to a kind of another synthesis—a possibility of it—is an advance in human knowledge, not the recurrence of the spirituality or something that comes to a civilization on the edge of collapse, maybe, which is what we've had in the past. This kind of going-into-the-self has happened in Athenian Greece and Rome and so on, just before decaying set in. Well, I would think that we have something *new* in history here, and this is the advance in science—science stepping up to, enlarging itself so that it's possibly big enough to take in what it couldn't take in in the nineteenth century: transcendent experiences and so on.

Well, in that spirit I would like you to read the Huxley thing. I don't think it will startle you in any way because we've talked enough about it, but it's very nice statement. It's a graceful—literarily graceful—statement. There are other books, other readings that I'd like to suggest to you. Not seriously for now because we've been overwhelmed with reading this semester, but you can put this stuff into your notes for the future when you've got time. Especially you women, when you have your first baby and you've got lots of time to kill—that's when the baby sleeps most of the time—I'll make this assignment on that time. [*General laughter*]

I'd like you to take seriously the Martin Buber[11] book *I and Thou*.[12] I haven't assigned it—partly it's just too damn difficult in a way—but it's worth sweating with and struggling with, especially if you have an infant around, because you can actually feel it. Then the Victor Frankl book—which I don't really *like*, but it has something. *From Death Camp to Existentialism*.[13] I think I've mentioned the P.W. Martin book, have I not? He's a Jungian and his book is called *Experiment in Depth*.

And then two books I'm not sure of. I don't remember if I spoke of this woman, Claire Myers Owens.[14] Did I speak of her? This is apparently a very simple, uneducated woman who wrote these naïve books. *Awakening to the Good*[15] is the name of the first book. She sent me a copy of it and that title just made it impossible for me to read the book, so it sat on my shelves for a couple of years until sometime when I had nothing else to read, and I found this a very good book, to my great surprise. It's a collection of her peak-experiences and what she made of them, and in a very good, phenomenological way. She's a good introspector in the way that I would have liked you to become. That is, this in a certain sense was her "notebook," you might say, and she did better than any of you did, I'm afraid, without her college degrees and so on. You may sniff at it because it's naïve, but psychologically it's not naïve. It's quite good. Another book of hers came out a week or so ago—the same kind of thing, naïve but good. It's called *Discovery of the Self*.[16] There's nothing new for you to learn in either of these books, but it's the manner, the simplicity, the willingness to be ludicrous, the lack of sophistication as a defense, you might say. She's perfectly willing to look simple, even, and her book is full of misspellings of every sort, and yet that was what I would have liked you to write in your notebooks, that kind of thing. So this could serve as a kind of example.

I told you that your mid-semester papers as a group were excellent, practically all very good, but your notebooks are practically all very lousy. There were a couple of quite good ones and three or four passable ones, and most of the others were just plain no good. Either you missed the point or you were too shy or bashful or something. For one thing, you simply didn't do part of the job that you were supposed to do—the matter of responding to these suggestions that I made, exercises about this and that and the other thing.[17] And I've asked Min to make a partial list of some of the exercises that were suggested, that I had wanted you to respond to privately in your notebook, which is your private conversation with me. Now that has just been passed out to you and I'd like you to take that seriously, please. Catch up on that.

There may be others on this list. For instance, here's a list I have:

1. Peak-experiences. Describe them. I have something to say about those in my notes in a little while.
2. The female's feeling of power over the male; I might add the male's feeling of power over the female.
3. What women think they would feel like if they hadn't seen a man for a long time. It sounds a little ridiculous as I read them off, but anyway these were suggestions, rather casual, off the cuff at the time, but you might as well respond to them.
4. Reactions to babies. I think most of you did respond to that.
5. What it would feel like to be in a nudist colony. I asked you to introspect on that, but none of you did. Your feelings about nakedness can strike very, very deep. They can be very revealing to you and certainly they would be revealing to me, if you're honest enough.
6. Reactions to the tape-recorder. I think most of you did take advantage of that to respond to. If you haven't, please write that down.
7. Do we ever experience a feeling of timelessness or eternity? If so, what does it feel like?
8. What kind of music seems erotic or romantic to you? What kinds of other feelings can music produce?
9. How do you feel when you are hurt; for instance, if someone says he hates you? I want you to say something about that.
10. What does it feel like to cry? What sensations are there?
11. Or, for most people: how does it feel to *feel* like crying, even if you don't cry? Some of you responded to that, but most of you did not.
12. Comment on the discussion of sex in class. I got some comments, some responses which were, for me, very instructive.

I feel, sometimes very strongly, the gap in the generations. It's as if I don't know what's in your heads, what you're thinking of and feeling, and some of the notebooks have been very instructive for me—which is very good. I should think educating the professors is a very desirable thing to do. Well, some of you did discuss, respond to the discussion of sex, and I'm grateful for it. It was very helpful to me. I think I know better how to handle it.

Oh, yes: I wanted you to respond to this suggestion about having informal sessions without a teacher around. [*Flips through papers*] That's all I have here.

I have an example of one of these exercises that are listed here. I could hardly suggest that you write poetry, for the suggestion probably would not work—I doubt that most of you could do it. Short of this, I had suggested, you may remember, as an exercise for yourself this business of being like a child—childish poetry, which you might very well carry on in the future. And I suggested the figures of speech, systematically breaking through the clichés. Do you remember that? To write down the figure of speech, whatever it's called—metaphor or something—"as white as ____," and then we would say as white as milk, as white as snow, something like that. And then your job would be to try to be like a child who doesn't know about our clichés. You ask him, "As white as what?" and then he'll give you something startling, very fresh, frequently. I have here just a few that I wanted to read. Here's one: how does it feel to sit in the sun?

One child says: "I feel like a snail curled in my shell and the curls of my shell are warm." It's obviously creative in the sense that it's novel, it's new, it's honest, it's authentic—that's the word: it's *authentic*. It's certainly not stereotyped, clichéd, rubricized. It's not like that at all. It's possible for adults to approach this whole business of being poetic via this technique, of trying to break through the stereotypes.

Or like this one again about the child sitting in the sun—it's marvelous, it's the one I like best: "I feel like a baked potato with my warm, crinkled skin"—marvelous!

And here the child was asked, "As slow as ____," to say what is slow. As slow as what? "As slow as a turtle walks" might be a good one; "As slow as growing" which must seem like the slowest thing in the world to an impatient kid. Or, "As slow as going to sleep"—there was one child, "Daddy, I've forgotten how to go to sleep." [*General laughter*]

Or a child describing a worm; this is cute too: "A worm has a way of walking; he wiggles into himself then flats himself along in a jiggering kind of way." [*General laughter*] That's the way a worm walks, obviously.

Well, that's the kind of thing that I had wanted you to try to do. If you're shy about it then keep it to yourself and try something else. If you're not shy, please pass it on to me and take these standard things—"as slow as, as fast as, as white as" something and so on—and see how you can describe it.

Paul: Dr. Maslow, we've done a lot of reading in this course on psychoanalytic ideas, concepts and psychoanalytic points of expression and associations. We've really done more reading in that area than in any other, I think. I was just wondering how we are to apply this to this general personality experiment that we're engaging in. You haven't really said anything in that regard. I don't quite know how to put it to use in terms of the objective of the course.

Maslow: Well, I'm interested to see just how you'll work that out. I think I'll throw it right back at you: that's *your* problem. Which reminds me of the one thing I wanted to add to here. I think I mentioned to you Mrs. Huxley's book. You remember that book by Laura Huxley[18] that came out sometime during the semester? It's called *You Are Not the Target*,[19] and there was kind of an effort to make therapeutic exercises that people could use for themselves. It's sort of simple. Some of them are helpful, and one is extremely helpful. The one that I like best of all, that Huxley liked best of all too, and gave it as the title of the book, is "You Are Not the Target." It would be a very helpful exercise and I would like you to make a special point of it, please. The job is to root out within yourself, your own paranoid tendencies, which we all have—the tendency to think of ourselves as the target, as if things were done on purpose to annoy us, when actually they are not. People may say at a very high level, "What did I do to deserve this?" Maybe a man says this as his daughter dies—I'm reading this Peter De Vries[20] book recently. This wasn't done on purpose to annoy him. He was not the target of anything. Most of us in most levels of living react in this paranoid way. If a rock gets in our way, we are apt to kick it as if it deliberately got in our way. Certainly in interpersonal relationships this happens very, very frequently. I can almost say that lifting yourself up to impersonality above paranoia—that is, if you can transcend your paranoid tendencies and your defenses against paranoia—that you are then at this higher level, this self-actualizing level in which you can realize that . . .

Well, I remember setting one example—it's the most extreme that I can possibly think of. If a tiger is about to spring upon you and kill you and you can look at it in a kind of detached way without anger and see how beautiful the tiger is, then this would be the most extreme example that I can think of—of this impersonal, "you-are-not-the-target" kind of thinking.

There's another example I'd like you to keep in mind in your notes, if you don't know it already. It's kind of a standard psychoanalytic joke, but it's not really a joke. It is the classical story about the two psychoanalysts at a party, and for some reason or another one got insulted and walked up to the other one and slapped him across the puss. And the psychoanalyst who was slapped got startled and thought for a moment, and then finally shrugged his shoulders and said, "Well, that's *his* problem." [*General laughter*]

In your notebooks and in our discussions in class, the question of hostility, of attack, of liking and disliking, of agreeing and disagreeing and so on was brought up often enough to recognize that on the whole you were too personal about too many things. Let me say it the other way about: you were not impersonal enough. Now, to become purely impersonal is impossible for the human being because we are persons after all; we can't become non-persons. This is a kind of a limit to which, apparently, psychologically healthy people approach. They are *more like that* than other people, even though they can never get there altogether—except maybe for the moment, the transient moment of peak-experience or B-cognition, which is transient, not permanent.

In effect, this is the kind of thing that would come up after a year and a half of psychoanalysis, if I were the analyst, trying to make this point that you are not the target. That is, you'll find characteristically in people who have got access to their unconscious after this training of psychoanalysis, you'll find dreams, or fantasies or impulses—if you can catch them, if you're a good enough introspector to catch unconscious impulses—a great resentment against your mother who died, maybe, and you can dig up out of the unconscious what you felt at the age of four, a real resentment and anger and hostility against your mother because she abandoned you. And then you have to discover at a higher level of maturity that you were not the target; this was not done on purpose to annoy you. Or if your father went off to the wars and left you without a father for a time, and so on. Again, this is the business of becoming impersonal, supra-personal about this.

The psychoanalysts I think have the best training in this—better than any other that I know in the world—in developing this attitude of being able to take hostility in an impersonal way. That is to say, to recognize it and say, "Well, I'm not the target." This is transference analysis: "I am not the target because I stand for somebody else. This guy may punch me in the nose; it may hurt my nose and make my nose bloody, but he thinks he's hitting somebody else's nose, or that's what he is trying to do." Well as we say, it's very difficult to be impersonal about it, but the good psychoanalyst under these professional conditions, with some experience, does manage to do that. It seems miraculous in the situation that they can do this with such calm and take abuse of all sorts. One of my friends was a psychoanalyst and he got so tired of it. He's a little fat and every once in a while, every time anything went wrong, one patient after another would call him a fat slob. [*General laughter*] You have to take it and realize what this means. It's like the two-year old child, perhaps, kicking his mother in the shins because she didn't love him enough.

Now the question is: Can you respond to my professorial talk, the words, my confrontation, my interpretation to you in general—can you respond to this in any personal way? Can it make a difference? Can you see in the next couple of weeks—for me of course, when you're reporting to me, but in the next couple of years even for yourself? Can this insight—if it is an insight, if it does percolate into your insides—can you use it? In other words, the old question that I started the semester with: can we short-cut psychoanalysis? Can we pass out via the radio, via the television set, via just words in a book maybe, an insight which hitherto has been considered to be requiring a year or two of work? Is that possible? So, I'd like you to put that down as an exercise for you to respond to me in your notebooks.[21]

Ben: In what form?

Maslow: I don't know. That's your problem again. I don't really know because we haven't tried this. What I want to know is: do my words click off anything in you or don't they? Have you thought of some experience in a different way while I was talking here? Have you reinterpreted something, or will you during the next couple of weeks? I might suggest even to go further: pick somebody you're mad at. Many of you are mad at me, perhaps—well, pick me. I have disappointed you in one respect again and again—it has been this business about your coming into this course because you thought it was a course in psychotherapy. Now some of you weren't aware that you thought so consciously and yet you've been trying—there has been the therapeutic effort all the time and I have pushed it off and pushed it off, and occasionally I can see a real anger. Well, perhaps take that, if you like, as an example to work on. That would be standard transference analysis, if you want to call it that. See what you can do with it yourself, on your own.

Charlotte: Are you saying that these feelings of paranoia should not be with us at all?

Maslow: No. [*Pause*] Alright, let me anticipate something I was going to say later on. We talked about this a little when we talked about that B-humor thing. Which, by the way, too few of you also responded to. I wanted you to tell me, how did you feel about that? What difference does it make? Would you add that to your exercises for those of you who didn't do it?

If you'll remember, I must have spoken about this B-humor as the resolution of what some people call the existentialist dilemma. Or other people, for a longer time than that, have called it the human predicament. One aspect of the human predicament is what the old theologians used to call the problem of hubris. The truth is that we are a peculiar species in this sense that our imaginations can carry us way, way, way beyond our actual possibilities. In our dreams, certainly, we can do all sorts of fancy tricks that we cannot actually do in the physical world. But this is true also for our aspirations. I might have aspirations for being simultaneously a great athlete and a great Don Juan and a great philosopher and a great musician and so on and so on. We can do this sort of thing even though we know it's realistically impossible.

Well, in our society at this time we have too many defenses against our grandiosity, put it that way. This was what I was trying to break through a little bit with you when I suggested that you look at each other and think of yourselves as world leaders, let's say; or think of yourselves or each other as fulfilling, you know, the U.S. Senate. If I could only look into your heads and see what your own particular fantasies are, what you would like to be in your deepest guts and that you've undoubtedly renounced for fear of paranoia, for fear of grandiosity, for fear of hubris, the sin of pride, the sin of being god-like. See, we're talking now about the punishment of Prometheus[22] and the punishment of Adam[23] and so on. This is an old, old theme of the human being having the tendency to be god-like and yet being afraid of it because of the evil-eye, because the gods punish and so on. Well, the question is: how can you be, in fact, more god-like than you are? As a group, you are—of your culture and of this time—afraid generally, or renouncing your own god-likeness, your own heroism, your own nobility, your own highest potentialities—with humility as a defense.

Humor of a particular kind—this B-humor, this high humor—has one good function: it permits you to be god-like without feeling paranoid, without being grandiose. It permits you, just so you'll keep your sense of humor. Then you can say: "I am going to change the world," and then you snicker and nobody gets mad at you. Or, "It's my ambition to be the greatest living poet," you might say, or "I'm going to be a famous actor" or whatever—fill it in for yourselves. But these are the things you keep to yourselves generally, because other people will regard you as crazy or puffed-up or whatever, and when this happens we know, as you will find out, that if—for instance, I were to tell you what my I.Q. was; well, I've never told anybody. You might imagine it would be pretty high, but I don't dare. There's practically no portion of our whole society, except maybe in the American Psychological Association, and then only in small portions—not even there, by gosh. I can't come in and say "Oh, I've got a wonderful I.Q., a very high I.Q." I can't look at somebody in the eye and say, "I've got a high I.Q.," much less say, "Oh, my I.Q. is so much higher than yours." [*General laughter*] The society doesn't permit it.

Now, that's a localism, because in the Plains Indians, for instance, it was permitted. With the Plains Indians, part of the many ceremonies—the sun dance ceremony—was for everybody to run around—we could call it boasting. But it's actually realistic talk. "You all know what a great leader I am," the Chief would say, "how in this reign I captured such and such and did so and so," and another man will say "You all know that I am the most intelligent man in the tribe," and everybody will say "Uh-huh, uh-huh"—if he is.[24] [*General laughter*]

Well, we can't do that, so it's for us a problem. See, if you're *only* proud, then you are in fact paranoid. As a matter of fact, that's almost the definition of it—to be proud or god-like without any humility at all. Now I'd go further: to be without *humor*. This is an easy way for you to make the diagnosis of the paranoid character—he's humorless. Well, B-humor, this particular high humor, is a way of reconciling the opposition between humility and pride in such a way that you can go on shooting at your highest aspiration levels without becoming psychotic, without being paranoid.

Our paranoid characters gave us plenty of trouble—Hitler and Stalin were paranoid characters, it seems pretty clear. Senator Joe McCarthy looks like a paranoid character. This John Birch fellow looks like a paranoid character. They make an awful lot of trouble for us, and I think it's best for us to understand them and our own paranoid tendencies too—not to be so afraid of them that it will cripple you. Many of us avoid being paranoid in effect by castrating ourselves, by making ourselves too small, too humble, too meek, too mild—renouncing ambition, renouncing high goals, renouncing aspirations and saying: "You don't have to be afraid of me. I'm no challenge to anybody. Poor little me; I'm no threat."

I wanted to talk about the obsessional in a kind of a hurry but I think I'll hold that for a time, because I want to make more comments on these notebooks. These are not in any special order.

First of all, about the group therapy. There are possibilities for group therapy which you will run across in your communities, things like the Unitarian fellowships which are spreading on the West coast anyway, much like the old Christian communion, the family communion, the group that meets together regularly over the course of years. One of our problems was we just simply don't have enough time. We couldn't manage group therapy in one semester of meetings—12 hours. Now, if you have 200 hours or 300 hours stretching out ahead of you, then it's quite possible to manage these things, and there are many approaches to it.

There are self-analysis training institutes which are starting up all over the country—T-group stuff. I just got a call yesterday from one guy who's going up to Bethel in Maine where they are apparently now running these institutions right through the whole darn year, winter as well. Do you want to pass this around? [*Maslow passes around a brochure on T-groups*] I want to keep this, but you can take a look at it and just pass it around.

Anyway, group therapy shouldn't even be tried unless you have time enough for it. As we talked about this, the waiting for the patients to open up needs much time and is not possible if you're in a hurry. Dr. Abell made a very interesting point for me that I hadn't thought of at all, but you may have noticed it. It was pointed out that the main beginning of discussion—somebody asked, "What did you talk about? What started the discussions?" And he pointed out that it was essentially personal problems. But in our setup we had to, to a large extent, renounce that as a beginning, or technically and strategically leave it. Well, in the Unitarian fellowship kind of thing, that is possible—personal problems are possible to use. Well, for us and in our kind of experiment, the question is: what could take the place of these personal problems as the beginning of the dialogue within a group?

Dr. Abell made a couple of suggestions, but I don't think they were very good. I don't think there is any really good substitute for personal problems as a start. One, you remember, he suggested we might start with personal statements, poems and so on. I think myself, the best thing I could think of was what I tried in a previous class: using other people's personal problems. That is, using case materials and reading them out. For you what this might mean—as a suggestion you might find it very interesting—is to pick up the habit of simply reading all the case histories you can get, to browse through the psychoanalytic and psychotherapeutic literature. There are always case reports. There are now many books—I think I've listed some for you—on "the story of my psychoanalysis" or "the story of my mental breakdown" and so on and so on. There is quite a bibliography. I'd be willing to say that exposing yourself to that kind of thing is a form of therapy. Your own defenses will take care of protecting you—you simply won't understand what is too dangerous for you to understand; let me put it that way. So that I think it's quite all right to read these things. It will percolate in rather than break your doors open altogether. It will just soak in gently.

Oh, another point that Abell reminded me of: if you ever do this kind of thing, and some of you will in the future, I imagine—if you have the teaching situation at any level and you would like to make it more psychodynamic, as Huxley or Professor Dick Jones[25] suggest, you'll have to keep in mind that you must have an escape valve there someplace or else it's too dangerous to start. You must have a way of quitting.

In group analysis of the sort that Abell did, if he makes a bad mistake for instance and starts interpreting, let's say, with a "schizie" person, this is dangerous. That is, it's easy for a borderline schizophrenic—somebody who is not schizophrenic but who has the potentiality for it—it's possible by pressing him with interpretations to break him over into open psychosis. And this is one of the kinds of experience that you need in psychotherapy—to be able to recognize this danger. Well, supposing we make a mistake, as every psychiatrist does, especially in his early years. He doesn't recognize the "schizie" person and then he presses him with insight, with strong interpretations which the person can't assimilate yet; it's too much, or the ego is too weak. What happens in such a situation, characteristically, is that the person quits; he just runs away with self-esteem-defending statements of one kind or another: "That guy is a jerk" or "He doesn't know his business" or "I don't like him" or something like that.

Now, if you have a classroom with a captive audience who must stay there to get credit and so on and so on, then you must not press. It's too dangerous, there's no outlet—especially if it's a larger group and you don't know everybody so intimately. You simply cannot— it's too dangerous to press and to push and to force. Never, unless there is a quitting point, an escape valve of some kind. And in a course like this, it's not possible to quit beyond a certain time without a great deal of trouble, and therefore it puts limits on the pressing, on the personal-ness of interpretations.

Joan: If you had a short time, say a month, would you still have these fears that it would be too dangerous? Or would you feel that that's too short a time to worry about it?

Maslow: Well, it would have to become practical. For me, yes; I don't have enough psychiatric experience. I don't have enough experience with borderline cases, with schizophrenics, with seriously sick people. My therapeutic experience was with *not* very sick people, with neurotics and so on. You get somebody like Professor Harry Rand, or some of our clinicians here who have a lot of experience, that's different. I'd say, well, what's possible for them might not be possible for me. With really experienced psychotherapists who have had lots of experience over a broad range of personalities, sometimes they can tell within an hour. It's like a really experienced dentist or doctor or surgeon or one of these osteopath people who can just—he is so sure of himself that somebody comes in who's all bent up and can't straighten and the osteopath looks at him—just looks at him— and then like that, he straightens up. I've seen it happen. Well, I wouldn't dare to do that. [*General laughter*] He dares to do that because he knows well. So I think I would make a big point about the adequacy of the leader. For myself, I'd be more cautious.

I've discovered something for myself. I wrote this for myself in my own journals on self-analysis, and this was your problem too, I'm afraid, because I was an important part of the group. I've discovered that I am very impatient about wasting time, and I had to analyze for myself the meaning of wasted time for me. I'm not a very good waiter about some things, I tend to break in if things are not going fast enough for me. In other words, as I was talking I realized I was speaking more rapidly than I would if we were sitting before the fireplace and having a cocktail or something, without limits of time. I was extremely conscious about the little time that we have so I sort of pushed a little bit there and I may have pushed into the middle of your conversations sometimes more than I should have. Well, that's *my* problem. [*General laughter*] I'll have to work that out.

Oh, one thing that came up again and again in the notebooks: the question of peak-experiences and their level. It's as a research strategy and as a pedagogical strategy that I chose to talk about the most extreme ones that I could find, the most undoubted, clean-cut cases. And apparently I didn't stress enough the foothill experiences, the low peaks, and the fact that most of our peak-experiences are not of that kind that I described in the extreme. It's that kind that might happen two or three or four times in a lifetime, once or twice a year at most or something like that. But my hope—or at least the pedagogical strategy—was that if you can become very aware of the pure radium, so to speak, then you could recognize it in lower concentrations in the pitchblende—did you get my figure in there? That you would then recognize the peaky quality that would come from simply smoking a good cigar or having a good meal or something mild like that, which is a peak-experience. You might call it an everyday one, a low one, with the quality of peakishness but not of the highest fusion of the universe kind of thing. I wanted to say that.

Paul: At the beginning of the semester I was very intrigued with this whole concept of peak-experiences. It was the first time I'd ever encountered even the term, never mind the concept, and I did a good deal of introspecting about this particular word and phenomenon itself. And I increasingly came to wonder, and I'd like to ask you right now, the question which I kept asking myself, whether it's not possible to have unhealthy peak-experiences in the sense that perhaps they can stifle your attainment of complete actualization of potential, by striving to keep yourself in those situations which give you peak-experiences which perhaps are here and rewarding rather than those up here, and you no longer ascribe to those up there because these down here seem to be rewarding in themselves. In this sense, do you almost stagnate your life as a result of your recognition of the value of peak-experience?

Maslow: You know, we've talked about that some. Just on your point I'd recommend again the book by C.S. Lewis,[26] *Surprised by Joy*.[27] It may be in your reading list. It mentions the way in which his consciously pursuing high peak-experiences actually messed up his life a little bit. I think we've also discussed the levels from health even to psychosis. The fact that you can have psychotic peak-experiences—or something that looks like them—neurotic peak-experiences—unhealthy ones—and that this is a problem for the workers in the field. They haven't straightened it out yet.

All I think you can say—everybody would agree—is that there is something like peak-experience in perversions, such as the arsonist setting fire to something. Colin Wilson[28] has a very interesting book that just came out on the sexual perversions. I think it is the best book I've seen on the subject: *The Origins of the Sexual Impulse*.[29] It's actually mostly on lust murders, which he analyzes very, very carefully and very intelligently. I could sum up his thesis. In effect he says what they are looking for are peak-experiences, and that's the best they can do. For "dead" people so to speak, it is the only recourse they have. I was going to speak about the obsessionals, too, on this point. People who absolutely cannot feel at all, and what we might suggest about that. *The Origins of the Sexual Impulse.* I ordered it for our library. It's an English book; it's not out in this country.

Yes, but I can't say much about it. Just that it's so—it looks like—and I don't know what to do about it exactly, except to just describe these differences and see what the research strategy will be in the future.

Another little note here. This may click after the course has ended, when the authority ambivalence is no longer needed. [*Maslow chuckles*] That is, when you don't have to fight me particularly, one way or another, you may find out that many more things will come into consciousness a year from now when our authority problem is gone—the grades and the power I have over you and so on and so on. If so, I would like you to write to me if you feel like it. If you feel scientific enough about this, help the onward march of knowledge via helping me. And I invite you to write to me. Please don't expect answers, but if you don't mind writing you know, tossing the data in, then please do.

Oh, another thing—I would like photographs of each of you if possible, if you have snapshots or something. I don't know, I may try to look you up five years from now, or something. I doubt it, because

I just don't have enough time, but it would be very interesting to talk with you a year from now or three years from now and see what's happening. For instance, it's my impression, after reading your notebooks and talking with some of you, that more has happened to you than you're aware of, as a group, as individuals—without regard to your feelings, as some of you for instance disapproved or had other expectations about what this semester would be and were frankly disappointed. Even there, I think, it's quite possible, if I smell the wind correctly, that more has happened than is now permitted to come to consciousness and which may very well come into consciousness two years from now. So I would very much like to be able to talk with you if that's possible in the future. Could you, if you have them at all—I don't want to press you on this too much—if it's not inconvenient, give me a photograph of your face so that you can be recognized two or three years from now. And on the back of it would be your name—I don't need the addresses. We'll have those here through the Alumni Office, if I ever do want to get in touch with you.

I want you to turn in your notebooks to me, those of you who are to turn them in, at least a week before the final examination. I must have time to read them. [*Pause*]

Here's a quote from someone's notebook:

> The first hour everyone had to contribute. There was a great deal of comradeship felt. Frankness was displayed. It was as if we were excited travelers about to explore ourselves together. The prospect of these new, exciting, perhaps terrifying vistas set us all aflame. Since that day the class has been flat. The original excitement and venturesomeness has been lost. Now the talkers talk, the listeners listen and the class is normal.

[*Chuckles from several people*] It's a good way of summing it up.

Now I'd say that only—there's sort of a split I want to speak about. First of all, I can tell you from my experience. See, I can just override your feelings because I just have the empirical facts. I can tell you from my experience that forcing people to talk in the way that I started with *does* work. Just as with the tape recorder, the uneasiness disappears very rapidly. The anxiety, even panic, terror in some cases—of speaking in public—disappears very rapidly for the shyest people. I didn't push that for other reasons. I wanted trial experiments.

It's interesting also—I would like you think about this—that most people in the group had a kind of ambivalent attitude toward their being pushed into openness. A little anxiety on the one hand and also the usual business about authority—the business of just simply resenting authority and resenting being pushed, being forced. It's interesting—watch for yourselves now—that there was the clear majority of you who felt that you didn't want that push, that it was better to leave it to spontaneity and openness. Well, obviously you read the situation wrong. I didn't mind spontaneity and openness, for one experiment is as good as another for me. But many of you who spoke against this being pushed, "Let us talk when we feel like it"—most of these people never opened their mouths for the whole semester.

And you've got here something that you have to work on for yourselves—that's late adolescent stuff. That's not yet adult reaction. It's not yet the mature person. This is still the fighting for freedom and not knowing quite what to do with it, or at least the fighting for freedom and not using it fruitfully, productively and well. This I think you could profitably analyze in yourselves, because I think this is very widespread. It's not only in this group. It's in the whole society, and the age goes higher and higher all the time. It used to be that this ambivalence toward authority was resolved around the age of 13 or 14, in the year 1900. Now it gets later and later and later, so that you have people at the age of 30. In some places, in the psychoanalytic institute here where a man sometimes isn't a full-fledged psychoanalyst until the age of 50—all his hair is gone and he's got grandchildren and he's still afraid of his teachers. People will make fun about it—they made a *bar mitzvah* ceremony for this white-haired man. [*General laughter*] *Now* he was a man! In our society, with the steady postponing of full citizenship, full economic self-support, full identification with your call, with your vocation, it gets later and later, and this is something you've got to work on. It seems to me, from my vantage point here, that there was a lot of this in this class—of this struggle for freedom and then not knowing what to do with it when you got it, or at least not using it as well as one might have expected from the protests.

I've referred you to my own investigation into dominance—the paper I spoke about comparing the dominance reactions of monkeys and the fantasies and dreams of patients in therapy.[30] This is the business of tending to personalize; that is, to make a dominance fight out of an order, a suggestion or a demand from authority. The fact is, I *am* authority. The only question is—I mean, the real contrast is not between authority and freedom but between *sane* authority and *insane* authority. The lack of authority can be just chaos altogether, not freedom, and this is something that you have to work out.

Now I saw here a fair amount of this, of the bucking of authority, which I think was sane, and not insane. It's not *authoritarian* authority but Fromm's *humanistic* authority for the sake of a common purpose.[31] That to transform this into a kind of king-of-the-hill, baboon kind of dominance struggle is, uh—well, let's say that needs analysis. I am now confronting you with it. That is, I am now interpreting and presenting you with that to think about.

My impression is that in this group the men did this more than the women. For good endocrinological reasons, the androgens seem to make more of this dominance struggle, aggressiveness, resentment against being overwhelmed and ordered about and so on. But still the task remains of coming to peace with authority and, if I may say so, even *identifying* with authority. For instance, I give you the example of loving the cops. In our society, policemen are generally regarded as, to some extent, to be outwitted, and in lower-class neighborhoods in this country, there is a continually rising amount of attack on the policemen who are trying to arrest somebody. This is a very, very profound and very dangerous thing with vast implications for the whole society. If you cannot identify with authority, then society breaks down. It's the end of it; there's no recourse.

Now, especially for intellectuals—you are supposed to identify with your teachers. That is, you're supposed to want to be like them in the psychoanalytic sense. They're supposed to be the models you identify with in the same way as ultimately, one would hope, you males will identify with your father and take him as the male model rather than identifying with your mother. And vice versa for the girls—of identifying with the mother rather than with the father and taking your role model there. Now, the young intellectual is supposed to, in this sense, be sympathetic with and identify with and not get into dominance struggles with the older, the *avuncular*—you might call them—intellectuals. Now, that's something to think about. Make what you can out of it. We can't go very far with it here. I think that's all I wanted to say about it. I'll toss it into your lap.

Now, this is another point from the notebooks that I want to throw back at you. Let's start from the positive: you have watched a pro at work and you haven't been quite enough aware of it. That is, here we are in a situation where we just don't know enough. You've watched *science being born*—put it that way if you want to make it very dramatic. The kinds of things that were going on here, which seemed so aimless and so unplanned and so on, have actually been the first steps in the advancement of knowledge. That is, of trying out, getting a kind of skill—the way a doctor would in some new disease that he was trying to cure and he didn't know anything about. You sort of play with it—you try this, you try that, you try the other. The doctors call that *empirical*, meaning using medicines even though they don't know why they work or how they work.

This kind of venturing into the unknown and trying things out, of going someplace even when you don't know where you're going, is itself I think a very good experience for you to try to feel, to try to experience. I'd like to point out—my notes here have it—"It is like the explorer mapping the unknown land." Your picture of science is of the end product; that is, of the kind of experimental work which is done when you already know a great deal. But in your education generally, at all levels, including the grades in high school science and college science, there has not been instruction enough or awareness enough about the beginnings, of how you start from ignorance—of ignorance as the beginning point.

The comparison I wanted to make here was with the explorer in absolutely unknown territory. You go into the wilderness, you know. If you have no maps, you don't know where to go, then it doesn't make any difference whether you turn left or right because either one has equal probabilities of being wrong or right. It just doesn't make any difference. If somebody suggests "Well, let's go that way," okay, let's go that way. It doesn't matter. Because if you go down that way and find that you've hit the *cul de sac*, that is an advance of knowledge. Then you can put on your map: "*Cul de sac*, don't go that way. I've gone that way and it's a blind alley." You don't have to go that way anymore. And I think if you take this business about making a map, about learning where the blocks are, or the pitfalls or the quicksand or whatever, what'll work or won't work—this is all fruitful and profitable.

[*Maslow chuckles*] Well, I picked up someplace the statement about the mid-Western farms, the pioneers—something that applies very, very nicely to this kind of experimentation which I would like to encourage you to do. Somebody said it took about five bankruptcies to make one good Nebraskan farm. That is, the first one who came out to farm was bound to fail but he would sweat his life away and his guts away building it up a little bit. Then, on his dead body somebody else would come along and build it up some more. It took five dead bodies before you had a good, functioning, fruitful farm. Was the first one a failure? In the sense, now, of the advancement of knowledge? I think we would say not.

Another point that came up several times in several notebooks was the statement about learning that "**sex** is not evil, sinful, dirty." And then I have to add, this was frequently taken as "therefore everything is fine." I would like to say that neither is it necessarily beautiful nor desirable under all circumstances. In fact, it can be evil, it can be dirty, it can be sinful—you can besmirch it. It can be very, very beautiful; it can be very, very dirty. It often is neither, so that I just simply had to point out this error in logic at least. It's true: sex is not necessarily dirty, sinful, and so on and so on—but it *can* be. All you have to do is make it dirty and there it is.

John: Don't those terms cloud the issue a little bit? I mean, you have beautiful on the one hand and dirty. The implications of each of them are so far off. Both dirty and sinful have so many associations. I bristle when you say that.

Maslow: I know. It's a first approximation, to save an awful lot of time. I think most people will know what I mean. Well, the simple error of logic is that somebody discovers sex is not merely dirty, sinful and rotten as my mother had taught me. It's a discovery. Now, it is illegitimate logic—I forgot the exact name for the logical mistake—to say therefore it's always beautiful. Or whatever words you want to choose. [*Pause*]

There are some casual notes for you to think about. On the whole, as a group this was a *privatistic* group, to use David Riesman's[32] term. It's characteristic of the culture. Everybody agrees now, at your age level approximately, privatism is the word to describe the difference between American college students and Indian college students for instance, or African students or whatever, in any other society. If you ask them, as people have, what are your ambitions in life, or what would you like to be doing and so on, they'll characteristically say something impersonal: "I would like to die leaving my society better than when I was born into it," or, " I would like to do something for mankind."

On the whole, American students are apt to say, "I'd like a nice, good, secure job," "I'd like to have two cars," "I'd like to have 3.2 children and 4.8 rooms," and so on—practical. And the list is generally a matter of "what I would like to have for myself." American college students in study after study differentiate themselves off from the college students of every other known society that has been tested so far. They're selfish—it's a simple way to put it if there are no others—or self-absorbed or self-preoccupied. Part of the etiology that most people agree on is that this is one of the consequences of indulgence. If you're interested to read on this stuff, I recommend again David Levy's *Maternal Overprotection* book about indulged overprotection and the consequences, which turn out to be on the whole what we would now call self-absorption, self-preoccupation. That's for you to work with.

For instance, I've just heard that Sarah Lawrence College, which was a beacon light in education and which was the result of one fight after another and all sorts of heroism and self-sacrifice to give the girls there the right to self-government and to run their own lives— and it *is* run by the girls themselves—well, what's happened? Nothing. It's the same way, you know, about people dying for women's suffrage and then not bothering to vote. Bennington College apparently still has that old spirit. At Sarah Lawrence I'm told it's gone.[33] The girls have the right to govern themselves and they just don't bother—nothing happens. It's a flaccid group. That's the way it was described. A flabby community. [*Pause*]

I'd suggest for you to respond to these words now. Write down a couple of these words, will you? Altruism, dedication, patriotism, self-sacrifice. There's little mention of them in your notebooks or in your talks with me. Nobody mentioned what they would be willing to die for. This term doesn't come up in the United States much anymore. Well, let's talk about another culture where people actually do die, literally, for good values. I might ask you what *you* can do, since you didn't bring up the question about improving the world or improving the society or improving yourself for that matter. Rather than "what I would like out of life" kind of thing. [*Pause*]

I don't remember hardly anybody being thrilled over the opportunity of helping scientific experiments, or of teaching me something, improving me in some way. I'm your eyes on the world, so to speak; I'm your liaison officer with the technical journals and the corpus of psychological knowledge. If you teach me something, it's quite important. If it goes through me, you can teach a lot of other people. On the whole, the questions about this class are: "Did I enjoy it?" "What good did it do me?" "Am I pleased?" "Did I have a good time?" "Was it interesting?" And I don't remember people saying, "I'm glad that I was of service." I'd like you to respond to that. [*Pause*]

I should tell you that you did a beautiful job as a group—an intellectual job. For instance, I expect fine final papers—these examination papers. You're very capable in this respect. I'm sure they'll be practically all good; some will be excellent. First, this is too large a group, but even that's a test. Good group functioners will be able to function well even in a large group. You function—practically everybody—[*Maslow hesitates*]—let me pick my words carefully. [*Pause*] Let's say it this way: I'm very glad I had the individual meetings with each of you. I don't know how to say this without being misunderstood. [*Pause*] How does it happen that you're all more "lovable" one by one? [*Some general laughter*] More lovable, more respect-worthy? Somehow it's more possible, easier to be open and honest, easier to relate to another human being—privately than in a group. It's something to think about. Every single one of you was able to talk with me alone but not in a big group. Rather few of you were able to talk with me or with each other in the big group. What can you make of it? Think about it. I'll stick with that word: "more lovable." Why is that so, and what do you think about it?

Paul: Was it really so surprising, Dr. Maslow, that when we came in to talk to you—

Maslow: I'm not surprised by it.

Paul: Well, regardless, when we came in to talk to you we were assured individually and personally by you that this was completely confidential, that we could say anything without any fear that it was going to go outside of that office, yet here we have no such assurance. First of all, we never even made the statement that this was so really, and secondly, we don't have the assurance even that the statement was made.[34]

Maslow: Let me pick up your word there—the word *fear*. This is something for you to analyze. [*Now talking to the group*] By the way, you do *fine* by comparison with other groups in other places. *Relatively*, everything's very nice. But *absolutely*, in terms of the ideal I'm trying to push you toward right now with all this talking that I'm doing—you have too much anxiety, too much fear about exposing yourself in a group like this, I would say. More than is necessary. That is, there is, I would say, unrealistic expectation about being hit on the head. The truth is that you wouldn't be. The truth is that you can apply this old lesson to what we've learned from the psychotherapists, for instance in that situation. As a person drops his defenses and shows his nakedness, the patient becomes more lovable, not less. That's what he has been fighting against; he has been hiding all his sins. He stops hiding and shows his sins and then you love him more, not less.

Well, that can happen also in a group. In the first place, I would like you to think about what punishments could be given. Supposing you did say, as many of you mentioned, that you were simply afraid to talk up because somebody might laugh at you. Now supposing we could set up an experimental lab situation in which we had three laughers, and then you said something and the three people would laugh at you, then what? [*General laughter*] Do you see my point?

The point is that the fears are essentially unreal—the fears are the fears of childhood, the fears of the youngster afraid of losing face, losing status, losing self-esteem and so on. But the fact is actually the opposite—that if you opened yourself up for even a larger group like this, that would be nicer rather than not. That you'd be closer to others rather than more distant, on the whole, and that would be in the long run. It's perfectly true that in the short run it might not be so—people might laugh, you might be hurt, you might feel rejected and so on. It would take patience, and courage, and continuation to stick it out and then to find out that nobody kills you even if you show yourself to be naïve, or even if you're stupid about something. Nobody murders you. They rather like you for it more rather than less if you reveal your simplicity or your authenticity. That's what *authenticity* means—just to admit you don't know something when you don't know it, or that you're not such a big shot or you're not so bold or you're not so all-fired courageous all the time, or you *do* have anxiety, or your guts *do* turn over, or you *do* get an impulse of one kind or another that you're trying to control. This is the point that I would like you to think about.

Let's see, I think I have some more notes here. Try to figure out why the group situation inhibited you more than it should. I hope I made myself clear: this group situation was far more "groupy" in the good sense—more open, more authentic, more honest, more intelligent than you would get in most colleges and university situations in this country. That's relative, so let's keep that in mind. I'm speaking absolutely; that is, in terms of what you might push yourselves toward: the group inhibits you, too many of you. You still feel too inhibited by shyness, too many of you. I think it's possibly good when you're encouraged or permitted to open yourselves up more—try to do it. [*Pause*]

This is my last note—about suggested remedies to forget self-absorption. To make this brief, it's the old platitude: the best way to forget self-absorption, self-awareness, the crippling self-consciousness, is to become interested in someone else or something else or some other job. This is the easiest and quickest way of relieving self-consciousness of the inhibiting sort. You can become absorbed in something which is unselfish, which is outside of you, which is somebody else, some job. If you're no good for yourself, be useful to others, or the *MANAS* type—I think I recommended that you look at that magazine—of taking responsibility on your own shoulders. Find work in which you can forget yourself. Seeking personal pleasure is not the answer. Also, seeking personal salvation, by the way, is not the answer.

If any of you are particularly interested in what I have just said, in my *Summer Notes* there's a section on "self-actualization via duty."[35] Another one is on this business of seeking personal salvation. The best way to seek personal salvation is actually to become enthralled with something other than yourself, and this particular direct, running head-on about "my own happiness" kind of thing is, our experience tells us, is not the way to do it.

Okay. We will reconvene in 15 minutes for that third hour. Remember that you can talk back to me on all of these things. I want you to. If it turns out to be better privately in your notebooks where you can talk at length and I won't interrupt you, or you can come in during my office hours, individually.

JANUARY 6, 1964

Laboratory for Self-Knowledge

Note: In this session Maslow shares slides of cartoons from Saul Steinberg's book, The Labyrinth, *each of which invites discussion on the relationship of humankind to the modern world. Figure 1 is apparently the only image not in slide form, so it is first placed on a table, then the blackboard. Figures 2-7 are displayed via a projector. The lights are dimmed throughout the class period.*

Maslow: I don't even have instructions to give you, exactly. The vague thoughts that I've had run something like this: for one thing I myself was very, very much impressed with Saul Steinberg's cartoons when I ran across them, and I still am. And I keep watching them. I think he's one of our great artists, even in the classical sense. I've seen his sketches and drawings and so on. The simplicity of the cartoons—don't take it too lightly. It seemed to me that they condensed so very much that you couldn't put into words very easily.

I want to pass this [*Figure 1*] around; this should be interesting to you. I think I'll make a bookplate, a bookmark for myself out of this one. I don't have a slide so I'll just leave it here [*on the table*] and you can look at it, because I think it expresses me very much. Somehow I identify with it.

Well, how much would I talk about it? I think if I wanted to talk about this I would have to go off on free-association really,

FIGURE 1

metaphorical, figure-of-speech kind of talk, what I call in my own journal "rhapsodic talk" rather than just straight, logical, sensible talk. It seems very real and very clear, yet the explaining or describing would be quite difficult. I remember that I made these up to show one class a couple of years ago after I'd been trying to talk about existential psychology and existentialism and the existential predicament and things like that, and had not succeeded very well. I didn't seem to get over somehow, but then I made these things up and said, well, look—that's what I'm trying to say, here it is.

Now, let's see what happens to you, if anything. Supposing I asked you: what do you think this means? Or, what is he trying to say? Then we could talk about that. Some of you I know are just going to be too shy to talk about it, so then you write that for me, if you can't talk about it. But in view of the background that we've lectured on, I would like you to try to talk about it even if you look ridiculous. This is guaranteed to make you look ridiculous, to cause you to start stammering. There really aren't any good words. There's nobody who can say this well, including Steinberg. It's just ineffable, it's beyond words. Therefore, since we all start evenly, you might say we're all cripples in this respect; maybe we can feel more easy about speaking about it.

I can't pass this around because it's falling apart. Supposing I put this here [*on the blackboard*]. Could I ask you to take a look at this? [*Everyone goes to the front and takes a turn examining the picture then returns to their seats*]

I choose this—it may be a little more meaningful to you, it may be a little more interesting—because this is the one that I identify with, that I want for my bookplate; it seems to be like the model of all my work. And it certainly expresses very nicely my own ambivalent feeling toward my own work. I don't know if you've seen that, a certain sense of the ridiculousness of these efforts . . . That's not quite right; of the amusing quality of it. Now the question is: what does it mean or what does it say to you, or how do you feel about it? I've set you off. I've told you roughly how I feel about it. What does it do to you, if anything?

Paul: I can well understand—at least I think I can—why this seems to represent you. Perhaps the best I can do is try to explain why I think it does. For one thing there is a man charging into a whole lot of things which really are pretty much unknown. You can see that there is something there, but you don't really know what you're jumping into, yet they look interesting, they look worthy of fooling around with. On the other hand, on a symbolic level what we've been trying to do in a sense is to reduce all reality to certain very simple adjectives of sensation and so on. We've been trying to describe things in terms of, well, here it says: "Draw the smell of an onion."[1] And in a sense this kind of symbolism of cubical shapes and roughness and smoothness and points and so on is really a symbolic way of experientially putting into a picture the way you might encounter any number of objects in the real world on an experiential level. This is what they might be reduced to in terms of your associations, and so on.

Sarah: Well, what I can see from here, I can see all the blocks and I can see the figure—that's all I saw—but when I walked up, I saw the spear for the first time and it seemed pretty funny and I kind of laughed, god-funny—well, that's B-humor in this sense—but because here is this man and all these things and he's charging in, armed with a spear. This is his weapon and it's powerful, yet it's absurd. You have to kind of congratulate him on his courage, even laugh at him and with him at the same time.

Maslow: That's what you get. Do you notice—in both of them—that one starts to talk about it's this and its opposite simultaneously?

Melissa: Also you have one man against a whole series of shapes which are basic shapes—circles, squares, triangles. He's attacking a series of basic things which are in shadows and he's all white in outline. Also the whole idea that he's charging on a horse, a noble steed, a noble duty going into the unknown.

David: First of all I think of Don Quixote[2] and the windmill, and also I think the very striking thing is the man on the horse is much smaller than the objects, and you know the spear is not something to defend the person. It's his means of offending, and this is what strikes up the idea of Don Quixote in mind.

Maslow: Remember: don't anybody get Freudian about this. Don't you dare! [*General laughter*]

Jacob: I don't know about the Don Quixote thing but I think that the B-humor and the existential thing comes out. It seems to me that those are children's blocks. They look like a set of children's blocks, which are small, and the fact that the man is so much smaller. But I also think it's—the whole Don Quixote business—a rather grandiose identification of self-image, that you can tackle these great things, best things.

Maslow: You know, you're adding things. Even my own joke about the Freudian—I never thought about Freud there at all. It suddenly dawned on me: people start talking about spears. [*General laughter*] I hadn't thought of it before—and then these things that you say, too. It might be that we could have a kind of group addition. We could function here as a group and add up to—each of you have added something to what the person before did. It accumulates, put it that way. But the interesting thing about these condensations is it's very hard to contradict anything. Do you know what I mean there? That the additions—you keep on adding opposites and adding opposites and even if they're inconsistent, it still adds on. It's hard to say "No, that's not so," because practically everything is so. And I must say already I see things in that that I didn't see, even though I've played with this a long time and hung it in my office and so on.

Charlotte: I don't think that it seems like a little man penetrating into the unknown. When you think of blocks you think of something hard. It seems like a little man, a human being in a great big, wide world trying with a little, thin spear, trying to penetrate something that's impenetrable.

Roslyn: I don't think the blocks are places so much as the unknown. I hate to say they represent Western civilization, but the fact is they're geometrical and yet there are all sorts of theorems backing up their existence. And here you are trying to approach things on sort of a supernatural or spiritual level.

Maslow: Did you notice the difference in style between the two? Even the difference in lines sort of supports that kind of . . . I don't know how to say it, but the lines are different: this is harder, sharper, stronger, firmer; the edges are definite and black. This is a little more sketchy, wavery, more poetic, perhaps.

Harry: Like the selfishness of our society and our goals versus another meaning of doing of things in society. I think here both elements are combined. There's not just the selfishness. The Knight on the horse by himself—certainly the self-importance of the individual is there, but also the greatness of the mission is there.

Clara: From here it looks as if he's stopped. He can't go on. The position of the horse is as if he were almost bucking and you have these two completely different worlds which are being forced apart, and they'll never really be able to reach each other.

Maslow: That too fits with a difference in styles. If you were closer you'd see that the lines are different; the style of the artistic line is different.

Saul: I think at the symbolic level it would represent your desire to fight for human elements against inhuman things, such as the American Psychological Association. From another point of view, the man on the horse is fighting something ridiculous—that might be a projection. He is fighting an ambiguous feeling. From our point of view, it is ridiculous things he is fighting. But from his point of view, it is something worth fighting for.

Doug: Well, I have the feeling that here are these fundamental, obvious things—triangles and spheres—and here he is with a spear, and here I go. There's a kind of silliness. These are basic things in life that we approach. It's kind of a funny thing to go about doing, and it makes me think of a poem—I don't remember it exactly but it's something like "the daffodils grow in the sunlight and never ask why."

Maslow: Anybody else? Take your time.

Sharon: Somebody over here set me off to thinking about what would be the next picture in free association. What would be the end of . . .?

[*General laughter and multiple voices talking at once*]

Maslow: It is an interesting thought. I bet you could use this as a projective technique. If we tried to write down what is the next picture, there would be different ones.

Sharon: I can see him turn that horse and go in the opposite direction. [*General laughter*]

Maslow: I know what my next picture would be.

Roslyn: Yours would be to go ahead.

Sharon: But she was right. It is bucking that way.

Maslow: That's an interesting thought. Maybe we'll try that for some of these slides that are coming up, or even for this. Let's [*then quickly changing his mind*] hold it. It would spoil it because I think if anyone spoke up then immediately that would freeze . . . It would suggest too much. If you have any thoughts about this next thing, could you write it for me. I'm very interested. I'm already interested to see that you've added so much to what I saw there, and I really studied this darn thing for a long time from different angles, and even personally.

This could be a kind of therapeutic technique. That is, supposing you would pick out some cartoon or painting or poem or something about which you had very strong feelings, and then listen to another group of people make associations with the painting or whatever, of the kind that you've been making yourself. It would be almost as if they were with their objectivity—greater objectivity about you than you could have about yourself—might be adding to your self-knowledge. That's an interesting thought. Try it; I think it would be of special personal interest to me. How different are your second pictures to the one that I clearly have in my head? It's very clear.

Sharon: Should this be a picture of what we think you would do?

Maslow: No, no! What *you* would do. This is a projective technique. I simply ask you what's coming next; just draw the next picture.

Paul: In action?

Maslow: Whatever it is. What's going to happen? What comes next? And then I'll leave it to you to interpret. Do you have any more thoughts for this? I'd like to try it once around for everybody before we make our second round. Does anybody, anyone of you *disagree* with anything that has been said so far—that seems to grate a little bit or is not quite right, or it didn't hit the right note?

Roslyn: Yeah, the Don Quixote approach in the windmill—he was making the windmill something more than it actually was. But in this, even though the rider is romantic, there's also a realism in it, because he sees just how large the task actually is. There isn't any soft illusion there.

Maslow: I think he tries. I'll tell you what it meant to me before you got started on it. Does anybody want to add anything?

Paul: I just think it's interesting that in the picture the objects themselves are fantastic things and really have a greater aspect of reality than the horse and the rider himself.

Maslow: It's a different style and can play many different themes.

Doug: Well, my reaction was not in agreement as to what those things were. They are vague, mysterious.

Maslow: Anything else anybody? This is very good because there is no right and wrong. I don't have any hesitation about telling you what I saw and there's absolutely no implication of greater virtue or validity or veridicality or anything. It's obviously projection, and your projections are absolutely as good as anybody else's projections. So we'd be comparing in the same way as some of those exercises, as the creative art educators do, where there's no right and no wrong in drawing the smell of an onion. You can compare different projections of that unreal task, so to speak.

Herb: I think a few years ago the *Brandeis Handbook* had a picture on the front of a little armored rider with a lance riding into the open mouth of a crane.

Maslow: That's very interesting. I don't remember it, but I must have seen it. I probably saw it.

Sharon: Even though these blocks are very definite shapes and all, I still somehow get the impression that this is somewhat a picture of something chaotic over there, anyway, even though there might be definite objects and that this figure on the charger, this figure representing you, might want to order it up a little bit—put the circles with the circles and the triangles with the triangles and so forth. It might not so much be fighting it but straightening out the mess a little bit.

Jacob: I've just got to add to that. I think that they're not as ordered, at least from your point of view of looking at it, as cubicle as they would be here. They're much more vague and non-specific and non-objective, more mysterious.

Saul: I just have a suggestion for the second picture.

Maslow: No, hold this. Keep that private because that will save the personal mess of all these suggestions so they won't be contaminated by anyone else's suggestions. I can tell you what it meant to me—it already means more. For one thing, when I saw it first I just laughed out loud. Now you don't often do that to a picture. It just seemed so funny, so terribly, terribly funny that I laughed and laughed and then brought it to my wife and friends and so on and then hung it on the wall and thought this was the most amusing darn thing. And I think I slowly identified—realized that I was sort of laughing at my own situation and reading myself into it. And it fits. For me, in the first place, the whole thing is a nonsensical situation and the whole thing is humorous, sort of funny, absurd a little bit—on both sides of it.

The way I saw it was all those geometrical things are sort of mechanistic. I think I felt much the way you said there, sort of mechanistic, cold, bloodless kind of thing, just the sort of thing that I'm fighting against in the American Psychological Association, let's say.[3] The quarrels that I'll have and the debates and so on are against the mechanistic conception of psychology. Now it's condensed there, I remember thinking they're very strong; they're more powerful than Don Quixote and this guy here. They're sort of frail by comparison to these huge, big, blocky, solid things that are heavier than he is and seem more solid and heavy. And yet they're also nonsensical because they're in a big clump. They're not really arranged, they're sort of all tossed around and they themselves are absurd too, or they looked absurd to me. I'm trying to remember my first looks rather than what it is now—with the accretions that you've added to it.

Yet, there's something . . . Well, I can like it, that is, I could identify with this. This is clearly weaker. That is, Don Quixote or whoever this figure with his spear is; it's all very nice. The association with me is of bravery, a kind of hopeless bravery, you might say—the ship going down with the flag flying and so on. Because this looks stronger and he can't break them; the spear isn't big enough for that; it isn't strong enough or powerful enough. So there's that kind of fundamental absurdity about the effort itself of— for me it's Don Quixote, or something like that. A Don Quixote-ish figure—and I *like* him. I like Don Quixote. And I like that—it seems like a nice thing to do. His spear will get bent or he can't crack it or break it or anything, but the fact is that he is in a certain sense stronger, you might say, because he sees how absurd all these big, self-important blocks are, all puffed up with pride and solidity. A kind of fake solidity, because they're all in a jumble anyhow. They make no sense, and he *does*, and even if they are stronger than he.

Now you'll be interested in the associations—Walter Weisskopf, a friend of mine, just suddenly called me up. He was in town for a meeting. I went over to talk with him and he was sort of depressed a little bit. It was the Economics Association, and in the Statler Hotel there were 4,000 economists or something and they wandered around and he thinks of them as so blind in general. But he felt he was just one against 4,000—he felt so weak. And I kind of bucked him up a little bit and said: the difference between the 4,000 and you is you're right—which he is.

And then he got into a better humor and—I like him, I like to see him, a great mind, a wonderful mind. It's a pleasure, an aesthetic pleasure just to watch it function. We then started playing this game about the Freudian myth—you know, about the horde, the Totem and Taboo myth.[4]

You know that one about the sons—the primal horde consists of the dominant father who is more powerful and strong and who has all the females for himself, so the other younger males get together and dethrone him and kill him and, if I remember, eat him, take his courage and strength and so on. And in that way they can get a female. And this, Freud used it. The anthropologists have been kicking like mad about it but he never meant it. It's a myth. It's a kind of a way of saying something, just the way this cartoon is. He was trying to say that you have to overthrow the dominant one or else you'll never be a man, and if you're not a man you don't deserve a woman and so on. That kind of association you can make to it.

We played the game there but we turned it around. Here the horde is of the fathers; it's the son who is weak. There is one son and there are 4,000 fathers around here and this poor one son—Walter Weisskopf has to fight all the 4,000 fathers. But in the long run he is strong because he's right.

Well, you can play that kind of game. That's the way this seemed to me; now I would see many more things in it. And it's *extremely* interesting that a psychoanalyzed man would never—I didn't even *think* of the Freudian interpretation of this. The spears and the charging on things, and so on and so on. It's a very simple possibility. Your psychoanalyst would start talking about the castration fears, anxieties and the phallic stage of fighting against the father and so on. The things you've added to make it richer.

Well, my attitude toward my work is involved here. I don't think it shows very much in public, where I'm just sort of talking like an authority, but the scientists. . . You see, the truth is I'm also this kind of a scientist. It doesn't show to you, I don't think, much. I'm partly identified with the blocks and the squares and the calculating machine, and I love them, and I've done very careful and rigorous experiments—that's a different kind of pleasure. It is a real pleasure too, if you do something obsessional well.

So that you might almost speak of double identification here, in a way, of the civil war within the person. This is like the dream interpretation where you should identify yourself with every part of the whole dream. Every member in the dream, every person in it is some part of you, and when you've got this kind of civil war . . . A civil war reflects it. It's true, because I have a great disturbance over this, great guilt for not doing rigorous experiments now, which I've done all my life until recently, and feeling somehow not quite decent. Guilty. I felt uneasy about all these big things without data, without support and all sorts of theories and hypotheses—a big, big balloon. And there's always the thought: which needle is going to prick that balloon? That's the thing about theories on the one hand and data on the other.

So this does reflect for me, and it made me understand in a way that perhaps you could use it too. It made me understand a little more about my guts, about my own self, about my own internal conflicts, which are really not settled and never will be. It's impossible—not till the day I die or the day you die. There's this kind of conflict in each of you—your obsessional side, your hysterical side, your impulsive side, your control side, discipline and so on, your orderliness and your anarchy and the like. They're all in you. You could play that game for yourselves. Well, that's what it means; that's what it meant to me. There were variations on this. Weren't there? A dozen at least,

FIGURE 2

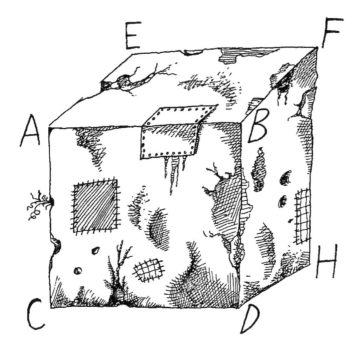

CREDIT: © The Saul Steinberg Foundation / Artists Rights Society (ARS), New York

different from this, equally sound. We could call this a projective test, couldn't we? Where you can insert yourself, so to speak, into the ink blot.

Maslow: Well, let's try and see what we can make out of these things. Do you want to talk about that? [*Figure 2*]

Paul: Can I just ask you a question? What were the letters [*in the picture*] for?

Maslow: Well, let me make it a little more clear [*Maslow adjusts the focusing*]. Yes, go ahead.[5]

Melissa: Well, first, the letters at the angles look like tenth-grade geometry when you're doing geometrical shapes and you letter the angles so you can work with the figure and work along. But the shape itself is so much more interesting than the triangles. It's just filled with patches and holes and dark spots and little leaves and things coming out of it. It looks sort of like a cell, and it looks like somebody's old overalls a little bit, and all of it sort of superimposed on a geometrical, kind of logical framework. It looks sort of silly, absurd.

Sharon: It's the story of my life. [*General laughter*]

Maslow: You know I just had the craziest association with that, "The Czarist Russian Empire." I've just been reading about it.

Maria: It's kinda like a closer look at one of those objects [*presumably from Image 1*]. That maybe this is what he's going in to.

Saul: It reminds me of Freudian defense mechanism.

David: It looks to me like a sick piece of Swiss cheese.

Cheryl: You might see a mouse trying to get at a piece of cheese and, you know, he has the corners labeled where you should start. And each time he goes to take a bite, something happens wrong.

Clara: It reminds me of a map of the world where they have all of these neat longitudinal and latitudinal lines.

Maslow: So, the world.

Doug: Well, if you think about trying to organize experience and make a code and think of what happens to a code.

Ruth: It makes me wonder whether that's from the inside or the outside business, or both. So what's inside?

Maslow: Okay. Let's go back to that. I think to some extent all of these overlap a little, at least to my eyes, that they have the same . . . For instance, supposing I were to ask you—you have to say it in figures of speech of course—in what respects is this similar to this thing that you just saw, or let's say to this [*Figure 3*]?

Figure 3

[Pause]

Charlotte: A doctor and his patient.

Paul: This is too Freudian.

Melissa: But just the absurdity of a man who is determined to fight or die.

David: It looks to me like a man in the hands of the psychoanalyst. *[General laughter]*

Clara: It's someone's conscience fighting back at him.

Paul: It looks like an atheist fighting God.

Melissa: But at least he's moving and the hand isn't.

Herb: It controls him.

Cheryl: Is there any significance about "Steinberg" [*the signature in Figure 3*] being written backwards?

Maslow: No, that's my putting it wrong. [*General laughter; Maslow has flipped the slide the wrong way around in the projector and inadvertently reversed the image.*[6]] That reminds me that I had hoped to invite Steinberg. I don't know where he is, but I'd certainly like to meet him. Maybe we should. How about this student government; don't they have money? We've run out of money for inviting people to our department. Why not invite Steinberg around to draw us a cartoon in public or something, talk with us?

Mike: Is the man's eye looking in the other direction? And afraid to fight the battle.

Herb: It looks fierce to me.

Harry: It's beautiful.

David: It's just very wary.

Maslow: Remember you're also technicians now. So you can ask the methodological question: in what respect are you the hand and in what respect are you the person? That's the way you'd handle your own dream for instance. You're everything in this dream, this is a dream.

Male student: Nightmare.

Maslow: Let's try the next one. [*Figure 4*]

Paul: It looks to me like a man running away from a "globbleglook." Whatever the thing on the right is, it looks like it's going to fall down. It's only balanced by the circular objects on the bottom, a golf ball.

Doug: I think that man has a problem.

Maslow: Any other thoughts?

Melissa: It kind of looks like something that has to do with the sea. At least that's the way I see it, with waves and maybe sea foliage and fish-like, and you know, a kind of sea monster. When we think of sea we think of basic origins and things. Maybe he's running away from that. Maybe he sees it and he's running like all get-out.

Sharon: To me it looks like a female-type figure, and he's running away from it. We did the same thing with stride drawings years ago at Antioch in psychology class, and half the class divided as to whether a figure was male or female.

Maslow: Well, just for fun, how many of you see that figure as female and how many of you as male? Well, isn't that interesting in itself—no answer to the male.

David: It isn't either one.

FIGURE 4

Maslow: How many of you see it as neither one? Supposing I forced the issue now. Make a forced choice: you must make a vote either for male or female. How many of you vote that this looks more like a female than like a male? And how many of you under that forced choice will say it looks more like a male than a female? [*Votes taken, some general laughter, but the result is not stated on tape*]

That's characteristic, by the way—remember we tried to talk about that physiognomic perception—that you'll get not a chance line-up. It's not 50/50. It's usually tipped very much one way rather than the other. Well, what's female about it?

Herb: Fanciness and curls. A man wants a simple life . . . [*General laughter*]

Sarah: This may sound terrible—but there's something female about it in the sense of nature, kind of, and he looks like he's the type of man who thinks he has organized everything so well and Nature just kind of gets up whenever she feels like it and becomes this fantastically complicated thing up there.

Sharon: Also it looks dominating to me. It's trying to dominate him.

Maslow: That's a very common male fantasy—confronted with a primal femaleness. You know, D. H. Lawrence-femaleness type.

Jayne: He has no awareness of the little thing that she's being balanced on, I think. [*General laughter*]

Paul: I think it needs something; maybe I can just point to it. I think if you put an eye—I don't know if you can do this—right there. I don't know how it changes your appearance of this whole thing. It makes a much more [*unintelligible*].

Maslow: You notice again the difference in style between the two figures?

Roslyn: I prefer to see it as neuter, though. This looks like somebody in an intense anxiety situation where they're running away from something and they don't know what. But whatever it is, it feels like it's going to fall in on them.

Maslow: Doesn't this remind you? Everybody here, you've had dreams like this, haven't you? Frightened at some vague, unknown . . .

Mike: He looks more surprised than frightened. Yeah, he doesn't look like that—it would be in his mouth more—anxiety—wouldn't it? He would be more tense.

Clara: He's not getting so well-ordered.

Saul: It's like a modern version of a dragon, mysterious. He's sort of like a hen-pecked husband. [*General laughter*]

Maslow: Okay, let's . . . [*Switches to Figure 5, pause*]

Clara: I think this is definitely Freudian.

Figure 5

Melissa: He keeps doing that to his "no's." All his negative things are blocks and solid and they don't move; they have this immobility. But the "yes" is on wheels and the whole thing is floating and moving and somehow much more dynamic—even if it's more delicate and more tasteless.

Maslow: That suggestion about the Freudian thing—am I being anti-Freudian? It's obvious enough, but I hadn't seen it. Psychologists all do. [*General laughter*]

Paul: If you really want to be Freudian about this—if you interpret that spear coming out of the "yes" as a phallic symbol of some sort, it might be pointing toward the desire of sexuality with the big social "no," which—

David: Social "no"? It's the female "no"!

Paul: Well, whatever it is, I don't know. [*General laughter*]

Maslow: Well, if you could convince it, if it is. It's the female's job to say no, not the male's—in this culture anyway.

Paul: Yeah, but that doesn't look like a female "no."

David: Sure, it is! It's a fortress!

[*Car horn heard outside*]

Maslow: That's my wife. I'd better tell her. [*He gets up and walks to the window, then returns and displays Figure 6*]

Maslow: Can you see that one now?

Saul: Not too well.

Maslow: It's a pity about the light. If you look closely you see that these are all—there's an A and a B—these are all paths between A and B. [*Pause*] Gee, I just hate to hurry this.[7]

Sharon: That looks like my husband in the upper left-hand corner, and the rest looks like me.

FIGURE 6

CREDIT: © The Saul Steinberg Foundation / Artists Rights Society (ARS), New York

Maslow: Do you know what I think? I think we should look at these again.

Herb: It looks like all the complexes you go through in a relationship.

Mike: Well, between A and B—there's always the space between A and B. I mean it's never one thing, it's never any one set pattern.

Maslow: Well, see what you can make out of it. I'll be back in a second.

[*Students talk to one another*]

Paul: I think it's saying that there's all kinds of ways to get nowhere.

[*Maslow returns and displays Figure 7*]

Maslow: You got that alright?

[*Pause*]

Paul: I think it's saying Steinberg is out of his mind.

Maslow: I ask you, how many words would it take to describe that as well?

Paul: It's not a dialogue.

Maslow: No?

Herb: No. Imagine what is being said. [*Pause*]

FIGURE 7

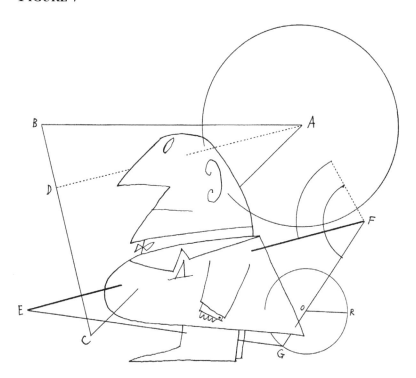

Randal: He's abbreviated as being the [*unintelligible; general laughter*].

Saul: This picture is an analysis of modern man.

Maslow: Well, again, you can ask the question: how does this relate to the other? Supposing I think of this as a single series—as a matter of fact I chose them that way. These were chosen out of perhaps several hundred. I saw—at least one human being saw something common in that whole series, starting with my thing that you looked at—

Herb: What did you see in common with A and B?

Maslow: Well, I'd rather—I know what I saw; how about you?

Melissa: These are like men's tools; the things he has to arm himself, you know? He takes everything. It's his knowledge—he knows about circles and triangles, his measuring devices, his compasses and things like that; it's what he goes to work with.

Maslow: Well, I've only got through half of them. I'd like to continue. I'd like to show you all of these things, and then also we have another kind of thing altogether that we can save for next time. I think I'll bring these slides back next time and start from the beginning. That is, I'd like to run them over again. Let's see what your unconscious can do with them in one week. Only one thing I'll say to get you going: I saw something common in all of these.

Sharon: What book are the pictures in?

Maslow: I think these are all in his book *The Labyrinth*.

JANUARY 13, 1964

Lecture

Maslow: I wanted to meet with you about getting this *MANAS* paper around. Remember that what you're supposed to read there is the paper by Weisskopf. Then I wanted to be sure that you knew about the final examination. Do you all have that? Did any of you miss that question that I passed out? Then also I would like you to get your notebooks to me as soon as possible. I have time for reading now and I won't when we get jammed up with the final exams. So get those books to me just as soon as you possibly can. Now also, I can't find— when is the examination time, anyhow? Wednesday the 22nd? In the morning? When and where is that, exactly. [*Several students answer: 9:30 in the morning, the 22nd*] Now you remember, you can bring in your notes, but you're not allowed to bring any books in. I'd much prefer it in a quieter room.

What I wanted the time for was to go over the dream psychology stuff, but I'll leave that to you. Perhaps I'll make a recommendation for those of you who are especially interested: put in your bibliography a new book on dreams—a clinical approach to dreams— which looks very good. I haven't read it thoroughly, but I was going to use some of the dreams there today. It's by Walter Bonime[1] and it's something like *The Clinical Use of Dreams.*[2]

Bonime, if I remember, was one of the Horney psychoanalysts. He's got psychoanalytic training and has a good reputation in New

York City as a therapist. He's a good clinician and he's more open. The reason I liked his stuff was that it was more open on dreams—it wasn't theory-bound as so many of the writers are apt to be. And this would have been one of the points if we had time to discuss it. I want to discuss dreams as—my own phrase for it—the *parallel languages*.

The illustrations are easy enough to make; for instance, Richard Jones' *Ego Synthesis in Dreams* is very good on this.[3] It is excellent just for making that point that you can take a dream and you can interpret it in any darn old language you want to. The Freudian interpretation is not correct or incorrect; neither is the Jungian or the existentialist or whatever. They all approach it from a different angle and what's nice for you if you get interested enough to pursue this further is to have in your armamentarium six or eight possible approaches so you can play with your dreams. You can turn it over in your head and look at it from a different angle. It may be from the point of view of the straight Freudian interpretation, which is usually what we'd begin with. This will carry you so far, and then you're finished. Then you turn it over like a relic perhaps that you're looking at; you simply look at the other side and say, "Now what would an existentialist say about it?" And it frequently happens that something new occurs to you so that you progressively enrich the dream by taking it from angle after angle, and point of view after point of view. It gets richer that way—more useable.

I had planned also, I had written down some various notes about how to use your own dreams a little more for your own purposes, but we don't have time for that. Dick Jones, as it happens, has promised to write a chapter for this book that Harry Rand[4] and I are playing with. We haven't worked at it very hard yet. On self-growth or self-help. What we'd like to do is discover a good word which doesn't sound snotty or too boy-scout-ish either and yet is *not* self-analysis or self-therapy—it would have to be something else. We don't have the word for it, but when we do find it, that's what the book is going to be about. Instead of trying to do it all ourselves, we've decided to ask people to make contributions of chapters where they're specialists. And Dick Jones is going to write a chapter on suggestions for the person himself about interpreting his own dreams. And there isn't anybody in the country who could do better with it than Jones, so it should be as good as it's possible to be. We're going to have other people doing various special recommendations—mostly toward the goal of self-knowledge of various kinds. I think that's all I'll say about it.

I wanted to tell you about this thing: there's kind of a wave going on here. I think I've mentioned it to you before. Practically every week, I come in with something new that has been mailed to me, and it looks as if this is popping all over the country and not so much elsewhere. I've got only one letter from England. There's something of the sort—a kind of self-actualization institute there. But that was the only one I got. In this country it looks as if in every darn town something is popping, under various guises, various names.

Now, this came a few days ago. It's called the Human Growth Institute. If you want to be put on the mailing list, then it's Village Corner, Suite D, Los Altos, California. [*Maslow reads from a brochure*] "The Human Growth Institute announces its school for the development of human potential. For persons interested in human health and growth, this is the beginning of a totally new program"— maybe for him, but I know that it's not. There are dozens of these things popping up everyplace. Some of them are in the hands of nuts; there's just no question about it. And some of them are in the hands of, strictly speaking, pollyannas—that is, people who deny, whose major defense is denial and who run around smiling at everybody all the time thinking that will settle the world.

And there are places like that that are being set up. Some of them are in very good hands. The National Training Lab people[5]—the Bethel group—are developing in various directions. It's spreading out from the T-group kind of thing over into what you might call therapy or self-growth or some darn thing. They're avoiding the term . . . The term that was used last summer in Bethel was the "continuing labs," but the clear implication of the description was that they were doing approximately what we've been trying to do this semester. I got some reports from it that some things worked and some things didn't— that's the usual report. Nobody has really struck on anything perfect yet. There is no panacea; that seems quite clear, and we'll all have to struggle with bits of ideas and try out this and try out that.

Well, this one [*Maslow picks up another brochure*], I don't know the guy at all. And I must confess that when I got this, I got depressed. My wife had to pull me out of that one. You know, partly I'm responsible for this stuff, and I don't know in which hands it is. I don't know this guy. It looks over-ambitious to me; I'd be more cautious. But in effect this is announcing a school, a three-year course, after which a diploma will be given—a school for the development of human potential and with no indication here that "We don't know how to do this yet; we're just trying, just experimenting." There's nothing said here about research or about the humility that you have to have. I'm happy he's trying it out, but he doesn't *say* he's trying it out. In effect he makes a promise; he's delivering something. It's almost a money-back guarantee kind of thing—self-actualization or else double your money back, you know, that sort of thing. [*Chuckles from the class*] Well, there's absolutely no question about it. We just don't know enough, as you have very well discovered this semester, I'm sure. We just don't really know enough to make any promises about anything. This is in the stage of just the first pilot exploring.

We had a meeting about this just a few days ago—some people who were involved with the National Training Labs—and then a debate is coming up. For instance, what should I do about this? I don't know the guy. He may be a joker of some sort, or he may be a fine psychologist, a responsible citizen, I don't know. The debate that rages now is about standards and controls and you might say caution, conservatism in doing this kind of thing. We know people can be hurt by being handled in the wrong way. On the other hand, there are some, like myself—I'm in the school of thought of letting it all . . . we must try out things, let it be done. I hope to minimize hurt, damage and danger, but some I think we must take a chance on. I'm willing to take a chance on it on just about the same grounds that bacteriologists are, cancer people are. The goal is a big one and it's worth taking chances for, I feel. Some people don't, and they want to set up licensing bureaus and so on. I don't know who you'd get to give the licenses.

Or as with the drug stuff for instance, which we had no time to discuss at length. The final windup has been that Tim Leary and Dick Alpert[6] are gone. Over at Harvard, someone told me, no research can be done in the Department of Social Relations that has the slightest social implication without getting the okay of the campus physician. Well, that kind of restriction is a hell of a lot worse and more dangerous in every respect than passing out psilocybin drugs. So I feel open about this stuff.

Then, another guy wrote me this; this is from San Francisco. "Axioscope," it's called, and that refers to axiology. Axiology is the technical name for the abstract study of values, ultimate values and so on. And what this guy did was to put out this sort of guide to the events that are going on that have to do with values, in this whole San Francisco area. [*Maslow reads*] "Northern California's guide to the exploration of ideas, ideals and values in philosophy, sociology, psychology, religion and the arts." And then he has announcements: symposium on existentialism, lectures by Alan Watts, something from the Buddhist association, general semantics, then an auto-suggestion, lecture by the Balanced Living Club—it says "no relation with *Balanced Living Magazine* or it's ideas." There are already splinter groups among the balanced living. [*General laughter*]

[*Maslow goes on to read about another program*] "Seminars on human potentiality." That's at this Big Sur Hot Springs place that I think I mentioned to you, which is sort of a gathering place for any old ideas from anybody, good ones, bad ones. "The Varieties of Religious Experience" is two seminars being given by the ones who own that Big Sur Hot Springs. "Cultural integration fellowship," Sunday morning discourses by Dr. Haridas Chaudhuri,[7] and then there's one about the tree of life—this is a Buddhist group apparently. "Art and Religion" and "The Development of Human Potentialities," a series of four lectures by Paul S. Kerr[8]—so that's the guy who runs this thing. And then the titles are just . . . Lecture 1, "Health: how to maintain it." That's for one hour. Lecture 2: "Growth: how to sustain it," in one hour. "Joy: how to attain it"—that's an additional hour. [*General laughter*] "Self-actualization: how to attain it"—that's one hour. Four hours for all of this.

Then there's something—a new group, "Dialectical Humanism." Well, you get the picture of something popping. Here's one sponsored by the Unitarian Church on the Monterey Peninsula: "The desire for self-knowledge: an inquiry into the problems of identity." And then a series of lectures on the self by well-known people: "The Religion and Philosophy of Martin Buber." A seminar at the University of California: "Education of the Imagination," "The Human Relations and Creativity Workshop"—creativity takes more than one hour, I think, it takes at least three or four [*general laughter*]—"with emphasis on discovery and removal of emotional blocks to personal growth, and on learning techniques for developing creative capacity. This includes participation in a sensitivity training group and relating this experience to classes and dance, acting and creativity games." Now this is run by William Schutz.[9] He's one of the experimenters in this field. I wish he'd say this was an experiment instead of this implication—"education of the imagination," *period*. A hundred and ten dollars, that costs.

Lectures on LSD, humanist fellowship, the American way of death, Jessica Mitford,[10] psychoanalysis and existentialism, Heidegger.[11] The theories of Abraham Maslow I notice is one of them [*Maslow laughs*]. That comes next to tantric yoga. [*General laughter*] There I am sandwiched in, right in between Theravada Buddhism and tantric yoga and the new concept of evolution, the problem of psychical research.

So it goes, and you're going to be tangled up in the middle of it. You can't help it because there's no stopping this wave. All you can do is try to make it more sensible if you can and a little more cautious and a little more scientific, insofar as that's possible. And try to keep the schizophrenics and the psychopaths out of it and so on. Do you have anything so say about this? I'm very curious about your reactions. [*Pause*]

Doug: I was going to tell you before that Los Altos is a funny town.

Maslow: Where is it?

Doug: It's near Palo Alto—south of Palo Alto about ten miles. There's a lot of strength of the John Birch Society there and they have campaigns to ban the works of Marx from the public library and all kinds of things like that going on.

Maslow: Well, the Birches won't like this. They're against mental health is the way they say it. [*General laughter*]

It's true. And you'll get involved with that too, if you go back to the towns where there are any Birchers. That's part of the campaign for the next couple of years—it's against the mental health conspiracy, as they call it. Well, it's your job. Have any other thoughts about this? [*Pause*]

Herb: When is this book due? Do you have any idea when it will be coming out?

Maslow: Two or three years at least, not before.[12]

Herb: I think if there's a lot of specific exercises in the book—specific things to do instead of just saying, "Well, let's do something," I think it may work.

Maslow: Well, my reaction is that this stuff comes along where I feel so shaky. I wonder what's going on and I'm a little worried. And then my feeling is of more sense of duty, and so is Rand's also—more sense of duty about that book, because that book is so conservative. That is, it's leaning over backwards about making no promises.

I think I told you about the first page in that book. "Do you want to improve yourself?" says the first page. "There's only one really good way that we can recommend that: get a personal psychoanalysis, period!" No if's, but's, footnotes, modifications, amendments and so on. It's the end of the page. Then, turn over the page: "But since, however, we realize many of you can't afford it, is there anything that is sensible or useful, or are there other possibilities? Yes, there are—they are this good or not good; one percent of the population can do so and so and one percent of the population can do this and that." Well, that's what I would call a conservative way to do it.

If you've read Horney's *Self-Analysis*, you know that she has been very careful about that too. Now, self-analysis to a degree is possible for powerful characters, strong people, especially for the non-projective types, I would say. You know, that "you-are-not-the-target" kind. As a major defense, most of us tend to blame somebody else for what's going on inside of us. Well, that's projection. Now, the non-projective type of person doesn't do that and is more able to use that kind of thing [i.e., self-analysis] and you get something out of it, although she holds out no promises about great revolutions for anybody, certainly not in four hours. [*Pause*]

Now if you have any thoughts about this stuff, any suggestions, again remember that I want still to treat you as a group of collaborative investigators, junior investigators, reporting back through me. That is, I'll be the one to pass it on to others—if you have any suggestions, or worries, or doubts, or thoughts, or any contributions, resolutions of your own, things that you would like to do.

The only thing that I just simply won't accept is a total rejection of the whole responsibility. I think you don't have any right to do that because you people are privileged members of society. You've been put in positions of responsibility, no matter what you feel about authority and responsibility today. You're going to run the society; you can either do it well or badly but you can't withdraw from it. You can't resign, not without being a son-of-a-bitch. You can't. You're the smart ones, you're the capable ones—you've simply got to do it one way or another. Now choose your way to do it. If you don't like the way, be critical. If, for instance, you disagree with some of the things that are being done, pound them, that's all, that's part of the job. The debate must go on over all this stuff: what can be done and what cannot be done and so on. But it's your responsibility.

Ben: I understand what you mean and I would agree with you for reasons of my own, but in the terms you put it, I can't quite understand it. Are you putting us on the level of technical responsibility, of moral, or what?

Maslow: Well, that's the way I said it, yes. But if I'm being cautious, I'll put it on a therapeutic basis that if you—you're a smart man—try to live a stupid life, you're going to destroy yourself in terms of simple illness: physical illness, mental illness, psychosomatic illness.

Ben: But in the way you phrased it, it sounds like a rejection of the responsibility in this particular place would inevitably somehow lead to this kind of illness, as you called it. I don't see the continuum there.

Maslow: Well, it's easiest to say for intelligence because there we have some data already. Smart people cannot lead stupid lives. You cannot renounce your intelligence.

Ben: Smart people could use their intelligence to reject something that they didn't believe was valid.

Maslow: That's alright.

Ben: Didn't you just say you would not accept a rejection or something?

Maslow: Oh, I see. I meant something else. I won't accept just simply having nothing to do with the whole business. Do you feel hot about this? For instance, do you feel antagonistic to what I've just been talking about? Then it's your job to kill it, or to try to kill it, to make a case against it. I would say that was using your intelligence and accepting your responsibilities too. The only thing you can't do is *la dolce vita.*[13] You just can't do it; you haven't got a right to it, and insofar as I'm your superego or will continue to call down the wrath of Freud upon you—you can't get away with it.

Ben: I still don't understand on what level you're placing the responsibility. What responsibility?

Maslow: The responsibility for taking seriously the efforts to improve the world and to improve human nature, which are being offered by all sorts of people—nuts and good ones. You cannot turn away from that and go off to the racetracks. You just can't do it. If you agree with some of this then you support what you agree with, I'd suggest.

Ben: But is someone necessarily immoral?

Maslow: Yes. There is such a thing as immorality by the way. If you want to argue that I'm willing to argue it. People have attacked me in their criticisms about this business about my being judgmental, for instance, and being moralistic and the like. Do you want to argue it?

Ben: Yeah. I would like to understand what you mean.

Maslow: In practical situations where I will myself have come to a conclusion of a kind and then somebody says, "Well, who are you?" or will raise this question about—in effect, what it amounts to is ethical relativity—of "Who are we to judge? Who are you to judge?" For instance, the question came up in this class, you remember, with Edward G. Robinson, and I was so shocked about that television advertising business and so on and so on?[14] And the response to that by perhaps about one-third of people here was either surprise or disapproval about my being moralistic, that is, by getting so mad about it or getting judgmental and so on.

In a general, most abstract way, I would say that people who are not judgmental, people who do not have some feelings of right and wrong or good and bad are . . . It's very dangerous, let's say—

Ben: Must they judge a particular ethical issue? I think of one thing: say a guy who is doing very good work in any of the academic pursuits—a brilliant physicist or psychologist or writer or doctor— just decided to quit and decided he'd be much happier if he went to a little apartment in the middle of the city somewhere and just shaved pieces of wood off a block all day or masturbated all day. Now, I would say that this guy was sick but I would not—

Maslow: It's also physiologically impossible. [*General laughter*]

Ben: But I don't understand how you could say that he was ethically corrupt. That's the distinction, and this kind of a judgment just eludes me. I don't understand that. I can understand the necessity for making judgments, because if you don't make judgments you're a *schlemiel*. But in this particular case it's the kind of thing that I think could lead to dangers.

John: It's true that the moral men must make moral decisions about lots of things, but it's not true that he has to spend his life pursuing his decisions. It's just that he must be prepared to meet, in every opportunity that occurs where he must make a decision, he must be prepared to make a decision to follow it up. Not that I would spend my life running around throwing bombs at those places where they're having those things because I think they're a lot of baloney. It's just that I have to be ready.

Maslow: From a professional psychology point of view—and also social science professors in general—the minimal statement is that the business of not making moral judgments at all is extremely sick and dangerous. They start talking about cultural-breakdown and people-breakdown and whatnot. Well, that's the minimal statement, that—

Ben: I just don't see how you can control another person morally.

Maslow: Well, that's an advanced question, you might say, and is much more moot and debatable and so on. What is not debatable at this point, and what carries a cap and gown—you know, the toga of science and so on—is this general conclusion that all the workers have come to in sociology, anthropology, psychology, psychiatry: that the people whose system of values breaks down altogether, the people who become non-judgmental, who don't know what's right and what's wrong—that they're dead. They're finished. We have all sorts of anthropological studies of this, and the truth of it is actually that they become less viable people.

Ben: I guess what I was actually meant was: what is right and what is wrong? "Right" and "wrong" I think are the wrong terms.

Maslow: Well, you'll have to speak up on that. If you start from this fundamental basis that we must take a kind of responsibility, if only for our own psychiatric health, let alone other considerations, then you cannot duck the problems of right and wrong. Now supposing you've accepted that, then beyond that you're in a morass. I mean, ethics—the right and wrong about it—is extremely difficult.

I would suggest, again speaking for this whole group, that if you come to conclusions yourself, for whatever reasons, you'd better know about them. You'd better be willing to express them, you better be conscious of them and so on. If you're also intelligent about these things and if you've had some training of the difficulties of right and wrong and judgments and so on, then you'd express yourself and not necessarily get mad if somebody says they don't agree with you. And this itself gets to be a technical question.

I was just interviewed by someone. *Time* has a lead article on changing sexual morality, and one of the guys was talking with me about it, and I have all sorts of things to say about this. One of them, by the way, is item number one: sex is really not a very moral thing. Some of the things we know about values and so on indicate that sexuality is a matter of strategy and tactics rather than a basic morality. We know that practically any old system works. If you know any ethnology at all, you know that. Well, that doesn't mean I won't give advice to my daughters and my nephews and nieces and so on about this particular society, what we're living in around here, what you can get away with and what you can't get away with and what will make trouble and what you pay too much for and so on and so on. That's another story.

Well, you see, that's the passing on of information I'm talking about there. This is not just me as a person propounding some personal prejudice. I'm talking from experiences in anthropology, not to mention psychiatry and psychology and psychotherapy and the like. Well, this is an area in which the facts have something to say. There is some science, some knowledge here. We can set limitations on this and that and the other thing, but I wouldn't venture to say that this was an easy thing. All I'm afraid of—the only thing I would push and that David Riesman has been pushing recently—is for the college students particularly: don't ever let yourself get into this crazy delusion that you can be neutral about values. Want to try to do that? Do it easier: just cut your wrists. That would be faster.

Herb: As a therapist do you make moral judgments?

Maslow: Not as a therapist, no. [*Pause*] I still remember one of the first cases that I handled long ago. It convinced me that therapy was something more objective than propagandizing, because the effect of good therapy was that this guy took up tap-dancing, which I loathe. [*General laughter*] But I was able to help him simply to unwrap himself, so to speak. Let's put it this way: he was too shy and too bashful and so on and so on. Well, as we worked along, he discovered within himself his impulse to do this—which was strong. That's what he discovered and that's what he wound up with. I had nothing to do with it, directly. This convinced me—I remember I've used that as a kind of paradigm at the back of my head: *good* psychotherapy is really just *uncovering*.[15]

John: Do you think that the psychologist, though—not the therapist—who proposes let's say a theory of health, must he take a moral position? I would tentatively say that he definitely has to, but given that, all kinds of questions arise. For instance, some of the peak-experiences are no good from a moral point of view. The circumstances under which one gets a peak-experience may be those which we think are morally dishonest, but nevertheless it might produce a peak-experience.

Maslow: Sure. These are questions of fact—empirical questions. The moralism or the stronger ethical judgments, the firmer tone of voice, that kind of thing, comes from more subjective certainty than there was ten years ago, comes from the conviction that the guidelines in human nature direct us in certain ways. I can be more certain in the way the dentist scolds you about brushing your teeth or doing something of the sort, which is again in terms of the goals: if you want good teeth, you'd better do this, thus and so. He has no doubts, no qualms, no uncertainties at all.

Well, to some extent, it's possible to say this now about your fate, your lifetime. Certainly it's easy enough to say to the extent that our goals are shared. You know, about these ultimate goals. For instance, that you would like to live free of pain, rather than with pain, and so on. There's much that we know now, from this last decade, about how to… If you want to live a longer life rather than a shorter life, and you want to be free of pain and you'd like to avoid the psychosomatic diseases in general, we know something about how to avoid them.

I have an excellent example—it just occurred to me—how much more firm we can be today than we were three years ago about cigarettes, so I'm getting moralistic about it. For instance, there came the question of putting a cigarette machine in this building and I said no, and I'll debate it. On the other hand, I don't run around campus snatching cigarettes out of people's mouths [*General laughter*]—they have the right to smoke, as I really feel people have the right to commit suicide, which I feel *definitely*. If I ever want to commit suicide, I'd like to be able to do it without fighting a lot of people. And I can conceive circumstances under which I would want to. But that's up to me—it's about my suicide—nobody should help me with it.

And I feel that you have the right to smoke, and I think you have the right for marijuana also. But I'm not going to help along with it. My daughters smoke, for instance, and we've been having these arguments. Then, they got past a certain age and I had to stop telling them what to do, even about cigarettes. Well, the very least I can do is—when I quit smoking, my wife quit smoking and we don't have any cigarettes around the house. If my daughter wants a cigarette, she can go hike someplace else to get one for herself. I'm not going to supply them, and I don't, and she gets mad.

Well, now that's moralistic? I think it is. I feel very firm about it, but I think it's for good reasons and I think I can justify the position there. Where I cannot justify the position, then I had better also know that I am simply expressing a prejudice, my own judgment. I don't like my steaks rare; I like them medium rare. Well, I'm going to insist on that to the waitress, but *you* can like them any other old way. I would say for me that was an issue, but not for someone else.

Ben: What happens if two people are eating the same piece of steak?

Maslow: You've jumped over into the questions of social psychology now.

Ben: I think there is some bearing there—

Maslow: That's the little step there, as there is between married people.

Ben: I don't know what terms—

Maslow: They're sleeping together in the same bedroom. I know as we get older, my wife and I for instance—and my friends have told me too—being middle-aged people, our thermostats seem to be going in different directions. There is my wife perspiring when I'm shivering. I'd say those are social psychological questions, and at the moment they are matters of strategy and tact and power plays and things like that. [*General laughter*]

Well, this was all. All I would want to say would be this first point, and not to go beyond that, which is a very difficult thing. The point about—and that's what I meant to be saying here—you cannot resign from the ethical problems under pain of destruction of your own soul, your own psyche. But specific decisions—it's all debatable still.

Melissa: This isn't about any of that. Maybe I shouldn't go into that today; I know time is running out. But about this dream material, reading a little of Jung and Fromm can get very, very confusing. At least, I know *I'm* getting confused. How much can you do with it yourself? You wake up in the morning and you've had a dream. How valid is it in terms of what we're trying to do? And when we do pay attention to our dreams? Only on the occasions it follows us around and we're thinking about it during the day? Is this the time to start? Or if you just have an interesting dream when you wake up? Is this something good to go into?

Maslow: If you are interested in self-knowledge then your own dreams are one of the major paths to self-knowledge that you have available. Once you grab that goal, if you are interested in self-knowledge, then I urge you very strongly to hang on to your dreams whenever you can—any dream, any snatch of a dream, any piece of a dream—and try to make something out of it, try to free-associate to it.

The usual trick that is recommended is to have paper and pencil by your bedside. If you go into psychoanalysis or you go into psychotherapy, it's a general experience that people suddenly start remembering their dreams. They never have before; now they remember their dreams. Then they're in psychotherapy for two years and suddenly they stop remembering their dreams. It's to some extent under your own control, if you want them very badly.[16] Also, you pick up this business about people who want them very badly—just write them down on the spur of the moment and you can pick up the habits very easily. You have a dream, you sort of half wake out of your sleep—not fully—you write one word, two words, you know, something to recall the whole business to you, and then you fall right back into full sleep again. You can do it. You can pick up such a habit, and it's a very desirable thing to do. This is the best way that I can think of, of seeking self-knowledge or self-therapy—self-therapy via self-knowledge. It's the most transparent, the most easily usable, about which we have the most knowledge. There's a large fund of sophistication about this thing.

By the way, if you cannot use your own dreams . . . Supposing you were a rotten dream rememberer. One of the things that I did in this class that I told you about when I tried that other technique—you know, using clinical materials? But I didn't use it this semester? One thing I found very, very useful was free-association to somebody *else's* dreams. You can do that too. Which means that if you get yourself, let's say, the books on dream interpretation—perhaps a dozen good ones are available—run through those and get into that "psychoanalytic state," you might say. And associate to the dreams of someone else. You'll find again that you can get insight on yourself. Some of them are obvious even to the naked eye.

Well, the situation I'm in, for instance—I haven't worked it out but for three or four nights in a row I've had unpleasant dreams. One was a train wreck. I was in a train wreck and people were dying all around, but for some reason I wasn't hurt—whatever that means. Then one I identified . . . Uh, by gosh, I got it! [*General laughter*] By gosh, sometimes it's so easy! The man who had been my psychoanalyst died a few days ago, or at least I heard about it then. This was Felix Deutsch, who was one of the great analysts. I heard about three or four days ago that he had died. No wonder! I had the one dream in which gangsters—you know, the Hollywood style—had occupied the house and there was this little old man who was the father of the house. Deutsch was about five feet tall and very slight. He must have weighed sixty pounds or something. [*General laughter*]

And the man in the dream was like that—an old man, stooped over—and he was protecting his family against the criminals who had invaded. You know, standard plot number six. And he killed them all somehow by outwitting them. And then I remembered the association was with Felix Deutsch and the psychoanalysts and the way he was attacked and so on.

But this dream is so typical of me—there's the train wreck and even strong people die, but I remain alive. I'm unhurt. This is a very, very typical sort of half guilt . . . Well, I'll be darned. [*General laughter*]

Yes, there was another part of the dream there in which there were dead people and I was taking money out of their pockets. [*Roars of laughter*]

My gosh! Isn't that pretty. Well, Deutsch died, and I rest on his dead body and characteristically, I'll bet you, I'll be having guilt dreams also. You know, I'm alive and he's dead. I deserve it so much, you know? Why should he die and not me? Then also this business about using his wealth so to speak, getting money out of dead people's pockets.

Well, that's an illustration of the technique, by the way. It happens if you tell it to someone; for instance, if you can tell it to your friend. Well, look, how it just happened. I've been puzzling over those darn dreams—those unpleasant dreams have been happening each night. It's kind of mourning over poor Felix and again feeling that—which we all tend to do—why should I be alive? Feeling slightly guilty just being alive when other people die. You feel if somebody has cancer and you don't have cancer—well, why do you deserve so much not to have cancer? Speaking it out loud is better. As a matter of fact, one of the students here tried the technique even of speaking to himself— that is, into a tape-recorder—and then playing it back, and this will help you interpret the dream. I didn't mean to make such a visual demonstration but that's the way it turned out. [*Pause*]

Well, when your father dies—and this is a little of the father relationship—things happen. Read what Freud has to say about that in *The Interpretation of Dreams*. There's a very good passage there. And there's so many fathers we have. It is not just your blood father.

Melissa: This may not be a question at all—

Maslow: Let's see if this will be as fruitful as the other question.

Melissa: It's about archetypes. I've been reading all sorts of things and I keep coming up with different ones. You know, sometimes they're fairy tales or nursery rhymes or stories—old images or ancient myths and things like this. Is an archetype that will be helpful to you—and this is all in the framework of what is going to make you better, more aware, more conscious—is one of your archetypes what you relate to when you hear one of these basic stories, fairy tales? Now that you know this is the language you talk in? Do you know what I'm asking?

Maslow: I think a good way of saying it for yourself is that your archetypes are recurring personal symbols. Now if you take the basic things in life; for instance, while we're talking about these dreams, if you're in analysis you'll find that you have personal symbols of a kind for the good mother. Paul Bergman—did I read you that case? I guess I didn't. I wanted to. Paul Bergman is a psychoanalyst. Under LSD he dug up whole sets of symbols which were for him so deep, so basic, so enduring, that they would be called archetypes, especially since they were, you might say, universal.

For instance, for him the whole oral question came up. He saw a whole landscape full of breasts, is what it amounted to. He realized that everything he loved—the mountain tops were breasts, and then there was a flowing stream and that was a breast for him, and then there was a fountain and that was a breast for him, and so on. This has been published just recently. Anyway, this was *after* his analysis was over. Then he took the LSD and somehow the whole thing came to an end. It came to a closure where he worked out his relationship to nature as a breast, somehow—nature as generous and as free-flowing and so on.

Now, that's his picture of a breast—it's got milk in it. But remember that you'll find that as an equal archetype is the breast that has poison in it—the witch mother. The Balinese for instance, have it embedded right into the whole society. They act it out in their ceremonies. The female with huge flapping breasts that go down to the ground almost, and they're poisonous, and the young men try to stab her to death, and then they get paralyzed and fall into a faint and so on. If you read about the Balinese, that's the kind of thing you get there. The mothers are a bunch of bitches there, technically, and the children grow up hating them unconsciously, and then they work it off in these ceremonies.

Well, according to Jung, Melanie Klein and a lot of other people, the standard things are the good mother with the flowing breast with good, rich, flowing milk; generous, freely giving, feeding—and also the foul mother, the witch mother, the bad mother who has either dry breasts or no breasts at all, or the breasts give poison instead, or they have thorns on them. See, there your job would be to find out what are these recurring symbols for you. If you find them, you'll find that they tend to be more universal. It's from a sort of a limited repertoire; they're not infinite. They may take different shapes in different societies but if you really soak up the Fromm book, get a good feeling for it, then you'll be able to have a good feeling for these archetypes, I think, no matter what the culture. You'll be able to read, let's say, about the Balinese dance and make sense out of it, get a feeling for it—recurring, widespread, personal symbols.

I think we better get out of here. They want to clear the campus of all the cars, so we better go. I'll be around a lot during this week and next week and so on, for any discussion, consultations. Bring in your notebooks—if they're private, bring them to me; or if you leave them in my box, put it in an envelope; nobody will look. I've decided I will give you back your mid-semester exams after I make up the grades for the whole semester. I'm going to keep your final examinations, these final papers. I want to keep those. I can use those. I don't think I need your mid-semester papers anymore, so you can have them back. I'll return them after I've used them for making up these semester grades.

Mark: I'd like to pass these out to you. It's, uh, a study I'm doing—

Maslow [*calling students back*]: Oh, yes, can you wait just a minute for this? I forgot this.

Mark: I say, I'd like to pass these out. It's, uh, a study I'm doing, asking you to describe some things, on a voluntary basis. If you find it interesting, it would be particularly worthwhile for me. Maybe take a half hour.

Maslow: All for the sake of science, remember.

[*The class was cut short due to an unexpected snowstorm*]

JANUARY 22, 1964
Final Exam

Final Examination

What have you learned about the human personality? Answer using material from the readings, class discussions, exercises and other activities we've engaged in this semester.

APPENDICES

Appendix A

EXPERIENTIAL TECHNIQUES AND EXPERIMENTS

Abraham H. Maslow

(Used in Psychology 115a Experiential Approaches to the Study of Personality 1963, 1964, 1966)

1. Exercises in Suchness and concrete experiencing, use the *Sense of Wonder* by Rachel Carson. A good way of recountering the ability to perceive Suchness is to do as she did, is to take a little boy or a little girl to go look at the seashore or spiderwebs or surf or trees or to look through magnifying glasses at leaves or snowflakes or the like. To help the child look means to help yourself look. Also the child's reactions to what you overlook or pay no attention to may help to pull you back to seeing the world and its Suchness as a child does.

2. Try not to label things or ask for names on a nature walk. Just look at each bird or tree or flower of leaf in itself, per se, as if you were seeing it for the first time, or as if no other such existed in the world. Don't try to classify it or label it or name it. It makes no difference whether it's common or not; the robin or the sparrow is just as much a miracle as the cardinal or the oriole. Try the same thing with dogs. Most people don't see "dogness" (although

children do). They think in terms of pedigrees or lines or even clip their hair in particular ways which are not doglike but are dog-owner like. They fuss about "pure lines," and then of course you can tell that such a person doesn't really like dogs, but has acquired a property. The same thing is true of flowers. Make bouquets of meadow grasses or weeds and look at them as if they were quite rare. You will see them in a different way. In such looking also be sure that you push aside all questions of usefulness or uselessness, of good or bad, danger, etc.

3. Concentrate on one single natural small thing as children do. For instance, let yourself get fascinated with following an ant through the meadow grasses. Or let yourself get lost in a microscope, that is, to examine something wondrous and complex and to become absorbed in it. The same thing can be done with a telescope. The same thing can be even better done using Laura Huxley's technique of having a little two-inch cube made up of magnifying glasses and lit from below. If you put a little flower in this box and then stare at it, it is very easy to become lost in this world, and to forget yourself. The thing is to get lost in the narrowed down experience, to concentrate, to be fascinated. Of course this can be done with anything, for instance, the blue vase experiment of Deikman.[1] Or use the Agassiz[2] fish story. He would ask a new student in his laboratory simply to look at a fish carefully and then to report back what he saw. Usually the student learned to see more and more deeply, to look more and more carefully, less and less superficially as, time by time, Agassiz rejected his report and sent him back to look more carefully. This can be done with any object or animal or bird or flower or whatever. We can call this intensive looking with care and then recognize that we do this, for instance, with a sweetheart or a baby. This can be tried out even if you don't have a baby or a sweetheart around by observing nursery school children through a one-way mirror. It is possible to get "lost," fascinated, absorbed, etc.

4. Exercises in sentiment and sentimentality. For instance, see *Ecstasy* by M. Laski,[3] Appendix F, pp. 503 following, in which children's ecstasies are reported. The task is to recover the *first*

confrontation with what is now "sentimental" or square or corny or platitudinous or truistic. Generally truisms are true: the wonder is lost because it's all got so familiarized. It is possible to break through the familiarization and to recover the triggering power of a snowflake or a leaf or a sunset or even of corny or Victorian sentiments of various kinds as on postcards. One can make a list of platitudes and then try to freshen them to recover their triggering power as if they were being said for the first time.

5. Experientially empty people can't really taste food, or at least ordinarily. And of course this is true for all of us much of the time when eating food is the background to, let's say, important conversations that are going on at the same time. We don't notice what we eat. Try the Aldous Huxley exercise in deliberately and consciously focusing attention on the tasting and chewing and sipping, stopping the conversation, and giving one's full attention to the sip of coffee or wine or tea, etc. In Aldous Huxley's *Island*[4] he suggests deliberately chewing silently at the beginning of a meal for a certain number of chews. It is possible to do this when one is alone, to learn to recover the consciousness of food and drink. It is simply a matter of focusing full attention.

6. As a text, use my Chapter 14, "Cognition of the Individual and of the Generic," in my *Motivation and Personality*.[5] There are many examples of rubricizing and of losing the cognition of the individual because of this abstraction. Do this for various abstract concepts and words, and try to recover the concreteness of these abstractions, or at least to give concrete content to the abstract word. This chapter might be a very good beginning to the abstract word. This chapter might be a very good beginning to the whole enterprise of recovering the ability to experience. It might be used at the very beginning of the semester. Another good beginning to this type of education would also be reading in the general field of General-Semantics. A good book to start with is Hayakawa's *Language in Thought and Action*.[6]

7. In the same book, Chapter 15, "Unmotivated and Purposeless Reaction," many examples are given of unmotivated activities and

many exercises are implied. I would put the theoretical stress on the differentiation between end-experience and means-experience. I would stress the self-validating, intrinsically worthwhile, intrinsically enjoyable experiences which can be enjoyed for their own sake.

8. Use also in the same book, Chapter 11, "The Expressive Component of Behavior," starting with the examples of end-experiences in the footnote on page 186. This is an easy way to teach people to differentiate between means-experiences and end-experiences, that which is done for its own sake vs. that which is done for the sake of something else.

9. Introduce the Freud concept of free-floating attention. Pair off students in the class, one to be a talker and one to be a listener, with the listener trying to acquire the ability at distributed attention, or free-floating attention, non-concentrating attention, Taoistic attention, passive receptivity, non-active listening, etc.

10. I found it useful to set a class of students this problem to think about while they closed their eyes. The problem was for the girls, When do you feel most feminine; when least feminine? And for the boys, When do you feel most masculine; when do you feel least masculine? Here the intent is to help the development of awareness and insight. The reporting to the whole class could then take place and interesting discussions of various kinds ensue. One that I think of was the development both of the recognition of profound similarities, and also the recognition of profound individual differences. This is along the tack of comparing one's own inner psychic world with the inner psychic worlds of others.

11. I talked about the old self-confrontation experiments of Werner Wolff, reported in his book, *Expression of Personality*.[7] Now of course this could be done much better. I reported Ronald Shor's[8] experiment with listening, with mimicking the psychoanalytic situation all by himself and as closely as he could, but talking into a tape recorder rather than to a psychoanalyst. And then for the second hour, playing back the tape recording to himself and

listening to it and then erasing it. This kind of self-confrontation I generally encouraged, and no matter where it came from. For instance, intelligence tests, personality tests, feedback from other people, i.e., any objective information. The ideal thing to do of course would be the new video tape machines.

12. Various Taoistic exercises in trust, letting go, letting be, being receptive, etc. The Taoistic attitude was discussed at the beginning of the semester and referred to throughout the semester in many situations that came up spontaneously where I would try to make the differentiation between Taoistic and non-Taoistic as I caught the experience on the fly. I spoke about extreme instances to start with, like floating in the water, or not being able to float. Or of the body instances in which we must let go rather than control, e.g., urination, defecation, sleep, etc.

13. The general exercise was recommended to be used especially in moments of depression, unhappiness, or discouragement, of deliberately trying to help others, or quite verbally placing oneself at another's disposal, with the motto to oneself or to the other, "If I am no good for myself, then at least I can be good for someone else." This was encouraged with the report that often enough such a person would become absorbed in what he was doing so that not only was he useful for someone else, but he was actually curing his own discouragement.

14. With such a class there should go a voluntary T-group, run by someone else, I believe, rather than the teacher in charge. I lectured about feedback, about here and now, about sending out signals that could be heard, of checking back your hearing of the signals with the sender to see if you received it right, the becoming aware and conscious in the T-group situation of the actual feeling of anxiety in the face of silence, for instance, etc., etc. Of course this can be expanded a very great deal.

15. I didn't *do* anything about it in class, but spoke much about training for children, especially in rhythm, free dancing, simple music and the like, and reported to them on the Esalen-type of

body-awareness techniques and body-expressiveness techniques.

16. I also lectured about creative art education for children of the type invented at the Museum of Modern Art by Victor D'Amico. The essential point is about non-representational rather than representational work with very large papers and with poster colors.

17. I recommend it very strongly for those who could do it that they keep a journal of a sort that I keep, which includes thinking out on paper, almost free association. The Hayakawa exercises were mentioned as helping in this enterprise for people who had no experience with writing, or who blocked in one way or another, of simply to write anything on paper, if necessary just repeating one's name over and over again, or repeating nonsense words, or anything, just in order to get into the ability to free associate on paper, to write nonsense, to write stuff that would then be thrown away. Thus the ability to think on paper either in a directed or undirected way, or to free associate on paper is acquired. Then I suggested a well-bound journal or diary which they could keep for the sake of months later going back over what had been written and meditating on it, pondering, mulling.

18. Self-training in free association. I spoke about the psychoanalytic situation and suggested private practice in achieving the same relaxation from culture, from logic, from rationality, simply turning inward and then saying out loud, what passed through consciousness, without censorship.

19. The training in breaking clichés via unconventional metaphors, figures of speech, new ways of describing things, etc. The way I started it off was to read examples of the way in which children break out of our stereotypes, like as white as milk, as fast as lightning, etc. Such a collection of examples of children's freshness in creating new figures of speech is a good way to start. Then the exercise is given deliberately to the class of doing something equally unconventional or unstereotyped with a list of incomplete figures of speech, e.g., as white as. . ., as fast as . . ., as

tall as. . ., as strong as . . .

20. The synesthetic languages. Relating colors with numbers, etc. The exercises I used were mostly with food and drink, which foods would go together like ham and eggs, for instance? I asked them to match which would go better with Roquefort cheese, a particular this or that wine, or beer, or brandy, or whatever. Similar exercises for people. Which cheese would Abraham Lincoln prefer? Would he prefer tea or coffee? Which would Mrs. Roosevelt[9] like—tea or coffee, or beer or whiskey, etc. What would you serve Spinoza or Harry Truman[10] or Eisenhower?[11] Or which foods are more masculine and which foods are more feminine? Which foods go with blue and which foods go with yellow? At the two ends of the spectrum make a list of public figures and ask which belonged on the blue/green end of the spectrum and which belonged on the orange/red end of the spectrum. Similar games could be played in the classroom with the students themselves. They can be asked, all of them for a single person whether for instance she should have her portrait painted by Renoir[12] or by Picasso,[13] for instance.

21. Following Heinz Werner's exercises (*Comparative Psychology of Mental Development*[14]) of the gestalt exercises in matching nonsense words with nonsense figures. It is very impressive to a class to discover that practically everybody in the class sees a zigzaggy nonsense figure as [the word] "takete" and the curvy figure as [the word] "lumuma." I also had the sign made from Arnheim (I forget the source) of music manuscripts by Beethoven, Bach and Mozart, and then asked them to guess who had done which. It's always impressive that practically everybody matches them correctly.

22. It made a very good exercise to ask the students in a group to volunteer their peak-experiences. This generally touched off other people in the group. Also it tended to be progressively more intimate, i.e., starting from rather mild and not very intimate experiences, and going on to more poignant, more emotional, more shaking experiences being reported. The same thing can be

done for desolation experiences. I used the silence experience in class to show how anxiety-producing it could be even for five minutes, but then suggested that this is much more effective when it is done for some longer period of time. Or when it happens spontaneously in T-groups or at a party or in any public discussion. People get very uneasy with silences and have to fill them up. This can be personally experienced.

23. The question put was, "Who am I?" This who-am-I game produces much thought and much conversation.

24. I gave a little lecture on counter-values on jealousy, envy, hostility, to the good person, to the honest person, to truth, to justice, to excellence, etc., and then the exercise was for us to find our own counter-values, and to dredge them up and experience them. This can be helped along by example after example, to the group.

25. I suggested experiences in nakedness starting with each one privately in swimming, walking about the house, etc. But then suggesting that if this were socially possible first in like sex groups and then in mixed groups, that most people report a kind of spontaneous dropping of defenses, freeing of inhibitions, etc.

26. The inhibitions to speaking in public, to making speeches in front of the class were to be experienced and then discussed openly. Attention was directed to any signs of tension or anxiety within oneself.

27. Much was made of the difficulty of transmitting or communicating one's own subjective, private experience to another person. I read my Appendix, Rhapsodic Communication, from my book, *Religions, Values and Peak-Experiences*.[15] The effort to communicate ineffable experiences, experiences of Suchness, can actually be tried out so that one experiences for himself both the difficulties and the possibilities. I have tried having a girl try to communicate to a boy what it feels like to be a girl.

28. I tried deliberately to help the students recover the awareness of anxiety, of sadness or depression, of anger in whatever ways I could think of through the whole semester. Allen Wheelis' book, *Illusionless Man*,[16] in this book the peak-experience quality is missing; zest, joy in life, etc. He sees everything, he is very smart, he is fully aware, but he doesn't *feel*. What would you say to him? What can one say to a person who doesn't experience emotion, or pleasure, or joy? One can talk here about the general topic of joylessness, of the non-peaker, of emotional aridity.

Appendix B

NOTES AND QUESTIONS FOR PSYCHOLOGY 150b (UTOPIAN SOCIAL PSYCHOLOGY)

Abraham H. Maslow

March 30, 1967

On *Island*[1] by Aldous Huxley

Why does *Island* seem goody-goody even though it is based, all of it, on data and extrapolations from data? We get the impression that everybody is beautiful and good and wonderful. Could this in fact reasonably be expected? Even if there were such a society and it had been functioning for some time and it was not threatened from the outside, could we still expect that everyone born into it would grow up as well?

It should be stressed again that Aldous Huxley tried to base himself upon extant scientific and pre-scientific knowledge. He didn't raise the question of how reliable it was. But in fact, had he wished, he could have made footnote references throughout the book to publications by scientists.

Is *Island* one of [Frank E.] Manuel's "no progress" Utopias? Is it an end-state? Is it going any place? Is it changing? Developing?

Growing?

One general problem for all Utopian or Eupsychian thinkers is raised on page 91 of *Island*. Probably no society can function at its best unless there is respect for elders, at least *some* respect, at least *some* functional using of the old people. If they are rejected altogether, then it is as if the young cut themselves off from all traditions, from all experience, from all life teachings. They would then have to relearn everything for themselves.

Guardians on *Island* are wise and good people. Can this be taken for granted? Must it be specified for a good society that there be social mechanisms as well as intrapsychic preferences for wise leaders rather than stupid or foolish or sick ones? Of course no society could be a good society for very long *unless* it chose consistently wise leaders or guardians and respected and admired them. The psychological as well as cultural mechanisms for making this come about must be specified.

In Pala the higher life (ethical, value, spiritual, religious) is based upon the "lower life" (body, animal, lower needs, material needs). That is, they are hierarchically integrated, rather than being dichotomized or mutually exclusive from each other. The good body is the *condition* of the higher life. They are also seen "unitively"; that is, the body and its functions are sacralized. There is an acceptance of sex, of body, of sensuousness, of sensuality, of muscles, etc. Perhaps special attention should be paid to the sacralization of sex in this book. Is this necessary for any good society? Or is it expendable? Is it possible to build a good society by renouncing the lower life of the body in order to reach the higher life of the spirit? This is what most Utopias and most religions have in fact done throughout history.

There is implied throughout the book a definition of science which is not orthodox. It is naturalistic and empirical, and Huxley is certainly respectful of science taken in the broadest sense, and even bases his whole society on science. But his conception of science is different from the average person's conception. It seems more humanistic, one might say, or more human-centered, person-centered, etc. Is this necessary? Is it possible to renounce science altogether, as for instance the Mennonites have done in this country?

Separable from this question is the question of whether technology should be rejected or not. This problem must be faced at the very beginning in any small community or large society. Many of the Utopian communities base themselves upon the rejection of technology, considering it to be too great a danger. While this might be possible for small communities within a large technological society, as some religious sects in this country demonstrate, yet it has to be faced that if there were a broad-scale rejection of technology, that a large portion of the human species would be condemned to death very quickly.

Island is an oasis-type Utopia. That is, it is imbedded within an alien world, which is also hostile. In planning a community this is one of the standard problems that has to be faced.

Peak-experiences are valued and indeed much of life is centered upon them. This is different from the Utopias in which there is only calm serenity and eternal peace.

The goal of Pala is quite specifically the self-actualization of all its individuals, i.e., it is Eupsychian.

The question of power is solved on Pala by having leaders who are not dictators. Pala moves in the anarchistic direction. Power is spread around. It is Taoistic. Association is voluntary. This is a general question that confronts any society, i.e., which kind of organization of power within the society is best, and which is possible?

Island is individual-centered. It is not State-centered.

Will, the visitor, in a certain sense "loved" evil. The psycho-dynamics of this "love for evil," i.e., counter-valuing, must be worked out and understood more than it has.

The same thing is true for Murugan and his mother. Huxley implied that all three of these individuals were evil because they were not brought up on the island entirely. Could such a love for evil develop in a person who was born and brought up on the island? Contrarywise, could a "love for the good" develop in people who were brought up in a non-Eupsychia? How?

Could this oasis kind of Utopian experiment be actually done? Quite specifically as pilot experiments? Or simulation experiments? There is no reason why many such experiments should not be made simultaneously under different conditions with different kinds of people and in different parts of the world.

Huxley does not face one problem that any society has to deal with. Where are the biological inferiors, i.e., the feeble-minded, the insane, the senile, the brain-injured, etc.?

Any society has to deal with anger and aggression. In *Island* there is certainly catharsis of fear, but not much is said about the expression or catharsis of anger (but see page 207).

The theme of candor, frankness, honesty, feedback, is found throughout the book. This accords not only with modern psychotherapeutic techniques, T-groups, psychodrama, etc., but also with the beliefs of various religious groups, e.g., Bruderhof, etc. Huxley implies that this is *sine qua non*.

Consider the question of the dangerous mountain climbing. Many psychologists are beginning to think that some kind of overcoming of difficulties, of the confrontation of danger and hardship, is desirable and perhaps even necessary, especially for young men.

The book could be described as an integration of Eastern and Western thought and philosophy.

This Utopia is unusual in one respect: not only is the society described, but also the history is detailed of how it got there.

Observe the use of hypnosis, of concentration, of the focusing of attention, contemplation, meditation.

There is implied throughout the book that the "natural" Taoistic kind of medicine is better than the intruding or interfering or controlling type (*Vis medicatrix naturae*) Taoistic sexuality described on page 77 (see Alan Watts' *Nature, Man and Woman*[2]). Is this essential or expendable in a good society? Any society, any culture has traditions, customs, folkways, or habits about sex. There are good ones and there are bad ones, at least from the point of the intrapsychic point of view of the personal pleasure that is possible, and of what is "good for the person."

Huxley accepts and uses constitutional differences. He was much impressed with W. H. Sheldon and used his work. This is an acceptance; and even a building upon individual differences between persons. Many Utopians have proceeded as if human beings were all alike and were interchangeable biologically.

The question of possible escape from the family, not only for a child, but for any member of the family, see page 90. Benedictine synergy societies had such an escape as a possibility in one form or another. Compare also with the kibbutz. Compare also with *The Free Family* by Paul and Jean Ritter.[3]

Huxley was quite willing to use psychedelic drugs. Must this be considered *sine qua non*? Were sacral experiences possible in other ways? Peak-experiences are reported, but high ones and small ones, as obtainable from simple and natural things so that no artificial triggers are absolutely needed, e.g., alcohol, speed, etc.

Any society has to consider the question of population control or expansion.

See page 145 for consuming and over-consuming.

Huxley outlines a system of education which is completely different from the orthodox system in the United States. Is this essential or expendable? Notice that it includes transcendental experiences, the education of the body, of attention, etc. Is education with a goal of self-actualization different from U. S. education?

See what Huxley says on page 148 about the newspapers. What

would be a Eupsychian newspaper? Any society has to exert power and control (unless it is a highly selected group of people). The question then comes up of crime, of police, of the cure of criminal tendencies, etc. See page 155. How possible in principle is it to have a society which is completely "swordless and punishmentless"? Certainly some small preliterate societies have been described in which there is no punishment from the society as a whole.

It appears that a normal life history of progressive gratification of the hierarchy of basic needs leading finally to preoccupation with higher need gratifications and metaneed gratifications has the consequence of making lower need greeds unnecessary or less necessary (page 146). People at the higher need and metaneed level tend to lead a simple life and not to want a great many possessions. The desire for *things* becomes less and less pressing as one goes up the motivation hierarchy. The high peak-experiences then come from simple triggers. There is therefore less and less need or wish for more money for buying objects with (except that more money may be wanted for giving away).

About this particular Utopia, how realistic is it psychologically? Is it possible? How much of this is fantasy, wish fulfillment, illusion?

There are admired people on Pala. The totally alienated person who rejects his culture tends to have no heroes, no models, nobody to admire. Is it possible to have a good society without models and heroes?

The Palanese did not really protect themselves against their enemies. What was the right thing to do with the evil persons who might destroy the island? What right does such a society have to defend itself? How far can it go with military defense, for instance? Supposing non-resistance does not work, then what?

If you have advanced techniques or secrets that are too much for the surrounding culture, that would shock them or frighten them or anger them, to what degree should you keep them secret? Or slow your pace? Or compromise with the surrounding culture in order to fend off their hostile attack (especially if they are stronger)? Politics has been called the art of the possible. In this sense, how much politics and what kind would you advocate for such a society as *Island*?

To what extent can a person make his *own* Utopia? miniature good society? family? choice of friends? of job? of neighborhood? the way he sets up his home?

Appendix C

Notes on Classroom Recordings

Hung-Min Chiang notes of the original classroom recordings: "A Wollensak tape recorder was used: Speed 3 3/4 ips, 4 tracks. There were eight sound-recorded sessions, each with corresponding tapes:

Reel 1: October 28, 1963 & November 4

Reel 2: November 18 & December 2

Reel 3: December 9 & December 16

Reel 4: January 6, 1964 & January 13"

The following chart provides a general breakdown of the actual recorded material as it exists on cassettes made from the reel-to-reel tapes.

Note that classes were scheduled for three hours. The intention was that the first two hours would consist of a lecture by Maslow. The third hour was to be a "laboratory for self-knowledge." involving discussions with everyone in the class, including Maslow. Although there was a three-hour timeslot for the course, with breaks it seems that in practice lectures would usually run for about an hour and a half and the labs would run for about an hour.

Source Cassette Recordings

Tape	Actual time minutes:seconds	Date @ Start	Date @ End	Notes
1	92:29	10/28 beginning of lecture	10/28 end of lecture	
2	63:56	10/28 beginning of lab	10/28 end of lab	
3	97:58	11/4 beginning of lecture	11/4 end of lecture	
4	63:23	11/4 beginning of lab	11/4 end of lab	
5	98:47	11/18 beginning of lecture	11/18 end of lab	Exam; 1st hour not recorded. Starts with Maslow in mid-sentence. Transcript note: *The tape ends here, even though the session continues a little longer.* [HMC]
6	98:05	12/2 beginning of lecture	12/2 near end of lecture	Cuts out in mid-sentence and is continued on tape 7
7	92:57	12/2 end of lecture; 12/2 beginning of lab	12/2 end of lab	
8	97:25	12/9 beginning of lecture	12/9 near end of lecture	Cuts out in mid-sentence and is continued on tape 9
9	98:22	12/9 end of lecture; 12/9 beginning of lab	12/9 near end of lab	Cuts out in mid-sentence; continued on tape 10
10	94:59	12/9 end of lab; 12/16 beginning of Dr. Abell session with Dr. Abell	12/16 session with Dr. Abell continues	There is a slight overlap between the end of cassette 10 and the beginning of cassette 11
11	71:12	12/16 session with Dr. Abell continues	12/16 end of session with Dr. Abell	
12	100:39	1/6 beginning of lecture	1/6 end of lecture	
13	51:58	1/6 beginning of lab	1/6 end of lab	
14	59:21	1/13 beginning of lecture	1/13 end of lecture	Class cut short because of snowstorm

ENDNOTES

Notes from the original transcription by Hung-Min Chiang have been reproduced in this updated transcript and are indicated in the endnotes as [HMC]. Other notes are by Chris Nelson. If a note combines comments by both editors, then both [HMC] and [CN] are indicated. The Introduction is referenced independently of the Lectures and Lab transcripts that follow it. Throughout, only the first instance of a name or text is noted, unless subsequent mentions include substantive material requiring further reference.

INTRODUCTORY NOTE

[1] See Appendix C: Notes on Classroom Recordings
[2] See Lecture, December 2, 1964, note 16. For a further exploration of Maslow's views on gender and other issues in context, see also Dye, Mills and Weatherbee (2005).
[3] See Lecture, January 6, 1964.

INTRODUCTION: A HUMANISTIC PSYCHOLOGIST IN THE CLASSROOM

[1] This essay, in a slightly modified form, originally appeared in the second edition of *The Healthy Personality* (Chiang & Maslow, 1977).
[2] Chiang (1968).
[3] Maslow (1965). Later published as Maslow (2000).
[4] Maslow (1971).
[5] Maslow (1971).
[6] See Lecture: November 4, 1963.
[7] See Lecture: November 18, 1963.

---

[8] See Lecture: November 18, 1963.

[9] Maslow (1965, p. 157). Later published as Maslow (2000).

[10] For instance, see Tenenbaum and Rogers (1977, pp. 174-188) and Smith (1977, pp. 153-163).

[11] See Lecture: November 4, 1963.

[12] See Lab: December 2, 1963.

[13] Maslow (1971, p. 183).

[14] Maslow (1965, p. 159).

[15] Karen Horney (1885-1952) was a German psychiatrist.

[16] Maslow (1971, p. 170).

[17] Sigmund Freud (1856-1939) was the founder of psychoanalysis and profoundly influential in the fields of psychiatry and psychology. Maslow distinguished between 1) behavioral psychology, 2) Freudian psychology and 3) humanistic psychology (the "Third Force"). In his view humanistic psychology includes the first two and is thus "epi-behavioristic" and "epi-Freudian." He writes, "I am Freudian and I am behavioristic and I am humanistic, and as a matter of fact I am developing what might be called a fourth psychology of transcendence as well." (Maslow, 1971)

[18] This extract was likely taken from Chiang's notes on a date before the class was recorded, as it does not appear in the recorded transcripts.

[19] Kubie (1977).

[20] A Maslowian term for an unhostile, philosophical humor that has an uplifting quality. [HMC]

[21] Courtesy of Mrs. Bertha Maslow. The memo was dated November 16, 1967. [HMC] A longer list is included in the present volume as Appendix A: Experiential Techniques and Experiments. [CN]

[22] Carson (1965).

[23] Rachel Carson (1907-1964) was an American biologist and writer.

[24] The "desolation experience" is a kind of parallel to the peak-experience. In his notes for Maslow's lecture on October 21, 1963, Chiang writes: "Maslow believed that any life experiences, when they rise to a certain level of completion and intensity, can lead to ecstasy. This means that ecstasy could be induced not only by positive events, as Maslow previously reported, but by negative events as well. Any sad or painful experience that produces an ecstasy and a heightened sense of consciousness was referred to by Maslow and Laski as a 'desolation experience.'" Maslow also offers additional specific examples in *The Farther Reaches of Human Nature*: "psychotic regression, confrontation with death, destruction of defenses, illusions or value-systems, tragedy and tragic experiences, failures, confrontation with human predicament or existential dilemma." (Maslow, 1971, p. 130).

[25] Allen Wheelis (1915-2007) was a psychoanalyst and writer of fiction and non-fiction.

[26] Wheelis (1966).

[27] Books mentioned throughout the class are listed in the Bibliography.

[28] Horney (1942).

[29] Fromm (1951).

[30] Erich Fromm (1900-1980) was a German-born psychologist and philosopher.

[31] See Lecture: November 18, 1963.

[32] Fritz Perls (1893-1970) was a German psychiatrist who coined the term "gestalt therapy."

[33] D. T. Suzuki (1870-1966) was a Japanese writer.

[34] See Lab: January 6, 1964

[35] Maslow (1970b).

[36] The Laughlin Foundation (possibly also known as The Saga Foundation) is located in Menlo Park, California, which is where Maslow relocated after leaving Brandeis University. The grant was "to study the philosophy of democracy, economics, and ethics as influenced by humanistic psychology." (Kelland, 2017)

[37] Maslow (1962c).

[38] Maslow (1970a).

LECTURE: SEPTEMBER 30, 1963

[1] Maslow (1954).

[2] Maslow (1954, p. 93).

[3] Maslow (1962c, p. 133).

[4] Maslow (1963).

[5] Maslow, A. H. (1962a).

[6] A.H. Maslow and Bertha Maslow. This test is discussed in, for example, Morant and Maslow (1965). This paper examines the hypothesis that there is a close correlation between "the ability to judge visual art skillfully and the ability to judge other persons skillfully." A test created by Maslow and his wife, Bertha, measured an individual's ability to "select paintings done by the same artist from a group of paintings done by various artists."

LECTURE: OCTOBER 7, 1963

[1] James (1902). The class was assigned Chapter 7. [HMC]

[2] We have been unable to find this exact quote in a published resource.

[3] Bucke (1901).

---

[4] Timothy Gallwey in *The Inner Game of Tennis* (1974) has much to say on the question of spontaneity. He has made a useful distinction between what he has called Self 1 (conscious ego) and Self 2 (experiential self). [HMC]

LECTURE: OCTOBER 21, 1963

[1] Marghanita Laski (1915-1988) was an English writer.
[2] Laski (1961).

LECTURE: OCTOBER 28, 1963

[1] Carl Rogers (1902-1987) was an American psychologist and one of the pioneers (along with Maslow) of humanistic psychology..
[2] Felix Deutsch (1884-1964) was an Austrian psychoanalyst and physician.
[3] See Lecture & Laboratory for Self-Knowledge, October 14, 1963 in this volume. [HMC]
[4] Women today are certainly more expressive and outspoken on the issue of sexuality—more so today than in the early 1960s, and certainly more so than decades ago. Addressing the class in 1963, Maslow showed a considerable amount of hesitation in deciding at what level the question of sexuality should be discussed in the class. His ambivalence is apparent in the following material. [HMC, writing in the mid-1970s.]
[5] D. H. Lawrence (1885-1930) was an English writer known, among other things, for the exploration of human sexuality in his novels.
[6] DeMartino (1963).
[7] Manfred F. DeMartino (1924-2002) was an American psychologist and former student of Maslow's.
[8] Maslow (1962c, p. 67).
[9] Maslow is perhaps referring to the article by Clark Moustakas, in the same volume, entitled "The Sense of Self." Moustakas (1961). [HMC]
[10] Adrian Van Kaam (1920-2007) was a Dutch humanistic psychologist and Catholic priest.
[11] Van Kaam (1958).
[12] Richard Maurice Bucke (1837-1902) was a Canadian psychiatrist.
[13] The writer mentions two experiences, but as Maslow notes above, he only reads one of them to the class.
[14] The subsequent quotes are drawn from James (1920, pp. 76-77).
[15] Maslow must have made this reference when the class was not being recorded.
[16] James Pratt (1875–1944) was an American psychologist and philosopher of religion.
[17] The ensuing questions and answers are from James (1920, pp. 212-214). As noted therein: "The following document is not a letter, but a series of answers

to a questionnaire upon the subject of religious belief, which was sent out in 1904 by Professor James B. Pratt of Williams College, and to which James filled out a reply at an unascertained date in the autumn of that year."

[18] Arthur Koestler (1905-1983) was a Hungarian-English writer.

[19] Koestler, A. (1960).

[20] Simone de Beauvoir (1908-1986) was a French writer and philosopher.

[21] The ensuing quotes are drawn from Koestler (1954: pp. 350, 351, 352).]

[22] Immanuel Kant (1724-1804) was a German philosopher.

LAB: OCTOBER 28, 1963

[1] Béla Mittelmann (1899-1959) was an American psychoanalyst.

[2] Maslow and Mittelmann (1951).

[3] Carl Gustav Jung (1875-1961) was a Swiss psychiatrist and the founder of analytical psychology.

[4] Benjamin McLane Spock (1903-1998) was an American pediatrician and writer on childcare and psychology.

[5] John B. Watson (1878-1958) was an American psychologist and prominent proponent of behaviorism.

[6] Solomon Eliot Asch (1907-1996) was a Polish-American social psychologist.

[7] Asch has written several books, one of which is *Social Psychology* (1952). The experiment referred to here is reported in Asch (1955). [HMC]

[8] Hadley Cantril (1906-1969) was an American psychologist known in part for his work on public perception and opinion. We could not find the specific experiment involving poetry that is mentioned by Maslow.

[9] Muzafer Sherif (1906-1988) was a Turkish-American psychologist.

[10] Sherif (1956).

[11] Irving Lorge (1905-1961) was an American psychologist.

[12] Maslow is perhaps referring to Lorge and Curtiss (1936). [HMC]

[13] David M. Levy (1892-1977) was an American psychiatrist.

[14] Levy (1943).

[15] Stacey and DeMartino (1958).

[16] Chalmers L. Stacey (1908-1995) was a Canadian-American psychologist.

[17] There are some reported instances of peak-experiences by fathers. One such case is found in Tanzer (1977). [HMC]

LECTURE: NOVEMBER 4, 1963

[1] Bodkin (1934).

[2] Maud Bodkin (1875-1967) was an English writer and literary critic.

[3] Martin (1955).

[4] Percival William Martin (1893-1972) was an English civil servant and writer.

[5] Thomas Stearns Eliot (1888-1965) was an English poet, playwright and literary critic.

[6] Arnold J. Toynbee (1889-1975) was an English historian best known for *A Study of History*.

[7] Constance A. Newland was the pseudonym for Thelma Moss (1918-1997), an American actress, psychologist and parapsychologist.

[8] Newland (1962).

[9] Jane Dunlap was the pseudonym of Adelle Davis (1904-1974), an American nutritionist and writer.

[10] Dunlap (1961).

[11] Alfred C. Kinsey (1894-1956) was an American sexologist, applied biologist, entomologist and zoologist.

[12] Maslow and Sakoda (1952).

[13] Knight (1953).

[14] John Knight is a pseudonym for an individual whose identity remains undisclosed.

[15] Lucy Freeman (1916-2004) was an American writer.

[16] Freeman (1951).

[17] Alan Watts (1915-1973) was an English-American writer.

[18] Watts (1958).

[19] Watts (1962).

[20] Watts (1960).

[21] "Science pursues the . . . measured and controlled . . ." (Watts, 1962, p.9)

[22] "The transformation of . . . habits and opinions." (Watts, 1962, p. 11)

[23] "Consciousness-changing drugs . . . are insufficient." (Watts, 1962, p. 24)

[24] Maslow has conversationally altered this quote here, which in Watts (1962, p. 24) reads as saying that the hallucinations have, "proved of less interest to me than one's transformed impression of the natural world . . ." He has not changed Watts' meaning but rather taken a sentence fragment from further down the page to cement the point Watts is making.

[25] "To begin with . . . richness of articulation." (Watts, 1962, p. 27)

[26] Maslow (1959).

[27] Red Skelton (born Richard Bernard Eheart) (1913-1997) was an American entertainer.

[28] "Normally we do not . . . structure and color." (Watts, 1962, pp. 27, 29)

[29] "At the same time . . . pretending to be." (Watts, 1962, p. 44)

[30] Timothy Leary (1920-1996) was an American psychologist especially known for exploring the therapeutic uses of psychedelic drugs.

[31] Watts (1962, p. 44).

[32] Thomas Henry Huxley (1825-1895) was an English biologist. We have been unable to trace the source of the quote that Maslow attributes to him.

[33] "They appear rather . . . before all words." (Watts, 162, pp. 44-45, 47)

[34] Maslow (1954, pp. 181-202).

[35] Abraham Lincoln (1809-1865) was the 16th President of the United States.

[36] Maslow is here likely referring to the Irish poet Thomas Moore (1779-1852) and not the American psychotherapist Thomas Moore (1940-).

[37] On the whole, the Eastern religions are not as severe in their general outlook as many other world religions. For instance, the Taoist and Zen literatures are full of the humor Maslow is talking about. Two relevant books here are: *Chuang Tzu*, a Taoist classic, and *Zen Flesh, Zen Bone*, by Paul Reps (1957)—a collection of delightful Zen stories. A very appropriate symbol of the Zen-Taoist humor is P'u tai (in Chinese) or Hotei (in Japanese), more popularly known as the laughing Buddha in the West. He is humorous, easy-going, and accepting, as a Taoist always is. He is a collector of junk and discarded things which nobody wants, which he keeps in a huge sack slung over his back. [HMC]

[38] François Rabelais (c. 1494-1553) was a French writer, physician and priest. His alleged death-bed utterance was: "I am going to seek a grand perhaps; draw the curtain, the farce is played."

[39] Gertrude Stein (1874-1946) was an American writer.

[40] Alice. B. Toklas (1877-1967) was the life partner of Gertrude Stein.

[41] Watts (1962, p. 56)

[42] "The problem is . . . at level 96." (Watts, 1962, pp. 56-58)

[43] Hermann Hesse (1877-1962) was a German writer. Hesse, H. (1929). *Steppenwolf*. New York, NY: Henry Holt & Company.

[44] Hesse (1943).

[45] Saul Steinberg (1914-1999) was a Romanian-American illustrator whose work was featured prominently in *The New Yorker* magazine, among other places. Several of his illustrations are discussed in class on January 6, 1964.

[46] Charlie Chaplin (1889-1977) was an English actor and filmmaker.

[47] It is not clear to whom the student is referring here. One contemporary with a similar sounding name is Philip Wylie (1902-1971), an American writer, but he was not generally known as a humorist.

[48] Bob Hope (1903-2003) was an American entertainer.

[49] Jack Benny (1894-1974) was an American entertainer.

[50] Maslow is probably referring to Godfrey Cambridge (1933-1976), an American comedian and actor.

[51] Jacques Tati (1907-1982) was a French actor and filmmaker. The film the student is referring to is *Mon Oncle* (Tati, 1958).

[52] Steinberg (1960).

[53] The Steinberg slides were eventually shown in class on January 6, 1964. [HMC]

[54] Maslow is referring to Lecture: October 28, 1963. [HMC]

[55] This refers to an exam question announced two weeks before, which reads, "How could you use all of your experiences gained this semester to bring William James' notion (as expressed in *The Varieties of Religious Experience*) up-to-date? What stands up, enriches it or rejects it?" [HMC]

[56] Aldous Huxley (1894-1963) was an English writer.

[57] The list referred to includes, among other things: Aldous Huxley's *The Doors of Perception* (1954), *Heaven and Hell* (1956), and *The Perennial Philosophy* (1945); William James' *The Varieties of Religious Experience* (1902); and Maslow's *Toward a Psychology of Being* (1962c) and *Religions, Values and Peak-Experiences* (1964). [HMC]

LAB: NOVEMBER 4, 1963

[1] Pagliacci is the name of a clown in the two-act opera *Pagliacci* (1892) by Ruggiero Leoncavallo (1858-1919) [HMC]

[2] Martin (1955).

[3] Victor D'Amico (1904-1987) was an American artist and teacher.

[4] See an article on the subject: Marks (1975).

[5] See Appendix A: Experiential Techniques and Exercises.

[6] Heinz Werner (1890-1964) was a German psychologist.

[7] Werner (1940).

[8] Bernard Kaplan (1925-2008) was an American psychologist.

[9] Werner & Kaplan (1963).

[10] It seems that Maslow must have written the "nonsense words" on the board as illustrations of the concept he is sharing, but they have not been preserved in the transcript. However, in Appendix A, item 21, in this volume he writes about "gestalt exercises in matching nonsense words with nonsense figures. It is very impressive to a class to discover that practically everybody in the class sees a zigzaggy nonsense figure as takete and the curvy figure as lumuma." Because it is reasonable to assume this is what he wrote on the board on this day in class, we have inserted the words and figures here.

[11] Maurice Ravel (1875-1937) was a French composer of the late nineteenth and early twentieth centuries, while Johann Sebastian Bach (1685-1750) was a German composer from the Baroque period. Their styles are markedly different, and Maslow believes that students will be able to identify each composer from the difference in appearance between their musical scores.

[12] Max Wertheimer (1880-1943) was a Czech-born psychologist and one of the founders of gestalt psychology.

[13] Rudolf Arnheim (1904-2007) was a German-born writer and psychologist.

[14] Richard Wagner (1813-1883) was a German composer.

[15] Maslow is perhaps referring to Arnheim's 1954 book entitled *Art and Visual Perception: A Psychology of the Creative Eye.* This same author also wrote *Toward a Psychology of Art: Collected Essays* (1966).

[16] Werner Wolff (1904-1957) was a German-born psychologist. Maslow is likely referring to W. Wolff (1943).

[17] There is a very interesting and fun game that can be played in small groups, utilizing the metaphors and physiognomic perceptions Maslow is speaking of here. One person is chosen as "it" and his/her job is to choose one member of the group as "the subject," the name of whom he/she keeps to only himself/herself. In turn, each member of the group is to ask one question of "it," the object being to guess as soon as possible who "the subject" is. A few sample questions might be:
- if this person were a light bulb, what watt would he be?
- if this person were an animal, what kind would he be?
- if this person where a piece of furniture; a book; a piece of music; a type of vegetable; a building, etc.

This continues until someone feels he has guessed who the subject is. If the guess is incorrect, the game continues. If it is correct, the guesser becomes "it" and he/she chooses a new "subject." [HMC]

[18] A koan is a problem posed by a Zen master to test the student's intuitive understanding of Zen. A correct answer usually requires a specific nonverbal demonstration. Example:
Master: What is the sound of two hands?
Student: (clapping two hands)
Master: What is the sound of the one hand?
Student: (extending one hand forward) [HMC]

[19] Henle (1961).

[20] Mary Henle (1913-2007) was an American psychologist.

NOVEMBER 4, 1963: ARMISTICE DAY

[1] Daniel Boone (1734-1820) was an American explorer.

LECTURE: NOVEMBER 18, 1963

[1] Somerset Maugham (1874-1965) was an English writer.

---

[2] S. I. Hayakawa (1906-1992) was a Canadian-born writer, English professor, and U.S. Senator.

[3] Maslow here refers to a book he and his psychoanalyst friend Harry Rand were planning to write. He refers to it again on January 13, 1964. [HMC]

[4] Ralph Waldo Emerson (1803-1882) and Henry David Thoreau (1817-1862) were both American writers and philosophers as well as friends. Both were known for keeping extensive journals.

[5] Betty Friedan (1921-2006) was an American writer and feminist. Maslow is probably referring in particular to Friedan (1963).

[6] Maslow is here paraphrasing a Bible verse, Mark 4:25.

[7] Louis Terman (1877-1956) was an American psychologist. The research Maslow is referring to here is Terman (1926), Terman and Oden (1947) and Terman and Oden (1959).

[8] Dove (1935).

[9] Maslow is here stating his *belief* that may or may not fully be substantiated by facts. He was "skating on thin ice," as he used to say. [HMC]

[10] Kurt Goldstein (1878-1965) was a German-born neurologist, psychiatrist and psychologist. The work the student is referring to may be Goldstein (1939).

[11] Mathematician Évariste Galois (1811-1832). Note that the student actually says "Gauss" here, but he seems to be confusing Galois and another mathematician, Johann Carl Friedrich Gauss. Gauss (1777-1855) was a contemporary of Galois, but he lived to age 77 whereas Galois died at age 20. Maslow also refers to Gauss moments later; this has also been changed here to refer to Galois.

[12] Samuel Herman Reshevsky (1911-1992) was a Polish-American chess grandmaster.

[13] Pitirim Sorokin (1889-1968) was a Russian-American sociologist. The research Maslow is likely referring to here is Sorokin (1956, pp. 57-62).

[14] E. L. Thorndike (1874-1949) was an American psychologist.

[15] Thorndike (1940).

[16] Frederick A. Woods (1873-1939) was an American biologist.

[17] Although reported in Thorndike (1940), the reader may also refer to Woods (1906, 1913).

[18] Francis Galton (1822-1911) was an English anthropologist and polymath also known for his research in the field of eugenics. See, for example, Galton (1869).

[19] Lawrence LeShan (1920-) is an American psychologist.

[20] In 1963 LeShan had not yet extensively published in this area, but one early paper was Leshan & Reznikoff (1960). In his original note, HMC references LeShan & Greenawalt (1966).

[21] Wilhelm Reich (1897-1957) was an Austrian physician and psychiatrist.

[22] Maslow (1964).

[23] Maslow (1962c).

[24] This was later published as *Eupsychian management; a journal* (Maslow, 1965).

[25] Erich Fromm (1900-1980) was a German-born psychologist and philosopher.

[26] Karen Horney (1885-1952) was a German psychiatrist.

[27] Horney (1942).

[28] Kurt Wolff (1912-2003) was a German-born sociologist and a colleague of Maslow's at Brandeis.

[29] K. Wolff (1962).

[30] The Esalen Institute [HMC]. This is a retreat center in Big Sur, California. [CN]

LAB: NOVEMBER 18, 1963

[1] Aldous Huxley never made the trip as he died just a few days later, on November 22, 1963, in California. [HMC]

[2] "Dystopia" refers to negative utopia or inverted utopia. See, for example, Walsh (1962). [HMC]

[3] Huxley (1962b).

[4] Maslow wrote a five-page memo on *Island* on March 30, 1967. See Appendix B: Notes and Questions for Psychology 150b (Utopian Social Psychology). [HMC]

[5] Robert E. L. Masters (1927-2008) was an American writer.

[6] M. Laski also used the term "desolation experience" in her book *Ecstasy* (1961). [HMC]

[7] Maslow occasionally uses the term "foothill experience" to describe a minor and less intense peak-experience. But the experience of rejection this student is reporting here should really be called a desolation experience rather than a low-peak experience. [HMC]

[8] Some books on the importance of openness and authenticity: Jourard (1964), and Derlega and Chaikin (1975). [HMC]

LECTURE: DECEMBER 2, 1963

[1] Upton Sinclair (1878-1968) was an American writer.

[2] Nevitt Sanford (1909-1996) was an American psychologist. The book Maslow refers to is Sanford (1962).

[3] Walter Toman (1920-2003) was an Austrian psychologist and one of Maslow's colleagues at Brandeis.

[4] Maslow has not handled the question of grades as skillfully as he could have. But his intention is clear: he uses the question as a pointer for many other important issues which he is passionately concerned with. This point will become clear as the discussion continues. [HMC]

[5] Lester Kirkendall (1903-1991) was an American sociologist.

[6] Kirkendall (1961).

[7] Edward G. Robinson (1893-1973) was an American actor.

[8] Maslow expresses a view here that may seem odd to twenty-first century eyes and ears accustomed to celebrity endorsements, but at the time his view was common enough: prestigious actors did not do commercials. Hints of the changing opinions towards this view are visible in some of the students' reactions.

[9] What Maslow said about women here might have been true in the past, but is no longer. [HMC]

[10] At the time (1963), both Sarah Lawrence College and Bennington College were women's colleges.

[11] Note: Maslow is apparently in hot water here because of his earlier reference to Robinson. Some students disagree with Maslow and keep going back to the same issue. [HMC]

[12] Maslow differentiated between B- (being) and D- (deficiency) aspects of human nature and cognition. In general, the concept of deficiency relates to the physiological needs for things like food or sex, whereas the concept of being is more connected to the desire for self-actualization.

[13] Maslow was a firm believer in the feasibility of developing a value system based on scientific knowledge rather than dogma. He believed that psychoanalysis and related studies have provided a wealth of psychological data upon which a sound value theory could be constructed. See Maslow (1962c, "Values"). [HMC]

[14] Walter Winchell (1897–1972) was an American journalist and broadcaster known for both news and gossip commentary.

[15] The John Birch Society is an advocacy group formed in 1958.

[16] Maslow's statement here has not done full justice to his own position on the issue of sex stereotyping. He is, in fact, very much opposed to the male-female dichotomy: "The man who thinks you can be either a man, all man, or a woman, and nothing but a woman, is doomed to struggle with himself, and to eternal estrangement from women." (Maslow, 1971, p. 161). He was also one of the first psychologists to question the traditional concept of femininity. See, for instance, two of Maslow's earlier papers: Maslow (1939) and Maslow (1942). [HMC]

[17] Victor Frankl (1905-1997) was an Austrian psychiatrist, neurologist and founder of logotherapy. Maslow here refers to the book Frankl (1959). It is now frequently known by its newer title *Man's Search for Meaning*.

[18] A little book by Erich Fromm could also serve as a useful introduction to the subject of love: *The Art of Loving* (1956). [HMC]

[19] This was included with minor revisions as an appendix in Maslow (1964). [HMC] Maslow reads extracts from this paper throughout this lecture. [CN]

[20] Maslow (1964, p. 103).

[21] Mircea Eliade (1907-1986) was a Romanian writer, philosopher, and religious historian.

[22] Eliade (1961).

[23] "This can also be seen . . . particular symbol." (Maslow, 1964, p. 103)

[24] Herman Witkin (1916-1979) was an American psychologist.

[25] Witkin showed his subjects films and asked them to keep on talking as they were falling asleep. The taped dreams were from a hypnagogic reverie state. See Witkin and Lewis (1965) and Witkin and Lewis (1967). [HMC]

[26] Maslow (1964, p. 103).

[27] Rubin (1961).

[28] Theodore Isaac Rubin (1923-2019) was an American psychiatrist and writer.

[29] Melanie Klein (1882-1960) was an English psychoanalyst.

[30] David Rapaport (1911-1960) was a Hungarian psychoanalyst.

[31] Rapaport (1951).

[32] Otto Pötzl (1877–1962) was an Austrian neurologist.

[33] Herbart Silberer (1882-1923) was an Austrian psychoanalyst. Maslow may be referring to representative works like Silberer (1909).

[34] Medard Boss (1903-1990) was a Swiss psychiatrist and developer of an existential approach to psychoanalysis known as Daseinanalysis. See Boss (1958) and Binswanger and Boss (1973).

[35] Similar findings were reported by Maslow (1942).

[36] Boss (1949).

[37] George S. Klein (1917-1971) was an American psychologist.

[38] Although not explicitly stated, Maslow is likely referring to Klein, Spence, Holt, and Gourevitch (1958).

[39] This individual could not be identified.

[40] "It is possible . . . or fleshy enough." (Maslow, 1964, p. 104)

[41] "In the critical situations . . . the D-woman—" (Maslow, 1964, p. 105)

[42] John F. Kennedy (1917-1963) was the 35th President of the United States and was assassinated on November 22, 1963.

---

[43] There is a moving account of Aldous Huxley on his deathbed by his wife which seems to support Maslow's statement. See L. A. Huxley (1968). [HMC]

[44] "Somehow it is necessary . . . of the major sex pleasures." (Maslow, 1964, p. 105)

LAB: DECEMBER 2, 1963

[1] The goal set by Maslow and the desires of some students are apparently at odds with each other at this point. "Group spontaneity" is also interpreted differently by both. [HMC]

[2] At this point Maslow has decided to play a passive role and turns the class over to the students themselves. [HMC]

[3] President John F. Kennedy was assassinated 10 days earlier on Friday, November 22. [HMC]

[4] As indicated, each statement by students has been followed by a silence in the class, indicating that other participants do not know how to respond. Some are very critical of the whole attempt, as the following shows. [HMC]

[5] He knows, in his head at least, the distinction between intellectual knowing and experiential knowing. He does not seem to have a feel for the latter. [HMC]

[6] A question of what is therapy, what is education and how to tell one from the other, has surfaced here again. [HMC]

[7] A discussion such as this often brings forth two sharply contrasting views on the value of experiential learning. The exchange that is taking place in this particular session is very typical in this respect. [HMC]

[8] Maslow, who has remained mostly silent since the start of this non-structured session, finally decides to step in at this point. [HMC]

[9] Bertrand Russell (1872-1970) was an English mathematician and philosopher.

[10] Issue: How is this form of expression and verbalization different from labelling and rubricizing? [HMC]

[11] In the last portion of this section some of the students seem to be having difficulty getting a good grasp of the topic at hand. The conversation does not seem to be moving clearly in any one direction. [HMC]

[12] For example, Maslow (1954).

[13] Calvin S. Hall, Jr. (1909-1985), was an American psychologist. It is possible that Maslow is mis-speaking here, because the most well-known book called *An Outline of Psychoanalysis* is by Sigmund Freud (1949). Calvin S. Hall did write *A Primer of Freudian Psychology*, which was first published in 1954, and perhaps Maslow is referring to this book here.

LECTURE: DECEMBER 9, 1963

[1] James Bugental (1915-2008) was an American psychologist.

[2] Robert Tannenbaum (1915-2003) was an American psychologist.

[3] Bugental and Tannenbaum (1963).

[4] See the Introduction for more about Maslow's thoughts on T-groups.

[5] K. Wolff (1962).

[6] Walter A. Weisskopf (1904-1991) was an Austrian-born economist, a Professor at Roosevelt University in Chicago.

[7] Weisskopf (1963).

[8] Paul Tillich (1886-1965) was a German-born philosopher and theologian.

[9] Max Weber (1864-1920) was a German sociologist.

[10] Karl Marx (1818-1883) was a German political theorist, philosopher and sociologist.

[11] Richard G. Abell (1904-1998) was an American psychiatrist who was also a guest speaker in Maslow's class on December 16, 1963.

[12] Cornelius Beukenkamp, Jr. (1918-1999) was an American psychiatrist. The birth/death dates given here are uncertain, but likely correct

[13] Beukenkamp (1958).

[14] See Lecture and Lab for November 4, 1963 in this book.

[15] Arthur J. Deikman (1929-2013) was a psychiatrist known in part for his study of mystical experiences.

[16] Deikman (1963). (Maslow is incorrect about the exact title of the article.)

[17] A few years later Maslow would report his personal experience of what it feels like to be really alive following his first heart attack. See Maslow (1970a, August). [HMC]

[18] Paul Bergman was a researcher at the National Institute of Mental Health at the time he published the paper to which Maslow refers (Bergman, 1963). Additional information about him was unavailable.

[19] Bergman (1963).

[20] Maslow has written about this in a very revealing article published in *The Journal of Transpersonal Psychology* (Krippner, 1972). [HMC]

[21] Ricardo B. Morant (1926-) is an American psychologist and was a colleague of Maslow's at Brandeis University.

[22] Harry Rand was an American psychoanalyst and a colleague of Maslow's at Brandeis University. Additional information was not found.

[23] Maslow's views on homosexuality will seem remarkably insensitive and ill-conceived to modern readers. To put his comments in context, in 1960s America most states still had anti-sodomy laws and homosexuality was often considered a disorder and a danger to society. That said, it would be difficult to underestimate the challenges faced by gay men and women because of the prevalence of these views.

[24] Harold Abramson (1899-1980) was an American physician.

[25] Abramsom (1960).

[26] Steinberg (1960).

[27] D. T. Suzuki (1870-1966) was a Japanese writer.

[28] Baruch Spinoza (1632-1677) was a Dutch philosopher known, among other things, for his nuanced ideas about God.

[29] Satori is a Zen term for enlightenment or awakening. [HMC]

[30] The original Zen version reads: "In carrying water and chopping firewood: therein like the wonderful Tao." *Ch'uan-teng Lu* (Record of the Transmission of the Lamp, chapter 8). Compiled by Tao-yuan in 1004 A.D.—an important source on Zen. [HMC]

[31] Maslow may be referring to Robert Latou Dickinson (1861-1950), an American physician.

[32] Maslow is here trying to make a distinction between *dichotomy* and *polarity*. In dichotomous thinking, two things are pitted against each other and made mutually exclusive. According to the polarity kind of thinking, the two are recognized and accepted—including some inevitable tension between the two elements. A good example of the latter way of thinking can be found in the yin yang symbolism of Taoism. [HMC]

[33] Maslow is probably referring to a show by György Kepes (1906-2001), a Hungarian-born artist, at the Swetzoff Gallery: November 26 - December 31, 1963.

[34] Note: Is an altered-state of consciousness possible for an entire population? Are there any drawbacks or dangers if the whole culture enters that state (as in Tibet)? [HMC]

[35] Another incisive statement on the same subject can be found in the preface to the 1970 edition of Maslow (1964). [HMC]

[36] Maslow, Rand and Newman (1960).

[37] Maslow appends the following: "If you want to look that up, that's in *The Journal of Nervous and Mental Disease* from a couple of years ago." Maslow, Rand and Newman (1960). Reprinted in DeMartino (1963).

[38] Marion Milner (1900-1998) was an English writer and psychoanalyst.

[39] The two books by Milner are: Milner (1936) and Milner (1950) [HMC]

[40] What would a feminist have to say on this? And who is right? [HMC, writing in the mid-1970s]

[41] John Rosen (1902-1993) was an American psychiatrist known for his approach of "direct analysis" and whose later career was marked by controversy.

[42] The emphasis here is on the *transcending* of dichotomy and of, in this particular case, the B- and D-realm. One can carry the analysis further and apply the idea of transcendence to sex stereotyping as well. If the discussion in this section appears to have accentuated sex roles, it certainly was not the intention of Maslow, who often rejected conventional sex stereotyping as

psychologically unsound. He believed that the individual should accept the fact of psychological bisexuality, and even enjoy the feminine within himself, or the masculine within herself. Self-actualizing people have been found to be both masculine and feminine at the same time. See September 30 lecture. Also, Maslow (1971, pp. 160-163.) [HMC]

[43] Therese Benedek (1892-1977) was a Hungarian-born psychoanalyst. Maslow is probably here referring to Benedek (1952).

[44] Helene Deutsch (1884-1982) was a Polish-born psychoanalyst.

[45] Albert Schweitzer (1875-1965) was an Alsatian physician known for his humanitarian work.

[46] A novel by D. H. Lawrence, *Sons and Lovers* (1913), is a good illustration of what Maslow is speaking of here. [HMC]

[47] *Who's Afraid of Virginia Woolf?* is a play written by Edward Albee. See Albee (1962) and Schneider (1962).

[48] Edward Albee (1928-2016) was an American playwright.

[49] See Watts (1977).

[50] It is impossible to know whether Maslow had any particular studies in mind when making this comment, but his expression of this idea will no doubt strike modern readers as insensitive an unscientific.

LAB: DECEMBER 9, 1963

[1] Several people did not stay for the optional third hour of the class, at least on this day.

[2] *Issue*: Is this sex-stereotyping or not? [HMC]

[3] *Issue*: Is this an exercise in fantasy? What is the difference, if any, between fantasizing, imagining and seeing potentials? [HMC] The students speaking do not seem to understand Maslow's goals with this exercise, which seems to be an act of imagination to make them aware of the potential within others, and therefore by implication themselves. [CN]

[4] Maslow (1948). Also Goldstein (1940).

[5] Charles Dickens (1812-1870) was an English writer and author of well-known works like *A Tale of Two Cities* and *A Christmas Carol*.

[6] The Greeks actually used four words for love, offered here with generally accepted basic translations: *eros* ("desire"), *philia* ("brotherly") *agape* ("higher love") and *storge* ("familial").

[7] Could it be that the hysterical reaction itself was culturally determined also? [HMC]

[8] This statement by Maslow is not clear. It seems he has misunderstood what the student has just said. [HMC]

[9] Maslow is here referring to adherents to the ideas of Carl Rogers (1902-1987), an American psychologist.

[10] Maslow believed that good psychotherapy uncovers the intrinsic needs of the person in a Taoistic fashion. [HMC]

[11] Maslow is referring to Maslow (1942). [HMC]

[12] Maslow's simple, affirmative answer of "yes" to the question is somewhat unexpected. [HMC]

[13] She actually says "a man looking at a man," though it seems in context that "woman" is what she means.

DECEMBER 16, 1963: GUEST SPEAKER: RICHARD G. ABELL, M.D.

[1] *Road to Reality* was an American daytime television show featuring dramatized group therapy sessions based on sessions conducted by Dr. Richard Abell. It premiered on the American Broadcasting Corporation (ABC) on October 10, 1960 (note that the IMDB date of October 17, 1960 conflicts with other sources). It was shown five days a week at 2:30 p.m. Eastern Standard Time, a slot it shared with soap operas. It was cancelled March 31, 1961. See also Mulcahy & Genovese (2015), Crosby (1960) and Road to Reality (1960).

[2] Note that Barnard College is an all-women's institution.

[3] *Breaking Point* (aired September 16, 1963 to April 27, 1964) was an American fictional television series aired by the American Broadcasting Corporation (ABC), and which focused on a psychiatrist and his patients. See also Breaking Point (1963).

[4] *The Eleventh Hour* (aired October 3, 1962 to April 22, 1964) was an American fictional television series aired by the National Broadcasting corporation (NBC) and featuring stories about a practicing psychologist, psychiatrist and their patients. See also The Eleventh Hour (1962).

[5] Loretta Young (1913-2000) was an American actress whose popular *The Loretta Young Show* apparently ran alongside *Road to Reality* while the latter show was on the air.

[6] Harry Stack Sullivan (1892-1949) was an American psychiatrist.

[7] These summaries were written by HMC for the original transcription and have here been lightly edited by CN.

[8] Beukenkamp (1958).

[9] Alexander Wolf (?-1997) was an American psychologist and psychoanalyst and a pioneer in group therapy.

[10] Emanuel K. Schwartz (~1912-1973) was an American psychologist and psychoanalyst and a pioneer in group therapy.

[11] Wolf and Schwartz (1962).

[12] Werner Wolff conducted experiments in which subjects were filmed or otherwise recorded engaged in specific actions. They then "confronted" the

resulting images of themselves as played back to them, and therapy was developed based on their reactions. See W. Wolff (1943).

[13] Maslow is probably referring to Henry Murray (1893-1988), an American psychologist who conducted controversial experiments at Harvard in the late 1950s and early 1960s. If these are indeed the experiments to which Maslow is referring, his comment that "There were no huge consequences. There were no obvious consequences . . ." is certainly debatable in light of events that occurred subsequent to Maslow's death. See also Murray (1963) and Chase (2003).

LECTURE: JANUARY 6, 1964

[1] The final examination was scheduled for January 22, 1964. [HMC]

[2] Huxley, A. (1962a).

[3] Frank E. Manuel (1910-2003) was an American historian who was teaching at Brandeis when Maslow mentions him here. It is possible (based on the content of his subsequent comments) that the paper Maslow is referring to is Manuel (1960).

[4] Franklin L. Baumer (1913-1990) was an American historian.

[5] Baumer (1960).

[6] James Klee (1916-1996) was a psychologist and a colleague of Maslow's at Brandeis University. It is not clear where the quotation Maslow uses comes from, but a relevant paper is Klee (1977).

[7] This joint seminar, given at Brandeis in the spring of 1965, was called *The Psychology of Religious Experience*. It also dealt with the psychological significance of utopian thought. Both men *did* indeed have a very different approach to the issue, and a different teaching style as well. [HMC]

[8] Georg Wilhelm Friedrich Hegel (1770-1831) was a German philosopher.

[9] Lewis Mumford (1895-1990) was an American historian.

[10] Stuart Chase (1888-1985) was an American economist .

[11] Martin Buber (1878-1965) was an Austrian philosopher.

[12] Buber (1937).

[13] Its newer title may be more familiar to modern readers: *Man's Search for Meaning.* See Frankl (1959).

[14] Claire Myers Owens (1896-1983) was an American writer.

[15] Owens (1958).

[16] Owens (1963).

[17] These experiential exercises have been mentioned throughout the course. For another list prepared by Maslow, see Appendix A: Experiential Techniques and Experiments. [HMC]

[18] Laura Huxley (1911-2007) was an Italian-born writer, filmmaker, musician and counselor. She was also the wife of Aldous Huxley.

[19] Huxley, L. (1963).

[20] Peter De Vries (1910-1993) was an American writer and editor. Based on the context of the discussion, this book is probably *The Blood of the Lamb* (De Vries, 1961).

[21] A follow-up study is being planned to find out from the participants the effects of the course after all these years. [HMC] It seems that nothing ever came of this plan. [CN]

[22] In Greek mythology, Prometheus stole fire from the gods to give to man; as punishment, Zeus chained Prometheus to a rock, then sent an eagle to eat Prometheus' liver. Each day the liver grew anew and the cycle repeated itself.

[23] Adam, of the Bible's Adam and Eve story in "Genesis," was banished along with Eve for eating from the forbidden Tree of Knowledge.

[24] A similar custom is practiced by the Blood Indians of Alberta, Canada, during their Sun Dance ceremony. There is a scene in the documentary film *Circle of the Sun* (Low, 1961) where a man is seen telling a tall story in good humor, sending a group of women into a laughing fit. [HMC]

[25] Richard (Dick) M. Jones (1925-1994) was an American psychoanalyst and author.

[26] C. S. Lewis (1898-1963) was an English writer and Christian apologist.

[27] Lewis (1955)

[28] Colin Wilson (1931-2013) was an English writer and philosopher.

[29] Wilson (1963).

[30] Maslow (1973).

[31] Fromm (1955). "Rational authority" and "irrational authority" are the terms used by Fromm. [HMC]

[32] David Riesman (1909-2002) was an American sociologist

[33] As noted earlier, Bennington and Sarah Lawrence were all-women's colleges at the time Maslow was discussing them. Both were founded as liberal arts colleges, and Bennington in particular utilized what at the time were innovative approaches to higher learning.

[34] Note: The question of confidentiality was discussed when a tape recorder was first brought in (October 28). Although no definitive statement on the issue was made, there was a tacit agreement that the real identity of the speakers would not be disclosed. There was also an understanding that the attendance in the Lab was optional and had no bearing on the grades. [HMC]

[35] Maslow is referring to his mimeographed book, *Summer Notes on Social Psychology of Industry and Management at Non-Linear Systems, Inc.*

(1962b). It was published in 1965 with a new title, *Eupsychian Management*. The section of the book mentioned is called "The attitude of self-actualizing people to duty, work, mission, etc." [HMC]

LAB: JANUARY 6, 1964

[1] "Draw the smell of an onion" is an exercise on physiognomic perception mentioned in an earlier class. [HMC]

[2] Don Quixote is the titular character of the Miguel de Cervantes (~1547-1616) novel *The Ingenious Gentleman Sir Quixote of La Mancha* (or *Don Quixote*). The idiomatic phrase "tilting at windmills" is a reference to fighting imaginary enemies which is drawn from the novel as it reflects Don Quixote's tendency to joust with windmills which he sees as giants.

[3] It is somewhat ironic that he was elected president of the American Psychological Association only a few years later. (1967-68). [HMC]

[4] Freud (1919).

[5] Pictures 2-7 are all slides projected onto the screen at one end of the room. [HMC]

[6] There is no signature in the original illustration from Steinberg's *The Labyrinth*, so it is not clear why there is one on Maslow's slide.

[7] Fifty minutes have passed since the session began. At this point Maslow is under time pressure. [HMC]

LECTURE: JANUARY 13, 1964

[1] Walter Bonime (1904-2001) was an American psychologist.

[2] Bonime (1962).

[3] Maslow references Jones (1962) and HMC adds the additional reference of Jones (1970).

[4] Harry Rand and Richard Jones were colleagues of Maslow at Brandeis. Rand was also a practicing psychoanalyst. [HMC] It does not seem that this book was ever completed. [CN]

[5] The National Training Laboratories Institute for Applied Behavioral Science (NTL Institute) was founded by German psychologist Kurt Lewin (1890-1947) in Bethel, Maine.

[6] Richard Alpert (1931-) is an American psychologist and spiritual teacher now better known by his adopted name of Ram Dass.

[7] Dr. Haridas Chaudhuri (1913-1975) was a Bengali philosopher and founder of the California Institute of Integral Studies in San Francisco.

[8] This individual could not be identified, and because the present book is transcribed from audio, even the correct spelling of the surname is uncertain.

[9] William Schutz (1925-2002) was an American psychologist.

[10] Jessica Mitford (1917-1996) was an English writer.
[11] Martin Heidegger (1889-1976) was a German philosopher.
[12] This book project was never carried through. [HMC]
[13] Meaning "the good life," as popularized by Federico Fellini's 1960 film on modern Roman high society, *La Dolce Vita*. [HMC]
[14] As discussed in the class on December 2, 1963.
[15] Maslow has elaborated on this idea in Appendix H of his book, Maslow (1964). [HMC].
[16] The following book contains many useful suggestions on conscious control of dreams: Garfield (1974). See also Stewart (1977). [HMC]

APPENDIX A: EXPERIENTIAL TECHNIQUES AND EXPERIMENTS

[1] Deikman (1963).
[2] Presumably Louis Agassiz (1807-1873), a Swiss biologist and geologist.
[3] Laski (1961).
[4] Huxley, A. (1962b).
[5] Maslow (1954).
[6] Hayakawa (1949).
[7] Wolff (1943).
[8] Ronald E. Shor (1930-1982) was an American psychologist known in particular for his work on hypnosis.
[9] Eleanor Roosevelt (1884-1962) was an American diplomat and activist and the wife of Franklin D. Roosevelt (the 32nd President of the United States).
[10] Harry S. Truman (1884-1972) was the 33rd President of the United States.
[11] Dwight D. Eisenhower (1890-1969) was the 34th President of the United States.
[12] Auguste Renoir (1841-1919) was a French painter.
[13] Pablo Picasso (1881-1973) was a Spanish artist known in particular for his painting, but who worked in a number of other mediums as well.
[14] Werner (1940).
[15] Maslow (1964).
[16] Wheelis (1966).

APPENDIX B: NOTES AND QUESTIONS FOR PSYCHOLOGY 150b

[1] Huxley, A. (1962b).
[2] Watts, A. (1958).
[3] Ritter and Ritter (1959).

BIBLIOGRAPHY

Note: For a comprehensive, contemporary bibliography of the works of Abraham H. Maslow and related publications, see:

www.positivedisintegration.com/maslow.htm

Abramson, H. A. (1960). *The use of LSD in psychotherapy: Transactions of a conference on d-lysergic acid diethylamide (LSD-25)*. New York, NY: Josiah Macy Jr. Foundation.

Albee, E. (1962). Who's afraid of Virginia Woolf? New York, NY: Atheneum Books.

Arnheim, R. (1954). *Art and visual perception: a psychology of the creative eye.* Berkeley, CA: University of California Press.

Arnheim, R. (1966). *Toward a psychology of art: Collected essays.* Berkeley & Los Angeles, CA: University of California Press.

Asch, S. E. (1952). *Social psychology.* Oxford: Prentice-Hall.

Asch, S. E. (1955, November). Opinions and social pressure. *Scientific American*, November 1955. *193*(5), 31-35.

Baumer, F. L. (1960). *Religion and the rise of skepticism.* New York, NY: Harcourt, Brace & Co.

Benedek, T. (1952). *Psychosexual functions in women.* New York, NY: The Ronald Press.

Bergman, (1963). A drug-induced ecstatic experience. *Psychotherapy Theory, Research & Practice, 1*(1), 44-48 doi: 10.1037/h0088569.

Beukenkamp, C. (1958). *Fortunate strangers.* New York, NY: Rinehart & Company.

Binswanger, L., & Boss, M. (1973). Existential analysis or Daseinanalysis: Binswanger and Boss. In: J. F. Rychlak, (Ed.), *Introduction to personality & psychotherapy* (pp. 443-470). Boston, MA: Houghton Mifflin Company.

Bodkin, M. (1934). *Archetypal patterns in poetry: Psychological studies of imagination*. London, England: Oxford University Press.

Bonime, W. (1962). *The clinical use of dreams.* New York, NY: Basic Books.

Boss, M. (1949). *Meaning and content of sexual perversions: A daseinsanalytic approach to the psychopathology of the phenomenon of love*. New York, NY: Grune & Stratton.

Boss, M. (1958). *The analysis of dreams.* New York, NY: Philosophical Library.

Breaking Point [Television show]. (1963, September 16). Retrieved from https://www.imdb.com/title/tt0056743/?ref_=fn_tt_tt_7

Buber, M. (1937). *I and Thou.* New York, NY: Charles Scibner's Sons.

Bucke, R. M. (1901). *Cosmic consciousness.* New York, NY: E.P. Dutton and Co. Inc.

Bugental, J. F. T., & Tannenbaum, R. (1963). Sensitivity training and being motivation. *Journal of Humanistic Psychology, 3*(1), 76–85. doi:10.1177/002216786300300107

Carson, R. (1965). *The sense of wonder.* New York, NY: Harper & Row.

Chase, A. (2003). Harvard and the unabomber: The education of an American terrorist. New York, NY: W.W. Norton and Co., 2003

Chiang, H. (1968). Experiment in experiential approaches to personality. *Psychologia, 11*(1-2), 33-39.

Chiang, H., & Maslow, A. H. (Eds.). (1969). *The healthy personality: Readings.* New York, NY: Van Nostrand Reinhold.

Chiang, H., & Maslow, A. H. (Eds.). (1977). *The healthy personality: Readings* (2nd ed.). New York, NY: Van Nostrand Reinhold.

Crosby, J. (1960, October 1). TV-Radio Today: New Program for Housewives. *Steubenville Herald Star*, p. 4.

De Vries, P. (1961). *The blood of the lamb.* Boston, MA: Little, Brown & Co.

Deikman, A. J. (1963). Experimental meditation. *The Journal of Nervous and Mental Disease, 136*(4): 329-343.

DeMartino, M. F. (Ed.). (1963). *Sexual behavior and personality characteristics.* New York, NY: The Citadel Press.

Derlega, V. J., & Chaikin, A. L. (1975). *Sharing intimacy: What we reveal to others and why.* Englewood Cliffs, NJ: Prentice-Hall.

Deutsch, H. (1944). *The psychology of women: A psychoanalytic interpretation. Volume 1: Girlhood.* New York, NY: Grune & Stratton.

Deutsch, H. (1945). *The psychology of women: A psychoanalytic interpretation. Volume.2: Motherhood*. New York, NY: Grune & Stratton.

Dove, W. F. (1935). A study of individuality in the nutritive instincts and of the causes and effects of variations in the selection of food. *The American Naturalist, 69*(S724), 469-544. doi:10.1086/280623

Dunlap, J. (1961). *Exploring inner space*. New York, NY: Harcourt, Brace & World.

Dye, K., Mills, A. J., & Weatherbee, T. (2005). Maslow: Man interrupted: Reading management theory in context. *Management Decision, 43*(10), 1375-1395. doi:10.1108/00251740510634921

Eliade, M. (1961). *The sacred and the profane: The nature of religion* (W. R. Trask, Trans.). New York, NY: Harper & Brothers.

Farrow, E. P. (1948). *Psychoanalyse yourself: A practical method of self-analysis ; Enabling a person to remove unreasoning fears and depression from his mind*. New York, NY: International Universities Press.

Fellini, F. (Director). (1960). *La Dolce Vita* [Motion picture]. Italy: Cineriz.

Frankl, V. E. (1959). *From death camp to existentialism*. Boston, MA: The Beacon Press. [Now better known by its newer title: Frankl, V. E. (2006). *Man's search for meaning: An introduction to logotherapy*. Boston, MA: Beacon Press.]

Freeman, L. (1951). *Fight against fears*. New York, NY: Crown Publishing.

Freud, S. (1919). *Totem and taboo: some points of agreement between the mental lives of savages and neurotics*. London, England: George Routledge & Sons.

Freud, S. (1949). *Outline of psychoanalysis*. New York, NY: W.W. Norton & Company.

Freud, S. (1953). *The interpretation of dreams (second part) and on dreams*. London: The Hogarth Press.

Friedan, B. (1963). *The feminine mystique*. New York, NY: W.W. Norton & Company.

Fromm, E. (1951). *The forgotten language: An introduction to the understanding of dreams, fairy tales and myths*. Oxford, England: Rinehart.

Fromm, E. (1955). *The sane society*. New York, NY: Rinehart & Company.

Fromm, E. (1956). *The art of loving*. New York, NY: Harper and Row.

Gallwey, W. T. (1974). *The inner game of tennis*. New York, NY: Random House.

Galton, F. (1869). *Hereditary genius*. London: Macmillan & Company.

Garfield, P. (1974). *Creative dreaming*. New York, NY: Ballantine.

Goldstein, K. (1939). *The organism: A holistic approach to biology derived from pathological data in man*. New York, NY: American Book Company.

Goldstein, K. (1940). *Human nature in the light of psychopathology*. Oxford, England: Harvard University. Press. doi: 10.4159/harvard.9780674492103

Hall, C. S. (1954). *A primer of Freudian psychology*. New York, NY: New American Library.

Hayakawa, S. I. (1949). *Language in thought and action*. New York, NY: Harcourt, Brace.

Henle, M. (Ed.). (1961). *Documents of gestalt psychology*. Berkeley, CA: University of California Press.

Hesse, H. (1929). *Steppenwolf*. New York, NY: Henry Holt & Company.

Hesse, H. (1943). *Magister Ludi* [The glass bead game]. New York, NY: Henry Holt & Company.

Horney, K. (1942). *Self-analysis*. New York, NY: W.W. Norton & Company.

Huxley, A. (1932). *Brave new world*. London, England: Chatto & Windus.

Huxley, A. (1945). *The perennial philosophy*. New York, NY: Harper & Brothers.

Huxley, A. (1954). *The doors of perception*. London, England: Chatto & Windus.

Huxley, A. (1956). *Heaven and Hell*. New York, NY: Harper & Brothers.

Huxley, A. (1962a). Education on the nonverbal level. *Daedalus,91*(2), science and technology in contemporary society, 279-293. This paper also appears in Chiang and Maslow (1977).

Huxley, A. (1962b). *Island*. London, England: Chatto & Windus.

Huxley, L. A. (1963). *You are not the target*. New York, NY: Farrar, Straus & Company.

Huxley, L. A. (1968). *This timeless moment: a personal view of Aldous Huxley*. New York, NY: Farrar, Straus & Giroux.

James, W. (1902). *The varieties of religious experience: A study in human nature. Being the Gifford Lectures on Natural Religion delivered at Edinburgh in 1901–1902*. New York, NY: Longmans, Green & Co.

James, W. (1920). *The letters of William James* (Vol. 2) (H. James, Ed.). Boston, MA: Atlantic Monthly Press.

Jones, R. M. (1962). *Ego synthesis in dreams*. Cambridge, MA: Schenkman Publishing Company.

Jones, R. M. (1970). *The new psychology of dreaming*. New York, NY: Grune & Stratton.

Jourard, S. M. (1964). *The transparent self*. New York, NY: D. Van Nostrand.

Kelland, M. (2017, July 07). *Personality Theory*. OER Commons. Retrieved June 03, 2019, from https://www.oercommons.org/authoring/22859-personality-theory.

Kirkendall, L. A. (1961). *Premarital intercourse and interpersonal relationships*. New York, NY: Julian Press.

Klee, J. (1977). The absolute and the relative: Two aspects of dynamic experience. In Chiang, H., & Maslow, A. H. (Eds.), *The healthy personality: Readings* (2nd ed., pp. 79-88). New York, NY: Van Nostrand Reinhold.

Klein, G. S., Spence, D. P., Holt, R. R., & Gourevitch, S. (1958). Cognition without awareness: Subliminal influences upon conscious thought. *The Journal of Abnormal and Social Psychology, 57*(3), 255-266. doi:10.1037/h0042824

Knight, J. (1953). *The story of my psychoanalysis*. New York, NY: Pocket Books.

Koestler, A. (1954). *The invisible writing: The second volume of an autobiography, 1932-40* (pp. 350-352). London: Collins.

Koestler, A. (1960). *The lotus and the robot*. London: Hutchinson.

Krippner, S. (Ed.). (1972). The plateau experience: A. H. Maslow and others. *Journal of Transpersonal Psychology, 4*(2), 107-120.

Kubie, L. (1977). The forgotten man of education. In H. Chiang & A. H. Maslow (Eds.), *The healthy personality: Readings* (2nd ed., pp. 164-173). New York, NY: Van Nostrand Reinhold.

Laski, M. (1961). *Ecstasy: A study of some secular and religious experiences*. London: Cresset Press.

Lawrence, D. H. (1913). *Sons and lovers*. London, England: Duckworth & Co.

Leshan, L. L., & Greenawalt, J. C. (1966). Mobilizing the life force: An approach to the problem of arousing the sick patient's will to live. *Pastoral Psychology, 17*(7), 19-30. doi:10.1007/bf01845888 [Note: the original transcript references: LeShan, L. L. (1966). Mobilizing the life force: An approach to the problem of arousing the sick patient's will to live. *The Ethical Form,* (3), 1-11.

LeShan, L., & Reznikoff, M. (1960). A psychological factor apparently associated with neoplastic disease. *The Journal of Abnormal and Social Psychology, 60*(3), 439-440.

Levy, D. M. (1943). *Maternal overprotection*. New York, NY: Columbia University Press.

Lewis, C. S. (1955). *Surprised by joy*. London, England: Geoffrey Bles Ltd.

Lorge, I. & Curtiss, C. (1936) Prestige, suggestion, and attitudes. *The Journal of Social Psychology*, 7(4), 386-402.

Low, C. (Director). (1961). *Circle of the sun* [Motion picture]. Canada: National Film Board of Canada.

MANAS. (n.d.). Retrieved from http://www.manasjournal.org/

Manuel, F. (1960). In defense of philosophical history. *The Antioch Review, 20*(3), 331-343. doi:10.2307/4610269

Marks, L. E. (1975, June). Synesthesia: The lucky people with mixed-up senses. *Psychology Today*, 48-52.

Martin, P. W. (1955). *Experiment in depth: a study of the work of Jung, Eliot and Toynbee*. Oxford, England: Pantheon.

Maslow, A. H. (1939). Dominance, personality, and social behavior in women. *The Journal of Social Psychology*, 10(1), 3-39. doi:10.1080/00224545.1939.9713343. Reprinted in Maslow (1973).

Maslow, A. H. (1942). Self-esteem (dominance feeling) and sexuality in women. *The Journal of Social Psychology*. 16. 259-294. 10.1080/00224545.1942.9714120. Reprinted in Maslow (1973).

Maslow, A. H. (1948). Cognition of the individual and of the generic. *Psychological Review*, 55(1), 22-40. Reprinted in Maslow (1954).

Maslow, A. H. (1954). *Motivation and personality*. New York, NY: Harper & Brothers.

Maslow, A. H. (1959) Cognition of being in the peak experiences. *The Journal of Genetic Psychology*, 94(1), 43-66, doi: s10.1080/00221325.1959.10532434

Maslow, A. H. (1962a). Lessons from the peak-experiences. *Journal of Humanistic Psychology*, 2(1), 9-18.

Maslow, A. H. (1962b). Summer notes on social psychology of industry and management at Non-Linear Systems, Inc. Del-Mar, CA: Non-Linear Systems, Inc.

Maslow, A. H. (1962c). *Toward a psychology of being*. Princeton, NJ: D Van Nostrand.

Maslow, A. H. (1963). The creative attitude. *The Structurist*, (3), 4.

Maslow, A. H. (1964). *Religions, values, and peak-experiences*. Columbus, OH: The Ohio State University Press.

Maslow, A. H. (1965). *Eupsychian management; a journal*. Homewood, IL: R.D. Irwin. Later published as: Maslow, A. H. (2000). *Maslow on management*. New York, NY: John H. Wiley & Sons.

Maslow, A. H. (1970a, August). Editorial. *Psychology Today*.

Maslow, A. H. (1970b). Humanistic education vs. professional education: Further comments. *New Directions in Teaching*, Bowling Green Univer., *2*(2), 3-10. Reprinted in (1979) *Journal of Humanistic Psychology*, *19*(3), 17-25.

Maslow, A. H. (1971). *The farther reaches of human nature*. New York, NY: Viking.

Maslow, A. H. (1973). *Dominance, self-esteem, self-actualization: Germinal papers of A. H. Maslow* (R. Lowry, Ed.). Monterey, CA: Brooks/Cole. [1942 paper is: Maslow, A.H. (1942). Self-esteem (dominance feeling) and sexuality in women. The Journal of Social Psychology, 16, 259-294.]

Maslow, A. H., & Mittelmann, B. (1951). *Principles of abnormal psychology: The dynamics of psychic illness*. New York, NY: Harper & Row.

Maslow, A. H., & Sakoda, J. M. (1952). Volunteer-error in the Kinsey study. *The Journal of Abnormal and Social Psychology,47*(2), 259-262. doi:10.1037/h0054411

Maslow, A. H., Rand, H., & Newman, S. (1960). Some parallels between sexual and dominance behavior of intra-human primates and the fantasies of patients in psychotherapy. *The Journal of Nervous and Mental Disease,131*(3), 202-212. doi:10.1097/00005053-196009000-00002 Reprinted in DeMartino (1963).

Milner, M. (as Field, J.) (1936). *A life of one's own*. London, England: Chatto & Windus.

Milner, M. (1950) *On not being able to paint.* Madison, CT: International Universities Press, Inc.

Morant, R. B., & Maslow, A. H. (1965). Art judgment and the judgment of others: A preliminary study. *Journal of Clinical Psychology,21*(4), 389-391. doi.org/10.1002/1097-4679(196510)21:4<389::AID-JCLP2270210411>3.0.CO;2-G

Moustakas, C. (1961). The sense of self. *Journal of Humanistic Psychology, 1*(1), 20–34. doi: 10.1177/002216786100100104

Mulcahy, Jr., K., & Genovese, J. (2015, August 17). FLASHBACK: A complete, concise yearly history of TV soap operas—1947 to 1977 (Part 4) (The Soap Box, Vol. III No. 10, September 1978). Retrieved from https://www.welovesoaps.net/2015/08/History-of-TV-Soap-Operas-4.html

Murray, Henry A. (1963). Studies of stressful interpersonal disputations. *American Psychologist, 18*(1): 28–36. doi:10.1037/h0045502

Newland, C. A. (1962). *Myself and I.* New York, NY: Coward-McCann.

Owens, C. M. (1958). *Awakening to the good.* Boston, MA: The Christopher Publishing House.
Owens, C. M. (1963). *Discovery of the self.* Boston, MA: The Christopher Publishing House.

Perls, F. S., Hefferline, R. F., & Goodman, P. (1951). *Gestalt therapy.* New York, NY: Dell.

Rapaport, D. (Ed.). (1951). *Organization and pathology of thought: Selected sources. Translation and commentary by David Rapaport.* New York, NY: Columbia University Press.
Reps, P. (1957). *Zen flesh, Zen bones.* Rutland, VT: C. E. Tuttle Co.
Ritter, P., & Ritter, J. (1959). *The free family.* London: Victor Gollancz, Ltd.
Road to Reality [Television show]. (1960) Retrieved May 18, 2019, from https://www.imdb.com/title/tt0053532/?ref_=fn_al_tt_1
Rosen, J. N. (1953). *Direct analysis: Selected papers.* New York, NY: Grune & Stratton.
Roszak, T. (Ed.). (1972). *Sources.* New York, NY: Harper and Row.
Rubin, T. I. (1961). *In the life.* New York, NY: The Macmillan Company.

Sanford, N. (Ed.). (1962). *The American college.* New York, NY: John Wiley and Sons.
Schneider, A. (Director). (1962, October 13). Who's afraid of Virginia Woolf? by Edward Albee. Live performance at Billy Rose Theater, New York, NY.
Sherif, M. (1956). Experiments in group conflict. Scientific American, *195*(5), 54-58.
Silberer, H. (1909). Report on method of eliciting and observing certain symbolic hallucination-phenomena. In: D. Rapaport (Ed.), *Organization and pathology of thought: Selected sources.* (pp. 208-233). New York, NY: Columbia University Press.
Smith, H. (1977). Two kinds of teaching. In H. Chiang & A. H. Maslow (Eds.). (1977). *The healthy personality: Readings* (2nd ed., pp. 153-163). New York, NY: Van Nostrand Reinhold
Sorokin, P. A. (1956). The American sex revolution. Boston, MA: Porter Sagent Publisher.
Stacey, C. L., & DeMartino, M. F. (Eds.). (1958). *Understanding human motivation.* Cleveland, OH: Howard Allen.
Steinberg, S. (1960). *The labyrinth.* New York, NY: Harper & Brothers.
Stewart, K. (1972). Dream exploration among the Senoi. In H. Chiang &

A. H. Maslow (Eds.). (1977). *The healthy personality: Readings* (2nd ed., pp. 127-37). New York, NY: Van Nostrand Reinhold. Also in Roszak (1972).

Tanzer, D. (1977) The psychology of natural childbirth. In H. Chiang & A. H. Maslow (Eds.). (1977). *The healthy personality: Readings* (2nd ed., pp. 96-105). New York, NY: Van Nostrand Reinhold.

Tati, J. (Director). (1958). *Mon Oncle* [Motion picture]. France: Gaumont/Continental Distributing.

Tenenbaum, S. & Rogers, C. R. (1977). Student-centered teaching as experienced by a participant. In H. Chiang & A. H. Maslow (Eds.). (1977). *The healthy personality: Readings* (2nd ed., pp. 174-188). New York, NY: Van Nostrand Reinhold.

Terman, L. M. (1926). *Mental and physical traits of a thousand gifted children* (Vol. 1, Genetic Studies of Genius). Stanford, CA: Stanford University Press.

Terman, L. M., & Oden, M. H. (1947). *The gifted child grows up: Twenty-five years' follow-up of a superior group.* Palo Alto, CA, US: Stanford University Press.

Terman, L. M., & Oden, M. H. (1959). *The gifted group at mid-life* (Vol. 5, Genetic Studies of Genius). Stanford, CA: Stanford University Press.

The Eleventh Hour [Television show]. (1962, October 03). Retrieved from https://www.imdb.com/title/tt0055669/?ref_=fn_tt_tt_1

Thorndike, E. L. (1940). *Human nature and the social order.* Oxford, England: Macmillan.

Van Kaam, A. L. (1958). *The experience of really feeling understood by a person* (Dissertation). Western Reserve University, Cleveland, OH.

Walsh, C. (1962). *From utopia to nightmare.* New York, NY: Harper & Row.

Watts, A. (1958). *Nature, man and woman.* New York, NY: Pantheon.

Watts, A. (1960). *This is it, and other essays on Zen and spiritual experience.* New York, NY: Pantheon Books.

Watts, A. (1962). *The joyous cosmology: Adventures in the chemistry of consciousness.* New York, NY: Pantheon Books.

Watts, A. (1977) On the Tantra. In H. Chiang & A. H. Maslow (Eds.). (1977) *The healthy personality: Readings* (2nd ed., pp. 75-78). New York, NY: Van Nostrand Reinhold.

Weisskopf, W. A. (1955). *The psychology of economics.* London: Routledge and Keegan Paul Ltd.

Weisskopf, W. A. (1963). Existential crisis and the unconscious. *MANAS,*

16(49), 1-6. doi:10.1177/002216786700700107

Weisskopf, W. A. (1971). *Alienation and economics*. New York, NY: H. P. Dutton & Co., Inc.

Werner, H. (1940). *Comparative psychology of mental development*. New York, NY: International Universities Press, Inc.

Werner, H., & Kaplan, B. (1963). *Symbol formation: An organismic developmental approach to language and the expression of thought*. New York, NY: John Wiley.

Wheelis, A. (1966). *The illusionless man*. New York, NY: W.W. Norton.

Wilson, C. (1972). *New pathways in psychology: Maslow and the post-Freudian revolution*. London, England: Victor Gollancz.

Wilson, C. (1963). *The origins of the sexual impulse*. London, England: Arthur Barker.

Witkin, H. A., & Lewis, H. B. (1965). The relation of experimentally induced presleep experiences to dreams: A report on method and preliminary findings. *Journal of the American Psychoanalytic Association, 13*(4), 819-849. doi:10.1177/000306516501300406

Witkin, H. A., & Lewis, H. B. (1967). *Experimental studies of dreaming*. New York, NY: Random House.

Wolf, A. & Schwartz, E. K. (1962). *Psychoanalysis in groups*. New York, NY: Grune and Stratton.

Wolff, K. H. (1962). Surrender as a response to our crisis. *Journal of Humanistic Psychology, 2*(2), 16-29. doi:10.1007/978-94-010-1526-4_6

Woods, F. A. (1906). *Mental and moral heredity in royalty: a statistical study in history and psychology*. New York, NY: Henry Holt & Co.

Woods, F. A. (1913). *The influence of monarchs: Steps in a new science of history*. New York, NY: The Macmillan Company.

Wolff, W. (1943). *The expression of personality: experimental depth psychology* (G. Murphy, Ed.). New York, NY: Harper & Brothers.

INDEX

Publisher's Catalogue

The Prosperous Series

#1 The Prosperous Coach: Increase Income and Impact for You and Your Clients (Steve Chandler and Rich Litvin)

#2 The Prosperous Hip Hop Producer: My Beat-Making Journey from My Grandma's Patio to a Six-Figure Business (Curtiss King)

* * *

Devon Bandison

Fatherhood Is Leadership: Your Playbook for Success, Self-Leadership, and a Richer Life

Sir Fairfax L. Cartwright

The Mystic Rose from the Garden of the King

Steve Chandler

37 Ways to BOOST Your Coaching Practice: PLUS: the 17 Lies That Hold Coaches Back and the Truth That Sets Them Free

50 Ways to Create Great Relationships

Business Coaching (Steve Chandler and Sam Beckford)

Crazy Good: A Book of CHOICES

CREATOR

Death Wish: The Path through Addiction to a Glorious Life

Fearless: Creating the Courage to Change the Things You Can

How to Get Clients

RIGHT NOW: Mastering the Beauty of the Present Moment

The Prosperous Coach: Increase Income and Impact for You and Your Clients (The Prosperous Series #1) (Steve Chandler and Rich Litvin)

Shift Your Mind Shift The World (Revised Edition)

Abraham H. Maslow

The Aims of Education (audio)

The B-language Workshop (audio)

Being Abraham Maslow (DVD)

The Eupsychian Ethic (audio)

The Farther Reaches of Human Nature (audio)

Maslow and Self-Actualization (DVD)

Maslow on Management (audiobook)

Personality and Growth: A Humanistic Psychologist in the Classroom

Psychology and Religious Awareness (audio)

The Psychology of Science: A Reconnaissance

Self-Actualization (audio)

Weekend with Maslow (audio)

Albert Schweitzer

Reverence for Life: The Words of Albert Schweitzer

William Tillier

Personality Development Through Positive Disintegration: The Work of Kazimierz Dąbrowski

Margery Williams

The Velveteen Rabbit: or How Toys Become Real

Join our Mailing List:
www.MauriceBassett.com

MAURICE BASSETT